MYSTERIES OF PARIS

MYSTERIES OF PARIS

PARIS

The Quest for Morton Fullerton

❖

MARION MAINWARING

Foreword by Richard Howard

UNIVERSITY PRESS OF NEW ENGLAND

Hanover and London

Published by University Press of New England, Hanover, NH 03755
Printed in the United States of America
5 4 3 2 1

Library of Congress Cataloging-in-Publication Data

Mainwaring, Marion.
   Mysteries of Paris : the quest for Morton Fullerton / Marion Mainwaring.
     p. cm.
   Includes bibliographical references and index.
   ISBN 1-58465-008-7 (alk. paper)
     1. Fullerton, William Morton, b. 1865. 2. Journalists—United States—Biography.
   3. Wharton, Edith, 1862–1937—Relations with men. 4. Americans—France—
   Paris—Biography. 5. Paris (France)—Intellectual life.

   PN4874.F774 M35 2000
   070'.92—dc21
   [B]   00–027745

To Barbara Proctor

To the memory of Dennis Proctor,

Fredelle Maynard, Christopher Herzig,

Stuart Murrie

To the memory of my parents

Contents

Foreword by Richard Howard   ix

Acknowledgments   xi

Prologue to a Detective Story   1

Part One   9

Part Two   66

Part Three   83

Part Four   145

Part Five   192

Part Six   224

Part Seven   253

Epilogue to a Detective Story   279

A Short List of Fullerton's Writings   283

Notes   285

Archival Sources   317

Index   319

Illustrations follow page 164.

Foreword

For nearly two centuries, say from Voltaire (*The History of Charles XII of Sweden, The Age of Louis XIV*) to Carlyle (*History of Frederick the Great, Cromwell's Letters and Speeches*), history was biography, curriculum of the great man, articulation of the character and accomplishments—including debacles—of kings, heroes, tyrants, and saints.

Then for another century this conception was rather neatly reversed: history was discerned to be anything but an account of human life, and "mere" biography was declared irrelevant to time's veridical structure; in its place, a perception of process wrung from mensuration, statistics, means no longer golden but of lead!

Yet now, in our incomparable modernity, we enlist biography once again to render the historical (Duby, Schorske); but of course we have inverted the terms—true history, as Shakespeare liked to call it, is to be a confrontation with a person frequently unknown to fame, a secret sharer—a *mystery,* as Marion Mainwaring calls him. A "minor" life is now the proper litmus, more likely to reveal the intimate architecture of an age than our good old (or even bad new) *monstres sacrés.*

Seemly and indeed painstakingly scrupulous as her procedures are, the grand title of Marion Mainwaring's "quest" for Fullerton (a man whose career and sensibility constitute just the oblique marker our contemporary historicism requires or at least prefers) nevertheless reminds us that the facts of the matter are anything but matter of fact: they are sensational. Eugène Sue himself, whose "original" *Mystères de Paris* seem so patent and tribal in the face of all that is, in the ineffable Fullerton's case, latent and scribal, would have been hard put to match the chronicle of this darkened and dissembled career; certainly he could not have proceeded with the vigilant circumspection that Marion Mainwaring has constantly invoked to such powerful effect. We have here the historian as conscientious psychopomp, inquisitor of the soul's own structures.

Which leads to my ulterior and perhaps more luminous point in this little foreword: there is a second subject in Marion Mainwaring's (perhaps fanatic, certainly obsessional) pursuit, excavation, archaeology of a man whose talent for intimacy with genius (James, Wharton, the Ranee of Sarawak, *e tutti quanti*) yielded only to his genius for betraying any and every intimacy by his talent for sexual . . . betrayal. This shadow subject is the story of the pursuit itself, the conduct of the quest for Morton Fullerton as the articulation of Miss Mainwaring's own literary identity (elsewhere evidenced in her subordination to problematic achievements of Turgenev and Wharton, and further in the parodies of nine masters of detection anatomized in her 1954 *Murder in Pastiche,* reprinted in 1989). The writing of history, the very possibility of history as understanding, becomes the *subject* of history in the Mainwaring enterprise. The biography (it is, ultimately, that) of Fullerton becomes the enunciation of Mainwaring's identity: Morton is as much the author of Marion's being as she has been the scribe of his.

Wherefore the peculiar mastery of *Mysteries of Paris,* a work of great probity and equally great discretion, an indictment (as I read it) as well as a confession. Though so great is the literary tact wielded here that I am no longer sure who is indicted, who confesses. And in that uncertainty resides (I dare not say *lies*) the triumph of modern history, no?

Richard Howard

Acknowledgments

I must first of all thank three generous men. Hugh S. Fullerton, William Morton Fullerton's literary executor, shared with me his memories of a man he admired and deplored, and gave me Morton's notebook. Leon Edel, who also had personal recollections of Morton Fullerton, sent me Fullerton letters and read drafts of this book with extraordinary kindness. Richard Howard has encouraged, understood, and inspired.

Morton Fullerton's family have been exceptionally helpful in discussing "Will": Gertrude Worcester, Dr. James Worcester, Gay Fullerton, Mabelle Fullerton, Dwight Fullerton, and Christopher, Mireille, and David Gerould.

Mary Pitlick, working bravely against illness, gave advice and information at long distance as she did pioneering research toward "The Unknown Edith Wharton," a book her friends hope will be published soon. Nadya Aisenberg read sections of the manuscript while working on what proved to be her last poems.

My brother David Mainwaring, who guided me from typewriter to word-processor, has come to the rescue in countless crises, and I have had invaluable help from others in my family, and from friends both old and new: Terence and Prue Bird, Virginia Boegli, Marc Cazal, Kay Daniels, Arlene Pitlick Graham, Capt. David Healey, Pepper Healey, Col. (Chap.) Matthew Imrie, Anthony and Helen Langdon, Dorothy Mainwaring, H. J. Mainwaring, Fredelle Maynard, Joseph McElroy, Sir William Stuart Murrie, Kaethe Peters, Sir Dennis and Lady Proctor, Bob Seaman, Nancy Seaman, Douglass Shand-Tucci, and Professors Max Maynard, Anna Mill, Adeline Potter, and Cornelia Veenendaal.

Of the many people who provided information in personal meetings and appear as characters in this detective story, I am especially grateful to

Paul Andrieux, Georges Clemenceau, the Eldins of Alès, Eugène Fleuré, the Comtesse de la Forest-Divonne, Maîtres Guerre and Radet, Eric Hawkins, Annette Langlois-Berthelot, His Exc. Roland de Margerie, the Comte de Noailles, George Nolan-Whyatt, and Gabrielle Roy-Bretaud.

I am much obliged to Marjorie Edel and Deborah Edel, and to Louis Auchincloss, Paul O. Blanchette, Arthur Crook, Sharon Hecker, Alan Hollinghurst, Nicholas Kilmer, Danila Marsure-Rosso, Robert Meteyard, Gerald Morgan, Jr., the Hon. William Royall Tyler, and Professors Franklin Brooks, Jackson R. Bryer, Jacques Cotnam, William G. Holzberger, Lyall K. Powers, and Walter B. Rideout.

So many curators, public officials, and other record-keepers have kindly provided information and enabled me to explore their archives that I cannot thank them all individually. My debt to them is great. They include Daria d'Arienzo, A. G. Battle, Alan Bell, Messrs. Bollet and Higelin of Saint Rémy, Susan Brady, Lisa Browar, Francisco J. Carmana, Kathleen Catalano, Joseph P. Cheevers, Stephanie Copeland, Margot Cory, Wallace Dailey, Edna C. Davis, Cécile Debrie, Jean Delmas, Rodney Dennis, Eleanor Dwight, Eamon Dyas, J. A. Edwards, Karen L. Esterl, Cynthia Farar, David Farmer, Mark R. Farrell, Ralph Franklin, Kristine W. Frost, Manuel Garcia Gallardo, Donald Gallup, Jane Golas, Milton O. Gustafson, Cathy Henderson, Janice Hodson, Catherine Johnson, Violet Kellogg, Laura Enaro Loseri, Scott Marshall, Leslie A. Morris, Michele Ostrow, Gordon Phillips, Michael Plunkett, Dean Sturgis C. Riddle, Julia Simic, Roger Stoddard, Carol Trabulsi, Kathleen Whalen, and Pasteurs Fred. LeNoury, C.-R. Muess, and G. Ruckwied.

Many thanks also to Mary Crittendon, Katherine B. Kimball, and other patient staff members at University Press of New England, to Linda Nelson, who helped proofread, and to my agent, Christina Ward.

M. M.

Mysteries of Paris

Prologue to a
Detective Story

Paris

There was a note under the door when I came in. Yale University letter-head. The writer was the official biographer of the novelist Edith Wharton, and the U.S. cultural attaché had suggested . . . Could I telephone?

Up the long dusty Rue de Lourmel, empty in the dead of August. Hôtel-café, baker. Le Roi des Fournaux, the Stove King, with his display of electric heaters. Four vacant shops awaiting demolition. Wine merchant. This undistinguished Left Bank arrondissement, the Fifteenth, is being upgraded by construction of *résidences de grand standing*. On past the high wall with the iron gate at the corner which sometimes swung open and disclosed a house set back in a garden. A convent, MAISON DES DAMES DU CALVAIRE was painted over the wicket door. House of the Ladies of Calvary. On across the broad leafy Avenue Emile Zola to the post office and its telephone booths in the basement.

Yes, I could come. . . . Tomorrow? Yes.

Edith Wharton brought to mind novels bound in old-rose buckram with titles stamped in gilt, *The House of Mirth, The Custom of the Country,* and a dynamic woman who swooped Henry James up for motor tours. With James or—what was his name?—Walter Berry, she would walk around a cathedral studying the clerestory while her husband followed after, burdened with wraps and boredom. Stereotype, doubtless wrong . . . Why Yale?

Yale had the Wharton Papers, a professor of American studies explained next day in the bar of the Hôtel Port Royal. Access had been limited for years, but now, as biographer, he had the use of them.

He summarized Wharton's life: Born in 1862, raised in Old New

York, Edith Jones had a disappointment in love, Walter Berry, and married Edward Wharton. She and "Teddy" lived in New York and Newport and built a house in Lenox, Massachusetts, the Mount. She was a successful writer by 1907, when they took a flat in Paris. Teddy broke down, and after scandals involving women and money Edith divorced him and settled in France. She died here in 1937.

Obviously, there was routine research to be done, legal records and so on. But there was more.

Specialists had known for a long time that when she was in her forties Edith Wharton was in love, because she had left an unpublished journal written as a love letter to an unnamed man. It was taken for granted that the man was Walter Berry, that she fell in love with him again—and again in vain, since he didn't marry her though he was her constant escort till his death ten years before hers.

The Wharton biographer, however, had been let in on a secret by the literary representative of the Wharton estate, William Royall Tyler. Mrs. Wharton had indeed been in love, around 1907–1908; had even had a love affair. But the man was not Walter Berry. He was a William Morton Fullerton.

Morton Fullerton, though an American, had succeeded the famous Blowitz as chief correspondent of the London *Times* in Paris. His liaison with the novelist was also known to his literary executor, Hugh Fullerton, a retired American diplomat now living in Paris, for when Morton was dying he had boasted to Hugh of having "had" Edith Wharton, and he'd given Hugh a poem she had written to him, which Hugh destroyed, convinced that it would damage Mrs. Wharton's reputation.

The dying Morton had divulged another fact startling to Hugh. Long ago, in France, he had been secretly married and divorced.

On top of all that, unpublished letters of Morton Fullerton's friend Henry James reveal that at the time of the Wharton affair Morton was being blackmailed by a Frenchwoman, perhaps a landlady or housekeeper, and that James and Edith Wharton paid the woman off.

Such was the background offered by the biographer.

Morton Fullerton, then, was of paramount importance in Wharton's history: as her lover, of course, and also because the blackmail might have had to do with her. She might have sent him compromising letters. His wife might have been the blackmailer. His divorce and Edith's might have been linked.

When Wharton and Fullerton were old and no longer in close touch, a graduate student beginning a life's work on Henry James, Leon Edel, sought them out as people who had known James well.

James and Fullerton had met in London around 1890, when James was in his late forties and Morton his mid-twenties. James, Edel found, had drawn on Morton for the journalist Merton Densher in *The Wings of the Dove*, who "looked vague without looking weak—idle without looking empty."

Edel worked backward imaginatively to this indeterminate young journalist from the solidity of a "handsome, heavy man working in a comfortable office" at the *Figaro*, in the Champs-Elysées: Morton Fullerton at sixty-four. *That* Fullerton—"his large moustaches were waxed; a fresh flower reposed in his buttonhole"—played to perfection the role of "an *homme de coeur*," a man of feeling, "creating a haze out of his past in which nothing was sharp or clear; everything was soft and impressionistic."

When Edel went on to visit Edith Wharton, he noticed a copy of James's novel *The Golden Bowl* inscribed to Fullerton. "Oh dear," she said, "I guess I still have some of the books that Morton once left with me." She pulled down other James volumes, all inscribed to Fullerton. Something gave Edel an inkling of "a greater intimacy than might have been supposed, by a researcher coming into their lives so late in the day."

Long afterward, Edel saw Fullerton at eighty, frail and unkempt, in a Paris barely freed from Nazi occupation, and Fullerton pointed to piles of boxes in his study: "letters from Henry James . . . from Edith Wharton . . . there you are—there is my life."

James, Wharton, Fullerton: an association eventful, not long-lived, never quite stable. If in every couple there is one who loves, etc., in this trio James and Edith loved Fullerton, and Fullerton let himself be loved. "You absolutely add," James told him, "to my wish, and to my need, to live the life of—whatever I may call it!—my genius. And I *shall*, I feel, somehow, while there's a rag left of me. Largely thanks to you."[1]

Edith Wharton's relations with him can be traced in what may be the most various written record of a lover left by any woman, ranging as it does from business letters to love letters to poems to highly wrought pornography to novels—for Fullerton is recognizable as a character not only in James's *Wings of the Dove* but in two Wharton books, *The Buccaneers* and *The Reef.* Moreover, he believed himself to be the original of the pivotal anti-Puritan in *The Last Puritan,* a "memoir in the form of a novel" by the philosopher George Santayana, a Harvard classmate and friend who became an enemy.

When I took on the job of investigating him, no William Morton Fullerton appeared in any Who's Who or Who Was Who: which seemed odd for a man who had held a key position in journalism and—usually a *laissez-passer* to such compendiums—had published books.

His absence was all the stranger as it became apparent that there was much more in his life than was needed for a biography of Edith Wharton. His coverage of the Dreyfus case, *the* case of the nineteenth century, caused an "explosion of public indignation" in the Anglophone countries at racist persecution of an innocent man. During the First World War he advised U.S. military intelligence on policy toward an emergent USSR and a Yugoslav union of the "suspicious, vindictive, parvenu little Powers" Serbia, Bosnia-Herzegovina, and Croatia. In the 1920s and 1930s many French readers, oblivious of Gertrude Stein, Fitzgerald, Hemingway, Henry Miller, regarded him as a spokesman for "Anglo-Saxon" culture.

During the Second World War the Gestapo raided his study and removed some of his letters, leaving thousands more from a most impressive array of correspondents. His was a curious case history in the holocaustic Occupation of Europe, which people had begun to think of as past and gone but is now being reexamined in more than one nation, sometimes grudgingly, by institutions of justice, religion, art, and banking.

Had the public, publishing man figured in *Who's Who,* an entry based on the data given me at the start of work would have read:

FULLERTON, William Morton, b. 18 Sept. 1865, Norwich, Conn., s. Rev. Bradford Morton & Julia (*née* Ball) Fullerton. Educ. Phillips Acad., Andover; Harvard Coll.; Lit. Ed. *Boston Advertiser.* Staff *Times* London 1890,

Paris 1891, Chief Corresp. 1902. Resigned partially 1907, fully 1910. *Problems of Power* 1913. Staff *Figaro, Journal des Débats,* d. Paris 26 Aug. 1952.

Several items would have been incorrect, and of course the episodes that I was to explore would have been absent:

> Marriage and divorce: dates and identity of wife unknown. Possible blackmail: grounds, date, and identity of blackmailer unknown. Ca. 1907–1909, liaison with Edith Wharton.

In her memoirs, *A Backward Glance,* Wharton mentioned men and women she met in aristocratic salons of the Belle Epoque: the Marquis de Ségur, Comtesse Rosa de Fitz-James, Comtesse Anna de Noailles, others. I should trace their descendants and learn what they knew about her and possibly about Fullerton, to whom she made no reference whatever in her book.

That he had one connection in that circle was known. Anna de Noailles, born a Romanian princess, had great prestige as writer, conversationalist, and beauty. Fullerton reviewed a volume of her poems in 1907,[2] the year he met the Whartons, and sent her the review with ornate compliments. Now, if she knew both Edith Wharton *and* Fullerton, did she perhaps know of their liaison?

"Morton Fullairton? *Non.* I don't think my mother knew him. I don't believe I ever heard of M. Fullairton."

This was in a dusky boudoir, dark wood and yellow satin, shaded against the afternoon sun and hung with portraits of a woman with a famous horizontal face[3] and two pitch balls stuck in it for eyes, the mother of Comte Anne-Jules de Noailles.

"I wasn't old enough to know the salons before the First War," said M. de Noailles. "Later there was Mme Mühlfeld's, where you worked at getting people elected to the Académie. The only literary salon now is Mme de la Rochefoucauld's, two Wednesdays a month. You used to have a day once a week. You didn't invite people; they came, and there were petits fours."

The name Edith Wharton meant nothing to M. de Noailles. He was *désolé.* He went down a list of names culled from Wharton's memoirs and a few writings I'd found by Morton Fullerton. "I know—I *knew—*many of these people. It will be very difficult to document your study because almost everyone is dead. . . . Mes hommages, Madame."

* * *

But some people still alive remembered Morton Fullerton. Their recollections, as well as books, newspapers, government records, and letters—above all, letters—gradually brought information.

Today he can be found on the Internet. He can be seen, or rather characters based on him (but with a difference) can be seen, in films. He is the journalist loved by two women in *The Wings of the Dove,* the heroine's true love in a televised version of Wharton's *Buccaneers.* He comes into all the books about James and Wharton. Many readers and viewers know something about him.

Not much, however; and a good deal of what is thought to be fact is error. A systematic liar, Morton Fullerton hinted at mysteries to divert attention from secrets. Misinformation has accumulated, and mistakes about him have led to mistakes about Wharton (the story of their liaison has never been fully or accurately told) and to a lesser extent about James.

When he applied for his first passport,[4] at twenty-two, Fullerton's height was one meter fifteen point five, five foot six. Eyes blue, nose aquiline, hair brown, complexion fair, face oval, chin round. In later applications he gained an inch, his nose straightened, and his chin became firm. He had a big moustache. Everyone called him handsome. He had a strong heart, serviceable lungs in spite of lifelong smoking, a tricky gallbladder, an agile, catholic penis; he had a soft voice, and charm. The charm hardly ever comes through in things he wrote; but we don't see the wind, only the reeds that bend and the oaks that break, as in Aesop; and from his impact on intelligent and sophisticated people we have to accept that he was very charming.

This book tells the story of the research into his life. The first part covers work done for the official biography of Wharton. The following parts cover work done independently later, and for a longer time, that concentrated on *him.* Throughout, questions arose and answers bred new questions, answers to which shaded into mysteries. Often what seemed to be true at one stage of work turned out to be false or had to be reinterpreted.

The quest for Morton Fullerton led to discovery of events more appropriate to drama than to literary biography. Kings and queens crossed the stage. Treason, stratagems, and spoils abounded. Hundreds of the letters that document his life, now decorously housed in some of the world's great libraries, are extant because after his death one woman took them from another woman at revolver point.

Research has its dangers. "Enter these enchanted woods, you who dare!" as George Meredith, Fullerton's literary idol, wrote in a different context. Unposted trails may lead to buried treasure, but also to bias, overconfidence, folly—may even lead, and in this search did lead, to *folie*, madness, or to the brink of it.

PART ONE

Paris

A Point of Departure

His sense of the far away and long ago came naturally, Morton Fullerton told his French readers. As a boy he read about the French and Indian Wars under trees planted by his Massachusetts forebears on land their English forebears had cleared in the 1600s. On holiday, when he and his brother and their father were tired of hunting and rowing they read Homer in the Greek.[1]

Their father was a Congregational minister who did no more to prepare them for success in American life than did the "sheerest idealistic instruction" boys received at school and college. Morton was born at the end of the civil war, which the elders thought had settled the nation's destiny forever. Familiar with the Bible, at home in antiquity, and unaware that an economic revolution was in progress, his generation assumed that the "triumphal advance of American democracy" would never halt.[2]

Those bits of autobiography were imbedded in the few works by Fullerton that I could lay hands on during a rough survey of his life. Additional items came from an outline of the Wharton book provided by the biographer from Yale. After Harvard, and a stint on a Boston newspaper, Morton went abroad with the son of the poet Longfellow. By 1890 he was in London, with a job on the *Times*, and—

But you can't say casually "a job on the *Times*." The *Times* was a national institution and a force in international affairs. Its staff was an elite. ("There's three reporters at the door, sir, and a gentleman from the *Times*.") How in the world did W. M. Fullerton—young, inexperienced (two years' book reviewing for a provincial paper), and an American— get a job on the *Times?*

Whatever the explanation, the following year he was sent across the Channel to work under Henri Opper von Blowitz, the famous Prague-born, French-naturalized—and always capitalized—Chief Paris Correspondent of that quintessentially British newspaper.

A Notebook for the 1890s: Clues Galore

> A worm walks over the fairest things
> Though life as pleasure runs death close
> Clink glass to glass for the girl who sings
> Of laudanum tomorrow an over dose
> Will make her as dead as a cobble stone
> And stab a regret half maddening.

Morton Fullerton wrote this doggerel in a little leather-bound notebook he kept in the 1890s.[3] When he was dying, he gave it to Hugh Fullerton. Hugh lent it to the biographer, who passed it on to me as of interest for "a curious dream, otherwise nothing much."

The entries are mostly blurred, soft-pencil scribbles, many of them made as Morton reported political events for the *Times,* with some fairly precise drawings of courtroom scenes and faces.

> March 8 1892 Assize Court, Palais de Justice. Trial of Deputies . . . for Corruption. Same hall as Ravachol . . . Clemenceau's brother for the Daily News. At five minutes to 12 appeared the witnesses, bustling through the narrow door. . . . Zola trial . . . Versailles 22 May '98 . . . contest publication of Aurore Paris.

The entry marked the beginning of Morton's coverage of the Dreyfus Case, which he reported as "an eye and ear witness . . . from the trial of Zola to the tragic August at Rennes."

The Dreyfus case, a landmark in the history of nationalism, racism, and militarism, is gripping even today. In August 1899, Captain Alfred Dreyfus, who had been found guilty of treason and sent to Devil's Island mainly because he was a Jew, was famous the world over. In simple news value the court-martial at Rennes in Brittany for which he was haled back for retrial was unparalleled. The case—the Case—tore France apart. Newspapers everywhere sent reporters; heads of state, observers. Covering the story must have realized a journalist's dream of glory; and the newspaper accounts are source material for historians, as well as the

leaden mass of official and unofficial depositions, memoranda, and correspondence that makes the Dreyfus archive one of the most daunting in
existence.

In time, the hunt for M.F. led to that archive. At the outset it was
enough to register that the *Times* entrusted him with a choice assignment
shortly before making him Chief Correspondent.

Since his private life was more relevant to the search, it was encouraging to find that his notebook had nonpolitical passages:

Feb. 4, 1894 . . . I dreamed that I was in a splendid palace in the midst of
a luminous green country. . . . I heard just behind me the step of a woman
who I knew occupied a room just near mine . . . there were many splendid
& beautiful women in the palace but among them all she alone . . . had
held my vision and I had sought to ingratiate myself with her without
avail. She was of perfect classic beauty, divinely tall & divinely fair, mag-
nificently serene in her movements, big-browed & gentle-eyed, & with
warm round arms & fully modulated curves of breast & ~~stom~~ belly, I was
sure, like the goblet belly of Canticles. . . . I would have drawn swords
with him who denied that she would one day reward my patient unselfish
adoration . . . by mingling me with her, and giving me the only sense of
dignity a man can know namely that born from his self-knowledge of his
utility.

The "dream," which is carefully written in ink, goes on and on for
pages. The notebook is also sprinkled with personal names:

First week in April 93 Marquis Lorne & Princess Louise Ronald Gower.
Hotel Choiseul all lunch at Le Doyen & I bring James. Afterwards M. of L.
&. R.G. chez moi.
All this month James

In a different handwriting:

Nov. 19 Après dîner s'en aller sur la mer! [After dinner off to sea!]

                                                          P. Verlaine

The poet. Did Morton *know* Paul Verlaine? Did he know Guy de
Maupassant, whose house he visited after Maupassant's death?

The week ending July 2 at Etretat. . . . Visited La Belle Ernestine where all
the house filled with literary and artistic souvenirs. She tells me that Maupassant "had" 14 women in one day. He wrote a great deal under the apple
trees there at her cottage.

The notebook also sets Morton in villages like Bougival, Mantes-la-Jolie, and Corot's misty Ville d'Avray, resorts of ordinary Parisians on their rare holidays.

> June 15 1895 Adèle & I Ville D'Avray Mais hélas Corot est mort et les saules commencent à pousser au delà du cadre[5] [But alas Corot is dead and the willows are beginning to grow out of the frame].

Still faceless, Morton began to take shape as a figure in the radiant landscapes that were being painted by Renoir, Sisley, Pissaro, Monet.

Holiday Travels. A Mission to Madrid

A "sort of amorous curiosity"[6] led him farther from Paris on his summer holidays. As he jounced in trains or sat over carafes of the local wine in country bistros, he made notes on talks with peasants and curés. On local history. The witch trials of the Franche-Comté recalled Salem, Massachusetts. On topography: with passion, Morton studied high and low relief—an approach in sharp contrast to that of the Impressionists. He related geography to history, mountain ranges and watercourses to invasions and migrations.

But he abjured "aesthetic rambles," foreseeing world war:

> from an observation point in Madrid, where I was detained on a prolonged and urgent mission, I saw over beyond Gibraltar, in the heart of Morocco, the weaving of that web of intrigue which the great Delcassé, the Richelieu of the Third Republic, was already secretly undoing. . . . I could not, in all decency, turn away.[7]

France and England were negotiating the Entente Cordiale. A wire Morton sent the *Times* from Madrid was the first public mention of the secret. He refers to his wire so often that, whatever its actual importance, you sense it had a deep private meaning for him.

He turned some of his travels into a book. *Terres Françaises*—French Regions—is low-keyed, literary, and *in French*. Few foreigners write the language well enough to publish in it, and this book was "crowned" by the Académie Française. Graceful French!

"Hmn," says Marc, a friend who joined in the hunt, "mais . . . Morton has the style of my grandmother."

"But it was crowned by the Academy."
"Justement."

Terres Françaises came out in 1905, which brings us up close to Edith Wharton's appearance in Morton's life. And at some time, it seems, he was married, divorced, and blackmailed, not necessarily in that order. His travel book may help in detective work, for it records every change from train to mule-back, every overnight stop. For the time being, I traced his itineraries with a felt-tip pen on a big Taride map of France on the kitchen wall.

The Beginning of a Love Affair

So, the man whom Edith Wharton met in early 1907 was engrossed as a journalist by world politics and plagued by mysterious maybe sinister complications in his personal life.

He was forty-two, though Henry James spoke of him persistently as "young." She was four years older, widely traveled and widely read, with a straitened social, emotional, and sexual experience; intelligent; a witty observer of New York society and a gifted storyteller, compulsively readable. Morton was a seasoned journalist, and *Terres Françaises* had just had a critical success, but Edith was a "name." At once dignified and fidgety, she was unhappier than she knew in the yoke with her mismatched husband.

According to the Wharton outline, the liaison began as follows:

The Whartons were renting a flat at 58 Rue de Varenne when Morton met them. Henry James came to stay there while their acquaintance with his young friend was still new. After they returned to America, Morton went over to see his family, near Boston. Edith invited him to the Mount, in the western part of the state, and during his visit she fell in love with him.

A Veiled Figure

The journal "The Life Apart," "L'Ame close," the life shut in, which Edith Wharton wrote as an unsent installment letter to M.F., still bears the stain of a flower she put between its pages in the year 1908.

The biographer had left me the journal for study, along with Morton's notebook and a third original document, Wharton's "Line-a-Day" diary—her ordinary engagement book for 1908. In the journal Morton is "you"; in the diary he is "M.F." or "*Er,*" German for *he.*

Edith began the journal at the Mount in October 1907, when she received Fullerton's bread-and-butter letter. A second entry noted the receipt of a second letter, from Paris. With her third entry, in February, she too was in Paris, again at 58 Rue de Varenne.

The diary lists people she entertained there and people she met elsewhere. "M.F." appears repeatedly in both categories. She notes encountering him by chance and giving him a lift—to the Chamber of Deputies,[8] to his office in the Boulevard des Capucines.[9] She records the weather, mentions plays and lectures. Nothing on public events except, February 1: "King of Portugal and Crown Prince assassinated at Lisbon" (odd exception!). She records in prudent and not always correct German a "sweet" or a "happy" or, once, a "sad" time spent with M.F.

Meanwhile, in "L'Ame close," she analyzed her hesitations and intently measured and marveled at what was happening in her shut-in soul. In a church she and M.F. visited, she wrote in her first Paris entry, "a veiled figure stole up and looked at me a moment. Was its name Happiness? I dared not lift the veil."[10]

M.F. intimated that a woman's "mental companionship" was not enough. Two unhappy hours were noted in the diary, in German; but in the journal Edith wrote: "You hurt me—you disillusionized me—and when you left me I was more deeply yours."[11] Later: "Nothing else lives in me now but you."[12] And later: "Alone with you I am often shy and awkward, tormented by the fear that I may not please you—but with our dearest H.J. I felt at my ease."[13]

James had come to stay with her (Teddy was ill and had left for a cure). Though he had his own engagements, he and Morton and Edith were together a good deal, and he was always a presence—enhancing friendship, inhibiting display of passion. Soon Edith wrote:

> Sometimes I think that if I could go off with you for twenty-four hours to a little inn in the country, in the depths of a green wood, I should ask no more. Just to have one long day and quiet evening with you, and the next morning to be still together. . . .—As I wrote these lines I suddenly said to myself: "*I will go with him once before we separate.*"[14]

"Go with" was literal as well as a euphemism for making love. She went with Morton; he did not come to her. "Zusammen," in her diary, meant being alone "together" with M.F., but not necessarily making love. Of their meetings *zusammen* in town, after James left, all but the last were in midafternoon, when lovemaking would have been impossible. Edith's "Line-a-Day" is filled with names not only of guests at mealtime but of guests calling without notice between meals, and there were always the servants. Nor did she and Fullerton meet in Paris hotels. They went, though not for twenty-four hours, to the "green wood" Edith had imagined. The day James left, on the page of her journal where she laid a flower she wrote only "May 9th" and:

> La Châtaignerie
> Montmorency

Otherwise that page is blank, but the "Line-a-Day" is specific. She and Morton saw James off at the Gare du Nord at noon, took a local train to Montmorency, also on the Northern Line, and were back in Paris at 6:30.[15] Montmorency village lay on the edge of Montmorency Forest with its glorious *Châtaigneraie,* or chestnut grove, then in bloom. "Châtaignerie" was probably a misspelling of the name of the restaurant where they lunched, La Châtaigneraie.

They'd have reached the village in under an hour, taken a room at one of its three inns—the Cheval Blanc, the France, the Deux-Tourelles—lunched, made love, and returned to Paris while James was still traveling home. It was their first time as lovers.

The train journey is significant. Horseless carriages were for the few. Edith had one; she had "carried" James and Fullerton on a "motor-flight" to Beauvais. She could take men, even one man, about, and the very publicity prevented talk. A matron with a motorcar and a chauffeur, she was hostess in a mobile annex of her own house. But if conspicuous locomotion manifested observance of the proprieties, it also enforced them. People noticed a car, and a chauffeur knew his employer's movements. Whereas arriving by train, in control, not a passive guest, bilingual, Morton could take a room without anyone's paying attention to the veiled lady with him (veils were common) who did not need to speak and thereby reveal herself as a foreigner.

A few days later they stayed in town, sightseeing—the Louvre, Roman ruins, two churches. But Edith longed to be alone with Morton. "There is no use in trying to look at things together. We don't see them any longer."[16] They saw only each other.

They went to Senlis in the Forest of Chantilly. Perfection, from their
meeting at the Paris station through their return trip, when, as they
watched a full moon and listened to a thrush, she knew for the first time
"the interfusion of spirit and sense."[17] The diary specifies: lunch in Creil
(a railway junction), then to Chantilly, then to Senlis (population 7,115),
with its little hotels du Grand-Cerf, du Nord, de France. An early evening
meal. The 7:05 train to Paris.

They boarded at the Place de la Concorde one of the steamboats that
plied the Seine—"Larks" and "Flies" (*mouches*, ancestors of our bateaux-
mouches). "Apt to be crowded and uncomfortable," Baedeker warned
the tourist; was it Edith's first exposure to mass transport? Landing at
Bellevue-Funiculaire, she and Morton mounted by cable car (fare 10
centimes) to the Terrasse in the Forêt Domaniale de Meudon. Panoramic
view. An inn near the top; another, first-class, near the river. They re-
embarked for Paris at five.

Meudon isn't far from Ville d'Avray, which comes into Morton's diary.
Yes, in June 1895: "Adèle and I Ville d'Avray *Mais hélas Corot est mort.*"

The brevity of these adventures would have been of *Edith*'s deciding.
She could not respectably be away overnight. *A cause des domestiques.*

Then, departure for America. The last entry was again headed "The
Mount."

Except in the poems Edith wrote and revised here and there, "L'Ame
close" is written with flowing hand and ready phrase. Shaken by emotion, she remains articulate: no disputed marchland between experience
and verbalization. It is girlish, romantic, American. Grateful, defenses
down, she was, and knew herself to be, a different woman from the self-
confident author of fiction.

During the year and more I had the journal, I reread it now and then
without discovering what Fullerton felt for *her.* Later, now and then, it
floated in and out of memory like an aria from an opera with a plot that
was only vaguely known.

To return to the biographer's Wharton outline: Edith came back to
Paris. When Morton went to America again in 1909, she accompanied
him as far as London, where they stayed at the Charing Cross Hotel. She
gave him a poem she wrote about their night together—the poem that
Hugh Fullerton was to destroy after Morton's death.

Elegance, Fashion, and the Faubourg Saint-Germain

Meanwhile, Morton had been having trouble with a woman who perhaps ran a *pension* where he lived; and later, it seems, Henry James and Edith rescued him from a blackmailer. It's cloudy. Was the landlady the blackmailer? When the Rue de Varenne lease ran out, Edith moved to a flat she sometimes borrowed from her brother Harry. (Both her brothers lived much of the time in France; both died and were buried there, like their parents—and Edith herself.) In her journal she told Morton she thought they were being "watched."[18] Was a servant in that flat the blackmailer? Where, incidentally, was it?

The *Bottin Mondain* lists all those who "through social position, celebrity, or wealth compose what is called elegant and fashionable Paris." It gives your townhouse, your chateau, your "day" for ladies, your "club" for men. Only okay addresses figure: the Sixteenth Arrondissement, alodium of the haute bourgeoisie; the Faubourg Saint-Germain and the rest of the Seventh; parts of the First, Sixth, Eighth, and Seventeenth; and Neuilly over the city line.

Edith's brother Henry E. Jones appears in 1903. Address, Place des Etats-Unis, near the Etoile. Edith herself, in Paris only sporadically, does not appear until 1914, after her divorce.

And Fullerton, who, oddly for a journalist, is never in phone books, surfaces here in 1921 as Morten-Fullerton, C*, 8 Rue du Mont Thabor. C* means chevalier de la Légion D'Honneur and explains his admission to the directory, in which he reappears yearly as Morton-Fullerton, Morteno-Fullerton, etc., rising from knight to officer, O**, and commander, C***. (But what explains the Legion?)

Tenants in the quiet Rue du Mont Thabor, Fullerton's listed street, parallel to the Rue de Rivoli, remember an elderly monsieur. Not often there. It was only a study, many flights up.

Walter Van Rensselaer Berry also appears in 1921.

Edith Jones had met Berry when she was twenty-one and Berry twenty-four, a beginning lawyer. According to received opinion, he failed to make the proposal she expected. She married Edward Wharton of Boston, an older, less intellectual, and less ambitious man. Decades later, Berry settled in Paris, and after Edith's divorce they were constantly seen together. Whereas the M.F. liaison was undreamed of by her friends, an affair she did *not* have with Berry was firmly believed in by friends and strangers.

The artlessly vulgar *Bottin Mondain* opens the not very heavily guarded circle of "society." The inner circle, the old hermetic *monde* of the Faubourg Saint-Germain, is indexed in the blood-red and broodingly intense, not to say mad, *Almanach de Gotha,* which carries great families back, *mariage de convenance* by *mariage de convenance,* through a changing Europe to a twilight where France and Germany merge in the Empire, and yet farther back to a night in which uncertainly humanoid forebears merge with eponymous half-gods and totemic beasts.

The Faubourg Saint-Germain: blank treeless streets with few cars and few pedestrians except during the ebb and flow of workers at the ministries and embassies that now dominate the quarter. But behind its gray façades private houses still stand in stone courtyards and silent gardens. The Rue de Varenne is at the geographical center of the Faubourg, as the salons Edith described in her memoirs were at its social center.

"She was *très snob,*" the Vicomte de Noailles says, at lunch in his chateau across from the Palais de Fontainebleau. "All the truly intelligent people I have known have been *très snob.* If she enjoyed going to the d'Uzèses' it was because they had the d'Uzès prestige since the sixteenth century. Nobody was so snobbish as Bernard Berenson. Nobody! The king of Sweden was the only person he liked having to his house. And Berry was excessively snobbish and brilliantly intelligent, but it was because he saw around a duchess the halo of two hundred years of duchesses."

Morton too knew some of these chateaux and these townhouses with their dim tapestries, polished parquets, lustrous lusters, Aubusson carpets Watteaux Fragonards *boulle sèvre . . . luxe calme et politesse. Someone* in that circle may remember him.

The Comte de Noailles had suggested friends who might remember. "Someone *très bien* will be His Excellency Roland de Margerie, who's a retired ambassador; we are very close."

M. de Margerie remembered Mrs. Wharton well as a friend of his mother, Edmond Rostand's sister. She'd often come to the house in the Rue Saint-Dominique where we talked, which shares a garden with Berry's former house. M. de Margerie pointed at Berry's windows. "He was an intimate friend of Marcel Proust, whose niece married a cousin of mine. And I have a cousin who used to know Mrs. Wharton—Mme Blondine de Prévaux, the great-granddaughter of the famous affair between Liszt and the Countess d'Agoult."

Many people remember Mme Wharton, though only from the First World War on. Fullerton draws a blank.

Fullairton? Morton Fullairton? *Non.* A shake of the head, a polite brief frown of concentration, but always the name is dismissed and the speaker rushes on to other matters.

Many people bring up the name of the man who had made Mme Wharton an *affreuse disgrâce.* "She divorced," says the Vicomte de Noailles, "and had the shock of finding that Berry didn't want to marry her. She had divorced in the hopes of marrying him."

"I suppose" (M. de Margerie) "her great sensitiveness and the difficulties of her private life made her reserved. Berry was *culture itself.* He spoke French—it was absolutely fantastic!—just as well as Henry James! But he must have been difficult for her because she was madly in love with him and he was of course frightfully egocentric and independent."

"She gave the impression of being in love with Berry?"

"Well: they were constantly to be seen together. I suppose that all passion was spent, but they were very intimate. I suppose that sometime before the 1914–18 war it was *la grande passion* for her. Her husband? He was never mentioned, that I can recall."

"Morally he was dead." (Mme de Prévaux) "I had the feeling she must have had a sentimental life, but there was an iron curtain."

Fullairton? Morton Fullairton? *Non.*

No use asking if they ever knew of a *Mrs.* Morton Fullerton.

In Search of a Marriage Record: The *Mairie* and the Palace

But knowing about *her* is essential to understanding Morton's affair with Edith, his divorce, Edith's divorce, his quitting the *Times* partially in the year he met Edith, and fully in 1910, at only forty-five—*and* to understanding the mysterious blackmail.

In France the only marriage legally valid is performed by the mayor or other official; any religious ceremony is optional. If Morton married here, there has to be a record in a *mairie.*

It was through Hugh Fullerton, Director of the American Hospital, that the marriage was known.

A harassed American voice came on the line:

"It's getting late, most of the people who knew him are dead. You go to the *mairie* of . . . the First. He married a French woman. Who was a kind of a terrible old thing. The marriage only lasted six months. I guess you see I disapproved of him. I—I liked the old fellow, he was a genius, but his moral life was lousy."

The *mairie* of the First Arrondissement faces the annex of the Louvre. *Tricoleur*, ʟɪʙᴇʀᴛᴇ́ ᴇ́ɢᴀʟɪᴛᴇ́ ꜰʀᴀᴛᴇʀɴɪᴛᴇ́, courtyard with policemen, concierge's lodge, directory. In the Bureaux d'Etat Civil (Registry) peeling paint, gloom, a counter with *guichets* for Marriages, Births, Deaths. Slowly, the queues move forward. At last:

"I would like to find the date of the marriage of this person" (typewritten slip produced) "and his wife's name."

"Are you a member of the family?"—"*Non.*"

"Quel est le motif de votre demande? The reason for your request?"—"Research."

"Hein?"—"Research, literary research."

"What was the date of the marriage? The name of the spouse?"—"Before the 1914–18 war. I don't know her name."

"How can we find a date if you do not know the date?" (Eyes to heaven.) "How can we find the name of the spouse if you do not know the name of the spouse?"

"Might one look at the indexes?" Behind the counter are rows of tall, tempting volumes labeled *Mariages*.

"Mince alors! When you give us the date we will give you the certificate. How can one find a date if one does not know it?"

Pressure behind and the murmur of innumerable queuers.

"Merci, Madame."

Quel est le motif?—Ignorance, Madame, sheer ignorance.

But you *can* look at indexes, *tables,* if authorized.

The Palais de Justice covers a quarter of the Ile de la Cité, looms over the Conciergerie, and encloses the Sainte Chapelle; it is easy to lose your way in its echoing galleries. In the vasty Salle des Pas Perdus black-gowned, white-stocked lawyers pace slow and aloof, tugged at by haggard gesticulating clients. Pure Daumier, even if many of the billowing robes conceal short skirts.

In the offices of the Procureur de la République a *huissier* takes your papers: *permis de séjour,* Kirschel listing, blood group, shelf mark (Cotton Vitellius A 15), and other annexes to a letter explaining how useful it would be in researches historical to be allowed to consult records of the status civil of certain friends of the writer Edith Wharton, *officier* de la Légion d'Honneur, and specifically the marriage *tables* of the First Arrondissement. "Vous serait-il possible, Monsieur le Procureur . . . ?"

Petitioners wait on a bench outside the office.

This is the Quai des Orfèvres side of the Palace. Maigret always comes through a door from the Police—that door at the end, maybe.

"Lucas!"
"Oui, patron."
"Ce type, Fullairton. It appears that he married. Before the 1914 war. . . . No, I don't know. Find out, my lad."

Time for a *fine* in the Place Dauphine while they look.

Next day the procureur scribbles on a yellow form—"Voilà!"—an authorization to search the indexes of the Premier for the marriage of a friend of Monsieur Edith Wharton, writer.

Across the river at the *mairie* they clear desk space.

Begin with 1903 and go forward a bit. Nothing. Do 1893–1902. No. On to 1920. No Fullerton. Try Morton. Morice Mortin Mouton. No. They may have thought William was a surname. Nothing under W.

Merci, Mesdames.

Another Puzzle

Still, at some point Morton *did* marry, did divorce. And in 1907–1908 he had an affair with Edith Wharton and was blackmailed—or was blackmailed and had the affair. In 1910 he left the *Times.* Why?

As a freelance, he published *Problems of Power,* a book so deeply rooted in the hard soil of pre–World-War-I politics that an ignorant reader can only mutter, with Huckleberry Finn, that "the statements was interesting, but tough." He talks of "occult powers behind the façade of

Governments," of "the great type-dilemma of Kowait-Flushing." He re-prints his 1903 wire from Madrid.[19]

Then came the world war he'd foreseen. Then his *Au Seuil de la Pro-vence,* On the Threshold of Provence, travel essays with a preface that exudes a self-importance not wholly absent earlier: "As an eminent statesman told me," "As I was the first to point out." Had success made him pompous, or middle age? When the war began, he was still Henry James's young friend, an under-fifty; when it ended he was fifty-four (and James was dead).

And a new puzzle:

He lived here for over sixty years. Yet none of the countless "My Memories of Paris" books for his day that I'd seen (not all, but lots) men-tions him. In a mammoth *Bohemian Literary and Social Life in Paris,* a vain Englishman, Sisley Huddlestone,[20] drops thousands of names, but not Morton's. Yet Huddlestone was on the *Times* in the '20s and must have known an ex-correspondent who was still around.

Had a scandal made Morton anathema? Or were colleagues jealous because he'd become Chief? Later, I found, Huddlestone called him, pa-tronizingly, "assistant and translator" for the great de Blowitz.[21]

Recollections of a Newspaperman

"Would a description be of interest?"

No one at today's *Times* bureau knows Morton's name, but the retired managing editor of the *International Herald-Tribune* does.

Spreads of the latest edition and classified ads desk in lobby, lift grind-ing up to city room. At the desk he still uses, Eric Hawkins—chubby face, North-of-England voice—folds his hands and proceeds slowly, precisely:

"He was rather short, extremely reserved and reticent. You would see him—I can see him now—in a long overcoat, walking along the Champs Elysées. When you met him, he was most affable and interesting, but I never got to know him well.

"He was on *Le Figaro,* writing in French, but he was a member of our Anglo-American Press Association. We had these phone numbers. . . . I have never seen him since the second war. He didn't become a French cit-izen, I think."

"No, but he married a Frenchwoman."

Mr. Hawkins rises in his chair, gripping the arms, and stares.

"Oh!"

A long pause.

"He was married?" Another pause. Sitting back: "Oh! he always struck me as a bachelor type. I always saw him alone. He had a silk top hat or a soft trilby, you know, always in black; that is how I remember him, walking slowly, usually with a cane. A flowing tie. A long moustache. I . . . He was *married?* I always saw him alone."

The Fourth Woman: Mme Pouget

From a desk by a window giving on a garden, Hugh Fullerton comes to shake hands: a short, slight, blue-eyed and white-haired man with a humorous, tired face. Overworked. Our talks at the American Hospital are always interrupted by the telephone.

"Mr. Hawkins called your cousin a bachelor type."

A snort. "Ho! He had lots of women in his life. When we met—just after the first war, I was in the embassy—he was a dapper little duck with his moustache. He'd talk part English and part French. I have not admired him from the moral point of view, but he was a genius. I met Mrs. Wharton, too. *She* was a funny person! Very retiring. I never had any contact with his wife, don't know her name even; must be dead by now. His old girlfriend the housekeeper or whatever she called herself—Mme Pouget—is probably dead too."

"Mme Pouget?"

"She lived with him in the Boulevard des Batignolles. A nice old thing, but not his class at all. When he died, she went to a niece down in Nîmes. When I first knew him he was living in a hotel, the Vouillemont. It was his high point, he was rather influential. Then he probably met Mme Pouget and went to the Batignolles.

"In the second war he was an enemy alien. During the Occupation he and old Mme Pouget had no heat. I got them coal and foodstuffs through the embassy when I came back after the Liberation. He had a study—had a lot of papers and never destroyed a thing. But the Gestapo took some, and he sold his books to the Chinese embassy and anyone who had money."

"Everything had gone?"

"He had a few things. Letters from Oscar Wilde; I sold them to Harvard. James. George Meredith. Santayana letters—didn't bring much. . . ."

I retired and went home; I was away when he broke his hip. This wife or former wife discovered he was here in the hospital, so Mme Pouget, his old companion, moved him to a little clinic. When I came back in '51, to this job, he was there. He died there."

"At the *mairie* of the First," I said, "they think I'm unhinged about that marriage—"

"I'd have sworn! It's a long time ago; I was up to the eyes in work. I had to get the certificate when I reported his death; I'm sure if I'd gone outside Paris for it I'd remember. I forget the wife's name. You see he was married and kept it secret till he was ready to die. He may have had trouble over the years; she may have contested the divorce. . . . But she must be dead. Mme Pouget, too."

"So there are four women." (Marc) *"There is Eydeet Wharton, there is Mme Fullairton, there is the* maître-chanteur, *and now there is the old Mme Pouget—"*

*(*Maître-chanteur, *singing teacher, because a blackmailer makes his victim sing. Blackmail is* chantage, *singing.)*

"—although one must contemplate the possibility that it was Mme Pouget who demanded money—the blackmailer was a landlady, a housekeeper?—and that they met again in later years, were reconciled, and lived together again."

"Or that the wife was the blackmailer! Suppose Morton, hoping to marry Edith, didn't want her to know of his encumbrance and paid his wife to keep silent. Then Edith found out, and by the time they were both free, she no longer wanted him because he'd concealed the truth."

Mme Pouget must have known things. But how to trace her? She didn't sound like one of the privileged few who have a telephone. I looked up old directories only pro forma—

But she *had.* Mme *Hélène* Pouget. From 1923. She moved from one house in the Batignolles to another,[22] and her phone numbers, changing with the move, were the numbers Eric Hawkins at the *Herald Tribune* had for Morton.

The Boulevard des Batignolles bridges the railway lines fanning out northward from the Gare Saint-Lazare to the suburbs and the Channel coast. The streets in this attractive quarter cross the rails and each other, tunneling under, flying over. Mme Pouget's sector has a wide center strip of grass. Sedate houses, expensive antique shops, a toylike theater with a painted façade.

But what matters is where he lived earlier, when Edith Wharton may have gone to his place and been seen by a blackmailer. Was he already in the hotel Hugh Fullerton mentioned—the Vouillemont?

The building, off the Place de la Concorde, has shops on the street front, but inside is a ghost hotel lobby, dark and disused, its reception desk furred with dust. "The guests have all checked out."

Divorce Lewis Carroll–Style

The grim Prefecture of Police is near the flower market.

"'Célibataire.' For us he was always 'unmarried,'" says an agent in the Aliens Bureau. "It's a small file. It means he was never in trouble."

"But the wife's maiden name should be on his death certificate," says an agent in Cabinet Direction (Mairies), and picks up the phone: "Fullairton, oui. Veeliam . . . Marie, Oscar, Raoul, Thérèse, Oscar, Natalie. D'accord. . . . Ah bon," writing on a slip of paper, "Merci!" and (Maigret!) pushing it over:

"Divorcé de Camille Victoria Chabbert."

A *name*—the view halloo!

Hurry back over the Pont Neuf to the *mairie* of the First. His name might have been omitted from the index.

C, Chabbert, Chabert. No Camille, no Victoria.

"Merci bien, Mesdames."

His death certificate at the *mairie* of the Ninth, an old building dank with glistening rain, has nothing new.

The marriage could be got at backward.

The Palace of Justice again. Opposite the Monument to the Dead, seventy, eighty . . . ninety-five wide marble steps changing to narrow marble and splintery wood. In the yard far below, *ci-devants* imprisoned in the Conciergerie washed their clothes as they waited for the tumbrils. Finally, the counter.

"The date of the divorce?"

"Probably before the First World War."

"Ten francs, come back in ten days for a copy."

In ten days, Camille might be linkable with one of the Chab(b)erts I'd been finding in directories and library catalogues. The Abbé Chabbert who wrote *Two Years on an Atoll*. The *Bottin Mondain* Chabert O** who lived cheek by jowl with Morton in the Rue du Mont Thabor. (Suppose *that* Chabert had a daughter!)

In twenty days the decree was ready. Pages of musty jargon.

7 NOVEMBRE 1904. TRIBUNAL DE GRANDE INSTANCE DE PARIS

Nineteen-oh-four! So early! One question is answered. Edith had nothing to do with it. Morton hadn't even met her.

> THE COURT having examined the briefs and heard the pleadings of CLEMENCEAU, *avocat,* assisted by Peyrot, *avoué,* for FULLERTON,
>
> > DECLARES Mme Fullerton in default for not having retained a solicitor although she was duly served with a summons on the thirtieth day of August. . . .
> >
> > AND WHEREAS the petition for divorce by Fullerton states sufficient grounds therefor, as it appears from the documents submitted at the hearing in court and in particular a letter dated the eleventh of May One Thousand Nine Hundred and Four which shall be entered with the Judgment from which it appears that Mme Fullerton accused her husband of having mistresses and therefore refused to fulfill her conjugal duties thenceforth [*la dame Fullerton accusait son mari d'avoir des maˆitresses et dès lors refusait de lui accorder ses caresses*], adding in injurious terms that her confidence in *him was lost,*
> >
> > GRANTS a decree of divorce . . . on the petition of and to the benefit of the husband,
> >
> > SENTENCES the defendant to pay the costs . . .[23]

It was Morton who sued. His grounds were that Camille accused him of infidelity and therefore refused him his marital rights. He had two lawyers. She was neither present nor represented. *She* was found to be at fault. A jumble. Extraordinary!

Morton's lawyer, Clemenceau: Was he related to *the* Clemenceau? the famous Georges Clemenceau who presided over the victory of a nearly defeated France in World War I? "Clemenceau's brother" came into Morton's notebook in connection with the Emile Zola trial.

Fifty years later, Camille was claiming to be Morton's wife. And in fact, *could* a wife be discarded just like that in those days?

In a dim Dickensian office, the very aged Maître Bourgain, admitted to the bar in 1920, holds the decree at arm's length and glares. "Bizarre!"—splutter—"The pretext is that he, the husband, had mistresses! The divorce is pronounced for the husband against the wife who did not appear! *Incompréhensible!* She could have appealed—didn't she? *Absolument bizarre!*"

Perhaps Camille, refusing to accept the divorce, learned of Morton's liaison with a rich American and threatened to expose him. "Kind of a terrible old thing," says Hugh Fullerton; but he's going by what Morton's housekeeper Mme Pouget said, the woman who hated Camille—

Morton may have married Camille in his early years in Paris, when he wrote that "dream" in his notebook, which went on:

> She was surely one of those rare great women of all time to whom the gods have given to be as beautiful as Aphrodite, & who can share their persons as others dispense kind deeds without loss of their integral beauty, or other sense than that of having been generous as their mother the Earth. . . . She turned her head and sent a whisper down the corridor: "My Morton, I will come to you." My heart seemed to crack and shattered fall[.]

But the wife he divorced doesn't sound like an earth goddess.

Those *Bottin Mondain* Chab(b)erts can be crossed off. No girl of family could have been divorced in hugger-mugger. Camille was obscure and defenseless. After all, a wife he hid from people! Discouraging. It is not easy to trace Fullerton, a writer with connections; when it comes to finding a poor old nobody . . .

Morton's address in the decree was the *Times;* Camille's, Rue de Chambiges near the Etoile, no number. I went, I saw, I quailed. A street too long for door-to-door inquiries about a woman who stayed there at the dawn of the century. Posh houses, but posh houses have attic rooms not much bigger than coffins, intended for maids, now occupied by maids, students, and miscellaneous poor.

Bus home. Champs de Mars, drab Rue de Lourmel, dolorous, mysterious Maison des Dames du Calvaire, bus stop.

Henry James: Advice on Blackmail

The blackmail puzzle was illuminated but not simplified when four letters from James to Morton, photocopies, came in the post with a request by the biographer to decipher a word.

(At that point in the Fullerton research, James's letters had not been collected and edited but were scattered in many archives.)

The letters are dated 1907, the year the liaison with Edith Wharton began. We find that, after the visit at the Mount that changed Edith's life, Morton returned to France via England, where he stayed overnight with James—to whom he wrote as soon as he reached Paris. What he said has to be divined from James's response, a torrent of concerned indignation and yet of gladness at Morton's having "after long years" spoken "of what there was always a muffled unenlightened ache for my affection in my not knowing."

For James had guessed at "complications" in Morton's life that he "was powerless to get any nearer to." Now surely, a man "as mortally, as tenderly attached" as he was to Morton must be able to help "somehow, bit by bit . . . by dividing with you, as it were, the heavy burden of your consciousness."

He returned a letter Morton had enclosed, from an unidentified person, showing such devotion that it might "be more than anything else" to see him through.

> So sit tight and sit firm and *do* nothing—save indeed look for that money; for which I wish to goodness I could *help* you to look, better than my present impotence permits. . . . P.S. *Destroy* those things—when you've made them yours.[24]

James hadn't been asked for money (or he'd have written "*could* help" not "could *help*"). But he answered three more cries for sympathy from Morton, who was *"hypnotized,"* James told him bluntly, by remaining "under the same roof with the atrocious creature" into exaggerating her power. No one could possibly see her except as

> a mad, vindictive, and obscene old woman (with whom, credibly, you may well, in Paris, have lived younger, but who is now only wreaking the fury [of] an *idée fixe* of resentment on you for not having perpetrated the marriage with her that it was—or would be—inconceivable you *should* perpetrate). She can only denounce and describe and exhibit *herself*, in the character of a dangerous blackmailer . . . [and get] "chucked out". . . her overtures to your people at home, e.g. simply burned on the spot, unlooked at, as soon as *smelt*.

No one, James continued, would *"touch"*

> anything with the name of the R[. . . .] in it—it will serve only to scare them. As for R.G., he is a very ancient history and . . . has all the appearance today of a regularized member of society, with his books and writings everywhere,

his big monument (not so bad) to Shakespeare, one of the principal features of Stratford on Avon. However, I didn't mean to go into any detail—if you've known him you've known him (R.G.); and it is absolutely your own affair, for you to take your own robust and frank and perfectly manly stand on. . . . If after this you make any pact or compromise with her in the interest of an insane (for it would be that in you, compassion), *then,* dearest Morton, it would be difficult to advise or inspire you. It is detestable that you should still be under the same roof with her— . . . take your stand on your honour, your manhood, your courage, your decency, your intelligence and on the robust affectionate [*sic*] of your old, old, and faithful, faithful friend

Henry James[25]

That was written from the Reform Club.

Lamps lit against the acrid November Pall Mall fog, the club claret, coffee and armagnac on the gallery, *luxe calme et dignité.* James rises, portly, passes Balfour or Asquith, moves to a quiet room with Morton's letter and writes his blazing exhortatory reply.

By the "same roof"—answering another letter—he'd only meant the same house, not the same apartment; but he understood the advantage of being able to "observe her proceedings. . . ."[26]

Dangerous Liaisons

With James's letters, what was happening begins to matter.

But, emotional impact apart, surely they contain some not very arcane clues? I am to find out, here, why Morton was blackmailed. But don't James's letters, there in America, point to reasons?

The person given as "the R[. . . .]"—the Rupert? Roman? Rodin? No. But "R[. . . .]" was one reason for the blackmail. So was the person called "R.G." But here things are practically spelled out:

First, "R.G." was a man. And he can't be all that hard to identify. A prolific writer, initials known, who had done a Shakespeare monument? Besides, somewhere . . . Morton's notebook—

April '93 First week in April 93 Marquis Lorne & Princess Louise Ronald Gower. Hotel Choiseul all lunch at Le Doyen & I bring James. Afterwards M. of L. & R.G. chez moi.

Beyond that: James's tone of voice. One topic would in 1907 have evoked that tone. Vivid in people's minds, though tabu in print and discreet talk, was the superscandal of a decade ago. The inference seemed imperative. Morton had had homosexual relations—criminal, at that time—which left him open to blackmail.

The library would still be open if I hurried.

Good, they had Oscar Wilde's *Letters.*

Wilde spoke at the unveiling of Lord Ronald Gower's statue *Shakespeare and Four of His Characters* at the Memorial Theater.

By God, he *was* this R.G.!

The Marquess of Lorne, later Duke of Argyll, was R.G.'s nephew. He was married to the Princess Louise.

In other words, the M. of L. who came with his uncle Ronald to visit Fullerton in his rooms was a son-in-law of Queen Victoria.

When Wilde was released from Reading Gaol, he went to France as "Sebastian Melmoth." His Paris base was the Grand Café at 14 Boulevard des Capucines. The *Times* was at number 35. He had his publishers send Fullerton a copy of *The Importance of Being Earnest,* then wrote asking his dear Fullerton to lend him a hundred francs.[27] In time, Fullerton apologized for not having answered his dear Melmoth's "touching appeal"; he had been away:

> You do me too much honour in asking me to come to the rescue of an artist such as you. . . . I grope at the hope that meanwhile the stress has passed, and that you will not have occasion to put, *malgré vous,* either me or anyone else again into such a position of positive literal chagrin.[28]

Wilde replied, with acidic gusto:

> But what a Johnsonian letter you have written me! . . . So might the great lexicographer have written (though perhaps he might have found tautology in "positive . . . literal"). In so slight a matter, my dear Fullerton, sentiment need not borrow stilts. . . . I return to Paris . . . and hope to come across you, but you must not be Johnsonian: Theocritean were better.[29]

Beneath the elegant snub, flirtatiousness.

Wilde and Fullerton were acquaintances having a common friend, Lord Ronald Charles Sutherland-Leveson-Gower. R.G. had introduced Wilde to aristocratic society.

R.G.'s father was the Duke of Sutherland. His mother, the Duchess, her friend Queen Victoria, and Queen Marie-Antoinette were, he said, the only women in his life.[30] He sculpted and wrote on art; art gave structure to his life. When his monument for the Shakespeare Memorial, of which he was a trustee, was unveiled in 1888 he had a bad name. Winning a suit against a journalist for defamation of character did not help.[31]

Lord Ronald Gower was the original of Wilde's Lord Henry Wotton in *The Picture of Dorian Gray,* who inspires in Dorian a passion for "what the world calls sin" and talks in epigrams so familiar it's as if he were quoting Oscar Wilde. ("The only way to get rid of a temptation is to yield to it.") Wilde explained to critics that Lord Henry "seeks to be merely the spectator of life. He finds that those who reject the Battle are more deeply wounded than those who take part in it."[32]

In his memoirs,[33] which were much expurgated in print, Lord Ronald comes through not as diabolical but as sentimental and proud of it, impulsive and rich enough to act on impulse. He had been second in a duel; had witnessed battles of the Franco-Prussian War in company with the famous war correspondent W. F. Russell. All told, a man to impress a romantic young American.

This discovery that Morton was bisexual suggests a Tiresian element in the "dream" in his notebook (pages 11, 27). After "crack and shattered fall," he wrote:

> She came, draped only like a figurine of Hellas. She flung aside the mantle. I seemed lost in her effulgence like an asteroid near the sun. . . . Lying on the cushions of a silk divan she seemed a goddess come on an errand of mercy. My soul was bursting in adoration of her & with sense of the goodness of the Earth. And so rarefied became my passion that actually as I glided over her I found myself envying her that

There he stopped. Envying . . . what? a woman's experience, being acted on, being "had"? Transforming his self into hers, assimilating his analogous experience with male lovers?

To return to the blackmail, it seems that:

(1) As a young man in Paris, M.F. lived with a Frenchwoman. (2) In 1893 he was visited, perhaps in her house, by R.G., a lover or ex-lover. (3) In 1899 he distanced himself, callously one may think, from the disgraced Oscar Wilde. (4) In 1904 he divorced Camille Chabbert. (5) In 1907 he wrote to James, whose replies indicate that Morton lived in the house of an ex-mistress who had evidence linking him with R.G. and the R[. . . .] and threatened to expose him.

Had Morton hidden his marriage and divorce from James; were they the "complications" James had only guessed at for "long years"? Had his marriage, like his dangerous liaisons, taken place long ago?

So much hinges on dating it. On identifying Camille Chabbert.

Letters came from Chab(b)erts[34] found in directories in and out of Paris. No one had heard of a Camille or a Victoria.

Buses, métro, walking in the rain, standing in line were becoming a bore. *I hate my love with a C because she is concealed camouflaged and chimerical and her name is Camille Chabbert.*

The Valise of Mme Pouget

"I have an idea she called herself Mme Fullerton," says Hugh Fullerton. "She denied the divorce. When he broke his hip, Mme Pouget, his old companion, said: 'I must get him out of the hospital, because that dreadful old wife of his has tracked him down.'"

"Have you any idea why he married her?"

"I never stopped to wonder *why*. Now, if he had married some society woman—! He was a very bad bet as a husband, I can assure you. Mme Pouget told me the wife was living in very destitute circumstances in a mansarde on the Champs-Elysées. Of course Mme Pouget never appeared in public with Morton, but he was sensible to get someone like that to do his cooking. She used to laugh at him. He had urinary troubles and walked like this" (demonstration) "and she'd say, 'Here comes the snail.' She had a bad time when he died because the government came down on single people having large apartments. They put her furniture in the street. She went down to a niece who ran a hotel in Nîmes. I went to say good-bye. I feel badly about that suitcase of letters."

"That—suitcase of letters?"

"It was there, open, with Morton's letters. I should have got my dander up and demanded them. But those old cousins of hers were there. The man had the Legion. He looked like a retired minor official. He was very hostile. . . . But I'm sure Mme Pouget is dead."

"Une valise pleine de letters?!"

"A suitcase-full! We have to find her. Or if she's dead, find the niece at the hotel in Nîmes."

But "we find no death record," writes a Nîmes official.

Would one have to write to scores of hotels in the city to ask if a manager had an aunt from Paris staying with her years ago?

No, only to hundreds of villages; for Mme Pouget's landlord in the Batignolles knows that her niece lived not in Nîmes, in the Gard Department, but *du côté de Nîmes.*

"Around Nîmes" could mean any of several hundred communes. I wrote to mayors. Mayors of Bouiallargues, Caissargues, Foissac, Rodhilon, Aigues-Mortes, Aigues-Vives, Arpaillargues-et-Aureillac, Collorgues, Saint-Bonnet du Gard, Garn, Comps, Mus, Mons, Grès, Mars, Molières-sur-Zèze . . . the slightly jangled bells of a Romanesque church across a valley . . . Mauresargues.

"Unknown here," wrote the mayor of Saint-André de Roquepertuis (population 241), "but I saw in this week's paper the death of *une dame Pouget* in Pouzilhac." "No one in our commune knows her" (another mayor) "nor is she in the Listes Electorales."

"When did women get the vote?"

"Just after the Liberation." (Marc) *"It wasn't voted, it was a decree of* le Général.*"*

Old Paris voting lists are kept at the Archives de la Seine on the tree-lined Quai Henri IV with its deafening traffic. Inside, quiet; faded prints, bleached flags, and yellowed street plans. A village museum. The lists stand crammed together, two feet high, two or three volumes per arrondissement per year.

By closing time I'd found POUGET Hélène, born in 1875. Her birth *acte,* duly obtained, names her parents, Etienne and Jeanne Pouget, and a note adds: Died Le Collet de Dèze (Lozère) 25 February 1958.

"It was her own name, then." (Marc) "She was 'Madame' by courtesy. The Lozère? It's true; Nîmes would be the nearest city. It's a godforsaken country, very depopulated."

I wrote to the mayor of Le Collet de Dèze asking how I could get in touch with Mme Pouget's family.

Camille Chabbert: Up the Street

And what of the woman Mme Pouget accused of persecuting Morton when he lay in hospital: his ex-wife?

The most recent lists stored at the Archives de la Seine have CHABBERT Camille Victoria, born 1879 in the Dordogne. Domiciled in the Eighth Arrondissement at 122 Avenue—Hugh Fullerton was dead right!—Avenue des Champs-Elysées.

Why, Camille Chabbert may be preparing her supper in a kitchen in the Eighth only four métro stops from where her . . . investigator . . . where I, in the Fifteenth, in a kitchen in the Fifteenth, am pacing up and down unable to eat.

But next day in the *mairie* of the Eighth a note beside her name in a later list says: "Died in the 15th."

Dead.

But why did she move here, to the nondescript Fifteenth? Was even a *garret* in the Champs-Elysées too costly for her?

The bus I caught jerked down through Paris in bumper-to-bumper pre-Christmas traffic. Cold gray light, tinsel and glitter, Dior, jewelers, Plaza Athénée, Revlon, jewelers, Balmain, over to the Left Bank, Lourmel, Emile Zola, Maison des Dames du Calvaire, past my own Rue de Javel to the Rue Jacquemaire-Clemenceau and the *mairie* of the Fifteenth with its sloping park and scowling guardians of the facts of life and death, where I asked for her death certificate. Name, date, one franc fifty; come back on Friday.

Camille's birthplace in the Dordogne—Le Buisson, near the then undiscovered Lascaux Caves—is a small town but an important railway junction. The wall map plotting Morton's travels shows that he went close by on a visit to Carcassonne. Was that how they met?

Friday. I collected Camille's death *acte* at my *mairie* and sat down on a bench to read it.

She was the daughter of Antonin Chabbert, mechanic, and his wife, Eugénie Auriol, both deceased. Unmarried. No occupation. Domiciled 122 Avenue des Champs-Elysées, Paris, 8th. Deceased 1964 at—at— 110 Avenue Emile Zola, Paris, 15th.

Emile Zola!

Where was 110? Breathless I went up the Rue de Lourmel, crossed my own street, followed the wall of the Maison des Dames du Calvaire as it angled obliquely into Emile Zola—

Number 110 is a side door in the convent wall.

Two blocks from home.

"Reverend Mother: For a long time I have been trying—"

By return post a letter from the Maison Médicale des Dames du Calvaire.

At nine next morning I opened the gate to the now bare and sodden garden, then the door to the house at the end of the drive. A smell of floor wax, antiseptic, and incense. An office with a desk. A woman in a coif with a crucifix on the breast of her gray dress. A strong characterful face.

Mère Louise had some papers before her. She asked no questions.

"We are an association of widows. We take cancer patients in the last stages, when nothing can be done. I remember Mme Chabbert. The separated wife of" (glancing down) "W. M. Fullerton. Divorced? *Non!* She was a practicing Catholic. Would you like to see . . . ?"

In the dim ward, two rows of beds with wasted, motionless shapes under white coverlets. A nun was bent over one of them.

In the office I said: "You're the first person I have met who knew her. I know she was destitute, but I don't know what she did. I suppose she was, oh, a waitress?"

"Why!" For the first time Mère Louise showed surprise. "Why, she was a singer at the Opéra Comique—*et du talent même! And* a gifted one!"

Montmartre: The Phantom of the Opera

The chastening discovery that Morton's wife was a singer meant that she would be on record. The Opéra Comique, like the Opéra, is a state institution. Its archives are at the Opéra Library, accessed by a double curving ramp, a porte cochère, a grand stairway, and a lush museum room with busts of Gluck, Gounod, and Pauline Viardot.

Camille isn't in Wolff's *Un Demi-Siècle de l'Opéra Comique,*[35] which lists every performance and every singer from 1900 to 1950. However, the Union Catholique du Théâtre et de la Musique know of her from their social worker at the Foyer des Artistes de Music Hall et de Cabaret, in Montmartre.

Utrillo's Montmartre, vineyards and windmills, is now neon and watered champagne by night and scruffy, sad, squalid by day. Girls stand one foot back against the wall like tired cranes, *grues.*

But the shabby Foyer blazed with flowers and posters. The old artistes who came for aid did not enter, they made entrances. A young probationer tried to help. M. Daigre's card said Deigre, *they* denied that he existed, how could he get his medical reimbursement? Actually he was better known as le Grand Alexis.

The phone would ring, the probationer would say that Mademoiselle apologized, she was at the hospital, the ministry.

Everyone knew each other.—Did they know of a singer called Camille Chabbert who had died recently, very old?—No one knew the name.—She might have called herself Mme Fullerton—*Non.*

Camille: The Concierge's Tale

From the moment Camille Chabbert's address was found, the obvious procedure was to go there and talk with the concierge.

Anyone who has been in the Champs-Elysées, north side near the Arc de Triomphe, has seen where Camille lived. Hers was the building with the Lord Byron cinema in that long broad shimmering stretch of tables, chairs, and bright umbrellas, bobbing with hundreds of waiters and thousands of tourists.

But there were delays. A concierge may stand mute if accosted in a foreign accent; help was needed, and it was Easter by the time Marc and I wove a way among tables and high-held trays of drinks and through the very high portal numbered 122.

A big lobby with the calm of business premises on a Saturday afternoon. Near the door, with the lobby ceiling for sky, stood a chalet with stairs running up its side. When the CONCIERGE button was pushed, a casement in the upper story swung open and, like a burgess parleying with besiegers from a rampart, the concierge put forth her head.

". . . information about Mme Camille Chabbert" (Marc).

"Elle est morte." The hand began to draw the casement in.

"You knew her perhaps, Madame?"

"Oh . . . vaguement." The head began to retreat.

Something else was said, something else . . . (gently does it). The head vanished, but the door at the top of the stairs opened and the concierge came halfway down. There she perched for—twenty minutes? Longer?

Then, with our "Au revoir, Madame," an exit, a weaving through tourists and trays, and a whipping around the corner into a crêperie for collation of notes.

The concierge's mother had the job before her. Therefore she knows a good deal about Mme Chabbert, a tenant with some rooms on the top floor and two offices, which she let, on the second.

Yes, in her youth she had been a singer. She had photographs.

She wasn't rich, but she did all right. "My mother told me she used to go to the Côte d'Azur every year; she had an apartment in Nice. Also her ex-husband would come and give her money."

What was his name? Why, his name was Camille Chabbert! She was called Mme Ixo Chabbert. He was an editor on *Le Figaro*.

She had a daughter married to an Englishman and a granddaughter raised in England. The daughter was brought up with the family of Clemenceau.

The husband was living with another woman.

"*Sympathique? Ah, bah,* she was *un numéro,* she was a sketch. She didn't seem poverty-stricken, but that didn't keep her from getting public assistance. When the husband died, she went to the deputy mayor and came in waving a bundle of franc notes and said 'He gave me a thousand, I can buy a bottle of liqueur.' Oh, she got by! She had a million in her drawer when she died."

The English Businessman's Story

Back to the concierge, alone. Again the bell, the head poking out from behind the crenellations, the semidescent.

Might there be tenants who'd remember Mme Chabbert?

"There were some old ladies. One used to go to Nice with her. But they're dead. I'm not sure how old she was when she died. Eighty-five? *That* old? She must have been very pretty in her youth. Even when I knew her she had very beautiful hair."

As if coming to a decision, the concierge added: "Next door in the Bureau Broux there's Monsieur Nolan. He knew her."

Out into the sunlight, through the tables, tourists, *garçons,* into the next high doorway. The Société John Brooks—ah, it was an English company.

"An appointment? In what connection?" The office receptionist was surprised.

"In connection with Mme Camille Chabbert."

The receptionist went into another room and returned looking more surprised. Mr. Nolan was tied up, but next week . . .

On a day that finally did arrive a dark-haired man shook hands, waved toward a chair, went back to his desk, and rapped out one sharp question: "What is your interest in Mme Chabbert?"

Explanation.

"Good." Mr. Nolan sat back and began to talk.

He had heard that Mme Chabbert had offices to let, and with his wife, who is French, he called at her mansarde.

"We saw that it was an extraordinary life. She was a friend of Pola Negri, theatrical people like that, before the war. She had a long arm— many friends from the old days. And dozens of cats.

"She was very theatrical. She may have exaggerated but she once told me that in Madrid or someplace, when she and her husband were there, she jumped out the window to get away from him. She must have loved that man! She kept talking about him. Probably when she was young she had a lot of charm, but I would have thought she was an impossible woman to live with.

"Anyway, he lived with some woman, a Madame . . . yes, Pouget. He was a most unusual man in many respects."

For the Nolans had seen a trunk, two trunks, with his papers.

"Mme Chabbert had gone, when she knew he was dying, to this Mme Pouget with a revolver. She always carried a revolver. Probably a stage effect. She used to brandish it. She went and got those trunks. She went through every piece of paper, but she didn't know a word of English and didn't know the value of anything.

"When she died, I knew that workmen had gone into her place. Everyone thought she had gold. You would see her in winter, in the bitterest weather, walking down the Champs-Elysées with no stockings on and no warm coat. But they thought she was miserly."

Nolan decided to save Camille's papers. He found her attic knee-deep in papers and feathers pulled out of the mattress.

"A shambles. Photographs. Fullerton and Mme Pouget on a steamer to America. One or two letters from Henry James. I thought I'd frame them. Was Mr. Fullerton homosexual? I thought he must have been. There were letters. And Camille told me he was a pederast."

I asked the all-important question: "Would you permit me to look at the papers?"

"Yes. You may look at them."

A date could be fixed next week.

"Oh, and she used to hide Jewish people in her apartment. Oh, not from altruism! She spent most of the war in Nice. For money."

"In your view," I asked, "would she have been capable of blackmail?"

"Oh yes. She would stop at nothing: nothing, nothing, nothing, nothing. She was a real phenomenon. Nothing."

The Social Worker's File

Until I could see those papers, concentration was impossible. However, there were things that could be done.

The concierge had supplied a stage name for Camille, Ixo; and IXO, says Wolff's compendium at the Opéra Library, "made her début at the Comique 7 June 1914 as Santuzza in *Cavalleria Rusticana.*"

Ten years after the divorce. Camille was thirty-five.

But Wolff says no more; and the multivolume small-print unindexed *Annales du Théâtre et de la Musique* say for June 1914 only that many sopranos were trying out for the part of Santuzza.

Faces at the Foyer des Artistes de Music Hall et de Cabaret brightened as a little woman with flying hair rushed in laden with bags and smiled around.

"*Voyons!*" In her office, Mlle Poitou-Duplessy found a card: "Mme Chabbert was befriended by Deputy Mayor Monnet of the Eighth." Dropping the card: "She was a personality! Dynamic! She lived in her attic with her cats; she talked of the past. She created the role of Madame Butterfly in Italy. She had a daughter, Mireille—but I believe she died in England—who was Fullerton's *fille déclarée,* recognized daughter. They married before a *pasteur* because he was the son of a *pasteur.* A Lutheran church, maybe?"

"*. . . named Mireille!*

"*C'est vrai, the concierge said Camille had a daughter. Was Mireille Morton's daughter, then? And is it possible that Morton married Camille in England?*"

"*I'll try to find out next week.*"

London

In Search of a Marriage Record: England

Morton may have met Camille here, on a visit.

In the U.K., wills and records of births, deaths, and marriages are open to the public. (When a French official heard this his eyes bulged: *"But there might be things the family did not want known!"*)

No FULLERTON William Morton; no CHAB(B)ERT Victoria Camille. But in 1930 CHABBERT Frederica Mireille, twenty-nine, and LAINÉ Robert Pierre, twenty-eight, were married in London. The groom was a "manufacturer's agent," as was his father, Paul Lainé. The bride did not fill in her father's name. Mother's name was not asked.

Paris

The Niece of Mme Pouget

Mr. Nolan had to postpone our appointment. Postponed it again. And again, and again.

I'd forgotten that I had asked the mayor of Le Collet de Dèze, where Mme Hélène Pouget died, how I could get in touch with her family, when a letter came. The mayor had passed my query on to the sender, who wrote: "I am Mme Pouget's niece and have lived here since leaving the Hôtel de Nîmes. Will you please explain—?"

I explained. Deferred asking permission to visit. It now seemed the papers Hugh Fullerton saw in Mme Pouget's valise did not go south with her. He said goodbye to her, and after he (and, presumably, her disapproving cousins) left, in burst Camille with her revolver.

Hélène Pouget, seventy-eight. Camille "Ixo" Chabbert, four years younger. Some episodes in this story are Jamesian; that confrontation was not.

A day came when the papers were on a table in Mr. Nolan's office in a laundry case. He pulled a few out. Names flashed. Clemenceau. Katharine. Grand Duke Alexander.

I lugged the documents home in a shopping bag on June 2nd, returned them on the 16th. The intervening fortnight was, as the French say, not banal.

Bundles of Letters

Piles of letters built up. Now and then a bee buzzed in from the geraniums on the balcony and settled on a note from Cousin Ella Clapp or Prince Leopold, Duke of Albany.

You could read by daylight till after nine that dry and hot June. *Télés,* laughter, the clink of plates sounded from across the court as the Great Bear wheeled above mansardes and chimney pots.

There were several thousand sheets of paper to match for size, color, ink, handwriting. I scanned for dates, arranged letters in rough chronology by writer, trying not to read for sense, yet—though now and then words compelled attention:

> Scorned by you as I am—treated as hardly a human being—I can hardly face him with ordinary human dignity. . . . I have simply never, by anything, been so *hurt.* I do not think any human being has the right to hurt another like this.[36]

Standard French, English, and American handwritings with personal variations niggardly, flamboyant, liliaceous, lazy, and downright illegible. Pastel notepaper coronet-embossed, brittle newsprint flaking at the touch, indestructible creamy vellum. Telegrams. Scraps of wallpaper. Sorted, there were about five hundred letters in two main groups: Fullerton's papers, with a few that were Camille's, and the papers of Charles Hamilton Aïdé.

Aïdé, whose name was vaguely familiar in connection with the theater, left Morton his papers "to manipulate, to publish, or to burn as you think fit. . . . I *trust you,*" he wrote. "I say no more."[37] Hence their presence in Camille's attic. (The letter that made Nolan ask if Morton was homosexual was among them, a distraught letter from a W. M. H[ardinge] whose signature looked like "W.M.F.")

Edith Wharton's hand appeared only in a 1931 note to Morton, late in her life and coolly amicable, to "cher ami" from "Yrs. E."

The papers came higgledy-piggledy with false juxtapositions and frustrating hiatuses. There was the thrill of discovery, occasionally the pleasure of a hunch confirmed. But above all, reading those letters was oppressive.

Like looking down into the oubliette of a ruined castle. The pangs of despisèd love, the law's delays, the insolence of office, all were there, and the room was too small to contain the revival of so much dead life.

Many letters to Fullerton ended: "BURN THIS."

Cambridge, Massachusetts: A Fiancée

The earliest letter was written by Morton himself in January 1888, when he was . . . was twenty-two, and working on the *Boston Advertiser*. He tells "My darling" that if she comes to Boston she can go to a concert with his mother ("who wants you to love her"). Shall he meet the Springfield train? "It is most delightful to be here in the Craigie House study writing to you, my Marian. Mr. Longfellow sits near by reading."

The study in yellow-clapboard Craigie House was "sacred to the Muses almost above all others on American soil"[38] as the room of "The Children's Hour." H. W. Longfellow, internationally famous, was one of the sights of America, visited by Wilde and R.G. among others, long before his house became a National Park Service monument because it had earlier served as George Washington's headquarters.

> . . . I tried to get a chance to lock my door in town and to answer your letter, but people kept coming. . . . [Here] I hoped to find a moment, but the hours were full of talk of Europe, and at bed time the letter had not been written. This is the last moment now, for you must have this letter Saturday night even if it takes a special delivery stamp. I wonder how it will find your cold, and whether really you cannot come. Oh, my dearest, you do not know how much I want it![39]

This letter (ten pages) loses in print. Morton's youthful hand has juicy loops and elaborate capitals. In a languishing "If you would only come" the *I* is a flower with petals on it, which he drew while talking about Europe.

Marian of Springfield does not appear again.

London: A Mistress

Next Morton is in the London particular, the foggy London, of Sherlock Holmes, of Whistler and Beardsley, of the Prince of Wales's philanderings, of misery, injustice, protest, and anarchism.

He is living in rooms off the Strand with Percy Anderson: late thirties, painter, theatrical designer. Both are hobnobbing with Ronald Gower; with Alec Yorke, a courtier with whom Queen Victoria sings Gilbert and Sullivan duets; and with Aïdé—oldest of the lot, born in 1826[40] of a Romanian father and a well-born English mother: novelist, painter, composer, concoctor of frothy West End comedies and private charades for the court.[41] A dainty, naughty, rococo man. Morton speaks of his "adorable Chesterfieldian charm."[42]

This was the milieu of the intimacy with R.G. that Morton revealed to James years later as one of the reasons why he was being blackmailed, the other being intimacy with the [R. . . .].

Morton told Aïdé that he thought his artwork "genius";[43] but as to writing, he was also getting to know James and recognized the real thing. Aïdé, with his stage successes, looked down on James, who felt for "poor dear" Aïdé a sort of exasperated kindliness. Morton did some tricky tightrope walking so as not to offend Aïdé:

> I confess . . . that I am quite ready to find something [in James's *Theatricals*]. In contrast I am in the presence of a dramatic *fait accompli,* in the promise of your comedy in October, which interests and delights me more—so far—[44]

He asked for a job on the *News* and got one on the *Times.*

But most of the papers for his London life are pages, hundreds, blotted and xxx'd by a lady who holds it a baseness to write fair, is not very strong on spelling, and dates her letters "4.30 p.m."

Morton met Margaret Brooke in spring 1890 and began to call at her Knightsbridge house. Hasty notes thanked him for roses; told him she'd be in town till 17.10. Soon they were meeting, or writing, daily. Why was he surprised that she liked Oscar? A brilliant talker, and "not at all black really—I imagine him to be rather good and true" for all his "contradictory looking décor."[45] Morton showed her poems. She too was writing, sketches of life in Borneo. He gave her advice and found her a typist. Her casual "Yours always" became "Thine always," *à toi.*

Margaret Brooke was an aristocratically scatty, unmaliciously arrogant, clever, semieducated, generous woman with a simple code of morals. "If people love each other—they may do as they like."[46]

Who she was is not clear. A friend of James and Maupassant; also of an *Almanach de Gotha* set, people like "little Alice of Monaco," wife of Prince Albert I.

Sublimely ignorant of a wage earner's life, she asked Morton to wire her Kettner's address, she'd forgotten it; she'd meet him there for lunch. And he might join her in Monte.—Morton's soaring letters encountered pockets of low pressure.

> I can't get on without seeing you and yet you go and hide . . . lest you should be bored. . . . Write to me that at least you know I am an honest fool, rather than a subtle one who has oerleaped himself. Now see how prosaic I may be. . . . There will come a [typist's] bill of £3.10. I hope this is all right.[47]

In an intense conversation aboard a train, he pressed Margaret to become his mistress. She dithered. She'd like to be the first woman he had ever really loved. She'd go to his rooms if he and Percy would be alone.[48] Percy tactfully absented himself. An hour after leaving, Margaret wrote to tell Morton of her bliss.[49]—She went abroad. He must write *every day;* he must seal his letters and *burn hers!!—But still no letter from him!!!* The hotel might be confusing her with some other Lady Brooke; Morton had better address her in full: Lady Brooke, Ranee of Sarawak.[50]

The Ranee of Sarawak. The word in James's letter was *Ranee.* She was a rani.

As a girl of twenty Margaret de Windt had married the middle-aged Sir Charles Brooke, "White Rajah" of Sarawak in what is now Malaysia. The marriage didn't work. Though appearances were kept up—she went to Sarawak around this time—the couple lived mostly apart. When Morton met her, Margaret was forty-one, "Winter"; he was "Spring."[51]

From abroad, more frantic postscripts. *Why hadn't he written?* At last, two letters arrived together.

> Come back to me, my darling, and you shall know I am panting my heart out in longing for one kiss from you. Ah me—. . . . We are both supremely self-reliant and intolerant of any laws that others make. . . . this may be sublimely, Satanically immoral, audaciously Promethean; but it is the way we are bound to live. . . .[52]

> I will guard your name, your reputation. . . . I *love* you I *love you.* . . . I could meet you in Paris. . . . I should have my sole difficulty in explaining to Percy why I deprived him of my company. . . . Frankly I would prefer to

meet you nearer home, but I throw myself into your hands. I will come at your bidding if you say break with me the bars of the kingdom of Pluto.[53]

In London again, Margaret bemoaned Morton's transfer to Paris. Superior to middle-class prudery, she told him that she had the curse three days early; still, they could dine at Pagani's and go to his rooms and talk.[54] Her feeling for him wasn't merely sensual.[55] If he were capable "of a mean or *little* action," she wouldn't love him as she did. "Never before have I loved intellectually and with my heart. You are my life companion."[56]

Paris: A Siren

The remaining papers, the great mass of them, date from Morton's long, long residence here.

The Ranee sent him introductions and London gossip. HRH was in love. "Burne-Jones and Oscar Wilde with their respective wives dined here. . . . The two women were dull, and the evening slow."[57] (But when catastrophe came, the Ranee not only helped Wilde in jail but had the dull Mrs. Wilde and the children stay with her in Italy.)

Swathed in shawls, she sat up late over letters. Morton said it was hard to find a room, Paris was expensive. Oh, not if one knew how to live, replied the Queen of Sarawak. She had a dear little Englishwoman in Paris, not young, a humble friend who'd helped her in dangerous scrapes and might help him.[58]

For a time, Morton was orientated toward London. He went over, staying with Percy, dining with James. He kept up gossip with Aïdé. A friend was jailed as co-respondent in a divorce case. "Only what a dull blundering instrument of justice a court is," wrote a now worldly New Englander. "When one thinks that it is possible to be arraigned as an adulterer or ess if you or elle put reciprocal hands contiguous upon a dining room table in presence of a parasite of a servant."[59] And month by month, singly and in droves, London friends came through Paris: R.G. and his friends. James, a different matter.

And Margaret, a difficult matter. Arrangements, altered daily, were made for meeting in Paris. Margaret asked Morton to find her a hotel; the Monacos, who had offered her their apartment, for one thing kept too many servants.[60] But why did Morton never *write*?

Whether they actually met in Paris is unclear. In April (?1892) Margaret wrote from Rome to "Dear Morton" at 5 Rue Vignon, Paris.

> I cannot think why you have not answered my letters. . . . Adeh [her son] and I may spend May in Paris, and I suppose in that case that you would condescend to come and see us sometimes. Now do write please and tell me all your news. Whether your fair haired syren of a landlady has made any further onslaughts on your virtue. . . . Give my love to de Blowitz.
>
> Yours alys Margaret
>
> *Write* you are a *horrid* little boy—and behave infamously to me. *So there.*[61]

A landlady! Ha, is this at last the blackmailer?

And an address for Morton before the Wharton affair. The Rue Vignon is near the Madeleine. A very short walk from the *Times*.

That was the last letter from Margaret.

And here, surely, are some of the letters a blackmailer later held over Morton's head. They are strewn with enough amorous French phrases for a nonreader of English to get the idea.

There are no R.G. letters. Morton must have destroyed them (though not the Ranee's!) when the blackmailer was paid off. In April 1893, we know from his notebook, R.G. went to his place after lunch. Did the siren landlady see, hear, something to alert her to the nature of their relations? That something did happen appears from a letter Aïdé sent Morton next month:

> How sorry—and how glad—I am at your little difference with R!—By "glad," I mean that I believe it is much better for your extreme intimacy to be stopped—even at the risk of some soreness on the part of our inconsiderate friend. Poor dear fellow! . . . With so much to make life happy, he has ruined his own prospects and would go far to ruin those of the friends he loves best![62]

Lord Ronald Gower, brother of the duke of Sutherland, the greatest landowner in England, and brother-in-law of the duke of Westminster, the richest private person in England. The marquess of Lorne, ex-governor general of Canada, duke-to-be, son-in-law of the queen-empress Victoria. The queen of Sarawak. Prince Albert I and Princess Alice, "the Monacos." Fabergé filigree on a matt Toulouse-Lautrec Paris background.

And Meanwhile . . .

From Julia Fullerton, Waltham, Massachusetts, 6 February 1893, to "My
dear Will":

> For some reason many trials large and small have come the last year. This
> illness of your father's . . . the supply of the pulpit each week. . . . Saturday
> your Insurance was due. . . . Sunday morning I got up to find the plate of
> my teeth had broken and that will be another twenty dollars, and now I say
> what next.—
>
> I worry about you, my dear boy. . . . You could give me untold joy if you
> would be willing to leave off your tobacco, and to retire early. . . . I long for
> you with such an intensity of feeling that it almost makes me sink from ex-
> haustion sometimes. . . . I want you a model in every particular . . . like our
> beautiful example Christ.
>
> K.'s 14th birthday—today. . . .
>
> Lovingly, J. M. F.[63]

A year or so earlier, Morton's parents had come to Europe, and his
father, Bradford Morton Fullerton, had had what sounds like a stroke.
After paying a "supply" preacher for a time, he gave up his parish and
went into an insurance company in Brockton, south of Boston.

The family structure becomes visible: Morton—William Morton Fullerton—"Will" to the family. Robert Morton Fullerton, "Rob." Then
Katharine, much younger. Rob follows Will to Harvard, visits him in
London. ("I have been upset tonight at my poor brother's going away,"
Morton told the Ranee; "the dear boy cried, and I felt so wicked; for all
the time I was thinking of you.")[64] Rob marries and goes into insurance.
At Thanksgiving dinner, Julia reads a telegram from Will aloud.[65] She
tells Will she's to talk to the Women's Alliance about Samuel Longfellow,
a clergyman. "What a friend you had in him. . . . I wonder what he would
say to you now if he knew your Paris life."[66]

Julia did the office work, looked after Will's insurance—a solemn en-
tity, usually capitalized—and opened a bank account for him. (1899:
"The money left after paying your Insurance was $28, which I depos-
ited.")[67] He must not worry about his father and her. "As we kneel every
morning he asks that our business affairs may be wisely directed and so
far we have not had to call for help from anyone."[68] But she worried

about Will's low pay. Blowitz was very selfish if he did not give the management any inkling of his value. "If you have any ideas for K. let us know."[69]

Katharine: rather a mystery. There are "you boys," and there is K. "K. is very far from being domestic but we enjoy each other very much,"[70] writes an oddly detached Julia who, when K reaches eighteen, tells Will they are not "planning any more" for her.[71] Still, she hopes that K's education is not ended.

Katharine

I will learn very much and be clever and wise write stories for the papers
                                                    Your loving Kathie

A letter from a six-year-old[72] who reminded Will twelve years later:

Do not forget to take my rosary to the convent if Aunt and Uncle bring it, please. I want it blessed in the Chapel. And give the nuns . . . my dearest love . . . the happiest days of my life were those I spent with them.[73]

A rosary, a convent, for a parson's child? Is K. a Roman Catholic? No, she teaches Sunday School at the Old South Church. But she is different from her parents and Rob in personal style. To Will:

De grâce! I appreciate all tender reminiscences of former happy days—but not those which bear the mark: "twenty years since." I am eighteen. . . . Cannot the memory which serves you so well for out-of-the-way phrases, enable you to keep in mind the age of your only sister? I promise you that it shall be constant, and never decrease or remain stationary longer than a year. Hang up the date, February 6, 1879, in some remote corner and bring it forward in times of doubt.[74]

In term time, Katharine boards with a wet-blanketing Boston lady and hates it. She'd even think of marrying if the man would let her alone sometimes. But no: she couldn't sacrifice her freedom.

You see that my own reflections coincide with your teachings; and marriage is as hideous an idea to me as to you. . . . Will, why do you not send for me to come to Paris? . . . I cannot stand the ocean between me and what is most inspiring—the atmosphere of art and beauty, the sun setting behind the Trocadéro tower, the garden of the convent—you![75]

She'd come to Paris with her parents, we learn, and spent a year in a
school run by Sacré-Coeur nuns. (Unusual. But Bradford Morton Fullerton seems to be an unusual man.) Will would call at the convent (now the
Musée Rodin) and take Kathie out. "The next time you dine chez Bré-
bant," she wrote six years later, "think of the twelve-year-old girl whom
you agitated beyond belief by telling her that she was flirting with the
youngest garçon."[76]

Though the parents weren't "planning," Katharine wins a scholarship
to Radcliffe. Julia is proud of her and misses her. Nevertheless, and although Rob is near, "My dear dear boy how can I live without you."[77]

As a student Katharine was stopped in Harvard Yard by a classmate of
Will's now teaching philosophy who asked when Will was expected:
"Mr. Santayana would rather give up half his holiday than not to see you;
and he is more than half of Harvard for you, I daresay."[78]

The austere George Santayana. A surprising friendship for the Will
who wrote that lush "dream" in his Paris notebook.

It was 1898, and the family was expecting a visit. There was no danger of Will's having to fight in the war with Spain, his parents assured
him.[79] "For a few years," Julia wrote after he left, "you were influenced
with the glamour and glow of the world, but now you have returned to
the simplicity, and sincerity, of your early years. . . . It seems to me that
you have grown heart-wise."[80]

As finals neared, Katharine panicked. If she didn't do well and
couldn't get a teaching post, she'd "be a drag on papa and mamma. . . .
They are just my whole life, and it is so hard to think that I have never
been anything but a drawback."[81] But she did well.

The Dreyfus trial came. Local papers published digests of London
Times reports. Though the work was anonymous, family and friends
knew who the "Special Correspondent" was. Katharine made a scrapbook. "You, at Rennes," she wrote, "seem to be at the very center of the
universe."[82]

Suddenly, in a coda to a chatty letter on "Mamma's birthday":

> . . . at last I have heard from my father about my adoption. He says that "he
> cannot conscientiously and in justice to himself and his family, consent to
> what I propose." So I must do it without his consent, if I do it. I feel badly
> about it. . . . He says that "his reasons he will convey to me personally at

some future time.". . . . Why didn't some of you foresee all this and arrange it otherwise? Isn't it maddening? Or are you so far away that you can't see?[83]

Adoption. It explains Julia's detachment. Katharine's fervent gratitude to Julia and Bradford. Her emphasis on sistership with Will. She emphasizes because she knows she is *not* his sister. Who her "real" father was isn't said.

Family letters stop for a while. Back to Paris, to the family's golden boy and cynosure.

Crisis: The Mission to Madrid, Second Time Around

For years, Will kept in touch with home, confiding plans and problems. Relatives came. Friends of relatives. Always he was begged to "do something" for them. He always did, and the returning travelers expressed themselves thrilled. He gossiped with Aïdé. Baron X was "an illegitimate son of old Gould who made his fortune." (Jay Gould the railroad czar?) Alec Yorke was in Paris, expecting to go to Ajaccio with Aïdé: "If, as you say," Morton told the latter, "Ronnie is to be with you the trio will lack harmony."[84] (Morton it seems was not the only friend with whom R.G. fell out.)

With a letter in a dashing hand signed "Blanche Roosevelt" (who was *she?*) the nineteenth century ends, and early in the twentieth a surprising letter signalizes a new phase in Morton's life.

The news item was true, he told Aïdé in October 1902. Yes, Lavino, the Vienna correspondent, was succeeding Blowitz. The *Times* had wanted to hold the news, but Lavino had "let the cat out of the bag, for his own private purposes":

[Blowitz] could have run on quietly 5, perhaps 10, years longer with me doing most of his work . . . if, by his jealousy of my position here he had not stupidly played into the hands of Lavino. . . . I am given the Madrid post, *without a sou additional*. There are strong and even peremptory reasons why I ought to be glad. No more night work at a bureau; a position of dignity and relative calm, where I shall be my own master. . . . Had my salary been raised (and it is shocking that it isn't: £40 a month, for a man in my position, with an insurance to keep up, and the whole future, in which his family is involved, constantly shadowing him—, this sum is absolutely inadequate . . .) I should go with joy.[85]

This is disconcerting. It's been understood that as soon as Blowitz retired, 1902, Morton took over.

So, his promotion was delayed by *Times* politics: Blowitz's jealousy—jealousy of a younger, more energetic man?—and the ambition of the Italian-sounding Lavino.

However, he spoke later of a "prolonged and urgent mission" to Madrid. There may have been more to the 1902 nonpromotion and transfer to Spain than he was free to tell Aïdé.

Did he take Camille Chabbert, whom (says the social worker) he married in a Protestant Church in (says Hugh Fullerton) Paris, and who (says Mr. Nolan) jumped out of a window to get away from him when they were in Madrid—?

So far there's been no mention of Camille in any of the Fullerton Papers, but suddenly, in May 1904, Morton's mother writes: "Your last cablegram is reassuring, that you intend to settle this matter as you say you have a good lawyer." It had "aroused" them all to see Will

apparently so dominated, and controlled by this scheming woman. Your "profound sympathy and affection" for her, and your saying no matter what happens you shall see that she is cared for has been very trying and painful . . . [your] not even telling us when you were in love, and surprising us by news of marriage, and *then* not writing . . .

Do tell me Will about Camille. She must be very tried. I have not heard from her since January. It would not surprise me if you were to separate. . . . What have you done with the household furniture and your belongings in Madrid? . . . Do write a full letter telling us the worst about Madame.[86]

Delay in promotion, marriage trouble, and now "Madame."

Well, the "scheming woman" is not Camille. And if it was this "Madame" who later blackmailed Will, Camille isn't the blackmailer. But at present Will has "profound sympathy and affection" for the schemer. Was she his landlady? If so, was she the "fair haired syren landlady" of the Rue Vignon alluded to by the Ranee?

By the time Will read his mother's letter, his lawyer, far from settling with Madame, had begun suit for divorce; and in November he informed his client of its successful conclusion: "At my request the court based its decision—not on the response to the summons—but on a previous letter of Mme Fullerton's injurious to you."[87] Signing "A. Clemenceau." Confirming the contents of the decree already seen. Leaving the divorce as queer as ever.

1905. Ella Clapp wonders at Cousin Will's silence after his kindness to Mama and her last year. She'd felt so sad leaving him so far from home she's probably sent "a regular love letter." Forgive her; come see her and Mr. Thompson when they were married,

> and bring your charming little wife. . . . I did not realize how disappointed I was at not seeing her until I got home. . . . How I should have loved to have heard her sing in Milan this winter![88]

So the family at large didn't know of the divorce. (Julia must have been sorry she'd made the marriage known.) For the Clapps, Will could use his wife's career to explain her absence. And *did* it explain her failure to appear in court?

5 December 1906: Morton's last letter from his "loving old Friend" Aïdé.

Again Katharine

October 1907. Katharine to Will, who is at the family house in Brockton, from Bryn Mawr College in Pennsylvania, where she is teaching:[89]

> Dear . . . if it is true that you could have found it possible to love me "ten years ago, five years ago, one year ago," how ironic it is that you did not! . . . If you could have loved, why not have saved us all this pain, this irrevocable confusion of our lives?[90]

Katharine, in the family house, November 1:

> You are saying goodbye to Annie in the kitchen, and I am trying to write a little note that you can get at the steamer. There is nothing to say except that . . . whether I ever marry you or not, I am yours to the deepest heart of me. . . . I push the pen on, while I hear mamma's tears in the next room. My tears are waiting for the moment when you will not be there to kiss them away.
>
> What more can I say? I have said it to you before this—yesterday and the day before—better than I can say it now.[91]

Letters so startling in themselves that it was a while before the dates made their impact.

October 1907 was when Morton visited the Mount.

Could the chronology be what it seemed?

Morton landed in New York in early October and went to Brockton, then to Bryn Mawr, where he gave a talk on James.[92] He had not seen Katharine since she was nineteen. She was now twenty-eight. They then went to Brockton, a day apart, for a stay with the family that was broken on the 21st–22nd by his overnight visit to the Mount.[93]

On the 27th or 28th, Will/Morton sent Edith Wharton the letter that led her to begin her secret journal.

On the 30th–31st he and Katharine became engaged.

On November 1st they traveled together to New York, where Will saw K off to Bryn Mawr. Before sailing he posted her a letter so agitating that she rushed out to cable him at sea. She couldn't think, she wrote next day, they'd *again* have to wait for years. He had called her his Beatrice, but she'd rather have been Dante's wife Gemma than his spiritual love. "'Wonderful in its wretchedness as is our fate,' you say. And I know well that you love me for the romantic strangeness of it, far more than you love me for myself."[94]

On the 9th: "in your own sacred words (only a week ago, my darling . . . !) 'without marriage there is no life for you nor for me.' . . . (*Please do not fail to destroy this at once.*)"[95]

The *Campania* reached Liverpool on the 9th. Morton spent the night at James's in Rye, reached Paris the next day, and began to fire letters at James—whose replies we've seen; they led to discovery of Morton's past relations with R.G.—and at Katharine, who wrote: "My own! . . . your letter from Paris."[96] ("Your letter from Paris . . ." Edith Wharton wrote four days later.)[97]

Katharine cherished a "passionate phrase" of Will's. But she had learned that she could live without him four years ago, when he was saying those words to another woman. (She could not bear to say "Camille.") She was much less the child he had "reared and taught; and it was that child that you loved in me." She had spent an evening with Mr. Gerould, from Princeton, whom she liked more than any man she knew who wasn't "kin." They'd talked of her work; he cared about her work. "We were gay and friendly."[98]

Will sent her Henry James's letters about the vindictive blackmailer:

they were "right and wonderful,"[99] Katharine said. (And the letters Will sent James showing a marvelous devotion (page 28) must have been from Katharine. But can he have shown James *these?*)

"Well," Rob wrote in January, "we got over Christmas without the promised rude shock. I confess I sort of held my breath. I see a change . . . you're just enough a different you to win out. . . . You've something ahead to work for that's worth it. You'll win."[100]

So: Katharine (and Will?) had confided the engagement to Rob, and over Christmas the parents were told. "And if I was ever glib with my Philistinisms about marriage," wrote Katharine, "I am punished now by my absurd fortnight at home":

> If we had both been there, we should have parted forever, neither one wishing to look on the other's face again. When I tell you that by the second day of my holiday, mamma had got as far as the details of the wedding breakfast. . . . I bear it not too ill when I am told how impertinently I have made love to you and how wholly a matter of chance it is that you have taken pity on me at last. But I am human—

—and when Julia said that if Will had spent three weeks at home with another girl he'd have wished to marry *her,* she stifled the retort: why hadn't they managed things better?[101]

> My heart bleeds for your loneliness, as yours must bleed for mine. But say to yourself faithfully, when you are alone after the long day and wanting me: "My little love would be here with me if she could."[102]

Katharine and Others

On January 10, when Katharine wrote those words, Morton dined at Edith's. On the 11th had tea at Edith's. On the 13th, dined. Then dined at Mme de Fitz-James's with Edith and Countess Anna de Noailles and Prince Bibescu. Had tea at Edith's. Lunched. . . .

Almost every night, on his way home, he wrote Edith a letter. "Instead of being stupidly sundered, we might have been happy together," he wrote after an opportunity to meet was lost.[103]

After January there is a gap in Katharine's correspondence. In the autumn she went to England on leave of absence with a colleague, Lucy

Donnelly, and sent Will letters that are bleak, distraught, hard to date and hard to follow. She dreaded Oxford: Lucy knew Bertrand Russell and his wife. Katharine loved her but heard that he was "the most brilliant man in England." In a U-turn: "Let me entreat you to write to our parents! You've a power, my darling, of inflicting pain—!"[104]

She went to Paris and saw Will—what happened isn't said—and went on to Tours, where her old friends the Sacré Coeurs took her and Lucy *en pension.* The two young women were taken up by local landowners, Comte d'Aulby and his wife, Francesca, an American who had known Will in Cambridge: "deliciously pretty in an artificial way and thoroughly nice and empty-headed," Katharine told Will; while the "wholly delightful" comte—a musician, an art collector, and a Sanskrit scholar—"believed about the universe exactly what, had I all the lore one should have, I should believe."[105]

Will went to visit. Soon Francesca was writing that she woke to his letter and her *café* . . . it had been painful to part at the too short moment of their first kiss . . . she'd written him three poems now burned . . . his letters were adorable but too short, he *would* burn hers? She pitied his hard life and longed to help him forget his cares.[106]

The inspirational count could not help Katharine for long. She told Will that she *should not* go to Paris; if she was to find peace it must be away from him.[107] But she did go, on the evidence of a *pneumatique* in atrocious French he received, postmarked 1909. In illiterate English, it might have read:

> *Chèr ami!* So you're with your sister all the time now. You play with fire too much. As you told me your little sister loves you. Don't break her heart if you are incappable of an atachment to her. I'm talking morals to you!! Wednesday or Thursday my freind arrives. He'll stay 8–10 days. Soon as I'm alone hope to see you. Je vous embrasse tendrement.—Doll.[108]

"She is a prostitute. A foreigner." (Marc) She makes all kinds of mistakes, chèr, je fait. Besides, you don't find the name Doll here. Is it English?"

"Doll Tearsheet. But if English, why write in French?"

Katharine was apparently still in Europe that June, when Will went to America after a night with Edith in a London hotel.

Six months later, early January 1910, she wrote to him from Bryn

Mawr. Mr. Gerould had asked her to marry him. How could she give an
answer, not knowing how she stood with Will?

This is the letter that had compelled attention out of any known context when the Papers were first sorted: "I do not think any human being
has the right to hurt another like this."

> How you can not have written to me—whatever your feeling, your attitude
> and your position in regard to me and to others. . . . Don't let me feel, with
> bitterness, that you have treated me unpardonably ill. . . . I wish I dared ask
> you—if you are as cruel as I fear, and still have not written to me—to cable
> me, if only one word— — —[109]

What word *did* he send? We have only her cabled reply, which he received on February 19th: "= COURAGE DEAREST LOVE = KATHARINE ="[110]

The next month he heard from his father that there was "a mix up on
account of Katharine." Mr. Gerould had asked for his consent to marry
Katharine, and he "did not oppose." Katharine had sent him the letter
from Will that she'd answered with COURAGE—in which Will had said,
we now learn, that he would definitely come home that summer and that
he had troubles at work.

Bradford wished she *had* waited to talk with Will. But she "seemed to
develop herself very strangely" and "went to her imagination for her
facts. . . . It seems to be the recurrence of the obsession of her childhood
of twenty-five years ago." And Mr. Gerould wanted to advance the wedding so that she would not be at home that summer "to suffer at our
hands. He knows you better than I do he intimates," Bradford told Will,
incensed.

Bradford says nothing about her announcing the engagement during
Christmas vacation, 1907. If she did not announce it but sent Will that
vivid report of having done so, then she—. But Rob's congratulations to
Will show that she *did*. How, then, can Bradford speak only of her *childhood?* Will had been home last year; there must have been discussion.
Had the family taken the line that she imagined things, and had Will not
gainsaid it? Bradford does not explain her "strange development." He
must know that Will already knows. But if so, why go back so far?—Ah,
but he continues:

> Your mother says that she thinks K. has . . . some letters, notes, diaries, etc.
> she does not know what in a lowboy here, and she cannot believe that you
> would like to have them fall into the hands of Mr. Gerould. If you will

write to me that you wish them left here we will see that they are carefully guarded. . . .

It is more likely that the parents couldn't face evidence that Will had led Katharine on than that she fantasized his having done so. Not delusion on her side, but protective prevarication on theirs.

"You see," Bradford ends, "that another burden is laid upon us, an experience which we could never have imagined. Come this summer and help us through it."[111]

Before Will went home (in October) he had two communications from Brockton. An announcement:

> Reverend and Mrs. Bradford Morton Fullerton
> announce the marriage of their daughter
> Katharine Elizabeth
> to
> Mr. Gordon Hall Gerould
> on Thursday the ninth of June
> nineteen hundred and ten
> Brockton, Massachusetts.

And a letter from his mother:

> . . . it was one of the prettiest, if not the prettiest, wedding I was ever at, beautiful for its simplicity but everything was choice as far as we could make it. Her gifts from the family are of the best. I have gotten her exquisite table linen and enough of it. . . . Of course the money had to come right out of the little we have saved . . .
>
> Your father . . . looked elegantly. He read the service as if nothing had ever happened to mar his speech. . . . Strange to say K. was the only one who blundered anywhere and that was not very perceptible.
>
> . . . You of course saw K's "Gemma and Beatrice" in the June Scribner's.[112]

Wars and Peaces

Will left the *Times* to work as a freelance, publishing *Problems of Power* in 1913. Katharine, a faculty wife in "dear, adorable, soporific, Presbyterian Princeton,"[113] had two children and published books and articles.

1914: Bradford Morton Fullerton fell ill. Will arrived too late to see him alive. The First World War had begun in Europe; he stayed in the United States for a while doing Allied propaganda.

After the war, a few personal letters to Morton and a welter of notes from Georges Clemenceau and other statesmen. Big names, petty contents. The lees of a significant political correspondence.

Dust specks in the sunbeams in the long-undusted room, names and dates and phrases dance about. Skim, study, linger; scrawl a note, who what where; go on to the next letter.

Soon the Second World War is upon us. Before the fall of France, Katharine writes: "I *don't* like to think of you in a cold, cold Paris—"[114] The last in a series of letters that began when she was six. She died before the Liberation.

Then the Fullerton Papers peter out.

Except for the things of Camille's that got mixed up with the papers she had liberated from her hated supplanter, Mme Pouget, after Morton died. Notes from admirers. Sheets covered with crazy curves by Camille herself, appealing to officialdom for help against Enemies.

End of Papers. Various 1907–1909 items photocopied for future study; slovenly inventory typed from scrawled notes and sent to Yale; originals returned to Nolan; myself returned to UNESCO.

UNESCO: in France but not of it. A high-powered smooth-running Picasso-and-Henry-Moore-enriched world, polyglot and polychrome, flawed but noble.

But a week later comes the clank and bang of the elevator and slipper-shuffles outside the door, *vera incessu patuit* concierge. "Excusez-moi, Mademoiselle, it's too thick to slide under."

Mr. Nolan has found more papers.

Another Bundle of Letters

Only a few. I seized a letter in a graceful hand from—*Camille Chabbert!* She wrote from Fiume (now Rijeka, in Croatia) in 1908—four years after the divorce—to *Mon bien cher Will:*

It's been impossible these last days to write you as I'd have liked . . . our correspondence seems so odd and so delicate, I truly don't know what tone to take. Can I write to you? *Ought* I? . . . I'm still dazed and stunned at all that's happened and the more I think of it the more I see the folly of it all! . . . meanwhile my career fills life so full that I wouldn't have time to think of anything else even if I wanted. . . . Last year they hissed because the manager hadn't engaged me. . . . You must admit that beautiful scenery, a balmy climate and a Massenet opera to sing are a dream for a sentimental artiste. . . . I'll write once the *Thaïs* première is over, Will dear. . . . Let me have news of you often, I love having it. Tell me how your amours with your sister are going—*if* you care to tell the truth . . . if not, don't say a word. Je t'embrasse bien tendrement, dearest Will. Mireille and I both wish you all kinds of happiness and great success in your *art littéraire*—

Camille[115]

Under Camille's swirl, in a child's big writing, is MIRELLA.

Camille's arabesques recalled an illegibly signed card. . . . Yes, the same hand, written small. Italian stamp, Paris postmark 10 *mars* 1908, and:

I hope my trunks haven't been too much of a nuisance. . . . Can you do an errand for me at Duverville's—the hairdresser in the Avenue de l'Opéra? Make my excuses for my sudden and precipitate departure and ask if he has sent my wig to Fiume, where I shall be on the 18th.—Many thanks, and affectionate regards from—

Squeezed in at the bottom is "[?] Cding et Mit." Once you know, you can see it is "Camille et Mir[eille]."[116]

("You loved her, you see; you surely loved her," Katharine had written a few weeks earlier. "To think of her is still pure torture for me. . . . I shall never, never, never, get over your marriage to her, though I myself should be married to you for twenty years.")[117] In Paris, Edith Wharton was eagerly awaiting Morton's next visit.

It was the erstwhile couple's first meeting since the divorce, and it ended cordially. Except for flippancy about the "sister," as to which she must have taken her cue from Will, Camille writes like a woman of sensibility. This is neither Mr. Nolan's turpitudinous foe nor the "dirty old thing" Mme Pouget detested. Her handwriting is as educated as Katharine's or Edith's, and her style is easy, airy. Why had such a woman put up with that irregular divorce? But she herself was asking why: "the folly of it all."

And Mireille—whom Morton recognized as his child, a hard-up eccentric old Camille was to tell the social worker at the Foyer des Artistes
de Music Hall et de Cabaret—Mireille was born before the divorce. Her
signature shows. The divorce had taken place three years and four
months ago. While the child who signed MIRELLA might be eight, seven,
six, she could not be three or four. Was she born before the marriage? The
old question when, where, the marriage? ("Just go to the *mairie* of the
First.")

Then two communications from Morton's college friend George Santayana, nothing memorable.

One letter remains, long and unenticing.

A Father's Sermon Reveals the Name of Madame

The first page, dated May 13, 1904, is typed single-space on the letter-
head of Glenn Falls Insurance Company, C. D. Fullerton & Co., Agents,
47 Centre St., Brockton, Mass.

My dear Will:—

. . . We have lately advanced money for the payment of the premiums three
times, and I do not feel that we should do this for the benefit of Madame
Mirecourt.

If money must be paid to that scheming woman who seems to have
complete control of you, and with whom you are so unwise as to dicker, we
will let you have a reasonable sum which you (not she, on your honor) may
name, provided you give me a legal title to the policy. This will involve real
sacrifice on our part, but I would rather make it than have you disgrace
yourself and your family . . .

It seems . . . you are beholden for the pay for half the rent of the apartment, for 200 francs a month beside, and that now a demand is made for
the insurance papers. This is simply bleeding you. You look upon these demands as legitimate, but do not recognize that you are under obligations to
others. . . . You are deceiving C., and in an effort to "liquidate" the situation to please her are simply getting yourself deeper and deeper into the
mire. . . . Mamma is weakening by your neglects, and, I am afraid, will not
last long. You seem to be wholly absorbed by Madame M. or by something
so that you do not think much of the people this side the sea.

Affectionately, B. M. Fullerton (over)

On the other side, handwritten: "P.S. I have asked Mamma because of my inability to get at the typewriter to add this post-script at my dictation":

> You remember the two or three early love episodes in this country which seem to me excusable because of your youth—then the lamentable Kellogg affair. Afterwards, Percy Anderson, Lord Gower, etc., associations—the dangerous complications with Lady Brooke, and as I infer Geraldine Ulman business and the cruel Gould matter in which you had proceeded even to house-hunting. Within the last few years Mde Mirecourt has reigned supreme . . . when you were home last you stated that she could always retain her present position. But now, by the act of marriage you have legally and morally annulled this. . . . No matter how "excited," hysterical, tearful, beseeching, insistent, rampageous, or threatening she may be in her demands that you tie up, restrict, limit, bound, bind, check, hinder, confine or hamper yourself you should concede these demands under *no conditions whatever*. You have now entered into a transcendent obligation, no matter what concessions [Camille] may have made to you . . . you have *amply* paid as you went. She has had a much better living on your account, and you decidedly ought not to allow yourself to be tied up so that your wife or children,—(if you have any), should reap meagreness. . . .
>
> Mde Mirecourt acts as if she thought that she struck a mild bonanza when she found an American Correspondent of the English Times in Paris. . . . It seems to me not unlikely from [Camille's] silence, and from your late silence about her, and her not joining you as you said you expected, that she may be cherishing some resentment. . . . Even if you and Camille were to separate permanently Mde. Mirecourt's case should be treated as I have indicated in my letter. . . .
>
> Always remember Will that your family are not condemning you. . . . We have looked to you with a not unworthy pride. Do not spoil a very promising career. Quit Mde. M. . . . She will fight this method but persist.
>
> [signed, shakily] B. M. F.[118]

"*Calme-toi, respire.*" (Marc) "*Breathe deeply. It is so important?*"
"*Like finding the Rosetta Stone. Listen . . .*"
"*Mais c'était un Don Juan!*"
"*It has been going through my head.*"
Ma in Ispagna, son gia mille e tre. Two flutes, two oboes, two bassoons, two horns, and strings.

How could they fall for that Edwardian masher?
Thou shalt be more beloved than beloving.
Un homme fatal.

Did he ever love anyone? No. Or—perhaps—this "scheming woman" whom he was defending even after his marriage.

And at last the scheming woman has a name: Mirecourt.

That Demn'd Elusive Mirecourt

I took time off from translating at UNESCO.

There were no Mirecourt births, marriages, or deaths in Paris from the earliest records through the witching year 1902, after which you need the *procureur*'s permission to search, item by item. No Mirecourt birth, marriage, or death in the Rue Vignon, Morton's address in the 1890s. Try telephone books, anything. Try the *Bottin Mondain.*

A Mme Jeanne de Mirecourt lived in the Boulevard des Courcelles and a Mme Daffis de Mirecour, *femme de lettres,* in the Boulevard des Italiens. Both women had the aristocratic *de,* and Daffis had no *t.* Morton's father might have misspelled. Mirecour and Mirecourt sound the same. However, our skimpy data are against the landlady's being in that exclusive directory.

Unless . . . Daffis was a *femme de lettres.* Was a woman writer eligible even if not well-born, rich, or celebrated? "Writer" could be anything from Anna de Noailles to a hack journalist. In other years she is "Mirecour, Mme Daffis de (Sewell)" or "(Sowell)" or "Swell, *publiciste.*" Evidently an English name, garbled.

Could the landlady have been a French Nelly Bly? A female reporter like the one in James's *Portrait of a Lady?* "Perhaps" (note to Yale) "she was a sort of French Henrietta Stackpole?"

Another cloudy possibility: Eugène de Mirecourt, writer, died in 1880. Since he went in for libel (did time for *The Novel-Factory: Alexandre Dumas and Co.*) and true confessions of courtesans, a wife who outlived him might imaginably have become a landlady with a nose for compromising documents.

But all this quick look shows is that no name that can be found easily is right. This is chopping and tugging like Procrustes. Mme Mirecourt will not be found by leafing through directories for a purpose too frivolous to admit to during the UNESCO General Conference, four-to-midnight shift, when one's office is a starkly lit cell in a long dark corridor, and messengers wing from halls below where global issues are under debate, with matter to be Englished. Resolved: that action be taken for cooperationand-aidinrestorationofthetempleatborbadurimplementationofthetenyearplan-forafricanlanguagesandoraltraditions

The Rue Fabert Fiasco

A free week. Requests had been coming from the biographer for identification of Mirecourt, probably "the most important 'other woman' in Edith Wharton's life." Also, he had been shown a letter James sent Edith in August 1909, apparently soon after the two of them somehow freed M.F. from blackmail. It was "a real luxury," James wrote, to remember that M.F. wasn't in the Rue Fabert.[119]

The Rue Fabert, then, was where, to James's horror, Morton was still living with his blackmailer in 1907. With a street, and a time frame . . . If the scheming Mme Mirecourt's husband was alive in the early 1900s (when only men had the vote), old voting lists might help. Try the Archives of the Seine.

Using recent lists had been easy. In earlier lists some years are missing for all arrondissements, some arrondissements for most years. Covers have fallen off, labels have disintegrated. Climb a ladder to extricate a volume from a tight-packed row without falling back under its weight as it comes free; manhandle it to a rickety table under a forty-watt bulb. Like tugging boulders out of a stone wall.

No Mirecourts anywhere.

What else? The Cadastre, a survey made every twenty-five years of every lodging in France. Here are filled-out forms for every building in every street. But the Rue Fabert forms are too early.

For later years there is the Enregistrement, where a man looks. No Mirecourt. At the Buildings Registry two men confer: These are tax records. To divulge an address would be *très grave*. For an authorization, go to the *mairie* of the Seventh. To the *greffier*.

In the *greffier*'s office is a counter, beyond the counter is a desk, on the desk is an outspread newspaper, bent over the newspaper hands folded is a *huissier* who looks slowly up, bares his fangs, and speaks.

"Que voulez-vous? . . . I have no idea what you are talking about, Madame. Cela ne me regarde pas. But que vous êtes stupide Madame! Why do you waste my time? What do I care? I have no time to listen, Madame. Idiote! Piss off!"

To the street, to the métro, to the Building Registry, to the two officials, who look at each other.

"Ça alors. You will return to the *mairie* and you will ask the Juge d'Instance to give you an authorization for the Receveur Principal, so that we may give you the information."

Plod home. Draft an appeal.

At the post office next morning the photocopy machine is out of order. On to the Invalides Aerogare machine. Copy appeal, copy credentials. The francs drop into the slot page by page. On to the *mairie*. Pick a way through the bones and gobbets of flesh outside the entrance to the Cyclops's cave.

A *citoyenne* cowers before the public servant; he breaks off his compliments, and she withdraws, quietly weeping. He looks at my papers, takes them into another room, returns and lays a folder on his desk, and picks up his *Figaro*.

Ten A.M. Sit down on the bench and pull out a P. G. Wodehouse, selected for the occasion. Bracing.

The newspaper rustles.

Ten thirty.

Eleven thirty. A happy Wodehouse ending. All went well, Jack had Jill, the earl had his pig again, and naught went ill.

Noon strikes. The *huissier* rises, dons his coat, and hands over the folder on his desk. The petition.

"Your answer."

"Merci." Stuff it in the shopping bag with Lord Emsworth. "But read it!" cries the *huissier,* eyes gleaming: "C'est un refus!"

"Merci, monsieur, tant pis."

Look at it in the street. The *juge* has written: "The petitioner appears to have no legitimate interest in the matter."

Punch-drunk, back to the Archives de la Seine. The stack houses hundreds of census cartons, each holding thousands of flimsy sheets, one per building, not in alphabetical order, and the houses in a street are not together or even in the same box. The earliest date seems to be 1914. Heave up a carton. A few flimsies for Rue Fabert. No Mirecourt. Which means nothing.

Quit, stagger to the métro, change at Jussieu, home, black with the grime of decades.

"Mais tu n'es pas un peu folle? Are you in your right mind?"

A letter from Yale. A hundred dollars or so might be put out toward identifying Mirecourt if there is a reasonable chance of worthwhile results.

Resign. Sweep Fullerton and his friends into boxes and store them on a high shelf out of sight, out of mind.

Out of mind. And yet, up the street ambulances drove through the gates of the Maison des Dames du Calvaire where Camille Chabbert died. Edith Wharton's secret journal was no longer stowed on top of a wardrobe, but the map on the kitchen wall, fading and blotched, was still magic-markered with Morton Fullerton's travels in the *Terres Françaises*.

PART TWO

Paris

The Quest Resumed

There would be things to discuss, things to return, when the biographer came through Paris. Get the cartons down before going to America for Christmas.

For the first time I read the material through steadily and as a whole.

But it was exciting! Not Fullerton, a strangely hollow man, but the story. When and where did he marry Camille Chabbert? Was Mireille his child? Edith Wharton's secret journal expresses her love for him during a few months in 1908, but what did he feel for her? How did she and James rescue him from blackmail? And was Mme Mirecourt, mysterious *dame sans merci*, the blackmailer?

Clear away debris. Shorthand interviews—save. Sleazy scratch paper used for jotting as I read the papers—leaf through before discarding.

One sheet had: "3 letters from a M. Alfroy, 1913, au sujet d'une Mme Mirecourt."

My writing.

I had read letters about Mme Mirecourt?

Of course. Morton's father's letter naming the evil landlady had arrived after I had returned the great bulk of the letters, including those three, to Mr. Nolan and sent a rough list typed from these scrawls to the biographer. At that time "Mirecourt" was one of hundreds of names calling for no special notice.

What the letters said is beyond recall. And I probably missed other clues. Send for copies of all the papers, get back to work, but this time go back to the beginning. To Massachusetts.

Massachusetts

Letters and Life

Henry James thanks Morton for some books, a "memento of the wonderful Rue Vignon."[1]—He had been there. Did he see Mme—

A man in an overcoat, on his way out, stops at the table where I have letters spread around and introduces himself as Leon Edel.

"Strange that it should be Morton Fullerton and not Walter Berry as people have thought, isn't it?"

This is in Houghton Library at Harvard.

Leon Edel had been editing James's letters. The letters for the period of James's friendship with Fullerton had not yet been published; many of them were here.

Pusey Library has Morton's class archives, and Widener must have his books. Besides, he grew up in these parts.

"I know some Fullertons in Dover," my sister says. "Why don't I ask if they know about your Fullertons?"

Blazing logs in the fireplace, a heavy snowstorm outside.

"Why not? But there are so many people of the name—"

She holds out the phone. "His father was Katharine's brother."

"Yes, my father had a sister Katharine," says Dwight Fullerton. "Their mother died, and they both lived with the Rev. Bradford Morton Fullerton when they were youngsters, and she stayed on."

Try another number, and from Quincy on the South Shore, through miles of blizzard, comes a voice familiar since my teens, the voice of Mabelle Fullerton, society editor of the *Patriot-Ledger*.

"Morton Fullerton? He crashed into my life like a comet!

"I was a child, in Washington; he'd been to a dinner party at the White House. He was very handsome. He had a silk hat and a cutaway. And he kissed my grimy hand. He said I had a talent for writing, I suppose that's how I became a writer. My father, Adelbert Morton Fullerton, was his cousin. Was it true he married some great actress? There was some mystery. Our family was so conventional about romance. Bradford Morton was a very devout man, and he kind of felt he had hatched a cuckoo."

Fullerton's Family

Bradford Morton Fullerton grew up in Whitman, near Plymouth.[2] His
father and three of his four uncles were shoemakers (the fourth was a
minister); generations of Fullertons had farmed and made shoes in the
Old Colony. Family scrimping enabled him to go to Phillips Academy
and from there to Amherst College in western Massachusetts, a land rising from the Connecticut River Valley to the Berkshires, where New
Yorkers like the Whartons were to build "villas" and live in a luxury
alien to spare, Puritan Amherst.

For Bradford, class of 1861, the Amherst norm was luxury. It was
hard to pay $3.50 for a room. But by a stroke of luck, the sort of luck his
elder son was to enjoy, the president's son invited him to his house, where
he lived for a while rent-free.[3] He may have glimpsed the treasurer's
daughter, Emily Dickinson—the town "Myth," who was not yet quite re-
clusive—at the tea her father gave at Commencement.[4] He fell in love
with another local girl, Julia Ball, a minister's daughter, and, after enroll-
ing at Andover Theological Seminary, dropped out in order to make
enough money to marry her, and roved, a scholar-gypsy, teaching and
working on newspapers. But after Will's birth, in Connecticut, he returned to Massachusetts to complete his course and was "called" to
Palmer, a village set in wooded hills near the big town of Springfield.

There, says the church history, Bradford inspired "a great spiritual
awakening." But his stipend was so small that the family lived at a boardinghouse during Will's impressionable childhood; Will was twelve by the
time a parsonage was built.[5]

Conflicting impressions of the vanity of worldly goods and the virtue
of saving. Impressions of his father's importance. And, perhaps, indefin-
able impressions made by ripples of a national scandal of the 1870s. The
famous preacher Henry Ward Beecher, brother of Harriet Beecher
Stowe, was tried for adultery. In the eyes of the church, he was cleared
by a council on which Bradford served. Guarded murmurs and pregnant
silences at the boardinghouse table may have given Will and his brother
Rob, three years younger, hints of forbidden fruit outside the Garden of
Eden.

Until Will ("a bright and pleasant lad who gave abundant promise of
a future of rich usefulness") was sent to Phillips Academy and Rob to

Worcester Academy, for finishing, the brothers attended a one-room wooden schoolhouse, now the home of Purina Grain. They competed in spelling bees there with Fred and Marian Kellogg, a merchant's children, and went to Sunday school with them. When the Kelloggs moved to Springfield, the families evidently kept in touch: Marian was the fiancée whom Will wrote off in that letter from Craigie House, replete with soulfulness and yawns, before sailing to Europe; she was the victim of what his father called "the lamentable Kellogg affair."[6]

A more lamentable affair had its origin when Will was fourteen. Elizabeth Fullerton, the wife of Bradford's half-brother Charles, died after the birth of her third child. The grandparents at the Whitman homestead took one boy; Bradford and Julia took the other boy and the baby, Katharine, whom they kept after Charles remarried and claimed the boy. Katharine was about thirteen when a stroke forced Bradford to quit his ministry and go into an insurance agency in Brockton, on the South Shore, which her "real" father had begun.

Katharine always knew her parentage. The shock she had at twenty was learning that her adoption was an ad hoc family arrangement. In a flare of loyalty to Bradford and Julia, she told her father that she wanted it to be official. It would make no "material difference," her brother Edward, a law student, told him, "except that you lose a daughter and Fred and I a sister, who although she existed as such only in name yet I think we were all proud of her."[7] When their father refused to help, Katharine made the arrangements herself, as she'd told Will she would. The adoption of Katharine Elizabeth Fullerton, twenty-one, is filed in the Plymouth County Registry of Probate.

Katharine learned her worship of Will from her elders. Julia adored and deferred. Both parents were remarkably lenient toward his "love episodes." Not till he married did Bradford lay down the law: Quit Mirecourt! Even then: "We are not condemning you." Rob's every reference to his brother was admiring. As Katharine told Will, "You have always had the imagination of the rest of us."[8]

Will's feeling for them? He dedicated his book *Patriotism and Science* to "my father," the range of whose library—Lucretius, the Puritan John Howe, Balzac, the *Arabian Nights,* Adam Smith—suggested the "social virtue of tolerance."[9] One of his letters from Paris has a ring of heart:

> It is wicked for me to tell you the whole truth of my sadness in not being
> with you four, for it simply enhances your own suffering. But on the other

hand I cannot refrain from saying it, and repeating it, because I should be
sadder still if I thought you doubted the aching loyalty of my feelings.[10]

But. Soon after writing that, he came home for the first time in nine
years. In those years there had been delay in promotion, marriage, divorce, blackmail. It was the momentous visit of 1907 during which,
besides awakening Edith Wharton at the Mount to the possibility of happiness, he persuaded Katharine that he wanted to marry her in a court-
ship conducted under the unobservant eyes of Bradford and even Julia,
which risked destroying the fabric of the close-knit, God-fearing, idol-
atrous other "four."

Veritas 1886

When Will Fullerton entered Harvard, chapel was compulsory, the pump
in the Yard was in use, and tuition cost one hundred and fifty dollars. The
Memorial Hall honoring students who had died for the Union was the
grandest edifice many students had ever seen. Blacks lived in shanties on
the banks of the Charles.

After freshman year, when he roomed in Story Street, Will commuted
from home. His father had moved to a new parish in the neighboring
town of Waltham, which permitted the economy.

In his class were George Santayana, later a philosopher; Alanson
Houghton, ambassador; Charles Loeser, art critic; and Richard Longfellow, nephew (not son) of the poet, with whom apparently Will was to go
abroad. T. W. Richards, a future Nobel Prize chemist, had entered at
fourteen. In overlapping classes were Charles Francis Adams III, J. P.
Morgan II, William Randolph Hearst, and Bernard Berenson,[11] who was
still wearing ritual locks—like the darkly handsome Santayana, an exotic
among the Boylston Adams Bealses, Bigelows, and Cabots.

Will joined the Hasty Pudding, the Everett Athenaeum, and the O.K.
Club. He joined the *Advocate* and published a story: A young man going
home for Christmas after a long absence shares a stagecoach with a young
lady too bundled up for her face to show; he is attracted; he discovers that
she is his sister. But, finding the *Advocate* unfulfilling, with Santayana,
Houghton, and others he started the *Harvard Monthly,* in order to print
the "strongest and soberest undergraduate thought."

* * *

More sober than strong. Those boys seem young for their age, cal-
low—and pious, though in sending sons to Harvard Bradford was unor-
thodox. Most Congregationalists saw the place as next to pagan.

Bradford's tolerance did not extend to the heretic Ralph Waldo Emerson, and Will respected his wishes enough to abstain from reading Emerson at college. When he read Matthew Arnold, who argued eloquently
that the Bible should be read as Literature not Dogma, his admiration
caused "maternal tears and un-Christian paternal anathema."[12] The class
of 1886 had missed Oscar Wilde's visit to Harvard during his American
tour, but they were there when Arnold came to lecture. He was a friend
of the learned, traveled, worldly Professor Charles Eliot Norton, with
whom Will took art history. From then on, Will tried to emulate Arnold's
urbane irony.

But not his clarity. Will's English instructor Barrett Wendell praised his
themes, yet diagnosed but could not cure his verbosity.[13]

If Santayana was "more than half" of Will's Harvard, Wendell was the
rest: "wonderful to look at," Santayana said, "red hair, cerulean eyes,
and a mouth that can breathe hot anger. Shelley, if Shelley had been a
Christian."[14] For calling his *Duchess Emilia* "the most powerful and original" American romance since Hawthorne in the *Advocate,* Will was accused of flattery by "Veritas" in the *Crimson.*[15]

Unexpectedly, a name signed to a lovelorn letter found in Fullerton's
papers in Paris turns up in one of Will's *Harvard Monthly* reviews:[16] he
mentions a life of Gustave Doré by Blanche Roosevelt. So she was a
writer. Everybody knew her *Home Life of Henry Wadsworth Longfellow,*
it emerges, and a musical based on Longfellow's *Masque of Pandora* had
been staged in Boston by the Blanche Roosevelt English Opera Company[17] when Will was at school. She inspires curiosity.

Santayana saw "generous intellectual sincerity" at Harvard, but "spiritual penury and moral confusion."[18] Will had other objections. He won
Bowdoin and Boylston prizes, election to Phi Beta Kappa, and a magna.
But what he coveted most he did not get, a fellowship for foreign study,
and he left college feeling "badly treated."[19] In his chagrin he retold and
later published the story of the third-century-B.C. student Apollonius of
Rhodes, who defied the pedantic head of the Alexandrian Library/Uni-
versity, read an epic poem aloud, met with scorn, went abroad "vowing

vengeance," and "lived to accept the highest honours in the gift of the university which had snubbed him in youth for his originality."[20]

"Of course I begin 'out of it,'" Will told Wendell later. "Harvard is democratic enough; and my brother, who had no more time nor money than I, having the personal qualities, 'got on' socially," but their parents' view of "Harvard and what they thought it stood for—Boston and Beacon Street—

> gradually percolated into my veins, until, at the end, not having been invited to join any of the clubs where the "peculiar people" dwelt in mutual admiration, and not having been successful in my final appeal for a fellowship . . . I began to move about the college-grounds with much the same mood that I imagine characterizes the average intelligent Jew as he goes up and down the world . . . hating and scorning it all. . . .

He assured Wendell that he no longer meant to "humble and abase" Harvard. "Beautiful things" had happened in his "dreaming soul" in the library.[21] In today's library, however, is a letter he sent Professor Charles Eliot Norton from Paris in 1906:

> . . . you may remember one of your former pupils who, appealing for a fellowship to study abroad, had not the good fortune to convince his University of the legitimacy of his candidature. Exactly twenty years have passed . . . and day before yesterday the French Academy "crowned" one of that boy's books: *Terres Françaises* . . . written by him in French. It seems to me that the event is one that honours Harvard and certain of my old teachers. . . . With a lively sense of what I owe to you personally. . . .
>
> Apollonius Rhodius[22]

The sense of injury rankled for twenty years.

The *Boston Record-Advertiser*

Nevertheless it does not come through in anything Apollonius Rhodius wrote in the course of his first job.

Events outside the two towns on the Charles were not neglected (A TRAIN CAPTURED: ROBBERS GET POSSESSION OF THE SOUTHERN PACIFIC.) Essentially, however, the *Record-Advertiser,* Will said, represented "Brahmin Boston" and Cambridge. A "Harvard News" column appeared daily.

Alumni were tracked in society items. (Edward "Teddy" Wharton of Boston, '73, married to Miss Edith Jones of New York, had "relaxed his fastidious scruples" about spending time with Mrs. Jones now that he had "accepted her money and daughter.")[23] Will's contributions were on a higher plane. He reviewed books, and

> everyone who sets forth into the undiscovered country of a new book is a
> kind of Livingstone wandering away into a Dark Continent. The opening
> lines of Meredith's poem "The Woods of Westermain" occur to me.
>> "Enter these enchanted woods,
>> You who dare!"[24]

Meredith was the greatest writer in English after Shakespeare.

The influence on Will Fullerton was not Henry James but George Meredith,[25] with his running fight against idées fixes and his own ideas—radicalism, feminism—which could fire young people able to get the swing of a style Will called "the most wonderful Gothic structure in England."[26] He had written a candid sonnet sequence on his unhappy first marriage. In his novels he assailed the "veiled virginal doll" ideal of woman[27] and advocated periodical renegotiation of marriage vows. Katharine was forbidden to read his *Richard Feverel*.

Will's reviews, sometimes presented as letters to Zadoc Everard, a classmate, are very personal. He reads a children's book to a little girl.[28] Kathie. *Scribner's* has something "fairly good" on Russian writers: "But I know of no one who writes better on these subjects than Mr. Bernhard Berenson in the *Harvard Monthly*."[29] He prints letters *from* Everard but derides him.[30] You begin to wonder, and, yes, Zadoc Everard was a hoax known to scattered classmates, friends still at Harvard like Berenson, now a senior, and Charles Loeser, doing an M.A., and two late arrivals there who opened vistas. Thomas Meteyard,[31] a "special" student not working for a degree, painted; he had been a pupil of Monet in Giverny. Bliss Carman, a Canadian graduate student, had studied at Edinburgh and made an effect at Harvard by having a poem printed in the *Atlantic Monthly*. Berenson took him up,[32] and "Mr. Fullerton of the *Advertiser*," he wrote, "very clever and at the same time perfectly sensible, gives me some reviewing to do, and is a good friend."[33]

Will met Francesca Lunt (Meteyard's aunt, though his and Will's age), who would write poems to him years later as Comtesse d'Aulby. Her uncle T. W. Parsons, already legendary as the Poet in *Tales of a Wayside*

Inn, and her mother were pillars of the old local culture. Meteyard and
Carman followed newer trends—after Will left. In Boston, a pioneer only
in proselytizing for Meredith, Will reviewed such products of the Establishment as came to his office.

One week Louisa May Alcott, next week Slavic literature, in translation, were wrapped up for readers. (He really had little hesitation about
entering that enchanted wood.) But his reviews had sparkling high spirits
and were bold—for a critic with avant-garde friends who was living in a
parsonage. It was *not* always wicked to read novels on Sunday! *Robinson
Crusoe* was fit for a boy's reading any day of the week.

George Santayana, who was studying abroad, urged "Fully" to join
him and other classmates in Germany. He had seen Will's letters to some
of them, and twice asked "Fully" to write to *him.*[34] He had read some
Advertiser pieces and assured Fully that he shared Zadoc Everard's "admiration for Mr. William Morton Fullerton's genius."[35] Santayana eventually received a sixteen-page letter, which he said he would frame and
leave to his nephews ("for like the Pope I shall have only nephews").
Noting that Fully, even living "among the leading men of the time," complained of "intellectual loneliness," Santayana sent him a fantasia on the
pages he tore from the Bible when he had diarrhea. Cleanliness, though
not godliness, enjoined him to "wipe thine ass therewith."[36]

Asked for "more stuff à la Rabelais," he sent Fullerton a letter on
"amatory attitudes." Even if a boy sees "dogs stuck together," he predi-
cated, he is innocent unless "corrupted intentionally and taken to whorehouses," but at twelve or so becomes "occupied with obscene things."
What to do? Masturbation? Whoring? "Seductions or a mistress" means
"scenes and bad social complications—children, husbands at law, etc."

> [Pederasty] has therefore been often preferred by impartial judges, like the
> ancients and orientals; yet our prejudices against it are so strong that it
> hardly comes under the possibilities for us. What shall we do? Oh matri-
> mony, truly thou art an inevitable evil!

He purposely left out "sentimental love." Knowing that Will was
skeptical as to "the ordinary talk" on such subjects, he wanted an honest
answer.[37]

How Will, approached as a man of the world at twenty-two, answered
is not known.

Santayana was heavily facetious—*partly.* He was not overawed by

Will's self-declared intellectual honors and glories but had an uneasy respect for what he called his *"succès de beauté."* "All these great friends of
yours have daughters, and all of these daughters have eyes. . . . Ergo,
when a handsome and fascinating young man, with the most brilliant
prospects, appears upon the scene as if by magic . . ."[38]

For some time, Will had been involved in the "love episodes" his
father was to tally. Already he was amorous and coldhearted and well
equipped to conquer, having magnetic good looks and fluency in appealing to a girl's higher nature. ("The *I* that loves you is a *soul*," he told his
fiancée, Marian.)[39] And on top of all that he now had prestige. He was
interviewed by the *Literary World*:

> The tiny room at the top of the . . . *Advertiser* building finds him busied for
> several hours each day, [but his] workshop is at his father's house . . . in an
> apartment book-walled and literally book-invaded, are written those Let-
> ters about Books which readers of the Sunday *Record* and the Monday *Ad-
> vertiser* turn to . . . there seems no reason to doubt his becoming before
> many years one of the foremost of American critical essayists.[40]

Will Fullerton knew everyone who was anyone in New England letters: John Greenleaf Whittier, Oliver Wendell Holmes, Francis Parkman,
and writers more obscure, *oscurissimi*. He invited them to participate in
a supplement honoring Whittier's eightieth birthday.

He published verse in the *Travelers' Insurance Company Record* and
elsewhere, alongside Adeline Treadwell Parsons, Francesca's mother, and
Constance Fenimore Woolson, whose death in Venice was to harrow
Henry James. He had a poem dedicated to him by Samuel Longfellow,
sermonist and hymnist,[41] and a volume of poetry dedicated to him by the
anthologist Oscar Fay Adams.[42]

He had built up a following by the age of twenty-three.

Then he left to tour Europe and, it seems, Egypt, for he wrote a book
entitled *In Cairo*, unobtainable in Paris, that ought to be at Harvard.

Grand Tour

It *is* here, deep in a dark stack under "Africa," and it has a surprising
preface. A letter to Samuel Longfellow: "Can we ever forget, we two, the
evenings in the garden by the Rhine . . . ?"[43]

So it was the *Rev. Mr. Samuel* Longfellow with whom Will talked of
Europe while writing to Marian! So, he went to Europe—Italy, Germany,
England, France—not with his classmate Richard Longfellow, nephew of
the poet, but with Richard's other uncle, Samuel, sixty-nine, a Unitarian
minister who in editing his brother's blameless letters had performed the
miracle of finding improper, irreverent, or unpatriotic passages, which he
silently deleted or corrected.[44]

Samuel had moved into Craigie House in 1882, the year his famous
brother died and the year Will entered Harvard. "A Man of Gentle Nature, Liberal Culture," he took Will under his wing. Julia held him up to
Will as an example. ("I wonder what he must say to you now if he knew
your Paris life.")

Julia's remark that Will ought to know about Mr. Longfellow as Mr.
Longfellow "leaned to young men"[45] was without innuendo. In her
world few people knew about "pederasty," as it was called by those few.
The "love episodes" Bradford excused because of Will's youth were with
girls, but there may have been same-sex experiments in his vacations
from home at boarding school, and at Harvard (though Santayana obviously did not think of him as gay when he wrote of "amatory" choices),
and of course when he was on the *Advertiser.*

Here in Massachusetts, working against clock and calendar to get an
idea of his pre-Paris life, there's time only for superficial research.

In Italy Will applied "scientific method" to the Old Masters he and
Santayana and Berenson had studied in poor reproductions under Professor Norton. He had decided, after discussion with Santayana, that beauty
is "pleasure in truth." He found that the original paintings often were not
beautiful. But if we reduce our truth to the narrow truth of the people who
believed in angels, they *will* be beautiful. They only *seem* "insincere."[46]

In England he took up an invitation from George Meredith, to whom
he'd sent articles. With an "uncertain umbrella," in an "impeccable silk
hat," through cinders, he made a pilgrimage to Box Hill by train, to be
met by a strong-stepping man with a "wonderful unique trick of high
god-like chaffing," the prodigality of whose genius was "like the prodigality of light."[47]

It was the first interview Meredith had ever granted. Will published it
when, returning to Boston late in the year, he produced another literary
supplement.

Then he again took ship. Mr. Longfellow's friendship may have been platonic and paternal; but, along the way with Longfellow, Will had met Lord Ronald Gower and Hamilton Aïdé and determined to seek his fortune in London.

But before settling down there he went on holiday with Aïdé to Egypt, Greece, and "Turkey."

Hebraism and Hellenism

Rob was at Harvard. Katharine was nine; Bradford and Julia just on fifty, hale and energetic. While they went about housekeeping, homework, sermonizing—brought in kindling and stamped snow from their boots—Will was in a white-hot world visiting ostrich farms and Heliopolis and taking coffee in bazaars heaped with carpets ("reds of damsons, of Pompeii, of burnt carnations"). By the Nile, the girls carrying water pots on their heads recalled the "sweet long rhythm of the Hebrew lines . . . 'I am black but comely.'" Too many women were fat, but Will commended "the swelling lines of the bust" and found departure sad. "Even the yellow-clad chain-gang making bricks like the Israelites had a certain joy in the sunlight not vouchsafed to us who were leaving the bright sun."[48]

On the verandah of Shepheard's Hotel in Cairo he had the refined pleasure of reading Emerson for the first time.[49] In lotus land, where he luxuriated in exotic sensation à la môde de Dorian Gray, reading a pure-minded Transcendentalist was a breach of the Fifth Commandment.

In Egypt, lisps about chain gangs' bliss. A more physically strenuous and, paradoxically, thereby more cerebral experience of Greece. Crammed with classical learning, author of an article on Theocritus,[50] he traveled a rugged land in which the Corinth Canal was just being dug and the Peloponnese had no railway.

He declared for Hellenism when he stood at Corinth "on a pinnacle raised far in clear sunlight above all the long shadows of all the anxiously wrought cathedrals of the Christian middle ages." At a sacred spring he poured libations, praying Zeus to "ease the long boredom of the tortured Sisyphus" and Aphrodite to bring him "that night the face of Nausicaa."[51]

"Boredom" was vintage Oscar Wilde. But Morton saw through myth to "the sediment of history." For scholars who wrote in studies, Greece was a flat map unrelated to the Mediterranean world. Now *he* saw

Mykenae as it was, a "castle upon a mountain route, where robber bar-
ons levied toll, and surrounded by the huddling homes of villains and re-
tainers." The importance of topography was revealed to him; he "un-
learned all, and began afresh."[52]

A London Life

"He is fresh from a ride over the picturesques of Greece," George Meredith wrote that spring, 1889; "has a lively mind, a classic taste (for my
work as well), loves music, aims at excellence, knows Henry James."[53]

In his article, Morton had mentioned Meredith's daughter Marie as "a
charming figure of a young woman in white" (an "intelligent nice girl"
the Ranee wrote, "as in love with you as ever she can be").[54] Her brother
William Mackse became his lifelong friend. Their genial father listened to
his anxieties about finding work.

Percy Anderson, with whom Morton was rooming, had private
means. Aïdé was rich. R.G. was very rich. All R.G.'s friends were "crea-
tive," even his nephew Lorne, ex-Governor-General of Canada and future Duke, published; but *pour le sport*. In that epicene, indolently cultured set, with its darts and swoops and progresses to Rome and
Baden-Baden, it would have been easy to drift. Morton, however, craved
fame and needed money and soon showed an essay on Cairo to the
coarse-grained maverick editor of the *Fortnightly*, Frank Harris. Whereas
James praised the "lovely golden haze" over its "kaleidoscopic surface,"[55] Harris submitted it to an irksome analysis; still, Morton liked
him: "his *brusquerie* even, his deep voice . . . the countless indications of
a Napoleonic will."[56]

He met Oscar Wilde, who was to ask him for a loan, and the "greenery yallery" butts of Gilbert and Sullivan's *Patience,* young poets and critics of the Mauve Decade. He made friends with Arthur Symons, who
hailed the new Decadent literature as "really a rare and beautiful and
interesting disease,"[57] and liked the "fragrance and colour" of Morton's
prose.[58] By offering help with a book on Meredith, Morton made enemies with Richard LeGallienne, who also felt proprietary rights in Meredith, and snubbed him. Morton was pushy; on the other hand, LeGallienne, unlike the overseas intruder, had never met their idol, let alone

become a family friend. When his colleague the bookman John Lane welcomed Morton, LeGallienne grudgingly accepted a five-page appendix, "Meredith in America"—but did not name Morton on the title page.[59] Morton took solipsistic revenge by publicizing his appendix as if it were an independent volume under his own name,[60] and he patronized LeGallienne, playing up his "in" with Meredith for all it was worth. LeGallienne ignored Morton in his *Literary Life in the Nineties, Paris from My Garret Window in the Nineties,* etc. But John Lane gave space in the *Yellow Book* to Morton's deformed sonnet on Meredith:

> No hand but thine is found to fit the gage
> The Titan, Shakespeare, to a whole world threw.
> Till thou hadst boldly to his challenge sprung,
> No rival had he in our English tongue.[61]

Harris rejected "Cairo" (it came out in another magazine with drawings by Percy Anderson)[62] but accepted "English and Americans":

The English obey conventions their reason rejects. Americans *believe* in theirs with a "blatant sincerity" that "drives hypocrisy crouching to a corner of the wall" (Meredithean image). Americans drink "cock-tail pick-me-ups," get rich, and break down. In England, a gentleman's park, lords "in the pay of Poseidon" import food. Their own fields are "a Circe's garden" where visitors cannot smell the hidden pigpens. But with the rumble of laborers on strike, "England takes another hue; and the critic has new light on Isaiah's fulminations, and the stern Thucydidean account of the Sicilian expedition."

Every American hopes to be president. Hence, vulgarity and conflict, but America has "more human beings with a growing sense of their own worth . . . of self and personality, than have ever before been congregated in history."[63]

What surprises is Morton's critical detachment from the clique whose patrician languor he was adopting in his demeanor.

Henry James found the essay "very charming"[64] and introduced its author to the "very charming and amiable" Ranee of Sarawak.[65] Soon Morton was helping her career, and James *his,* telling Macmillan that he and Morton saw the Cairo essay as the "nucleus" of a little immediate book.[66] An "extremely dainty book," Morton explained, "small-paged, wide-margined"; and, another thing, he told Macmillan,

Lady Brooke, Ranee of Sarawak [is writing] a small book upon her Borneo kingdom . . . full of colour and charm. . . . I am exceedingly anxious it should come out in *Macmillan's Magazine* where its almost first-rate literary qualities would find their proper setting.[67]

Macmillan took "Cairo." Morton suggested lunch. He might also ask Lady Brooke. "But that you should meet her at dinner one evening after Sunday week would please me better."[68]

Morton exuded indiscreet triumph. James (and Macmillan) may have guessed about the Ranee. Though James didn't guess about R.G.

Whether James's latent homosexuality ever took physical expression may never be known, but the evidence is overwhelmingly against an affair with Fullerton. Nature and art combined, he told Morton, "in the kind, fond way I think of you and your friendship."[69] It might almost have been a guideline for himself, in contrast to the elaborate buffoon protestations and physicality of some letters to Morton and other young men, and the pain of his letters to the sculptor Hendrik Andersen, with whom he really did fall in love.

When he learned of Morton's blackmail problem years later, James felt that he could have helped earlier by Morton's "admission of me (for I think *my* signs were always there)"; that there would not have been the waste of "something—ah, so tender!—in *me* that was only quite yearningly ready for you" and something "deeply and admirably appealing in yourself, of which I never got the benefit."[70]

And Morton, surely aware of the potential of James's love, maintained with him his character as lady-killer, because of a busy calendar—lack of sexual attraction—or perception that anything like taking up "signs" would irreparably harm their friendship.

"English and Americans" came out in Boston as *Patriotism and Science: Studies in Historic Psychology* (historic psychology was "the science of sciences").[71] Macmillan bought the British rights. Morton didn't care about rights, only wanted to hold the book, "of the colour of the red Matthew Arnold," in his hands.[72] Later: "I like the binding, I think, though I am a little afraid it is very red . . . the pleasure which I have in seeing my wishes so delightfully carried out I cannot help expressing."[73]

Reviewers praised *In Cairo* in its book form,[74] but for some reason the London printing of *Patriotism and Science* was not published. James soothed Morton over his "insulted volume."[75]

The *Times:* From London to Paris

"English and Americans" gave a hint that the aesthete who so ineffably patronized the Ranee might turn to politics. An event of autumn 1890 headed him ineluctably in that direction. The *Boston Journal* reported that Mr. W. M. Fullerton had wished to be Harvard Professor of English, but (burble of excitement):

> the London Times invited him—a youngster and, above all, an American— to become a leader writer. How he has enjoyed this work very few of his friends on this side know, for his correspondence has been addressed solely to his parents in Waltham and to a certain young lady in Springfield.[76]

Marian Kellogg. It must have been salt in her wounds.

In Massachusetts were simulacra of James's journalists, bright-eyed, bushy-tailed, and thick-skinned. Henrietta Stackpole in *The Portrait of a Lady,* the *Reverberator* man . . .

The Boston man was inaccurate as well as coy and indiscreet. Morton was a lowly copy editor. "Not so much a printer's devil," he told John Lane, as his "Satanic Majesty's ancestor" Prometheus Bound.[77]

"What says America," Meredith asked an American correspondent, "to our picking of her plums?"[78]

The following spring, Alice James wrote that a young man from Cambridge was being sent to Paris, to "undermine Blowitz, I suppose."[79] We don't know if "undermining" was her brother Henry's joke or hers. Morton's career was already being obscured by smoky inaccuracies.

Shortly after he departed for Paris, his parents and Katharine arrived in London. Bradford, now a D.D., spoke at an International Congregational Council.[80] Will's friends entertained the family until they went on to Paris, where (*why* is still a mystery) Katharine was left with the "Sacré Coeurs"—committed to the supervision of Will, who took her out on holidays, indulged her and good-naturedly teased her, and purposefully "formed" her. It was on a second trip, to collect her, that Bradford had a stroke. A Protestant clergyman was judged above all by his preaching. The impairment of Bradford's speech was catastrophic. There was heroism in his and Julia's acceptance of a diminished life in "Insurance."

Their son had blithely jettisoned a whole Sunday school past when he noted, after dining with James: "An example of well-brededness [*sic*] on

part of Greeks . . . they didn't send any missionaries." He planned a "scientific" study of Christ for people unable to accept the appearance of "a
quite alien and . . . unnatural force on this particular planet of our astro-
nomic system."[81]

At the *Advertiser,* he had defended keeping the *Heptameron* on Harvard reading lists; such works seldom show sin as "different from the
awful thing that it is!"[82] In London he had left the lilies of Palmer, Waltham, Cambridge, and Boston for the "roses and raptures of vice." The
"I" who loved Marian Kellogg had been "a *soul* with aspirations"; an
"I" living in London enthusiastically told the Ranee that he and she were
fated to be "sublimely, Satanically immoral, audaciously Promethean."
He had of course forgotten Marian long ago. (She married a Springfield
businessman.)[83]

But in Paris even some of his London friends lost their allure. The
Ranee, the first sophisticated woman he had known and perhaps the first
with whom he had an uninhibited sexual experience, a source of trium-
phant gratification, was a bore. And, telling Mr. Longfellow that he'd
heard from Meredith, he wrote:

> Poor man he's very unwell. What do they call it, locomotor ataxy I believe.
> Of him in general I think one could write a scathing article, but the fact re-
> mains that to me he is . . . the greatest natural force in our literature since
> Shakespeare. The criticism is careful: the stress falls on natural.

The defection must have taken mild Mr. Longfellow by surprise. He
and Will had read Meredith together in New Hampshire. But his protégé
was world-weary. Will's "amusements" were "the Opera."

> A dear woman, the Baroness Sal[omon] de Rothschild is charming to me
> and often offers me her box: then, of course, usually when I wish I can drop
> in here and there in the theatres . . . I am dragged into social life and am dis-
> tinctly bored. . . . James wrote to me last week: "I have at last learned to
> live with a decent selfishness: you won't attain to that, however, for a long
> time." He was wrong about me. It is coming fast—this desirable end.

"I sometimes think myself at the end of my career," he sighed. "I suppose it is because I have lived much, and seen many changes in quicker
succession than most men at 26 have experienced."[84]

In twenty-six years he had experienced parsonage, Harvard, book reviewing, travels, a start at the *Times.* So much has been learned in America. It clears the decks for the *real* investigation of Morton Fullerton.
Who was to live in Paris sixty-one years longer.

PART THREE

Paris

Review. Questions. Agenda.

Living here sixty-one years longer, he saw global changes as obvious as vast. The petty but intriguing vicissitudes of his personal life are entangled in clues, lies, lures, errors, and hints. Try to sort things out.

He joined the Paris staff of the *Times* in 1891.

In the early 1890s a "fair-haired syren" landlady at number 5 Rue Vignon attempted his virtue (source: letter from the Ranee).

By the late 1890s he was dominated by a scheming "Madame" (letters from his parents).

In 1900–1901, Camille Chabbert had a child (source: child's marriage record in London).

In 1902, Blowitz retired. M.F. was not appointed his successor that year (M.F. letter to Aïdé).

In 1903, M.F. and Camille were in Spain, married (family letters).

By May 1904 he was back in Paris, alone. A Mme Mirecourt was demanding money (same source).

In November 1904 he divorced Camille because she upbraided him for having mistresses (decree; letter from Albert Clemenceau).

In 1907 an ex-mistress, much older than himself, with whom he was living in the Rue Fabert, had evidence linking him with R.G. and the Ranee and wanted money (source: letters from James and Katharine). He met Edith Wharton. Became engaged to Katharine (letters from Katharine and Rob). Partially resigned from the *Times* (source: biographer's Wharton outline). *Why?*

In 1907–1908–1909 he was involved with Edith and other women; in 1908 he met Camille on friendly terms (letters from Camille).

Around then, Edith and James helped him pay off the blackmailer (Wharton outline; James/Wharton correspondence not yet seen).

In 1910 he resigned completely (Wharton outline).

By 1912 he was in the Hotel Vouillemont; a few years later the reminiscences of Eric Hawkins and Hugh Fullerton begin; by 1920 he was with Mme Hélène Pouget in the Boulevard des Batignolles.

So:

When did *he become Chief Correspondent?* Presumably before partially resigning, but when? See what they have at the *Times*.

Did Mme Pouget, his housekeeper, know about the blackmail?

Write to her niece again.

Who was the father of Camille's child?

The marriage certificate of Frederica Mireille Chabbert and Robert Pierre Lainé in London, 1930, gives Lainé and his father as "manufacturer's agents."

Find the Lainé family.

(Continuing hunt for record of Camille–Morton marriage: English, American, Scottish churches in Paris. Rooms where ladies fold bulletins. Removal from cupboards of hymnbooks and folding chairs. "Oh dear, afraid not!")

Who was Mme Mirecourt?

Who Was Mme Mirecourt?

It is a decent working hypothesis that the blond "syren" of the Rue Vignon, the schemer, the "Madame," the woman of the Rue Fabert, and Mme Mirecourt were one and the same. Who was she?

Was. She can hardly be alive. But people still alive may have known her.

For years she "reigned supreme." Will discarded Camille in her favor. By 1907 (when we came in) her hold had weakened. James's letters and Katharine's reflect Will's portrayal of a rapacious witch, lidless-eyed, wrinkle-trenched, with a tusk for teeth and a beak for a nose. Will was treating this monster with delicate chivalry (Katharine) and deplorable compassion (James).

The family knew about her as early as his visit home in 1898. He must have been strangely confiding. (But he *was* strangely confiding! He must have volunteered many of the names in his father's Catalogue of Lovers.)

In 1907 she wanted him to marry her. Had there been an impedi-
ment—a husband whose death now made marriage possible? The writer
Jacquet or "de Mirecourt" is said to have died at Ploërmel. His death certificate will name a widow if any.

The town has no record of him under either name.

Meanwhile, brooding over notes on the little notebook (returned long
since) that had yielded gold in "R.G." Many women are named, non-
committally. Two entries are tantalizing: "June 15 1895 Adèle and I Ville
d'Avray but alas Corot is dead and the willows are beginning to grow out
of the frame," and

> Sept. 11 '97 . . . glorious autumn mist with the metallic colours enswathing
> the yellow hay ricks. . . . Ascended Montlhéry & afterwards read to A.
> under tower Matve Bruvis's little pamphlet. . . . Glorious sunset westward
> of Montlhéry tower seen across pumpkin patches. . . . An old Benedictine
> Priory.

Was A. Adèle? Morton was with Adèle just when Mirecourt would
have been ascendant. Moreover, it's the only time he says "so-and-so and
I." The entry stood out for that reason when first read.

Not what you'd call evidence. But a conviction took obstinate hold: A.
was Adèle, and Adèle was Adèle Mirecourt.

The hunt in the Cadastre for the Rue Fabert had been futile, thanks to
the *greffier*'s henchman, but long before that Morton had lived at number
5, Rue Vignon. Try the Archives of the Seine.

The quiet reading room has a single table, eight readers to a side, and
a view through trees of the river and the sand barges tied up on the Left
Bank opposite.

Two pale folders for Rue Vignon were brought to the table. A thick
dossier for number 5, with many hands, faded ink, light pencil, minus-
cule note, erasures, deletions, addenda, page after page after page after
page. Hard to keep the attention focused. Then, on a righthand page,
faint as faint: "1891. Moutot Adèle dite Mirecourt loueuse d'une cham-
bre meublée."

Mirecourt.

And she was Adèle. Adèle was she.

Dite. "Known as" Mirecourt. No wonder there is no Mirecourt in
Births, Marriages, and Deaths. "Lessor of a furnished room."

Outside the window the Seine slid by oily smooth. Now and then someone breathed.

The apartment was on the entresol, that important floor between ground floor and first. On the landing, an anteroom and an *anglaise* or W.C. On the entresol, facing you, a dining room. Left, kitchen. Right, a bedroom with a fireplace, a salon, another bedroom with a fireplace, and a corridor to the dining room.

Mirecourt's lease began in April 1891, about when Morton came to Paris, and ended in April 1903, about when he left on his mission to Spain. Renting a room was a "taxable occupation."

Suppose she kept her later flat, Rue Fabert in the Seventh, till her death. My authorization for the *mairie* is still valid—

MOUTOT Adèle Augustine died at 40 *bis* Rue Fabert in 1924. No occupation. Unmarried. Born 1848. Older than Morton indeed: by seventeen years.

The Rue Fabert forms the west side of the Esplanade des Invalides. (It is the street airport buses take as they leave the Invalides Aerogare.) The front windows of number 40 *bis* overlook the trees that border the wide gravelly esplanade. Under the trees men are playing *boules,* as they played on spring evenings like this when Morton came out that door and strolled across to the Faubourg Saint-Germain on the east side.

In the months when he was going to Edith Wharton's for lunch, tea, dinner, and readings of Dante, it was the easiest of walks. Late in the evening he would leave the *Times* office, write a note to Edith at some café, drop it off, make a wearier way back here, creep past the concierge's cubbyhole, and tiptoe upstairs, hoping that a door would not fly open and a Fury swoop out.

Time to go. Past the Invalides moat, past the Rodin Museum where Katharine lived when it was a convent school. Zigzag over to the Ministères. Belle Epoque, soft mirrors, green banquettes.

"I've found Mme Mirecourt!"
"Non!"
". . . 'dite' Mirecourt. She might have been living with a Mirecourt and taken his name and—"

"*Non! 'Dite' means just one thing. The person is an artiste, a writer, painter. Wasn't Camille Chabbert at the Opéra?*"

"*Yes—much younger—*"

"*What does that matter? Fullairton meets a young débutante in the same milieu as Mme 'Mirecourt.' And Mirecourt is a fanciful name. It sounds good. It's good for someone on the stage.*"

Les Enfants du Paradis

Well, she may have been a bareback rider in the Circus. But, to start somewhere, try the Opéra Library again.

The *Annales du Théâtre et de la Musique* had been useless for Chabbert-Ixo, but the exceedingly fine print of a footnote listing the cast of a musical, *Pif-Paf,* gives—"Mademoiselle Mirecourt."

It was 1875. Adèle Moutot was twenty-seven.

In time, a dozen plays were resurrected in which Mlle or Mme (depending on the printer) Mirecourt had a billing, never at the top, and usually near the bottom.[1]

Newspaper reviews can also be found, on microfilm, though the search is not easy on the National Library's Merovingian machines. Fingers bleeding, twist a jagged screw up to January 1, descend delicately to January 2, and the reel whirls down to December. But winding those kilometers of blurry film, organ-grinding, produces music, whispery, then gaining vigor and bursting full force into the prance of the can-can and the *galope,* the music of Offenbach and *La Gaité Parisienne.* Those unprepossessing records tell us what songs the Siren sang. She sang:

Dans le pays des amoureux	All who live in lovers' land
Tout le monde va deux à deux[2]	Go two by two and hand in hand.

And:

Prenez, prenez ces menottes,	Take, O take these little hands,
Vénus ne sait refuser rien.[3]	Venus never can say no.

Her birth certificate comes. She was born in the village of Saint-Rémy, Haute-Saône Department, on 29 February 1848.

Then a blank until, on New Year's Eve 1872, we see her cavorting on the stage of the Menus-Plaisirs Theatre at the rowdy first night of the *Cocotte aux Oeufs d'Or*.[4]

Cocotte means hen and also tart, courtesan, demimondaine. In *The Hen That Laid the Golden Eggs,* some barnyard fowl are turned into women and launched in the demimonde.

"Make love, not war,"[5] sang Mlle Mirecourt, one of a septet of cocottes. Rather, those words were assigned to Folichonnette, whose part she played; but she, Cascadine, Nana, etc., sang each other's lines, and when they came to the chorus sang it to seven different tunes. An uproarious audience applauded as trapdoors refused to swallow persons slated to vanish. "White-ties" who had escaped from family parties eyed unescorted ladies. At midnight a spectator kissed an unknown woman in the next seat and had his face slapped. "Happy New Year!" yelled someone in the paradise.

(Midnight in Paris. Early evening in New England, and a Currier & Ives print. Fir trees black against dark-blue sky with stars, white church with steeple, white house with lantern over doorway, path of light on snow, and eight-year-old Will Fullerton pulling his little brother home on a sled to supper and family prayers.)

The premiere of the *Cocotte* provided gags for *The Bride from the Rue Saint-Denis,* a play about a play at the Menus-Plaisirs in which Mirecourt, petite artiste, played a petite artiste. "A first-night audience isn't fussy," she reminds the other artistes. "Anyway, we've nobody but friends out front."

Audience laughter.

The friends out front were the *cocadès,* keepers of cocottes. A cocotte went on stage to attract keepers. A resting actress took a box and was matter-of-factly named in next day's papers among "cocottes I noticed in the audience." A critic reported on the spectators first. Days later, after consultation with management, authors, *cocadès,* and actresses, he published a mature appraisal of play and performers.

It was the world of *Nana.* It was, literally, the source material for *Nana.* Zola did his methodical research for his fetid, powerful, misogynistic novel at the very moment when Mirecourt was on stage and in the very theaters where she played. Nana, *"la blonde Vénus,"* was alternately actress and courtesan.

Many of those plays had only one, two, or three performances, yet their librettos were printed in advance and purchased by the audience at the door. It is as if television guides provided sitcom scripts for viewers to follow.

In *The Transit of Venus,* singing "Venus never can say no!" Mirecourt was embraced by the Sun as excited astronomers aimed telescopes at her. She was a gypsy in *Pif-Paf,* Cleopatra in *Tant Plus Ça Change,* The More Things Change ("exquisitely Parisian, but perhaps too distingué, too *soigné,* for a revue"). Then:

The Palais-Royal and *Monsieur Blondeau's Tenants*

The Palais-Royal Theater was famous for actors who were comic gen-iuses and actresses with "intelligent faces, graceful bearing, and witty, provocative delivery."[6] In the "five-story vaudeville" *Les Locataires de Monsieur Blondeau* a retired barber buys a house and finds it tenanted by such people from his past as his ex-mistress (played by Mirecourt), now wed to a Portuguese marquis. She is also the ex-mistress of the great tenor Riflardini, another tenant, to whom she sends a note signed "The Veiled Lady" entreating a rendezvous, which he grants.

Mirecourt: I never intended to see you again. Then I saw you in *Rigo-letto:* It did something to me.
Riflardini: I am superb in *Rigoletto.*
Mirecourt: I didn't suspect when I left you that I carried a pledge of our love. Our son—
Riflardini: A son! What emotion! Oh my bronchial tubes . . . and my son—?
Mirecourt: I had a booking in Portugal, so I left him at Bayonne. Then I married an old Portuguese marquis in Lisbon and when I went back for him fifteen years later—
Riflardini: Fifteen years?
Mirecourt: One can't always do as one would like. When I went back—he had vanished!
Riflardini: My son! My bronchial tubes!
Mirecourt: Weep not! I have found him. A quarter of an hour ago.
Riflardini: What—only a—

Mirecourt: When I entered this house, he was leaving. Our blissful reunion took place in the entry.

As the landlord Blondeau, the fat comedian Montbars swung in and out of windows, floor to floor, on a rope to escape the Portuguese marquis's machete. "Impossible," cried a critic, "to give any idea of the headlong speed, the comical episodes; the dialogue moves at the tempo of a polka."

Henry James was sending "Paris Letters" to the *New York Tribune.* He discussed the revue with its "many bad jokes and undressed figurantes" in the year when the four-star revue was *Les Echos de l'Année,* with Mirecourt in three bit parts; he didn't name it. He called the Palais-Royal "exhaustingly exhilarating": Mirecourt wasn't yet there. At a public swimming pool he saw with abhorrence "Mlle X. . , the actress of the Palais-Royal," in "a single scant, clinging garment," her "nether limbs" trousered, "take a straight leap head downward, before 300 spectators"; he didn't name her.[7]

The *Locataires,* a smash hit, played in London as *French Flats* and was revived in Paris in late 1879.

Then, nothing until twelve years later a clerk, climbing stairs, knocking on doors in the Rue Vignon, recorded that Moutot Adèle *dite* Mirecourt was a tenant subject to tax on the room she sublet.

So:

Mirecourt was pretty. Looks were the first essential, and she was cast as Venus and as Cleopatra.

She was talented enough to be taken on by a company that was famous for a witty, stylish technique.

She was not famous. No Mirecourt in *Les Jolies Actrices de Paris.* Nor in the *Dictionnaire des Comédiens Français,* which lists players so minor that it says only: "played in Algiers 1883." Her protectors, if she had them, couldn't or wouldn't buy publicity.

Still, by 1891, at forty-three, she had enough money to take a large apartment in a fashionable neighborhood: though, on the other hand, not enough to dispense with subletting a room.

And so Mme Mirecourt, no longer in tights or Grecian tunic but in the garb of an elegant Parisienne, took a young journalist, foreign, his French not very good, as a lodger.

At Mme Mirecourt's: Press and Politics in the 1890s

"Between 7 and 11:30 at night I am at my office reading all the French journals or translating Blowitz." In a letter to Samuel Longfellow, Will parodied W. M. Fullerton:

> while the Chamber sits I am a little nervous as to what may happen there, as I am responsible for all of the local political life. . . . I am in constant relations with deputies ministers and even, through archbishops, the Pope. . . . It is very odd, it is very delightful and it is very instructive. It forces me to have the whole European movement at my finger-ends.[8]

We've been putting too much emphasis on Camille, Edith, etc. Blowitz meant more than any woman to an ambitious young man who never knew disappointment in love. For eleven years, Fullerton was in daily contact with a living legend.

The Paris Correspondent was an adventurer—not the confidence man but the condottiere. Short and fat, but active and audacious. He once got a scoop by jumping over a wall after a state dinner. Sometimes, Morton wrote in a magazine, governments denied what he printed. But he had "nipped in the bud" some scheme, "anticipated" a revelation, or set a trap for a "less wary diplomatist."

Morton laid it on thick. (Would he have dared call the *Times* "only the accidental projection" of Blowitz had Blowitz been more sensitive to English?) But stronger than any undertow of mockery is his swelling admiration of Blowitz's idea of journalism: to get at "political truth" and exert an influence for peace as a "self-accredited representative to every European court."[9]

As Morton himself would do one day.

Not so soon, though, as he expected. There was that letter in the Fullerton papers, 1902. He told Aïdé that he had been doing most of Blowitz's work and that another man had exploited Blowitz's jealousy of him to maneuver himself into the post. But when he wrote his article, he wasn't aware of Blowitz's ill will. Blowitz had a "good and amiable heart."

Morton went about the Senate and the ministries and the Palace of Justice and brought his findings to his chief, who assessed them and produced copy in French for him to translate. As Blowitz's assistant, he covered the major events of the early Belle Epoque.

A Beautiful Epoch for the rich. To aid the poor, laws reduced the miner's day, to twelve hours, and prohibited use of women and children, underground. Repression of protest spawned terrorism. One terrorist, Ravachol, mesmerized Morton, who followed his trial and deemed him an "individually distinguished man" as fit for psychological study as Mr. George Meredith, Marcus Aurelius, General Ulysses S. Grant, and Jesus Christ.[10]

Ravachol was guillotined in 1892. The following year Morton was in the Chamber when there "shot a sort of dull red gleam" and

> the sound of an explosion was heard. Smoke . . . a rain of something hard upon my head. . . . Half a dozen Deputies, guarded on either side by friends, with the blood running from their faces, were led out of the Chamber dropping blood as they went along. . . . Big horseshoe nails were lying everywhere. It was a bomb.

In the carnage he saw a woman with her breast almost torn off.[11]

Since the storming of the Bastille, France had gone from monarchy to republic to empire to restorations of monarchy to Second Republic to Second Empire. The Third Republic had sprung from the country's defeat in the Franco-Prussian War only twenty years before Fullerton began, perforce, to gain a knowledge of French history as he reported current events for a foreign newspaper.[12]

He discovered that the Republic was "fighting for its life." Born of revolt against divinely appointed kings, it was reprobated by the Vatican, which opposed "every manifestation of 'the modern spirit'"—religious freedom, separation of church and state, civil legislation on marriage and divorce, civil supervision of schools. It was constantly assailed by monarchists.

Morton sided with the Republic, progress, and "the scientific method of thought" and against the Vatican.

For the rest of his life his personal experience was inseparable from that of his adopted country.

At Mme Mirecourt's: Paris in the Spring, 1893

Many visitors were here. Richard Harding Davis and Charles Dana Gibson. James McNeill Whistler. Edmond Gosse. And of course:

first week in April 93 Marquis Lorne & Princess Louise Ronald Gower
Hotel Choiseul all lunch at Le Doyen & I bring James. Afterwards M. of L.
& R.G. chez moi. All this month James.

Gosse told a friend that "the austere and melancholy James" was "de-
coyed" into the Latin Quarter and could "be seen by mortal eyes . . . with
a certain 'Reine de Golconde' on one arm and a certain 'Bobbinette' on
the other."[13]
Austere and melancholy, James brought his talent for fun to a com-
radeship that glintingly recalls Falstaff and Prince Hal, even if he and
Morton bought books on the quais instead of ambushing travelers on the
heath: the older man frank and exuberant, the younger always keeping
something back.

Strolling with Morton in Bohemia, James would have encountered cocottes. When Morton took him along to the high-fashion Le Doyen, he
saw that his young friend was on terms with the royals lunching there—
though the intimacy with R.G. came as news years later.

R.G.'s visit *"chez"* Morton in the Rue Vignon is more resonant now
that we know the landlady is a woman aware of "names." It sounds spur-
of-the-moment. If Morton did not already have the run of the place, he'd
have murmured to Adèle: Might he venture to ask for the use of her
salon? . . . English of the highest distinction. Merci infiniment, Madame,
c'est très aimable de votre part.

Give Mme Mirecourt the habit of reading newspapers. On the front
page of *Le Figaro,* March 29, she has seen:

Arrived from London H.R.H. Princess [Louise], daughter of the Queen of
England, and her husband the Marquess of Lorne, accompanied by Lord
Ronald Gower and Miss Bulteel, lady-in-waiting. The Marquess and Mar-
chioness have been staying at the Hotel Choiseul.

She guesses who Morton's visitors are and knows that one of them is
a brother-in-law of the Prince of Wales, a familiar in the greenrooms of
her youth; friends of hers had, like Nana in the novel, been taken to bed
by him.

She did not necessarily eavesdrop. This was the occasion of the "little
difference" between R.G. and Morton that Aïdé was so glad to hear of
("much better for your extreme intimacy to be stopped"). Voices may
have risen. The altercation may have alerted her to the significance of letters from R.G. when she went through Morton's papers later.

But how did she know about the Ranee? From letters, but had Morton already *told* her? He told his parents and James about R.G., the Ranee, and Adèle; told Doll and Camille about Katharine. At what point did he pass from joking to the Ranee about the fair-haired siren to joking with Adèle about *la Reine de Sarawak?*

Verlaine: Poets and Poverty

After being in and out of prison—for shooting Rimbaud, for attacking his mother—after brutal orgies in "obscene streets"—ravaged by syphilis and absinthe, Paul Verlaine, angel-demon, was in and out of hospital, mostly in.

"Et O ces voix d'enfants chantant dans la coupole, the voices of those children singing in the cupola—"

Arthur Symons invited Verlaine to lecture in England and asked Fullerton to see the Decadent off on the boat train for Dieppe.

"Decadent? Verlaine said that art is being clear and absolutely yourself. If no one follows you, go on alone."

Morton found Verlaine living in a room "as big as a bathroom, with one coal, burning, I am sure, to receive me" and was informed that Mme Verlaine, who was "buttoning his coat and tying his plaid tippet," needed money. Morton gave her thirty francs and took the poet to the Saint-Lazare Station café-restaurant. It was November, and a bad night. Even in Paris the wind was howling. Verlaine took Morton's notebook and dolefully wrote in it: "après dîner s'en aller sur la mer," after dinner off to sea, and signed "P. Verlaine."

With the help of *le bon vin,* Morton got him aboard the train. "This morning, however," he wrote Symons next day, sending a bill for the thirty francs and other expenses, "when I read of the frightful tempest that has blown all day I had a sensation of choke."

Curious fact: in the three hours we spent together Verlaine appealed to me like Jesus Christ and Socrates. I thought of him as a Man of Sorrows, with the Socratic cheerfulness and winningness of spirit behind that ugly mask. . . . I could not bear to think he was being tossed about on the sea unaccompanied by the still more ugly woman whom he seemed to love tenderly.[14]

The Fullerton of the 1890s had a penchant for Dostoievskian characters, associating an anarchist with Christ and Marcus Aurelius, a *poète
damné* with Christ and Socrates.

Verlaine's journey, begun on November 19, had not ended as Morton
wrote. The crossing was delayed. Symons went back and forth from London Bridge Station to his rooms in Fountain Court. At 2:30 A.M. on the
21st he went out and saw, "moving slowly and with labour . . . a vague
figure, carrying a tiny bag and leaning heavily on a stout stick." Verlaine
had found his way across London in the dark. Plied with biscuits and gin,
he recovered in time to give his talks, wearing a white shirt, the essential
contents of the "tiny bag."

The next February, Verlaine sent Morton a macaronic postcard. "I am
divorced and have removed my premises. (Excuse my dog English.)" A
"young Irish poet Mr. Yeats" was coming, sent by Symons: "It would be
amusing if you came together between half past twelve and one for coffee."[15] But Yeats and Verlaine had to use a dictionary when they talked;
Morton was working on a story. That day a bomb went off in the Saint-
Lazare café-restaurant where he had dined with Verlaine, causing death.
(The place was targeted as a "haunt of the *petite bourgeoisie,* accomplices of Poverty and the State.")[16]

The Fullerton of the 1890s wanted to be more than a critic. He had a
few poems printed (the novels he began fizzled out).[17] His elegy "Three
Sonnets" ("Oh sweet communion of the vanished days / When his large
eyes looked calmly into mine!")[18] was probably on Samuel Longfellow. A
poor writer of verse, he recognized talent in others. Santayana, who was
teaching philosophy at Harvard, sent him manuscript poems, which he
sent on to James (who asked who "Santyana"[19] was, not deciphering the
name of a colleague of his brother William). He read verse by Richard
Hovey admired by Bliss Carman, who wrote:

> there is not an abundance of poetry in this world now. Somehow we have
> wandered out of that Fairyland where we lived once. How sunny it was.
> . . . good cheer to thy heart, and my kindest regards to your beautiful
> mother.
>
> With love, Your Bliss Carman[20]

(A new perspective on Julia. Carman, who sought both beauty and
mothers, had spent a Sunday in Waltham in the "once" he wistfully

recalled. Only five years ago, but that was when Julia was the contented mistress of a parsonage, not yet careworn by Bradford's illness and worry over money.)

Hovey had studied for the Episcopal priesthood but, finding that "Adam and Eve were punished for scientific research," had broken with dogma just as Morton was shuffling off his Protestant piety. At present he was in France, where his mistress was giving birth to their child. Till they left to arrange divorce and marriage in America Morton found him odd jobs in Paris.[21] For neither Hovey nor Carman could make a living by poetry. Hovey took jobs in theaters as an extra; Carman lived in friends' houses, with friends' mothers.

Whereas Verlaine appealed to Morton as a genius and a true *misérable,* Carman and Hovey confirmed his conviction of the need for a regular salary, as did his parents' reduced circumstances. On the other hand, Thomas Meteyard,[22] who designed the *Songs from Vagabondia* that Hovey and Carman co-authored, had money and could paint where and when he liked, moving with his mother between London, Giverny-Paris, and Boston-Scituate, Massachusetts, till he married and settled in England in a house next to Henry James's in Rye. Meteyard's situation heightened Morton's growing wish for a private income and a life in Europe unharassed by material problems.

Morton's friends rich and poor sailed back and forth and ambivalated as he steadily became more deeply French. They were James's subject matter. Matter of France, matter of Britain, matter of America the Great. Meteyard's young aunt Francesca, now Countess d'Aulby, was one of the many American women who married titles. Most of them came, like her, from conventional families in the East, but Morton met a noblewoman-by-marriage, as Europeanized as he, who had grown up in an America he never knew.

The Golden Girl of the Middle West

A scene in his office that must have been tempestuous was followed by a letter of apology, a letter found in the Fullerton papers, written with a swashbuckling pen and enclosing a rose leaf.

> . . . so forgive the vanity and think only of the sentiment—which had I your pen would be better expressed, and your mind—better conceived, but what

I wish to say is—I am not to be a worry a bother a trouble to you—and I am never again going to no 35 unless expressly invited—parole de bonne fille et de bonne camarade.

The *Times* bureau was at number 35 Boulevard des Capucines.

Yesterday I felt a thousand acute things—Remorse—regret—repentance, but I am an impossible woman—I know no law not my own caprice and recognize no will—not mine own—volition. Yours I might bend to—I say might—but not easily.

You are not coming this morning. I hear every footfall, even in the street—dont be surprised—my windows are wide opened. There is not even a thoroughbred passing man horse dog or child—there is nothing beautiful to look at but a rose on my table—I send you a leaf, and it beareth a message—discover it—"For now I follow yearning / to know and to be known." When am I to see you, Adonis—do you wish me to cry for the moon—and regret—my last ambition? I believe you do—I can believe anything of a man—Why must I sign myself—always

Yours

Blanche Roosevelt[23]

Blanche Roosevelt Tucker, raised in Wisconsin, Illinois, and Ohio, was a niece of Ferdinand Roosevelt, son of Nelson Roosevelt of Albany, who is believed to have been related to Theodore Roosevelt and Eleanor Roosevelt. After working in many states at many trades, from Wells Fargo clerk to gold prospector, Ferdinand became one of "the progressive men of Montana."[24]

With his backing,[25] Blanche went abroad to study under Pauline Viardot. Discovering that her voice was too small for grand opera, she turned to writing hectic murky novels like *Stage-Struck, or, She WOULD be an Opera-Singer,* articles for Oscar Wilde's *Woman's World,* and biographies that she researched by living with her subjects, sometimes as lover. Her *Longfellow* was popular, but at twenty-one she had captivated a greater writer: when she recited a sonnet on Victor Hugo's seventy-sixth birthday, Hugo gave the "Muse and Genius of the New World" a kiss that "went round the table."[26] "Eager always to do anyone a good turn," said Frank Harris, whom she introduced to Maupassant and Turgenev. Harris scoffed at her calling herself *femme de lettres.*[27] A French savant thought her learned,[28] and her *Doré* was crowned by the Académie.[29] She married an Italian marquis.

Morton may have met her in Montparnasse Cemetery when, as James put it, "the indignity that life had heaped upon poor Maupassant found itself stayed."[30] Guy de Maupassant died of syphilitic insanity. In disregard of the *Times*'s denunciation of his works for immorality "so repulsive as seriously to detract from their artistic value,"[31] he was given a public funeral with a eulogy by Emile Zola. Blanche was there; she had lived with Maupassant[32] and was the only personal friend present except his valet, who praised her in a life of his master as beautiful, kind, and unpretentious.[33]

Wherever they first met, Morton must have heard enough to make knowing Blanche piquant until—conjecturally—like him a heartbreaker not used to being the one who was dropped, she stormed into his office to confront him. Probably in her decline. She died in 1898; only forty-one,[34] but she had lived with a hard gemlike flame.

Serendipity: in her *Verdi* Blanche calls the crowd of admirers in the great composer's anteroom farcical, "quite like *Le Locataire* [*sic*] *de M. Blondeau,* a piece I once saw at the Palais Royal theatre."[35]

She saw Mirecourt. Playing a Portuguese marquise. Mirecourt, whom she, Marchesa Blanche Roosevelt Tucker Macchetta d'Allegri, might have seen again in the role of a female Blondeau had she pursued Morton not to his office but to his Rue Vignon lodgings.

In that "most literary of entresols," Morton ranged his old books. Books are a problem when you move, Julia had warned;[36] and, as if foreseeing problems he would have in escaping Mirecourt, he told Aïdé that they were the bane of his existence. "I resemble one of those *automobiles* that promise much, and when they have sizzled . . . a rattling kilometre or two, suddenly halt, blocking the way. . . . Not that I block the way to anybody but myself."[37]

To the south he browsed on the quais. Strolling north, he noted "the cocottes swoop down . . . Murillo boys . . . workmen eating on grass."[38] Right Bank, Left Bank, all about the town, his movements can be plotted, a red dotted line beginning and ending at 5 Rue Vignon.

The Dreyfus Case, 1: The Condemnation to Devil's Island

In 1893 and 1894 lines in other colors crisscrossed his.

A French army officer, Esterhazy, leaves his house in the Eighth Arrondissement. A German military attaché, Schwartzkoppen, leaves his embassy in the Faubourg Saint-Germain. Their routes converge at street corners, in dim alleys. Esterhazy hands over papers. From the German embassy there issues a French cleaning woman who enters a church where lurks a French agent. They meet. She empties her pockets of scraps from the ambassadorial wastepaper baskets.

It was the pastoral age of espionage. Spies donned false beards and signed women's names to forged love letters. Schwarzkoppen and Esterhazy wore disguises. Shredding was manual.

Thanks to the scavenging char, French army intelligence learned that secrets were being passed. Especially suspect was Captain Alfred Dreyfus, a Jew. When a Colonel Henry produced pasted-up scraps of a paper listing data that had been passed, Dreyfus was arrested.

CONDEMNATION OF JEWISH CAPTAIN DREYFUS
—*La Libre Parole,* 24 December 1894

People climbed trees to see into the courtyard of the Ecole Militaire as an adjutant "snatched off the epaulettes, plume, and red stripes" of Dreyfus's uniform, their stitching already "almost entirely unpicked," and broke a sword already almost broken.[39]

Dreyfus was sent to Devil's Island, a former leper colony off French Guiana, and most people forgot about him.

At Blowitz's house, Morton would smoke after dinner while Blowitz, on a divan "one leg curled under him," reminisced. You "had visions of Baghdad," wondering when he worked, but he'd have dictated an article, telephoned for his carriage, and invited you to the opera before he'd finished his cigar.[40]

Four summer holidays passed while Dreyfus was on Devil's Island.

On the "iris-coloured watery" shore of the Atlantic at Arcachon the oystermen were "as handsome in their sunburnt way as a terra cotta vase," the oyster that made Arcachon famous was becomingly humble, and the superstitiousness and Gascon dialect of his illiterate host Castro gave Morton pleasure. He wandered the dunes:

> Nor man, nor beast, nor bird was in sight or hearing. For company I had only this long cannon thudding of the ocean. It followed me everywhere, hauntingly. Not even the insistent individuality of Castro, nor even that of Arcachon, and most agreeable of all, not even that of myself, could make

the slightest impression. It was relief unutterable to be amid a few unadul-
terated, unsophisticated things, and to have for the moment the illusion
that things, but only these things, were.[41]

Even in his marine retreat, Morton did some academic reading, he told
Barrett Wendell later, confiding that at Harvard he had felt like "the av-
erage intelligent Jew . . . hating and scorning" the world. In a sequitur he
asked if Wendell had read a "simple little book," *Venetian Painters*. It
gave "the old Berenson" away. "A good new French word" for
Berenson's quality was *"narcissisme."*[42]

Neither the snide "narcissism" nor the "Everybody seems Jew nowadays"[43] of a letter to Aïdé prepares one for the total partisanship Morton
would soon give a victim of anti-Semitism.

The Dreyfus Case, 2: The Rennes Court-Martial

In a sweltering hut on another shore of the Atlantic, Dreyfus survived.
But it began to be said that his trial had been illegal: the defense had not
known of a "secret dossier" used against him. Col. Georges Picquart was
ordered to search for his motive. (*What is the motive of your treason?*)
He found letters by Esterhazy in the hand ascribed to Dreyfus and refused to keep his mouth shut.

Thereupon, the forger, Colonel Henry, created proof that Picquart too
was a spy, while Esterhazy created a "veiled lady" (she comes into
Morton's notebook) who had other proofs. Georges Clemenceau demanded "revision," review, of the case. When Esterhazy was acquitted of
forgery, Emile Zola published *"J'ACCUSE"* in *L'Aurore,* attacking the
government and provoking a libel suit in which Albert Clemenceau—
Morton's divorce lawyer four years later—defended the paper and
Maître Labori, Zola.

Zola's trial dominated the *Times* except on the day when the battle-
ship *Maine* was sunk off Cuba. Zola and Picquart were both found
guilty, but Zola went to England before he could be jailed.

Then someone found that Colonel Henry had pasted up unmatching
kinds of paper. He confessed to forgery and cut his throat.

(And died a martyr! cried Charles Maurras, a founder of the far-right
movement Action Française. Colonel Henry had committed a moral forgery so that a traitor should not go unpunished!)

An appeals court found Esterhazy guilty of forgery. He went to England, Zola came back from England, and Dreyfus was put aboard a ship
and taken to Rennes in Brittany, far from Paris, for trial, to reduce the
danger of riots.

Every day the *Times* gave its main page to verbatim reports of testimony, background pieces by Blowitz, and an atmospheric narrative, of
course anonymous, by "Our Special Correspondent," Fullerton.

Thirty long reports[44]—they would make a fair-sized book—testify that
Morton's elaborate syntax, the hallmark of his style, was not studied, for
he wrote under pressure. The trial was being followed throughout the
world. Tension was high among the journalists of many nationalities who
were working at close quarters in a foreign land. (Even to the French,
Brittany, with its own language and traditions, was half foreign.) There
was danger of civil war.

But the trial itself was a civil war, Morton wrote: war between "the old
reactionary conservative France and the perennially young and revolutionary France adventurously curious as to ideas and enamoured of progress."

RENNES, August 7. 5:30 a.m. The long corridors of the [Hôtel de France] re-
sound with the comings and goings of the hotel servants knocking at doors.
. . . A few moments later some 30 or 40 men are hastily drinking their coffee in the common dining-room. A hasty meal, and we are all making our
way through the still empty streets . . . hardly a soul is abroad, only a few
peasants arousing the echoes with their heavy *sabots*. 6.30 a.m. A double
line of mounted gendarmes has just been moved. . . . We are at last in the
Court-room.

ENTRANCE OF THE PRISONER

At 7.10 . . . behold a man in the brand-new uniform of an officer of artillery
with a close-cropped, white head, with features like and yet unlike the portraits scattered throughout the world, who marches rapidly across the sill
of the entrance door, and with head erect and firm and steady step advances . . . to his place. There he stands an instant and salutes the Court
with his white-gloved left hand.

In a tour de force of pretelevision immediacy, Morton had his readers
share the experience of the reporters who were their proxies, judging the
judges. He focused on a "little messenger" whose head sometimes
drooped, and on the stenographers, "busy fingers" who had to concentrate on recording each word and yet took sides. (One was arrested for

calling a general "assassin.") A bureaucrat who had claimed that a Dreyfus "syndicate" was pouring money into France was a "little white
mouse." Would he now make for a hole? But Colonel Picquart, who had
refused to keep quiet about the forgeries, had the "distinguished air of
force of character and gentleness combined which is so winsome in this
admirable type of French manliness."

While Morton's coverage was not quite the ideal journalism he envis-
aged for the successor of Blowitz (who would work behind the scenes to
influence the events he would openly report), he did not pretend to im-
partiality. He voiced indignation, humor, scorn, homoeroticism; he was
melodramatic. However, he exhorted readers who had not "followed
sedulously each movement of the opposing armies" to read the verbatim
stenographic reports.

ATTEMPT TO KILL M. LABORI

One evening, journalists in cafés, watching "the mysterious shifting
through the dark streets of this provincial town of scurrying bands of agitators," talked low of the National Anti-Semitic party—of a coming St.
Bartholomew's massacre of Dreyfus supporters. Next morning Labori,
Dreyfus's counsel, was shot in the back. His substitute, Demange, performed so badly that it was said Dreyfus's family might ask Albert Clemenceau to take his place.
"The choice," Morton wrote, "would not be a bad one."
The refusal of a recess inspired a "kilometric" sentence:

A Government commissary who, like Major Carrière, refuses to accede to
the legitimate request of a defendant who has lost his counsel to interrupt a
trial until he shall have been able to secure the support accorded to an accused man in every other civilized country but France, and who puts forward as the reason of his obduracy those miserable antiquated "considera-
tions of public order" which, under the name of *raison d'état,* have been
invoked as the sufficient excuse for all crimes of State, is a standing warning of the danger which individual liberty and social justice run from the
untrammelled development in our modern society of military institutions.

The "pale, strange" deviser of an "anthropometric" system for identifying criminals displayed portfolios proving that Dreyfus *was* a forger.
"The little messenger had not an instant to himself," handing them

around. Then Captain Freystäter, "a splendid and sympathetic type of masculine beauty," took the stand

> like the conscience of France incarnate, [lifting] our emotion into that sublime, strange sphere of mingled moral and aesthetic joy where, as in the finest scenes of Greek tragedy, wonderment before the beauty of the act seems ever shifting into admiration for the plastic perfection of its representation. Considered as a plot with a moral interest we had reached the culminating point in the drama of Rennes.

DREYFUS CONDEMNED

The sight of the guards at the door playing cards reminded journalists of the Roman guards who played dice while Christ was on the cross. When the court was told not to consider the evidence, merely the "quality" of the witnesses—to, as it were, "count the stars on the epaulettes"—"a sudden chill entered our souls."

> The hour which we now spent in the yard of the Lycée while the Court deliberated is one which none of us, I believe, will ever forget. . . . Suddenly a bell. We hastened to our places and waited there, an entire audience standing shoulder to shoulder for perhaps ten long minutes of profound silence as in a cathedral. My neighbour bade me place my hand upon his heart to see how it was beating. . . . The Court entered. When we learned the condemnation by five votes to two we trembled, and a pained, hushed cry traversed the hall. Not a word was said. We filed out silent and ashamed. . . . the Judges were still standing triumphant. . . . For us tonight Rennes is the *ville maudite*. Dreyfus alone is calm. He is beginning to comprehend the sublimity of his *rôle*.

The verdict: guilty of treason "with extenuating circumstances."

Rennes

Today, on an August Saturday afternoon, Rennes is as always clean and open. We gaze at the lycée through the railings of the empty playground where Morton saw military witnesses "promenading" with judges during recesses while "hundreds of kodaks were recording for all time . . . tell-tale proofs of [their] surprising intimacy."

The only passersby are two women in white lace Breton caps and a boy on a bicycle. Over the entrance of a nearby building, almost effaced, is the name of the HOTEL DE FRANCE, where Morton stayed.

Dreyfus accepted presidential clemency, insisting that he be allowed to work to clear himself. Fullerton did not cover the later episodes of the case; and by the time Dreyfus was exonerated, his own life had undergone revolutionary change.

The Turn of a Century: Camille's Child

"The century wanes and night cometh."
—JAMES TO FULLERTON, 30 NOVEMBER 1899[45]

And somewhere, around that time, a girl from the Dordogne became pregnant.[46] Somewhere, nine months later, her child, Mireille, was born. In 1903 she was in Spain, married to Morton.

Where had Camille Chabbert been, what had she been doing, before Mireille's father came into her life?

The Paris Conservatoire keeps records of prize-winning students only. Camille was not a prize winner. Moreover, if she studied there she had left home to do so: Paris has no record of her parents. Yet they were no longer in the town where she was born. Toulouse in the Pyrenees was a *bel canto* training center. Where they did not live.

Camille told her concierge that her mother, Eugénie Auriol, was related to Vincent Auriol, president of France. Though Eugénie married a mechanic, a kinship is not inherently unlikely; the president's father was a baker. The president's son, however, writes that no Eugénie existed in their family.

The port from which he set out was "the *essential loneliness*" of his life, James told Morton, hoping to help him in "a complexity, an obscurity, of trouble."[47] Did the trouble relate to Camille?

Where that Protestant marriage? Tick off English and American churches in Paris. Eliminate the Eastern Rites: Byzantine Greek, Greek Orthodox, Armenian, Chaldean, etc., leaving twenty-one Eglises Réformées, two Baptist, and ten Lutheran.

("Fullerton? So sorry," writes the rector, British Embassy Church, Madrid.)

A purgatory or a hell, a theologian could say which, of typing letters and trekking to far corners.

"Why *did he marry her?*"

"*Voyons. (Marc) One can conceive hypotheses supposing that Camille had a child who was born before the marriage.*

"*First, the child was Morton's; he regularizes and thinks to spend his life with Camille. Second, he regularizes, but they agree to separate.*

"*Now, supposing the child is not Morton's. First, he does not know the father. We return to the previous cases: either he means to stay with Camille or he does her a service. In that case there is another possibility. Having agreed to divorce, is it that she becomes* amourachée *of Morton? Or again, he is not the father but he knows the father, and it is a service to him. It is complicated. And all the cases are possible.*"

"*Did Camille conceal the fact that she had a child?*"

"*Or was it that he saw a way to free himself from Mme Mirecourt? It is conceivable that in the 1890s there was a sexual rapport and also* un cadre agréable, *tasty little dishes, but in the new century he wanted perhaps to* débarrasser *himself.*"

"*But it was Camille he debarrassed himself of.*"

By marrying, his father wrote, he had taken on a "transcendant obligation," whatever "concessions" Camille might have made, and he must not become "tied up so that your wife or children (if you have any), should reap meagreness."[48]

If the child already there was his, Will knew his parents would hear of her and realize that she had not been born in wedlock. Wouldn't he have announced her existence along with the other fait accompli of his marriage? If she was *not* his. . . . Perhaps he thought that news of his marriage would hit them hard enough without the additional detail that his wife, though not a widow, had a child.

"Concessions." Had Camille agreed that Will need not support Mireille (who is a piece in the puzzle whoever her father was)? Or had she agreed that Will, as disciple of a great English thinker, could end the marriage—as could she—at any time?

But again, why didn't he hold out for his new young wife against his old old mistress? We go in circles.

Camille, Morton, and the Brothers Clemenceau

The name is emblazoned on streets, boulevards, quais, avenues, squares, and schools throughout France. It is almost as ubiquitous in our documentation of Fullerton. Furthermore, the concierge said that Camille's child was brought up in the Clemenceau family.

Georges Clemenceau, prime minister of France, lord of a Vendée manor, was a doctor. ("I have a prescription he wrote for Morton," says Hugh Fullerton.) He published in many genres; he collaborated with Fauré on a musical; he was a member of the Académie and, said Morton Fullerton, "one of the best Greek scholars in Europe."

The Manet portrait and magazine illustrations show a sinewy neat man with an enigmatic, slightly Oriental face, peaked balding head, and drooping moustache. He is usually depicted shaking his fist at someone or something. He was known as the Tiger.

He was a man about town, at home in many a *foyer des artistes* in Mlle Mirecourt's time. He married an American, Mary Plummer.

("Whom he treated very badly," says M. Roland de Margerie. "He wanted to divorce her. He went with a policeman and took her in flagrante delicto, had her jailed to serve a term for adultery, divorced her, and had her deported as a common criminal. Yet he had several children by her, children who were then young. He was *très dur, très très dur* toward women. *Très dur.*")

Albert, Morton's lawyer, must come into some books on Georges, but the ones I saw, dryly political or fulsomely eulogistic, had nothing on his family.

The Musée Clemenceau is Georges's house in the Rue Franklin. In Morton's day, Georges might be "basking in the garden among his animals."[49] The fauna (storks, peacocks) are gone, and the flora. The house is hard to find, dark, and even dirty; and dull: the model of what a museum ought not to be. An aged man mumbles: "This is the desk where *le Tigre* wrote; there is the pen he used."

No one may look at what he wrote.

"Have you many visitors, Monsieur?"

"*Oh non*" (contentedly). "You are the first this week."

Morton's relations with Georges look like journalist-politician symbiosis. He might easily become friends with Albert, nearer his age. All three men were bonded by having fought on the same side in the Case, the brothers as actors and Morton as a very non-neutral reporter for the world's most powerful organ of information. He had given Albert a puff when Dreyfus seemed to need a new lawyer. (Albert "would not be a bad choice.") When he needed a lawyer himself, he might naturally ask Albert to act for him.

It is equally easy to suppose, as an unrelated event, that a Clemenceau got a young singer with child.

But would Morton have chosen a lawyer just because he happened to know him? The divorce being so off-color, mustn't Albert have had a special reason for acting?

But if Albert, father or uncle of Mireille, acted against her mother . . . and if later he or another Clemenceau took Mireille into the family. . . . Nothing fits together. Too few facts. No fixed point.

The Museum Board, writes the museum secretary, "does not authorize the communication of letters."

Send for Albert Clemenceau letters at the Bibliothèque Nationale, and what comes is part of the mountainous Dreyfus dossier: *Procès* Zola, Reinach MSS, tome on tome. Memoranda, articles, notes, proofs of "J'ACCUSE." Thousands of letters: Albert to Zola, Georges to Zola, everyone in the Case to everyone else. The cupboard door opens not on teacups but on explosives. Albert may have written letters about Camille Chabbert, but they would not be here.

Send more letters out into the regions where Chabberts are said to have pullulated since the days of good King Dagobert.

Camille could have been anywhere at the time of Mireille's conception; and as *Terres Françaises,* which is about his travels at that period, makes amply clear, Morton went almost everywhere.

Traveling Companions

But not alone. In the preface, he thanked "two persons."

L'une est celle qui m'a fait l'honneur de m'accompagner dans mes voyages, et dont les heureuses remarques sont les seuls mots d'esprit que j'ai retrouvés dans mes carnets. C'est encore elle qui m'apprenait le nom des fleurs.[50]

The first *personne* was "the one who did me the honor to accompany me in my travels and whose apt remarks are the only witty words I find in my notebooks. And he/she it was who taught me the names of flowers."

The second person is named: an André Godfernaux who helped with Morton's "barbarous" French. But the first person, the companion: man or woman? *Elle,* which looks like *she,* is *une personne,* and even the most macho male *person* has the feminine gender.

Collate Morton's travels with Chaix railway guide. Follow timetables to Zagreb and Thessaloniki and back to humdrum Paris with its *super-marchés* and its *pressings,* dry cleaners. Write to more communes in the peach, pistachio, and café-crème departments on the sun-bleached wall map.

In May 1901, by which time Mireille was born, Morton was in Burgundy. Next year, in the Franche-Comté, the old "Free County" between France and Germany.

He was living with Mirecourt, whose native village, Saint-Rémy, is in the Haute-Saône Department, which is part of the Franche-Comté. When he entrained at night in the Gare de l'Est and detrained next day in Vesoul, the departmental capital, he may have had her in mind.

Even had her *with* him! He could have escorted her, left her to visit family. . . . No. The screeching, acquisitive Madame could not be the person of his graceful thanks.

But it had to be a woman. He knew that precisely *because* he said "person," readers would assume that he was protecting a lady. Grammatically impenetrable, psychologically pellucid. It now seems.

It was on returning from the Haute-Saône that he learned that he wasn't yet to be The Correspondent but was being posted to Madrid. On a "prolonged and urgent mission," he said later.[51]

He told Aïdé that another man had exploited Blowitz's jealousy of him but he'd be glad of Madrid if the pay were better. He sent James a letter that James found "deeply interesting" as to the move but above all pleasing and gratifying in its comments on his new novel.

In *The Wings of the Dove,* Merton Densher and Kate Croy are in love but too poor to marry. Hoping for a legacy, Kate induces Densher to make the young, rich, mortally ill Millie Theale think that he loves her. When Millie learns the truth from a spiteful rejected suitor, she turns her face to the wall. But she leaves Merton money, a great deal of money. Remote from Morton's life.

Except that Merton Densher is a journalist, attractive, clever, not rich—Merton, Morton. Morton asked James if the journalist T. A. Cook was Densher. James gave a reply as oblique as the question: "Ah, que non . . . and of course you don't suppose it."

As to Madrid, James gave some jocular encouragement. Morton would "repay the debt to Columbus."[52] Morton must also have explained his mission obliquely. But what in fact *was* he up to in Madrid? The *Times* itself may explain.

The Mission to Madrid, Third Time Around

In the Periodicals Hall a man in a floor-length *blouse* trundles gigantic bound volumes of the *Times* to the table.

Backtrack a bit. The few reports from Spain are credited to agencies like Reuters up to February 2, 1903, when "France, England, and Morocco" appears, datelined Madrid, February 1, "From Our Own Correspondent." Fullerton had arrived.

The story is the wire he often mentions, and now that it has turned up in situ it had better be tackled.

Anglo-French rivalry in Africa was nurtured by a chortling German Kaiser. Morocco, which France, England, Spain, and Germany all yearned to civilize, was a trouble spot. Now Morton revealed that, unknown to Spain, the French and British foreign ministers meant to solve the problem between the two of them. He had discovered that, last summer, the French minister, Delcassé, had

made overtures to Lord Lansdowne for the complete and detailed settlement of the whole Moroccan question. [In return] for French official recognition of the British occupation of Egypt, France was to be allowed a free hand in dealing with Moroccan territory save on the North African coastline.[53]

The idea of negotiations was ridiculed, Fullerton wrote later, but he had been right. An agreement was reached:

France and England were face to face like birds in a cockpit. . . . Europe, under German leadership, was fastening their spurs, and impatient to see them fight to the death. Then suddenly they both raised their heads and moved back. . . . they had decided not to fight, and the face of European things was transformed.[54]

It was the genesis of the Entente Cordiale. France was already allied with Russia. The eventual Triple Entente was to face the Central Powers in the First World War.

The story had no follow-up.

A visit to Portugal by King Edward VII. Our Own Correspondent in Lisbon reported speeches, banquets. Skim.

At last, in June, July, and August, stories by Our Own Correspondent in Madrid. Contrast of old and new. The Vatican and obscurantism versus republicanism and progress. Favorite themes of Morton's.

By February 1904 he was back in Paris—without having had many stories on Spain published. In the year of his urgent mission, Spain was not news.

Curious. I'd thought his talk of a "prolonged and urgent mission" self-important. But there must have been *some* reason for his going. The dull reports the *Times* printed might have been a cover for investigative reporting.

A *secret* mission?

The Return to Mirecourt: Threats

Morton was in Madrid when he told his family he was married. Did he break the news to Adèle, too, from a distance?

Mirecourt, who had played a Cleopatra mad about Antony, would have been unpacking Morton's boxes in her new apartment.

Messenger: He's married, Madam.

Mirecourt (draws a knife): Rogue, thou hast lived too long.

Or did he confess to his marriage only on his return to Paris?

In either case, Adèle—"excited," he tells his father (who amplifies: "hysterical, tearful, beseeching, insistent, rampageous, threatening")—Adèle wants half the rent plus 200 francs a month and the insurance. His father sends money to pay her off. But Morton divorces Camille, moves in with Adèle, and for a while all we know is that he publishes *Terres Françaises* and it is crowned.

Then, in 1907, he tells James that he is being blackmailed, and James is grandly outraged by the woman who threatens to—do what?

To expose, James believed, the Ranee and R.G. affairs to the family. But the family already knew. Bradford had mentioned those "associations" when he told Morton to pay Mirecourt off. If James thought Morton dreaded his family's learning about Lord Ronald Gower and the Ranee, Morton must have lied to him.

Well, hell, Morton *did* lie.

But his alarm was real. So, what was he really afraid of?

Lord Ronald Gower himself was safe, oil was poured before his prow in the roughest sea; but a man known to be his lover would be ostracized.

When Oscar Wilde asked for a loan, Morton made excuses. Wilde had "too much delicacy and *esprit* not to sympathize with the regret of a man obliged to reply thus." Wilde sliced smoothly through the hypocrisy. "Sentiment need not borrow stilts." Annotating Wilde's letter, Morton wrote: "Parbleu! What he called stilts were the Johnsonian tongs!"[55] (*Tongs,* says Johnson: "an instrument by which hold is taken of any thing, as of coals in the fire.") Morton continued: "See Diary June 16." The diary-notebook that is so rich in clues covers the 1890s. Wilde's name does not occur, but parts of two pages have been torn out.

Wilde and Lord Ronald, his known associate, stood for danger. Morton had every mundane reason for secrecy, and no conflicting emotional bond. Nothing suggests that he loved R.G. or any other male lover as much as his job, which Mirecourt's proofs might have threatened.

On the other hand, would the *Times* have cared enough about past misconduct with top people to sack a valuable member of the staff—a future chief correspondent?

A man would not be discredited if known to be the Ranee's lover; but she herself feared scandal because she was afraid of being divorced by her old, honest, but dour, resentful Rajah.

Some years after the affair, and before he knew about it, James told Morton he longed to know "what the Ranee did to you. Are you very sure? She doesn't do things!"[56]

But James didn't know what cause she had to despise Morton for caddishly dropping her. And even *thinking* she'd "done" something would have made Morton the readier to name her when, later, he revealed the blackmail to James: who, thinking Morton was concerned for *her* reputation (and therefore excusing what he'd otherwise have thought caddish in Morton's naming her) said reassuringly that no one would "dare" touch her.

Whereas Morton was staring at the certainty that damages in a divorce suit brought by the Rajah would bankrupt *him*.

* * *

If only we knew what Morton said about the blackmail—about the urgent mission to Madrid—free of interpretation by James. But his truths and falsehoods went up in bonfires in the Lamb House garden and wafted over the fields and town of Rye toward the coast.

"Perturbation ondulante" over the Channel, says the noon *météo* report.

Voisins-les-Bretonneux

A Secret

"In his eighties, with his experience, he had secrets."

Eugène Fleuré, tanned from working in his garden, with very clear bright eyes, writes poems and *pensées* and writes and lectures on Simone Weil, the philosopher, laborer, and heroine of the Resistance in World War II.

"It was only after the war that I met the former Dean of the *Colonie Américaine*."

(Dean of the—?)

"And he had letters! M. Fullerton's study was a temple, with letters from Jaurès, Maurras, Verlaine, Léon Blum, Barrès. . . . The Gestapo had taken some, but fortunately not all."

"The Gestapo?" (Marc)

"Monsieur, they came twice! When I read his *Figaro* articles of before the war I was amazed that they let him go. Amazed! Ah oui, he had secrets. Above all"—M. Fleuré hesitates—"I can tell you, because he said: 'You may publish this when I am gone.' Above all, he had a historic meeting with Pope Leo XIII!

"You know that the Vatican opposed the Republic, and the monarchists and others who wanted to subvert it could call it their religious duty. Well, the Holy Father decided that monarchism was a lost cause and issued an encyclical telling the faithful to rally to the Republic. But before he did so, he gave Messrs. Fullerton and Blowitz an audience, and it was to them that he first spoke the words: 'L'Eglise ne s'attache qu'à un seul cadavre—the Church is attached to only one corpse: the one that was attached to the cross.' What he said was tout à fait extraordinaire! And they—discrets et gentlemen—did not repeat it till after his death."

As we were leaving, M. Fleuré ran back to his garden and returned with an armful of roses. "Another thing, one of the great joys of his last years was hearing himself quoted by the Reverend Père Riquet in a Lenten sermon, from the Pulpit of Notre Dame!"

"It was not to M. Fleuré that Morton would have confided the sleazy blackmail story you're so keen on."

"I had hoped he might know why Morton really went to Spain. It's true, there was a photograph—a card—of a pope."

I checked. Long before the pope died, Blowitz quoted the "body on the cross" as a "prophetic utterance" the pope had made at an audience in 1884[57]—when Morton was a college student in America.

Paris

Mme Mirecourt: Illusionism

But Leo XIII *is* the pope in the photograph, and he autographed it in "the fourteenth year of his pontificate," 1892, when Blowitz had a second audience[58] and apparently, for some reason, gave Morton the card as a memento.

It was in a sack of photocopies delivered by Bob Seaman, one of a camera crew who had flown in to do a documentary on the Eiffel Tower and were slumped, jet-lagged, in the breakfast room of a small hotel in, appropriately, the Rue du Mont Thabor, near the study where the original letters had once reposed.

Reduced to a common denominator of black on white, trimmed and stapled, the Fullerton papers were no less oppressive than on first reading. I knew so much more now, yet was more ignorant.

Here were the letters from a Monsieur Alfroy "about a Mme Mirecourt." On March 12, 1913, Alfroy told Fullerton that after hearing from him he had gone to Mme Mirecourt's.

I stood there dumbfounded, seeing how she looked, and considered her as
lost. . . . Yesterday I had a poor reception. She would only answer my questions by yes or no. . . . I think she should go into a nursing home or have a
full-time nurse. Unfortunately illness hasn't helped her temper and with her
continual observations she has trouble even keeping a cleaning woman. I
have known her for 25 years. . . . I have only one wish, to see that she is
taken care of during her illness.

On March 13:

Like you I went to Mme Mirecourt right away. . . . I don't think she can go
on much longer. . . . You and I should perform the last duties. . . . would
you know the names of her surviving kin? . . . [H]er notary, who lives in
Rueil and has her will, can pay; our only expenses will be the wreaths. . . .
It's very painful and sad, but I think it my duty to do the needful to take a
woman whom I esteem to her final abode.

And on March 15:

I trembled at the sight of your wire but once it was opened I was overcome with joy!!!! Tomorrow I'll go to see our friend and I hope she won't
refuse me entry.

Open-mouthed, I read those letters. What, four years after paying off
the blackmailer, Morton not only was in touch with her but was seen as
a good friend by—Was Alfroy a former protector?

"'Une femme que j'estime.'" (Marc)
"'A woman I respect.' Oui."

In his notebook, Morton wrote that when he and A. went to Montl-
héry he read a pamphlet by Matve Bruvis aloud.
So, I went back to the Bibliothèque Nationale.
Bruvis's *Montlhéry, son Château et ses Seigneurs: Notice Historique et
Archéologique*[59] is archaeological and historical. Dry as dustical. Not a
pleasure you'd expect Morton to have shared with—
Home again, look at everything we have on Mme Mirecourt—Cleopatra:

> Though Antony be painted one way like a Gorgon,
> The other way's a Mars.

Shakespeare was alluding to the "illusionist perspective" of paintings
like Holbein's *Ambassadors,* in which the circular object at the feet of the

fur-robed diplomats is seen from the right as a globe of the world but
from the left as a human skull.

Was the monster Mirecourt Botticelli's Venus?

Sinistrally	*Dextrally*
That scheming woman who seems to have complete control of you. . . . It has aroused all of us to see you apparently so dominated and controlled by this scheming woman. The atrocious creature. . . . A mad, vindictive, and obscene old woman . . . dangerous black-mailer . . . the poisoned air of her proximity . . . vindictive and de-mented calumny . . . ridiculous . . . vulgarity, vindictiveness, gro-tesque mal-adjustments . . . pain-ful and sordid manoevres . . . that brutal slut.[60]	Adèle and I Ville D'Avray but alas Corot is dead . . . on plateau the first revelation of the impor-tance of the role played by Montl-héry owing to geographical posi-tion. Ascended Montlhéry & afterwards read to A. under tower Matve Bruvis's little pamphlet. Walked back to Longpont. . . . Season of pilgrimage. . . . Glorious sunset . . . profound sympathy and affection for Mme Mirecourt . . . no matter what happens I shall see that she is cared for . . . our friend . . . a woman I respect.[61]

Data previously ignored bolster degorgonization. A brassy ex-Folies type would have bored and been bored by a man who related landscape to art and history. The termagant dulcifies into a gracious listener, and perhaps more: witty. The cameos in his notebook suggest the sedate rec-reation of a married couple, yet have a tinge of . . . Renoir. After all, if Adèle was more than a housekeeper, she must have had . . . appeal.

We have been misled by James. *He* was misled by a bias against Palais-Royal artistes—Did he know she had been one? No matter. He presumed depravity of her as the Newsomes of Woollett, Massachusetts, presumed depravity of the lady who held young Chad in Paris in the trick perspec-tive of *The Ambassadors* (James's not Holbein's). A denizen of Woollet-tian Gay Paree is what James saw in the Vénus of the Théâtre Déjazet at-tached tooth and claw to his forty-two-year-old young friend.

Alfroy is the first witness for whom Adèle is not the bad fairy in a tale he knows nothing about. In his unguessable story she and he are protag-onists; Morton has a supporting role as her friend.

Companions and Threats Reconsidered

There's another passage in Morton's notebook:

> Mantes & Limay. . . . Breakfast Grand Cerf Hotel. . . . Visited (Mantes) old
> prison deep down under the Palais de Justice. 5 little children piloted me
> thither while A. sat with the grandmother in a little Dutch-like room.

Adèle—and with the aura of "Adèle and I Ville d'Avray Mais hélas
Corot est mort," Alas Corot is dead. Vermeer not Corot this time, but
Corot-compatible. (Was the family hers? Write to Mantes-la-Jolie. . . .
No.)

Morton's sunlit weekends with Adèle suggest his longer holidays with
a *personne* who taught him the names of flowers, whose witty words he
jotted in his notebooks. (Lost notebooks, it must be, that succeeded this
one.)

Terres Françaises didn't come out till 1905, but the Franche-Comté
chapter is dated June 1902. It may—it *did* appear earlier, in the *Revue de
Paris*. In the book, *nous*, we, are in Joigny, but it could be the literary *we*
that means *I*. In the article, "I asked for two rooms with communicating
door. 'Oh!' said the host, 'you can communicate through the wall.'"[62]
Two persons, one a woman.

At that time Mirecourt was the woman who would have been with
Morton. In the book he thanked the companion in his "travels," plural.
The same woman on each holiday. Now that we see Mirecourt differ-
ently—it *was* she whom he thanked in his preface.

Another neglected letter in the Fullerton papers is a missing link.
When Bradford outlined his son's "love episodes," he recalled Will's
pledging "entire allegiance" to "the Madame" on his last visit home in
1898. It has always seemed queer that Will should have raised Mirecourt's name. But here in this letter, 1897, Aunt Sarah thanks Will for his
hospitality to her and Uncle Phillips. "Remember me kindly to Madame
Mirecourt. She did much for our pleasure."[63]

Sarah Phillips tells her sister Julia Fullerton about that nice Mme Mirecourt. Julia and Bradford ruminate. Next year, when Will comes home:
"Son, who is this woman?" The ball is tossed gently, until Will rises to as-
sign ranks in the seraglio. "Mme Mirecourt can always retain her present
position."

Incidentally, the letter shows that Mirecourt did not have the externals of a bad woman. Will could let her take his family about without embarrassment. (And Uncle Phillips was a clergyman.)

How does the hypothesis of a milder Adèle (never mind that her temper has worsened with illness) alter the blackmail scenario?

Morton is assigned to Madrid. Adèle's lease in the Rue Vignon is ending. They agree that she'll find a new place he will come to when his Spanish mission ends. Then: "He's married, Madam." When he returns, she is angry—and worried: "What about the rent?" He does *not* think her demands unfair. He tells his parents that he is *obligated* to pay her. He discards his bride, moves into 40 *bis* Rue Fabert—and compliments Adèle next year in *Terres Françaises*.

Not till late 1907 is blackmail spoken of—by James, in answer to Morton's scared outpourings. Adèle's tolerance had ended. Failing a marriage which would not have seemed so grotesque to her as to James, she wanted a firmer material base. Suppose that Morton owed rent, money she hadn't grudged till now. That he had enjoyed meals and housekeeping free: services she now estimated at 200 francs a month. That she made threats for leverage in what she did not regard as extortion. That she threatened to take him to court.

Then he so worked on his friends that, somehow, they enabled him to escape from her bag, baggage, and incriminating letters.

But four years later he is still visiting her, and the visits seem normal to Charles Alfroy, who is unaware of a cloud over the Fullerton-Mirecourt friendship.

Perhaps Morton felt renewed affection and pity when the strain of daily contact ended. Or was money still at issue? Did he hope to recoup as legacy what he had paid as blackmail?

If it was blackmail.

Adèle lived at 40 *bis* Rue Fabert till she died in 1924. Two apartments to a floor. Steepish narrow wooden stairs.

"I don't believe Morton," I said as we came out into the Esplanade des Invalides, "when he told James he wasn't in the woman's flat, only the same house. How could he have told her he had no money for her if he was paying rent, as she'd have known, for a separate apartment?"

"One wonders" (Marc) "why he didn't force her to hand the papers over, or pick a lock while she was out shopping."

* * *

The landlord of her day died two years ago.
Only two years ago.
Pursue her.

Mme Mirecourt's Family

"Being much interested in 19th-century theatrical history," writes the deputy mayor of Saint-Rémy, Haute-Saône, "might I trouble you [*pourrions-
nous nous permettre d'abuser de vos instants*] for information about this
actress, of whom I regret to say I have not heard?" He encloses handwritten copies of documents[64] which take us far from the boulevards of Paris.

Adèle's father was a blacksmith, her mother a farm worker, but they
left Saint-Rémy and came to Paris with their daughters Adèle Augustine
and Zélie and their young son Auguste. Why?
"Poor pelting villages and farms." The soil of no other region, Morton
observed when he visited the old Franche-Comté, seemed so "worn out
by invasion."[65] Huns, Vandals. . . . the most recent invaders had been the
Prussians, in 1870, whose victory ended the Second Empire in France and
inaugurated the German Empire.
Were the Moutots refugees? When Auguste reached the age of conscription in 1873, he was exempted. Reason, "loss of right eye."[66] Had
he been a war casualty as a boy?
Saint-Rémy is surrounded by Anchenoncourt, Mailleroncourt, Senon-
court, Melincourt, Cendrecourt. Nearby is the larger village of Mirecourt. Subliminal influences on choice of a stage name.
In Paris the family lived in a street that runs from the tranquil, narrow
Canal Saint-Martin to the Place de la République, which was then the
Place du Château d'Eau and the entertainment center of Paris. Mirecourt's workplaces were close to the Moutot lodgings.
Auguste became a typographer and married a sixteen-year-old laundress whose family and friends were printers, engravers, omnibus drivers.
Zélie, however, married a *rentier* or man of private means, Henri Napoléon Saint-Laurent. A marriage contract was signed. The mayor read
aloud an affidavit that the groom's father consented to the marriage of his
thirty-eight-year-old son (a widower). Witnesses: a *propriétaire*, an ex-
magistrate—

*"Contrat, magistrat—Zélie entered l'establishment! And the groom's
father absent. Had he consented reluctantly because the bride's sister
was an artiste?"*

Facts slowly collected, not in order. Arranged, what do they amount
to? Not much. Save that Mirecourt, first the evil extortionist, then the ar-
tiste/cocotte, then the softer Corotian Adèle, is now, this at least undeni-
ably, the member of a family. Losing a mother who died, losing a father
who left home never to return, attending her brother's wedding, standing
godmother to his daughter Berthe Adèle, going to the funeral of his son
Gabriel who died aged three months, who was dying while she took curtain calls for *Monsieur Blondeau's Tenants.*

Rueil-Malmaison

Mme Mirecourt Makes a Will

Forty-odd years later, when Adèle herself seemed to be dying and Charles
Alfroy was busy planning her funeral, he told Morton that a notary in
Rueil had her will. Why Rueil?

The quiet village of Rueil, just west of Paris, had one notary, Maître
Faribault. His successor Maître Radet is the one notary in the city of
Rueil-Malmaison.

The bus goes up one steep side of Mont Valérien and down the other,
as in an animated cartoon. In the fortress on top the brave Colonel Picquart was jailed when he refused to keep mum about the forgeries that
had doomed Dreyfus. In another cell the forger, Colonel Henry, jailed
after confessing, cut his throat.

Rueil is undergoing crash development. In the house that is still the
notary's "Cabinet" men with briefcases, men with blueprints, shake
hands with incomers, rush about; doors open and shut. A serious-faced
man in brown shakes hands and leads me into a high-ceilinged room.
"What was it—? Ah!" He hurries out.

Is this the chair on which Mme Mirecourt sat discussing the provisions
of her will? Belle Epoque office. Over the fireplace a tall mirror. On the
mantel a tall porphyry clock and two black marble candleholders. Parquet
floor. Bookcases with heavy curtains behind glass fronts hiding the books.

The porphyry clock ticks.

Maître Radet hurries in waving a folder. "*Bon.* You know a will is classified for a hundred years. This will was never proved, I will give you a photocopy"—rushing out and returning with two damp sheets: "I'll give you the first part and the last; the rest does not concern you. This names the witnesses. *Voyons.* Roze: I know his son; *très gentil,* I'll speak to him. *Non non,* no need for thanks. *Non non non,* no question of a fee."

Back home, I had a go at Maître Faribault's terrible hentracks:

in presence of four witnesses has appeared Mlle Adèle Augustine Moutot spinster of legal age domiciled in Paris but staying at 28 Avenue de Paris Rueil, 1911, 5 September at 5 p.m. The testatrix has signed . . .

She signed "A Moutot" in a spiky, curvy hand.

Words on page 3 showing through on page 4 of the will appeared as dots on the photocopy. Mirror-maneuvers yielded only "drawn in a bedroom *dans laquelle la testatrice est alitée.*"

In bed at five P.M.! She hadn't gone to the lawyer. She was so ill she'd sent for him. But again, why was she in Rueil?

Here, says the Town Guide, Napoleon Bonaparte bade farewell to Josephine, whose last residence it was. The Hôtel de Ville is a replica of the Palace of Fontainebleau.

The Etat-Civil staff in the replica *smile* and *ask if they can help.*—

Would there be any record of a Moutot, 1911-ish?—

"Oui. Mme Zélie Saint-Laurent née Moutot died. Also her husband."

The Rueil connection. Mirecourt's sister lived there.

Rueil has remnants of rusticity: orchards, gardens with pigeon cotes and gnomes, grassy lanes. The Saint-Laurents must have known Morton. Adèle would have brought him; his status would have exalted theirs, till her long friendship with him went bad. After which. . . . We wondered why he didn't break into her desk in the Rue Fabert when she was out. She may have kept his compromising papers in Rueil.

The Avenue de Paris has been renamed and renumbered and most of its buildings razed, but the house where Adèle made her will is still there, flush with the pavement and very narrow, its one window just above the low door. One of the witnesses lived in the next, bigger house. Summoned by the notary's clerk, he had only to walk down his path, go in

Adèle's door, and mount a few stairs—surely a few; a tall man outside could easily touch the windowsill.

The Saint-Laurents died, childless, shortly before Adèle nearly died. Her brother Auguste had died earlier. Zélie was her last bond with the time when they came to Paris, raw country girls, and Adèle found work among gold-digging artistes, rakish nobles, venal critics, obscene pimps and bawds, and cynical impresarios.

Joan of Arc became a soldier. Adèle of Saint-Rémy, a peasant girl who knew the names of flowers, went on stage. Why? To buy an apprenticeship for her young brother, to see her name on posters, to find a rich protector?

But what does it matter what she was like—or Morton Fullerton or Camille Chabbert or Edith Wharton? Why this laborious nosiness? When they ask *Quel est le motif?* the answer no longer comes glibly. It is just that somehow one wants to *know*.

Camille-Ixo: The *Mairie* of the Eighth

Adèle's friend Alfroy came of a line of landowners in Lieusaint, a hamlet that "belonged to them," says a young Parisian who goes there to shoot. "He could live in Paris without working, which isn't so easy nowadays!" When he reached the age of conscription, he was a student, another sign of privilege. He may well have gone on to be a boulevardier, a patron of artistes, a stage-door johnny.

On a scorching day, I went to the *mairie* of the Eighth Arrondissement and learned that he died two years after he and Morton visited Adèle.

This is where Camille Chabbert came for welfare decades later, her social worker told me, and the deputy mayor helped her.

The concierge's glassed-in cubicle has a sign INFORMATION and a glassless opening four feet above ground level. People wishing information stoop and talk through the opening, while the concierge reads his newspaper.

"Would M. Monnet, who was once the deputy mayor, still be here?" The paper drops. "Mais c'est le maire!"

"Ah bon; alors, would M. le Maire be—"

"But he is on *vacation!*"

Go home.

At nine the sky is cloudy, the moon gibbous with a star to the south-east. Waft of basil and thyme from windows open on balconies. To the left my neighbor the madwoman cries, "Un deux trois quatre cinq six sept huit neuf dix, O trà là là là là là O trà là là là O je l'aurai, ma villa." Down in the dark courtyard picked out in a pool of torchlight a young man bare to the waist works on his *moto*.

Write more letters to *mairies*.

Camille-Ixo: Peroration of a Mayor

With thirty years' difference in age, their careers did not overlap, but Ca-mille and Adèle could be hunted as a pair in the Secours Mutuels des Ar-tistes Lyriques and the Société Mutuelliste des Artistes and the Mutuelle Nationale des Artistes Dramatiques et Lyriques, where members talk of their past ("I often played opposite Pierre Fresnay, *un homme ador-able!*") while waiting to be called into a room marked CASHIER.

Nothing.

Next month the trade paper *L'Information du Spectacle* carried an ap-peal for information about Moutot *dite* Mirecourt and Chabbert *dite* Ixo, boxed in among "Merry Widow gown (new) F 500"; "Young man seeks D-J job sports resort"; "Director seeks script for creation Paris the-ater." The gown may have found a wearer, the youth a job, the director a script; but no word of the two old artistes ever came.

So I still didn't know much about Ixo's career when October, chest-nuts plonking, brought the day to cross the dreary public wastes of the *mairie* of the Eighth into marble halls with statues and vassals and serfs opening portals into a gilded chamber with cherubim and chandeliers, where a broad-faced fatherly person behind a vast mayoral desk talked for two hours about Mme Ixo Chabbert.

"You knew she was an artiste! She wore rings and bracelets; when she talked, she used her hands—there was a perpetual music!

"She was well-dressed. A gray suit, the first time, clean, *correct*. But she would wear *one* earring! Had she lost the other? She wore her hats with an air. They might have come from the Flea Market, but she thought nothing of it!

"The first time I lunched with her, it was absolutely curious. There was a chair with no back and a chair with half a back. She was poor, but she wasn't ashamed. I was secretly amused, but I wasn't offended because of being the deputy mayor.

"She was an *animatrice*. At her parties, everyone was merry.

"She was selling valuable books and stamps. She told me there had been a divorce and her husband had done nothing for her. But she bore no grudge—

"Oh, not only books but letters! She knew kings, princes, the highest personages in the countries where she sang.

"But, as she'd come for aid, I thought: great artistes aren't poor. They save their fortune for their old age. I thought she was inventing. Now I see that she had a deep sense of the dramatic art! She must have given grandeur to a role. I have understood that, since you wrote that you were treating her in a book.

"I hadn't seen her for some time—high office is engrossing, you know. Then a social worker told me that Mme Camille Ixo had died.

"Letters?" Mayor Monnet spread his hands. "She did write. You have shown me that there are real artists who are poor. But I always had a doubt, and it kept me from saving her letters. I am happy to have talked with you. It is a homage I pay her now that she is gone.

"In the noblest sense of the word, I loved that woman!"

Winnowing the Archives of the Seine

Letters from kings and princes to Camille. Oh, sure. Letters to Morton in the papers she stashed in her garret more like. And what the mayor said isn't evidence. What's needed is facts.

In the Corridor of Indexes, sieve Paris births, marriages, and deaths for every Moutot, Saint-Laurent, Pouget, Chabbert, Lainé (Camille's daughter Mireille married a Lainé). Swing index off shelf onto counter, scan, copy, swing back on, climb ladder to next row. Rhythm, like shoveling snow. With other shovelers. "Passez, Madame, je vous prie." "Mon cher Gaston"—"Mon cher Alphonse." Aerobics.

Mais quel est le motif de ton travail? What's your idea?

Why to get at people with those names who were in Paris when Adèle's family came and trace their children. To find people of those names living here now and trace their parents. To find some live connection. A hope of finding Moutot Papers? Pas si bête. But . . . some faint family legend.

Organize data culled from the indexes by commune. Ask the *mairies* of the communes for *actes;* enclose stamps to the value of *x.* SAS envelopes. November 20, forty letters mailed.

Re Camille: H.M. Consul, British Embassy, Madrid, has no record of a marriage, nor has the U.S. consul. Re Adèle Moutot: nothing.

Re Mme Hélène Pouget (whom one tends to forget): no progress.

December 1. "With the first frost" (8 A.M. news) "the first truffles have appeared in the market at St. Quelqu'un in the Dordogne. The price is thirty francs per hundred grams."

Massachusetts

Brockton and Cambridge

Research in America always requires struggling through snow. In New-bury Street, Brockton, the house where the Fullertons used to live is deep in drifts blindingly white on a day of bright sun and glacial cold. Nice house: medium size, white shingles with fancy edges. A garden or yard, exiguous in front, merges behind the house with skeletal trees and the top branches of underbrush jutting from the snow that blankets an undeveloped corner lot.

But think of this frozen extended garden in October when the maples are scarlet. As Lady Catharine de Burgh might have said: "Miss Fullerton, there seemed to be a prettyish kind of little wilderness on one side of your lawn." In October 1907 Will and Katharine went out there, probably, to talk away from the family, and at Halloween, the leaves yellowing, became engaged.

Two and a half years later, Julia arranged greenery in that bay window for Katharine's marriage to Gordon Gerould.

It is too cold to work up the appropriate emotions.

At Harvard there is time only to follow a snowplow to Pusey and send for the newspaper clippings in Morton's class archives.

From the *Boston Herald,* January 1902:

DE BLOWITZ AND SUCCESSOR

The news cabled from Paris this week that M. de Blowitz [has retired] and that his place has been filled by William Morton Fullerton, aroused much interest in Boston and vicinity.

The *Herald* interviewed a Boston journalist who had known Mr. Fullerton in Paris as a fine newspaperman and American gentleman:

> "[Blowitz has] $10,000 a year, plus his expenses, which include the keep of a horse and carriage. I think that the expenses amount to something like $5000 or $6000 more per year. . . . If [he gives] any large dinners or banquets . . . the bill for the same would be promptly met by the Times. . . . Mr. Fullerton's salary undoubtedly will be as large as that of Blowitz."

News *"cabled"*—for heaven's sake, *by whom?*

In the first place, Blowitz did not retire till eight months after this cabled "news." And when he did retire, a Mr. Lavino succeeded him, Morton told Aïdé. ("Blowitz by his jealousy of my position here stupidly played into the hands of Lavino.")

The *Record-Advertiser* reported that its former literary editor was stepping into "one of the notable positions in the world of journalism, like an ambassadorship at the French capital in a way."

A false report of Blowitz's resignation must have circulated, and Morton's heirship-presumptive was so taken for granted that some colleague jumped the gun.

Still, to *cable* the news?

When, then, *did* Morton succeed Blowitz—or, rather, Blowitz's successor, Lavino? Soon, to go by another clipping, which has "Springfield Union 2/7/07" penciled on it.

BROCKTON BOY'S SUCCESS ABROAD

Mingles with the Greatest of the World's Statesmen
For Years. Represents London Times in Paris

Interviewed by a local reporter, W. M. Fullerton stated: "I have resigned from the regular staff of the Times, but I may not sever my connection entirely with the paper."

This will be the Wharton biographer's source for Morton's 1907 "partial resignation." A crucial event, coming as it did at the onset of the Wharton affair, the engagement to Katharine, and the escalation of the blackmail.

But why did a Springfield paper interview a Boy from Brockton, eighty miles away? The answer is that it did not. Fullerton's parents live "here": their Brockton address is given. The date, too, is wrong. Morton is quoted as to floods and strikes in France "last winter": sensational events of 1909–1910. A "current" piece on Roosevelt came out in 1910. It is an

article in the Brockton *Times* of 1910 mislabeled by a careless archivist
and read by—

But there may be a true source for the 1907 move, and there must be a
record of his promotion to Chief. Which obviously was before he fully resigned in 1910.

No time to think. Photocopy now, use brain later.

Paris

Lucubrations of a Goosegirl

Answers to queries posted before Christmas had piled up. News, perhaps,
of Mirecourt, blackmailer—or, Humbert Humbert nuance, mauvemailer?

Envelopes bulge with *actes*. Birth, death, and usually marriage, three
papers equaled a life, naming parents, spouses, godparents. Try to connect, clambering through time with telescope at one astigmatic eye and
microscope at the other.

Pierre Moutot dying in 1897 is the infant who was presented to the
mayor in 1812 and certified to be the son of Pierre Moutot and is presumably the Pierre Moutot who married in 1838, since the bridegroom
lives at the address of the father of the son born in 1812. But what was he
to Adèle of Saint-Rémy?

Pierre Moutot, wool spinner's son, is baptized, 1782. The godfather is
Sieur Pierre Jacques Nicolas Royot, age five, represented by Dame Frontier, servant of Sieur Rosay, King's Guard. But soon King's Guards are
not calling attention to themselves. "18th Messidor, Year Two of the
French Republic, there appeared before us Citizen François Moutot—"

Wool spinner, coachman, bricklayer, milliner.

Moutot, *père inconnu;* Moutot, *père non nommé.* Father unknown,
unnamed. Under the Napoleonic Code a father need not acknowledge a
bastard, for lawful progeny must be protected. Harder for a mother not
to acknowledge, but this Moutot of the female sex born in 1869 was recognized by hers twenty-nine years later, when she married.

At the *mairie* of the Twelfth, with queues at every wicket, a youth,
Black, stepping up for his turn at Births:

Murmur.—"What?" (functionary of the female sex).

Murmur.—Functionary, louder: "But it's very simple. Why can't you understand? The child does not bear your name because it is the mother who has recognized him first. A child bears the name of the first parent to recognize."

Murmur.—"Non, je vous dis! There is no way for the child to bear your name unless you marry the mother. There is nothing you can do about it!" (Snatching up a ringing phone): "I can't talk now. J'ai une histoire absolument empoisonante, I've an absolutely filthy business to deal with. . . . Not now. J'ai une histoire empoisonante" (banging down the receiver). Over the young man's shoulder she directs her attention to the next in line:

"Que voulez-*vous?*"

1888: Paris. Death of Marie Alphonsine Moutot, laundress, age fifteen, spinster, parents not named.

On 17 December 1924 a clerk who lived near the Rue Fabert reported at the *mairie* that Adèle Augustine Moutot had died two days ago. Her funeral? "Celebrated on December 18." Abbé Miannaert of Saint-Pierre du Gros Caillou has no further information.

Death certificates do not give cause of death. Did she die of the illness she had in 1911, when she made her will, and perhaps also had in 1913, when Morton and Alfroy were planning wreaths for her funeral?

Fragonard was struck dead by lightning while eating an ice. Aristophanes died of laughing at one of his own jokes. The Duke of Clarence drowned in a butt of monembasia. Aeschylus was killed when an eagle dropped an oyster on his bald head. (Q: Who killed Aeschylus, the eagle or the oyster?—A: Who was Aeschylus?)

Sculptor, waiter, shepherd, banker. The constant is the *maire* sitting in his *mairie* pen in hand as fathers enter bearing babes in swaddling clothes, live, dead, or stillborn; as fiancés enter bearing affidavits of birth, parents' birth, and publishing of banns; as landlord or neighbor enters and states that Moutot Adèle Augustine has died. Teachers, milkmaids, clerks.

Sir Arthur Aston died in Drogheda Castle when Cromwell's men tore off his wooden leg and clubbed him to death with it.

The signatures of We the Mayor are classy swirls inserted among the heavy fists of laborers and the X's of *personnes ayant dit ne savoir écrire.*

Two reports arrive from the Paris Cemeteries Bureau.

MOUTOT Adèle placed 18 December 1924 in a temporary concession. . . . as the Administration periodically removes bodies buried in temporary or gratuitous concessions this plot has been repossessed and the remains transferred to the ossuary.

Os is bone, as in ossification. *Ossuary* is bone house.

CHABBERT Camille placed 10 March 1964 in a temporary concession. . . . If the family wish to keep the grave they should notify the Keeper as soon as possible to arrange renewal and thereby prevent transfer of the body to the ossuary.

Mme Mirecourt's bones are in the charnel house.
Camille Chabbert's will go there unless
And cursed be him
Morton claimed a French ancestor "so fanatical and sympathetic as to have got himself killed at the Battle of Ivry,"[67] i.e., fighting for Henri de Navarre, then a Protestant, against the Catholic Ligue. (Q: If Henri estimated that Paris is worth a mass and if Morton would give Paris and Saint-Denis to be with his blonde, what is to the fair-haired siren as his blonde is to the mass?—A: They grind our bones to make their bread.)

"Synesius, Bishop of Ptolomais under the younger Theodosius, counted an ancestry back to Eurysthenes, first Doric King of Sparta and fifth in lineal descent from Hercules. Such pure and illustrious pedigree of 1700 years" (grinned Gibbon), "without adding the royal ancestors of Hercules, cannot be equalled in the history of mankind." Hercules son of Zeus son of Chronos son of Euranus son of Gaia the Earth.

Camille-Ixo: The Flight of the Butterfly

As Adèle and Camille, old wraiths, fade into mist, a young Ixo rematerializes in three photographs from a museum in Trieste.[68]

That was Camille, then: the bejeweled bedraperied prima donna, the girl in a veil, and the girl of today with straight hair. *They* were Camille: Thaïs as courtesan and Thaïs as penitent.

When she was old, Camille claimed that she had created the role of Madame Butterfly in Italy. She told Mayor Monnet that she'd sung at La Scala. ("She sang an aria from *Tosca* for me. She still had a clear strong voice.")

She never sang at La Scala; and Storchio sang Madama Butterfly at the Italian premiere in 1904, when we have Ixo down as Madama Fullerton in Spain. But she *can* be traced, laboriously, in *Ars e Labor, Le Ménéstral, Musica, El Teatro, Musica e Musicisti*—thick, glossy, unindexed magazines[69] of an era when every self-respecting European town had its opera house. Camilla Ixo (Ikso, Yxo, Ickso, Yksô, according to the country's alphabet) toured Europe.

Soon after the divorce she sang in Milan. Next year Trieste praised her seductive Iris in *Iris*. Voice not perfect but fresh and brilliant; youthful spontaneity, dramatic range. In Catania, 1907, Ikso's Butterfly was superb. (So she *did* create the role, in *Sicily*.) When the Madrid Royal Opera produced the Spanish premiere of Massenet's *Werther*, the important Paris *Ménéstral* learned "by telegraph" that "thanks to Iksô's triumph *Werther* will always have a place in the Madrid repertory." Next, *Le Ménéstral* picked up Milan reviews of "a new Manon whose pretty voice, superlative dramatic sense, and delicate taste are praised by the entire press."

After which Camille went to Paris with Mireille, saw Will for the first time since the divorce, and rushed off to Fiume, leaving him to cope with her trunks and her wig (presumably the straight-haired one) to sing *Thaïs*. Then Trieste again, and so on.

And in June 1914, *Cavalleria* at the Opéra Comique in Paris.

Hugh Fullerton did not know that Morton's wife had been an opera singer until we talked one day in the Travelers' Club. Just across the Rond-Point of the Champs Elysées is the *Figaro* building. Hugh Fullerton pointed to a window high up: "Morton's office."

"His wife lived along there, near the Arc de Triomphe," I say.

"She was pretty discreditable," he says.

"Look." I show him the picture of the long-haired girl.

He looks. "Of course I only knew what Madame Pouget said."

"Can you remember, did he ever tell you where he met his wife?"

Mr. Fullerton thinks, frowning; says suddenly: "I have in mind he met her in Portugal. Does that make sense?"

"Yes!"

Portugal! Yes, yes; it makes sense. In 1903, Morton was in Spain, and there's mention somewhere of a visit to Portugal.

If Morton first met Camille in Portugal in 1903, he was not the father of Mireille, who was already two or three.

Back to the Clemenceaus.

Georges Clemenceau, tiger and man-about-town, might well have fathered a child by an opera singer, but would he have taken the child into his family? A man brutal toward women?

All we know of Albert Clemenceau, lawyer, is that he finagled a divorce for Morton. Pin him down. The Clemenceau Museum had a Mme Langlois-Berthelot on the board. There is a Langlois-Berthelot, engineer, in the Place du Panthéon.

Snowfall in Paris: Camille and the Clemenceaus

The last day in February is very cold. Snow, rare in Paris, has fallen overnight and still lies where there is grass. Snow in the Place Cambronne, snow in the Luxembourg Gardens. An Edinburgh day: the high-mounting Place with the domed Panthéon is noble, not pretty as in Paris's usual pale lavender. On one side of the mausoleum is the undernourished Bibliothèque Ste Geneviève, used by Sorbonne students, and on the other is the *mairie* of the Fifth and a terrace of high gray stone houses. No office fronts. Numbers 9, 7, 5 . . . It is *not* an engineering office: still, since I'm here—Shallow stone steps. Six stories up, a maid opens the door.

". . . no appointment, only to ask if I may make one."

A tousle-haired old lady in a wool dressing gown, her wrist in bandages, appears from a door to the right.

Confused apologies. . . . I hadn't realized . . . a book on a writer who was a friend of Albert Clemenceau—

Galvanic start; smile: "C'était mon père!"

The salon with its Goya and Hugo drawings looks over miles of chilly white-gray Paris to Sacré-Coeur.

"I remember the end of the case," Albert Clemenceau's daughter tells me, "when Dreyfus was reinstated."

(In 1906 the Rennes court-martial was reviewed by appeal judges, who annulled the verdict. The wheel turned. Georges Clemenceau, who had been out of favor, became prime minister.)

"It was very frightening, one or two nights we were taken to my grandfather's for safety. I remember my father and Georges and someone else were in a restaurant, and the people next to them got up and left saying 'It smells of dirty Jews here.'"

Mme Langlois-Berthelot can't remember a M. Fullairton.

With bated breath: "Would you by any chance, Madame, remember a little girl called Mireille Chabbert who was the protégée of someone in your family?"

"Non," says Mme Langlois-Berthelot automatically—then pauses. "Ah! mais c'était Oncle Paul qui s'occupait d'elle. It was Uncle Paul who had charge of her."

Don't say a word.

"He lived in the Avenue d'Eylau and the Château de l'Aubraie. I think he was taking care of her and then dropped her. I think he was disappointed in her. And it was we seven nieces and nephews who became his heirs."

"Your uncle Paul—Clemenceau?"

"He married an Austrian woman who was très mal. A daughter of Szeps—the friend of Rudolph of Hapsburg, the crown prince. She deceived him. I don't know why he didn't divorce her. Then Georges and Paul quarreled. Georges asked what would become of the château, and Paul said it would go to his Austrian nephew, who had fought against France in 1914. And Uncle Georges never saw him again. Now it belongs to young Georges Clemenceau."

"*. . . and she said: 'Albert Clemenceau was my father!'*"

"*Non!*"

"*She said, 'It was Uncle Paul who had charge of her!'*"

"*So there was a third Clemenceau? And you say Szeps—the friend of the Archduke Rudolph of Hapsburg?*"

"*Yes. Mayerling and all that.*"

The Liberal newspaper publisher Moritz Szeps had a part in that haunting tale from the Vienna Woods. His influence on the crown prince was such that Rudolph was hounded by the reactionaries who ruled his father's empire and in 1889 killed himself and his young mistress in a shooting lodge at Mayerling (Charles Boyer and Danielle Darrieux). Rudolph's harsh father lived to lose a second heir years later, the archduke who was assassinated at Sarajevo.

The uncles whose names had flitted through Mme Langlois-Berthelot's reminiscences were: Georges Clemenceau the statesman, born 1841; Paul, born 1857; Morton's lawyer, Albert, born 1861, father of Annette, now Mme Langlois-Berthelot.

According to Henri Mordacq, Georges's chief of staff, Paul was an engineer "renowned for work on gunpowders."[70] His château in La Réorthe, Vendée, is given in directories as a farm and its present owner, G. Clemenceau, as an *agriculteur*.

So: write to G. Clemenceau. Go to La Réorthe.

Camille and the Queen and King of Portugal

In the meantime there were other leads here in Paris.

Among the things of Camille's that got mixed up with Morton's in her garret was a draft appeal, all crazy curves, much crossed out, to the Procureur of the Republic for help against Enemies. In old age, despite her glories, she was in financial distress in a cruel and dishonest world. She mentioned a lawyer, Maître de Sariac.

"He is ill," I'm told when I telephone his office, "but his colleague has some interesting information."

Maître Guerre is young, with an eager face and dancing eyes.

"She wanted to make a will," he tells me, "not that I could see she had much to leave."

"Had she any family left? Her child was dead."

"Her child?"

Maître Guerre knows nothing of a marriage, a divorce, a child. He reads the divorce decree and looks up wide-eyed: "Nowadays, this might possibly be done, because the courts are more liberal—but at that time! To obtain a decree for something so slight!"

"Her husband knew the lawyer—and was she in collusion?"

"Oh, *oui! Sûrement!* She had to be. She never spoke of her marriage. But she was a bit gaga. She'd talk of her past glories. *Did* she have successes?"

"Yes." I bring out the photographs.

"I recognize something. Her look" (pointing to Camille in a veil). "She was anxious to leave what she had to someone. She was incapable of expressing her ideas, so it couldn't be done. I visited her at the Maison des Dames du Calvaire, to make her feel less alone. She was afraid of being thrown into the common pit, so I spoke to Mère Louise, who was *très très gentille,* and she assured me that it wouldn't happen. . . . I went to the funeral."

Maître Guerre looks at the photographs again, pushes them over to me. "Even in old age she was . . . attractive."

"I now think the marriage must have taken place in Portugal."

"She told me she danced before the king," says Maître Guerre. "She recited poems, she danced, and everyone was excited to find that she was also—that she could also sing like that."

"The . . . king?"

"In Portugal, before the king. Moreover, I believe she had been the king's mistress. Maître de Sariac told me she talked to him about Queen Amélie of Portugal, who'd come here after the king was assassinated, and she called the queen *une grosse vache,* a fat cow—as one woman speaks of another."

Home through the rush-hour traffic not even noticing. "Princes to act, And monarchs to behold our swelling scene—"

Wait. That was only what Camille, slightly gaga, said.

But Portugal fits. It fits what Hugh Fullerton said.

To the National Library at crack of dawn.

Maria Amalia, ex-queen of Portugal, died in Paris in 1951, says an encyclopedia. Good; that's when Camille was talking with the lawyers. Get *Figaro* on microfilm and start cranking.

Camille couldn't have missed the story. On a front page in October 1951 was: QUEEN AMELIE OF PORTUGAL DIED YESTERDAY IN HER CHATEAU, with a photograph.

Amélie d'Orléans, daughter of the pretender to the French throne, had married Carlos I of Portugal. In 1908 he and their elder son were assassinated. When she fled later, as a "Daughter of France" in the context of the old monarchy she was housed by the French Republic in the chateau where she died in 1951.

Portugal: Vasco da Gama, Camoëns, Ines da Castro the Dead Queen, oppression of colonies, revolts of colonies, juntas, revolutions, assassinations.

Who was this king before whom Camille had sung and danced?

He was Carlos Fernando Luis Maria Vitu Miguel Rafael Gabriel Gonzago Xavier Francisco de Assis José Suñao. He ascended the throne in 1889, when his cousin Rudolph of Hapsburg was shooting himself and the young Baroness Marie Vetsera. Camille was ten.

His ancestors included Alfonso the Conqueror and Alfonso the Fat, João the Pious and João the Perfect. Had his people continued to want monarchs, he would be known today as Carlos the Cultured: writer, painter, collector, science buff. His grandfather had, as a widower, married an opera singer mistress morganatically. Carlos himself patronized artistes as well as the arts.

The Mission to Madrid: Fourth Time Around

The *Times* for the period of Morton's 1903 mission to Madrid had something on Portugal. Send for that volume again.

March, London: King Edward VII is to visit Portugal.[71] Articles on the love of the British people for King Carlos. News flashes: King Edward has left Buckingham Palace! He is at sea! Meanwhile, wrote Our Own Correspondent in Lisbon, balconies on the kings' route were "being hung with the incomparably rich embroideries which are among the artistic glories of old Portugal."

Queen Alexandra of England was in Denmark on a family visit, and the queen of Portugal, whom Camille later called a fat cow, was at a spa. The queen mother acted as hostess.

The easy intimacy of the Portuguese strikes one used to "the well-ordered fêtes of France," says Our Own Correspondent. Sounds like Morton. He then reports the five-day visit in detail.

Except for alluding to "a talk with one of the most eminent of Portuguese statesmen" (definitely Mortonesque) he eschews political comment. The kings go to Cintra for "delicious holiday-making amid the woods and hanging gardens." They receive the diplomatic corps, watch fireworks, and attend a gala performance at the opera—

> in an atmosphere of pure sheen and radiance that plays on the bright colouring of the tiled façades of the houses, on the waters of the Tagus . . . whilst at night the vividness of the stars in the clear southern skies and the brilliant moon shed an almost equal beauty.

A banquet: On King Carlos's right, the wife of the British ambassador; on his left, the Portuguese premier's wife; opposite him, King Edward with Portuguese ladies to right and left. At a separate table the queen mother, the papal nuncio, and the prime minister. Then a bloodless bullfight. Finally, DEPARTURE OF THE KING, and the royal yacht sails off toward Gibraltar.

Yes, Morton was there.

Gala, state dinner, moonlit walks, and "golden hours under untarnished skies": rarely have *Times* stories been so lyrical—and stories about a state visit, dullest of assignments!

A little night music, and if he meets Camille . . . if he discovers her position at court, a new rosy light illuminates his marrying her. Royal mistresses have always been in a class apart.

And it makes sense of a letter from Henry James mentioning a "wondrous scrap" Morton had sent him with an explanation in which James found only "maddening mystification":

> "Out of the Palace . . ."? Well, you've inspired a hopeless passion in the Queen-Mother (as I believe the Queen-wife was then absent?). . . . I return religiously . . . awe-strickenly, the passionate little paper—only *not* arriving at *any* vision of the particular state function during which, driven to madness by your insensibility, she filched a leaf surreptitiously from the notebook of the Historiographer-Royal and, scribbling the wonderful words in some dissimulated attitude, got one of the pages to smuggle them into your hand.

Out of doubt and out of question, a billet-doux from Camille to Morton. How Ruritanian, rich, and romantic!

At the state banquet, the two kings at one table, the queen mother, prime minister, papal nuncio at another. A historiographer royal (why not?). And somewhere, below the salt—like Morton?—Camille, whose presence at court is, marvelously, established by, of all people, Henry James! Enamored, adventurous, she slips a note to the *bel anglais, représentant du Times de Londres.*

Wonderful. *Wunderbar. Thavmasio.*

James also mentions a "cryptic" allusion Morton had made to his "personal situation."[72] Would Morton have sent him Camille's note if they were already married? Who knows; but it does look as if they were married around then, in Lisbon or Madrid.

Still, it's out of character for Morton to marry. Was Camille in distress—needing to escape? In that small, feudal, extravagant realm anything was possible. Rescue would have been the action of a Meredithean hero (who like our hero would soon regret it).

But how came the child of a French mechanic to be set before a king? Maître Guerre says Camille told him that people were surprised that she sang "too." So it wasn't known that she'd been studying voice. But what *had* she been doing? A courtly environment would explain the worldly young woman who wrote to Will from Fiume after the divorce. But which came first—life at court providing polish and training in dance and elocution and, later, singing; or training in dance and so forth, that gave her a place at court and then, there, singing lessons?

The prima donna whom Carlos's grandfather married morganatically was Elisa Frederica Hensler—1836–1929—a Viennese. Camille was named Camille Victoria and named her daughter Mireille Frederica. The two second names are neither French nor Portuguese. Where facts are so sparse, the tiniest fact gives one pause. Two coincidences: names, opera singers. Elisa was still around, step-grandmother to Carlos. Can she have trained Camille? Befriended her when she became pregnant, and sponsored in baptism a child named for her Frederica? It still wouldn't explain why Camille herself, French-born, had been christened Victoria. Or why she was in Lisbon.

Revolutions

Well, Camille and Morton marry, cohabit in Madrid, divorce in Paris, and live their separate lives for a few years, she touring, he in Paris. He would often have been reminded of Carlos, who came to France—officially, incognito or "semicognito"—for lectures by Marie Curie, for the auto show, for private visits.

Meanwhile, Carlos's poor, corrupt, and backward country was crashing toward disaster. Peasant risings, student riots, anticlerical demonstrations. As the cost of his hobbies rose and tax collection became harder, he gave his prime minister dictatorial powers, which were used so harshly that in 1908 there came:

ASSASSINATION OF THE KING OF PORTUGAL AND THE CROWN PRINCE

In London, news and comment nearly covered the main page of the *Times* and poured over on others. Nothing shook the *Times* like an attack on royalty. In Paris a requiem mass was said in Notre-Dame.[73]

Carlos was assassinated on the first of February—a month we already know something about. Morton was cultivating Edith Wharton and ignoring Katharine's letters, and it was in February or early March that he and Camille met and she went off with Mireille to sing in *Thaïs* and had him send on her wig.

That meeting has a new aspect now. Whatever the divorcés' quarrel, Portugal had powerful personal associations for them both. Awkwardness would dissolve in thrill at being so close to a world event. Camille, in Paris when she heard the news or arriving soon after, would want to see the one person who knew the setting. Will would be glad to talk with a reliable inside source.

Camille, black-veiled, exquisite, drooping, enters Notre-Dame, late, and glides up the great aisle. Will is there as reporter for the *Times*. Afterward, dinner in a private room in one of his several excellent restaurants.

Camille in a trim suit at a post office counter sends Will a *pneu*: She's in Paris; she *must* see him!

"I'm still dazed and stunned," she told him when she wrote from Fiume after their meeting. Strong language if applied to a divorce three and a half years ago, but not inappropriate as response to the murder of a royal protector.

(And that's why Edith Wharton noted the event in her diary. When Morton called on her that day, he'd mentioned having met the king.)

Camille had Mireille with her. Did the child recognize a man who had, for a short time, been "Papa"?

Lisbon should have a record of the marriage.

Answers to queries arrive: British embassy, Lisbon. Registros Centrais, Lisbon. Archives Etrangères, Nantes. Archives Service, Washington. No record.

A *secret* marriage, arranged by Carlos—or, better, concealed from him? Camille and Will cloaked and hooded steal to the Chapel Royal by starlight. A hedge priest waits at the altar.

Go to Lisbon! But, the cost—

Besides, the archives may be barricaded. On every broadcast is news of LISBONNE: peasant risings, student riots, army mutinies.

Portugal's having another revolution. So, wait.

La Vendée

Mireille: Fairyland

In April we drive south in the Vendée. A country "exceedingly pretty," Henry James said. Today, here and there, the prettiness is enhanced, as an eighteenth-century pretty face was enhanced by patches, by dainty Klee-like pylons lifting arms and trailing wires against the blue-and-white sky.

*"Always a region apart." (Marc) "The last to accept the Revolution.
The chiefs still have clientèles, each Vendéen still has his chief and is
loyal to him. . . . so, what do you expect to find at La Réorthe?"*

*"A fairytale castle. An ancient retainer who will say, 'I knew Mireille
Chabbert.'"*

The tiny communal roads twist and curve, climb and descend. A narrow unparapeted stone bridge crosses a stream. La Réorthe is a straggle
of houses. The château? "Go on through La Féole and there's an allée to
the right," say some boys.

La Féole is two or three houses, a hamlet within a hamlet. The wide
grassy tree-vaulted allée becomes a grassy path, crossed with gates as it
passes through drowsy courtyards. Stone barns and outbuildings, a cat
asleep on a crumbling wall, farm not castle till you enter the last courtyard: then a manor house, its door set in a round mossy tower with a
mossy pointed roof; a moat, a bridge, a pond, soft tender April trees.

"Monsieur is in Paris," says the maid. "But there is a very old person
who might remember. Madame Gabrielle Roy Bretaud."

Off the allée, hidden by its trees, a terrace of low cottages borders a
patch of cabbage, lettuce, and beans.

"Entrez!"

A low-ceilinged flagstoned room, cool, dark, spare, and reposeful,
with a table and benches in the center. An old woman, tall and straight, in
black dress and black stockings, with a blue apron, turns from a modern
stove at the back.

"Madame, we are trying to learn something about Mireille Chabbert."

Madame Bretaud's grave wrinkled face breaks into a beautiful smile.
She puts down the pan she is holding and comes forward.

"I knew her very well—very well indeed. Are you family, Monsieur?
We heard that Mlle Mireille had married in London and then not long
after she died giving birth to a child.

"She was the adopted daughter of Monsieur Paul and his wife, who
was an Austrian. They had no children, so she was the daughter of the
house. She didn't wear an apron but little frilly sleeves and skirts with
flounces. You didn't have to say Bonjour, she'd speak to you first, and
when she came to La Réorthe, the whole village would say: 'Mireille is
here!' Elle ne faisait pas la princesse; she didn't put on airs."

* * *

Monsieur Paul, Monsieur Albert, *le Tigre;* the names come and go. Mme Bretaud's family has worked for the Clemenceaus for, oh, two hundred years. "Albert came rarely, Georges very often. And he was prime minister of France! Time flies. Tout ça, mes amis . . .

"She had a round face like yours, Monsieur. Dark. Thick black eyebrows, almond eyes. Healthy-looking, more like a country girl than a *citadine.*

Mme Bretaud looks at the photograph of Camille with long hair.

"It is the portrait of Mireille."

When had she come? Around 1908, later. "She was about eight, nine, but she was already very well formed. Her mother was dead. She was an Algerian."

"We think we have found out that her mother was born in the Dordogne and died fairly recently."

"Oh! Oh! Everyone thought her mother was Algerian! She simply came. Monsieur Paul brought her. Three men had started a club, Paul being one, and they had singers come, as the custom was in those days. They told Mireille's mother, 'Don't worry; we'll take care of her.' The other two quit, Paul kept her. She had a pretty little voice; she sang chansonettes. But she wasn't to be in the profession, or to work at all. She was the *demoiselle du château.*

"And then—something went wrong. Monsieur Paul was devoted to Madame. The best peaches, *'C'est pour Madame!'* And it seems that when Mireille was older, maybe eighteen, the servants told the Clemenceaus that she made remarks about Madame. And from that time Mireille no longer came to the château."

"They thought the mother was Mediterranean, even Algerian, but it could have been the father."

"A swarthy Portuguese?"

"It need not have been either the king or Paul Clemenceau—écoute, tu penses que dans ces clubs très fermés men got together simply to listen to a singer? It's possible that of the three men they didn't know who was the father."

"But at the time of the club, Mireille was eight or so."

"One can imagine jealousy between Mme Paul Clemenceau and Mireille. 'Mirror mirror on zee wall,' as in Blanche-Neige. Camille may

*have found herself with a child ready for school. Dis, Carlos was
assassinated when?"*

"1908."

*"And it was not long after that Mireille was taken in by the
Clemenceaus. Suppose that Camille was receiving a pension because
Mireille was Carlos's child, or even if she wasn't; the king was generous
to his mistresses, with the people's money. And suddenly, with his death,
she was without that source of income."*

Was it Carlos? Mireille, who didn't act the princess, was she the daughter of a king?

Paris

Mireille: A President's Grandson

May Day is Labor Day in Europe. In Portugal the revolution has succeeded. Today's *Times* Iberian Correspondent reports that people are weeping for joy in the streets at their first legal May Day.

In France it is also the Fête des Muguets; people are buying lily-of-the-valley sprigs for luck along the Champs-Elysées and the Rue de l'Elysée, all the way to the house where the present Georges Clemenceau's windows overlook the Presidential Palais de l'Elysée with its Garde Républicain sentries and police.

There will be presidential elections in a few days. Monsieur Clemenceau, a slim silver-haired man, apologizes for the valises in his hall. He's about to go to La Reórthe; as mayor he must be present for the voting.

"With the articles M. Fullerton wrote," he says, "if he had the Legion, it was my grandfather Georges who got it for him."

"He had another tie with your family, rather odd," I tell him. "He was once married to a singer who was the mother of Mireille Chabbert."

"Mireille—Chabbert!" M. Clemenceau repeats slowly. "Mireille Chabbert. *Mais oui,* her mother was an artiste, very well known. Mireille Chabbert! . . . What I shall tell you isn't confidential, but you make me think of things for the first time in many years, I am a little bewildered. I knew Mireille. I knew her very, very well. I remember going for walks.

"Paul and his wife gave their affection to Mireille and to me. Gossip had it he was her father; I don't know. But all at once the affection disappeared. She displayed a precocity that was so embarrassing that he put her out the door. It was sad for them. It also meant that they concentrated on me, and that's why I inherited not only the mayorship but the château.

"Though my grandfather, Georges, quarreled with Paul! He thought Paul's wife, who was Austrian, helped arrange talks with Austria during the war; he wanted Paul to divorce her. Paul said, 'Mind your own business,' and that was the end. I lost track of Mireille. I had the idea her mother was Italian?"

"She was French. She was in Portugal at one time; she told someone she had been the mistress of Carlos I."

"It wasn't a monopoly," Monsieur Clemenceau says dryly. "Mireille disappeared from my uncle's entourage very abruptly. She was scandalous. Advances to all his friends, even elderly men. They complained, either joking or really offended. And she was very young. But I think, though Uncle Paul showed her the door, he had indirect contacts with her. . . . I don't know."

Senlisse

Mireille: A Childhood Playmate

"M. Andrieux used to play with Mireille," Mme Bretaud writes from La Réorthe. "I often saw them in a little cart harnessed to a little pony. Sometimes M. Andrieux drove, sometimes Mireille."

In the lane mounting to Paul Andrieux's house in the green Chevreuse Valley, cuckoos sing and a lizard streaks out to sun itself on a stone.

"Paul Clemenceau," says M. Andrieux, in a room with books everywhere, "was my godfather, and his wife was my godmother. Today's Georges Clemenceau is the grandson of a man who had a fight with Paul; after that he didn't go to the house. He didn't really know Mireille. She went to the Versailles Lycée as a boarder, and she'd come to Paris on her free days and I'd see her. We'd go to the circus. And every vacation we'd go to the Vendée together, and then we were together every moment.

"Mme Clemenceau was nice to her; so was Paul, but she was not their child. They . . . left her a little to one side, from the point of view of affection. At school, where there was a very disciplined life, it changed her less than it did the other children, for she hadn't been spoiled by her mother, that's a certainty.

"One year, *en Vendée,* M. Paul Clemenceau, who was the mayor, married us! They dressed us up, and they had a wedding, and he married us.

"Nobody knew about her. M. Clemenceau brought her to the château one day. That was that. Her mother simply abandoned her. She never came. It must have hurt. At first she hardly mentioned her. My parents were amazed at the mother.

"I was mad on opera. I'd go without meals so I could go. Mme Chabbert must have sung in *Werther,* I think? Because Mireille and I went to *Werther,* and she told me that she was once in a chorus of children in the opera. They needed children, so she was in it."

"That was in Madrid, I think," I said. "She was seven."

(In an early scene some children take a singing lesson. At the end they are heard offstage in a Christmas carol.)

"Then, during the war, the '14–'18 war, I felt as if something had changed. But in reality something *had* changed. Much later, I understood. I had chums, a bicycle. Nowadays boys and girls go around together, but it wasn't like that for us. There was a donkey, not the one in that photo, who was gentle, but a ferocious creature; he'd bite. So I took the cart for errands, and it didn't occur to anyone that she could come; there was a bit of danger—

"We were separated by the customs of the time. I realize now that she suffered because of being alone all through the war. Mme Clemenceau came for two weeks; she was bored. M. Clemenceau came now and then. But a boy that age doesn't think of just talking. My parents moved, I did my military service, then I married. She wasn't at my wedding. She had already gone to England."

"Why did she leave, do you think, Monsieur?" I asked.

"I don't know why she left. She left without anyone's knowing. To look for a job. She wasn't trained for anything, but she'd had a prize for English at school. She was perhaps twenty. My sister was in London, and she stayed with my sister for a time. Then I learned that she had married and that she was dead."

"Madame Bretaud was very fond of Mireille, she says."

"Everyone was! Elle était gentille, douce, de bon caractère. She had all the qualities that make people love you. I never—never—saw her cross, never heard her raise her voice—never. She was douce et soumissive. She was fatalistic. That is the word. People decided for her, and she would do what they said. Maybe she thought differently, but she wouldn't say so."

London

Mirabelle: London's Daughter

Between two shops in Oxford Street a gate marked OXFORD CIRCUS AVENUE opens onto a grimy and dilapidated courtyard. Robert Lainé was working in his father's textile business here and living with his father in airy Highgate when he married Mireille Chabbert in a registry office on February 8, 1930.[74]

Now the pale green certificate of that marriage, obtained at St. Catherine's House on an earlier visit to London, the paper on which the bride did not fill in "Name of Father," can be supplemented by two other certificates, pink for birth, lilac gray for death:

April 18, 1930, at The Hall, Great Bentley, Essex, a girl, Mirabelle Janet, was born to Robert Pierre Lainé and Frederica Mireille Lainé, *née* Chabbert.

The Hall was a nursing home for unmarried mothers.
Mirabelle: wonderfully beautiful.
The birth was registered on April 23. Informant, the mother.

May 6, 1930, Essex County Hospital, there died Frederica Mireille Lainé, thirty. Cause of death: puerperal septicaemia. Death registered May 9th by R. P. Lainé, widower.

The Anglican priest in Great Bentley has the burial record.[75] There is no stone; he thinks Mireille was put in an unmarked grave.
Douce et soumissive. Gentle and biddable.
Lainé was granted letters of administration for her estate—£200. (More than she could have saved. Present, dowry, from Paul Clemenceau?) He vanished from the directories after the Blitz, when his daughter (still unwanted?) was twelve.
St. Catherine's House has no record of Mirabelle's death or his. When I tried Caxton Hall, the superintendent said: "I'll see if there was a bombing incident at one of those addresses. I'll get on to the Borough Surveyor's office. But I've a wedding at twelve; come back after lunch."

Lunch was bread and cheese and Guinness across at the Albert.

When Camille came after the war to get news of her grandchild, part of Caxton Hall was rubble. A huge chunk was missing even when I came to this pub years later. A direct hit there'd been, they said. Craters still lined Victoria Street, wildflowers jutted from chinks in naked cellar walls.

After lunch: "Nothing," said Superintendent Boreham. "They must have been blown to pieces and not identified."

PART FOUR

Still London

At the Times

At one minute to eleven the lobby was empty; at one minute past a moto-messenger with an envelope under his arm strode in, his helmet dripping rain; and after him, furling umbrellas, men in caps, men in bowlers, bareheaded women streamed into the big solid building near the Thames.

The story unfolded at the *Times* takes us back beyond the bare ruined choirs of the 1940s to the 1890s and the confident capital of the world's greatest empire. Morton lived in that London for a time: an initiate in a chic homosexual set, the lover of a rani, a contender in the Grub Street battle for print, and a friend of two writers who stood above the fray, George Meredith and Henry James. He went on to Paris, but for twenty years he wrote for the British public, and it was in London that his work was judged and his career decided.

In Paris, working under Blowitz, he covered political scandals, terrorism, the Rally to the Republic, legislation to separate church and state, the Zola trial, the second Dreyfus court-martial.

When Blowitz retired in 1902, Morton was not immediately promoted. *Why?* Was there a connection with his 1903 posting to Madrid, which produced, in print, neither much hard news nor much analysis? Was his "partial" resignation in 1907 or 1908 related to his affair with Edith Wharton and his renewed contact with Camille, whose daughter he had recognized and whose royal lover was assassinated in 1908? How did he free himself from blackmail by Mirecourt? Why did he resign completely when he was only in his forties?

The archive of the *Times* was in the basement. And of all the reversals, surprises, and upheavals experienced in the search for Fullerton, the profoundest, I think, came about in that calm, cool, usually empty room.

Fullerton and His Chiefs

"Anything from Paris should reach the office through the Correspondent, and that is Mons. de Blowitz and not you."
— C. MOBERLY BELL TO FULLERTON ON 30 NOVEMBER 1891[1]

Henry Opper von Blowitz in portrait and caricature looks down benignly on letters from Paris to Number 7 Printing House Square, the home office, and the manager's letter books—bound copies of letters sent to Paris, the paper thin as the film on the white of a hard-boiled egg.

At Number 7 are C. Moberly Bell, manager; John Walter III, of the founding family; his son Arthur; Arthur's son John; Buckle, editor; Valentine Chirol, foreign editor.

Morton went to Paris in April 1891 and after three months' trial had his pay set at £40 a month.[2] A book review he sent to London incurred the manager's rebuke above, his reply to which (missing) brought a PRIVATE reply: Bell thought he had a "complete misconception" of his duties. In Paris he was under M. de Blowitz just as in London he had been under the editor.

I am sure that when you were here it would not have occurred to you to send in to Mr. Buckle a long review of an important book, nor to reply that you could not attend such a meeting because you were dining with one friend or taking tea with another.

Reviews were unsigned and represented the paper. "Why even when we give a book for review to the greatest living authority we do not necessarily accept his judgment." They were apt to mistrust a young man "self-confident on subjects which have engaged the life study of much older men without producing that confidence."

What I want you to understand in all kindness is this: that your business is to assist Mons. de Blowitz. It is he whom you must satisfy and not the public, if you wish to remain in Paris.[3]

This, to a man who had ruled the world of letters in Boston. But Morton set out to please Blowitz, who soon informed Number 7 that, "since his first mistakes," Mr. Fullerton was "zealous, modest, and intelligent,"[4] and his improved performance was rewarded by marked social favors.

Morton was invited to Les Petites Dalles, Blowitz's gingerbread-Gothic pleasure dome overlooking a Normandy beach. There, he wrote in a feature for an American magazine, one saw the man who had emissaries the world over, whose "subtle influence" affected all Europe, chatting with the brightly dressed women who flocked to him under his umbrella.[5] In town, Blowitz took Morton to the opera. And at the office, a colleague said, hearing Fullerton and the great man "chaff" was "always a merry moment." Blowitz declared that a hundred words of his were put into ten words of English by one assistant, Alger, and two hundred by the other, Fullerton, whose Blowitz-Alger parodies amused him "hugely."[6]

In the *Times* archive, however, few peals of laughter sound. The effervescence of Morton's early letter to Samuel Longfellow—"I am in constant relations with deputies ministers even the Pope"—went flat. Three years passed, and Blowitz told Bell that Mr. Fullerton was troubled by, he thought, material preoccupations":

> When he came . . . he had no idea of France, of the Continent, of politics in general, nor even, really, of journalism . . . he had conquered this knowledge . . . is a good and zealous reporter . . . I do not know whether you have some objection to him, because it seems to me that he is not much liked on the other side.[7]

While he juggled his complex personal involvements, Morton, above all, worked hard. Blowitz recommended a pay raise. The "other side" refused.

It explains the advice Morton had from Meredith: "Do not be disheartened, hug your forces, bide your time"[8] and from James: "Sit as tight as you *can:* it's all we can ever do."[9]

Normally, Morton corresponded with Number 7 only during Blowitz's holidays, when he managed the office. He was in charge, with Alger assisting, when the decision to retry Dreyfus was announced. Bell rebuked him for sending five columns. He'd been told, no more than two. "PLEASE CONFORM TO INSTRUCTIONS." He answered lengthily:

> Mr. Chirol has, indeed, written me two letters asking us to condense the Dreyfus matter, but *it was after his first letter that your first letter arrived,*

and we both interpreted it as cancelling the order contained in the letter in question. . . . The next letter had crossed [etc., etc.].[10]

Morton must have cut; Bell sent him a check (Blowitz's idea) in recognition of his part in "the excellent work of the Paris office."[11] "We have documented honestly," Morton replied, "in the spirit of disinterested science, and I doubt if a future historian . . . will find anything essential to add."[12]

At the 1899 court-martial, Morton, we know, outdid himself in dramatic presentation of the actors and the issues. He wired copy direct from Rennes, to save time. (The London papers were in fierce competition.) James read the reports every morning transfixed, not writing to Morton, he told him later, "because it seemed kinder and wiser in every way not to interpose even a feather's weight into your so heroically overburdened consciousness."[13]

"He has done credit to you," Chirol told Blowitz as the trial went on.[14] But he sent a private wire:

FULLERTON CORRESPONDENT TIMES HOTEL DE FRANCE RENNES PRIVATE ADVISE KEEPING TONE RATHER MORE DOWN IN YOUR OTHERWISE EXCELLENT TELEGRAMS REMEMBER BRITISH PUBLIC INCLINED RESENT HIGH COLOURING ESPECIALLY OUR PUBLIC PLEASE UNDERSTAND THIS MERELY FRIENDLIEST HINT CHIROL.[15]

After the trial, however, Chirol criticized *content* and did more than hint. Of Morton's handling of a Turko-French incident: Events helpful to enemies of France should not be unduly stressed. France had been friendly during the Boer War.[16] Soon after: How could he send a dubious report of Anglo-French dissension when, as he knew, they wished to show friendship to France?[17] Two days later:

You really need not speak of "reproaches." . . . My wish is to establish such relations with all our correspondents that I can make whatever observations and recommendations I may think useful in the interests of the paper without giving rise to any such impression as is conveyed in the word "reproaches."[18]

At that time, Henry James was absorbed with characters in the novel he was writing—the journalist Merton Densher and Millie Theale, a Tennysonian "heiress of all the ages." He remarked to Morton on the censorship London writers endured, whereas Morton in Paris was free—Morton, "young heir not only of all the ages but of all the subjects."[19]

Morton did not feel free. Even after his triumph at Rennes he was sub-jugated to men of baser metal. But he was the heir of Blowitz and submit-ted to bondage while awaiting his inheritance.

The Dark Night of the Ego

In January 1902 the Boston papers announced the news cabled from Paris that the great Blowitz was being succeeded by W. M. Fullerton, who would have the same grand salary and enormous expense account.

Six months later, Blowitz notified the *Times* board that he meant to re-tire. They informed him that Fullerton (then on leave in the Franche-Comté) would not be kept on in Paris; Alger would.

Blowitz was scandalized. Alger had never "produced one single infor-mation." Mr. Fullerton lived "in an honourable fashion, being very hos-pitable, perhaps too, because like every American he is anxious to know many people, and he evidently imagines that it is a force to have numer-ous relations . . . to leave Paris will be very crushing for him."[20]

It was the most crushing blow Morton Fullerton ever experienced.

Bell wrote. There was a question as to his future: subediting in Lon-don or a foreign agency, perhaps in the Balkans.[21]

Morton, after his return, to Bell: M. de Blowitz had broken the news as gently as possible. ("He told me, by the way, that the whole thing arose out of an appeal to you to raise my salary.") The suggestion of subediting showed that his successful work had escaped notice in London.[22]

The new man, Blowitz told Bell, could ask no better aide than Fuller-ton. To return him to "the subeditor room where he certainly will not be considered with much sympathy nor with much friendly support would be an undeserved and hard punition."[23]

Talk of subediting stopped. Blowitz went on leave, still sending Bell pro-Fullerton letters.[24] Fullerton ran the office and the inept Alger. For some reason he declined a post in Russia and/or the Balkans.[25] Bell then told him that Blowitz would be succeeded by Lavino of Vienna, Lavino by Steed, and Steed by Hubbard of Madrid. "We shall in all probability ask you to go to Madrid."[26]

Fullerton to Bell, 25 July 1902:

This decision satisfies me completely. . . . The principle of [rotation] is, I may add, the one that I hoped would be adopted . . . although I had fancied it would begin with Rome, having completely forgotten Madrid. I am no less content for that, and I perceive that, on this principle, I am after all headed towards Paris.

Yours, dear Mr. Bell, devotedly.[27]

(This introduced a train of letters in which, after years of *faithfully*'s and *truly*'s, Morton signed more personally.)

Bell replied that they could not raise his pay. Except for unwillingness to "dispense entirely" with him, they would not be sending anyone to Madrid. Nor should he hope for "a regular progression culminating in Paris." His work had improved, but was far from what they had from Vienna Berlin. . . ."[28]

Coffee in the Times*'s dull canteen.* . . . Journalists and printers talk over pints of bitter, an editor comes up after a phone call from Our present Own Correspondent in Paris. . . . *Musing.*

We have seen MF as a sentimentalist, a bisexual Lothario, a cad, a crusader. But always it has been posited that he was a luminary in his profession. Whereas now—

Letters to and letters from are not collated in the archives. You couldn't read Bell letter, Fullerton reply, Bell reply, in order. Morton's letters read straight through revealed a new Morton. A worrier. Personal, unprofessional. You feel embarrassed on his behalf. And then to read Bell, and learn *why* Morton worried!

Yet he never doubted that he would succeed Blowitz. In fact—the news cabled to Boston that he *had* succeeded Blowitz—who but Morton himself would have sent it?—mad though it seems. Perhaps to precipitate an event he thought was imminent.

During the break in communication with his family that began when Blowitz decided to retire, a black period we've been relating to his private life, Morton was corroded by torments that had nothing to do with family, friendship, sex, or love. And he had learned nothing from experience.

For eleven years he had worked under men he thought inferior to himself. Yet Bell was an authority on Egypt. Chirol was knighted for services to India. Buckle, the editor, a fellow of All Souls, worked on a life of Disraeli and an edition of Queen Victoria's letters and turned down a baronetcy. Morton undervalued the men at Number 7 while taking pains to please Blowitz, whose influence he overestimated.

But even Blowitz, who was his generous champion, never thought of him as a possible chief correspondent.

Hotly defending an article on Turkey impeached by Bell, Morton sent him his documentation: private letters from the Turkish consul in Brussels. No, he did not "swallow stories" uncritically.

> I might have subserved British interests and secured for myself a journalistic success in publishing the fact of the theft by the French government of the Siamese cable cipher code. . . . I have not done so for the simple reason that I seek always to act on your good rules. . . . Yours, dear Mr. Bell, devotedly.[29]

Bell returned a document Morton had sent as proof:

> It is of no value whatever—first, because it is the statement of a Turkish official, second because on the one page out of the four which is in the remotest degree relevant the writer's testimony is against you.[30]

By this time, Morton had learned that France and England were secretly negotiating claims to Africa, but he could not get his story published. There is nothing about the matter in his file. His stock as political journalist was nil.

Meanwhile, the staff changes had been made public. With amazement Morton's friends read in the *Times* that Mr. Lavino had succeeded Blowitz as Our Correspondent in Paris.

"Blowitz by his jealousy of my position here," Morton explained to them, "stupidly played into the hands of Lavino."[31]

The Mission to Madrid, Fifth Time Around

The scoop on the Anglo-French intrigue was published three months later, February 1, as a wire from "Our Own Correspondent," Madrid.

Before and after that date, Morton was in Paris helping Lavino run in. He must have made the awkward journey to Madrid to publish his wire with a local slant, "In Spain they didn't know . . . " But he could not have done it secretly. How did he contrive it?

* * *

14 March, Lavino to Bell: Fullerton "left last night for London and will proceed to Madrid shortly after his return." His "friendly and cheerful" help, his "ability both literary and journalistic," had made working with him a pleasure.[32]

In London, Bell gave Morton credentials and informed him that in Spain he would get £50 a month instead of £40.

When Fullerton returned to Paris, it was announced from Buckingham Palace that there was to be a royal visit to Portugal.

Fullerton, Paris, to Bell: "I start tonight and if all goes well I shall be at Lisbon at 4 on Sunday . . . not a second too soon if I am to post a letter for publication before the King's arrival."[33]

He left seared and shredded by being devoted to Bell and smilingly serviceable to Lavino and, hardest of all, saving face before his family, his friends, and his public.

Then, instead of assuming his new post routinely, he found himself banqueting with kings and dallying with a royal favorite. The British minister commended his "appreciation of the situation," and he "had to refuse a Portuguese decoration."[34] His stories were euphoric—even after being toned down, we learn, at Number 7.

The visit, Chirol wrote, was doubtless brilliant. But they'd had to prune severely, while its political results were unlikely to be as great as Fullerton "somewhat cryptically" indicated. "Feel your way" in Madrid, Chirol advised, "and don't be in a hurry to take either the Escurial or Printing House Square by storm."[35]

20 APRIL 1903 BELL TIMES LONDRES. NEED MONEY TO TELEGRAPH AND EXPENSES ON LEAVING FOR MADRID AFTER WEEK STUDY PROVINCES FULLERTON[36]

23 APRIL 1903 FULLERTON AVENIDA LISBON SENDING FURTHER LETTER CREDIT BUT REQUIRE NO TELEGRAMS TIMES[37]

When he reached Madrid, Morton sent Henry James Camille's love letter and Moberly Bell his Lisbon expenses.

James: "You bear I won't say a charmed, but certainly a charming, life."[38] Bell: "Not quite our idea of an account."[39]

Morton explained to Bell that he'd had to "return courtesies" to high officials;[40] and though he'd given notice for his Paris flat, he'd had to pay taxes and insure his books and belongings.[41]

* * *

In Portugal, circumstances had shed charm on the medieval past. Analyzing Spain as a modern man, Morton reported that "new forces" were affecting a government that was an "executive committee" for the Vatican.[42] Chirol advised him not to show partisanship for the republican movement in a country where he represented the paper.[43]

But mostly letters from London varied two directives:

1. *Condense!* For Spain, they did not want telegrams "except in the possible event of a very important (in the European sense) crisis."[44] "Too long." "Too diffuse."

Spain *was* of European interest, Fullerton retorted.[45] ("You'll bring Spain back into the family," James had assured him.)[46]

2. *Keep accounts straight!* Bell would patiently copy out an account and correct it; he enjoyed giving bookkeeping lessons.

The prelude to one lesson set me back in my chair:

> I received the notice of your marriage and should have written to congratulate you but I assumed that you had gone away for your honeymoon and holiday—

He *announced his marriage to Moberly Bell?* That settles any doubt as to its having been bona fide.

> permit me to congratulate you and to hope that in the comparative leisure of married life, you will find time to keep your accounts a little more in order . . . you have asked the Crédit Lyonnais to advance you 500 pesetas and express your confidence that I will "gladly facilitate your movements"- —Whither? . . . Now my dear Mr. Fullerton I really must ask you to put matters straight.[47]

A query about another bill goaded Morton to abandon his determined winsomeness in a letter Bell returned to him, saying:

> I can only suppose [it] was written in a moment of temporary excitement and . . . will consider it as unwritten. [Else] I should be compelled with regret to tell you that your connexion with us must cease.[48]

Fullerton to Bell, 29 January 1904:

> The growing interest of the situation here forces me to appeal to you [to let me] draw up to £60 upon you through the *Crédit Lyonnais*. I promise not to make an abuse of telegrams, but I feel . . . [49]

(Would he *never* learn?)

Two reprimands came lightning swift. Bell: "To be perfectly frank we regard the whole—or nearly the whole—of the expenditure at Madrid as so much money wasted."[50] Chirol: "You must surely be able to realize that with this crisis in the East interest in Spanish affairs is as limited as the space we can afford to devote to it. Yet you continue to handle them with a diffuseness which merely adds quite unnecessarily to our work."

("All we want is just to keep in touch with what is going on," Chirol said. "Of course if you like to write privately at greater length. . . . One is always glad to be kept abreast.")[51]

Morton sent Bell's next letter on to Chirol for Chirol to read and was icily reproved: "a very improper proceeding and in returning it to you I wish to forget that you sent it to me."[52]

In Paris, Lavino too was having troubles: a salary dispute, removal of the bureau from the Boulevard des Capucines to the nearby Chaussée d'Antin, and illness among the staff. A telegram sped from London.

22 FEBRUARY 1904 FULLERTON 11 MONTESQUINZA MADRID DURING O'NEILL'S ILLNESS PLEASE GO ASSIST LAVINO ARRIVING PARIS BY NEXT SUN-DAY BELL[53]

Morton returned to Paris on as short notice as he had quit it to go to Portugal and Spain.

Back in Paris, I could collate the *Times* records with others.

Paris

Demotion and Divorce

As normalcy returned, Bell told Lavino to keep Fullerton on as second assistant. "We have absolutely no use for him anywhere else, and unless he can be made useful to you in Paris I do not see how we can continue to employ him."[54]

He and Fullerton were "capital friends," Lavino replied.[55]

Fullerton, however, had been under a misapprehension.

Bell to Fullerton, 13 April 1904:

[You] charge the Madrid salary and in addition living expenses in Paris. Now this clearly will not do. My intention was—though I see my telegram, which I forgot to confirm by mail, did not express it—to close the Madrid

agency which was both useless, expensive, and troublesome, and, temporarily at least, to reinstate you as assistant. . . . That change implies also I
am afraid a return to your Paris salary.[56]

John Walter, the chairman's son, a peaceable man eight years
Morton's junior, had become a friend. Morton wrote to him in despera-
tion:

> My Madrid obligations were, and remain, my monthly loyer [rent] and
> monthly payments on the relatively meagre furniture which you yourself
> have seen. I had settled down there as your correspondent, and secured for
> the *Times* a respectable position. I was living, as a married man, exactly
> within my means. My life was satisfactorily organized. . . .
> The post which you gave me has been taken from me without a warn-
> ing; the salary . . . has been reduced without any reason; and the bare ex-
> penses incurred by my change of residence the Manager refuses to pay. The
> extreme urgency and seriousness of this special situation prevent me from
> alluding to the other contents of the Manager's letter. It is impossible for
> me to suppose you can be aware of them.[57]

"I think," Bell wrote, "you have quite fairly and reasonably ques-
tioned the justice of my last letter—written somewhat hastily." They
meant no injustice, but

> we do want you clearly to understand—and Mr. Walter asks me to put this
> very plainly—that except as an assistant to Mr. Lavino we have really no
> opportunity of employing you. . . . Will you let me personally address one
> word in sincere friendship. . . . Many very ordinary men make good journal-
> ists. Many very clever men can never make good journalists. . . . My friends
> say I am an instance of the first and in my opinion you are an instance of the
> second. Why persist in a career for which I honestly think you are unfitted.[58]

Lavino told Bell that he would "try to make things pleasant" for Fullerton. "He has even said that he had learnt something from working
with me. He is rather an old pupil but I will try."[59]

Meanwhile, Morton's marriage was coming to its predictable end.
In Lisbon, Camille had seen Will mingling with dignitaries, handsome
and open-handed. In Madrid, his splendor tarnishing, he vented on her
the spleen he stifled in letters to Bell.

A flat with rented furniture. A small child about the place. Even though there were servants in that time and land of cheap labor, Mireille was *there*. If Camille went on tour, was Will to look after her? Or was Camille's "concession" a promise to take Mireille with her? Was he already unfaithful? They were already quarreling. He may have "satisfactorily organized" his life, but Camille jumped out a window to get away from him. After January she stopped writing to her mother-in-law in Brockton, U.S.A.

When Will learned that he was to stay in Paris as a junior with a 20 percent pay cut, his first terrified concern was, how could he live on that pay—and where? He had been putting up at a big hotel.[60] His "books and belongings" were in Adèle's new flat. He went to see her. If she did not already know he was married, he told her. He could also assure her that she need not be jealous.

For it was clear that he must divest himself of Camille, and divestiture was feasible. He knew a lawyer, Albert Clemenceau, and Camille, a girl used to *le biglif* who wouldn't care to play the thrifty housewife, would go along with it.

After his colloquy with Mirecourt he told his parents that he owed her half the rent and 200 francs a month *and* that she wanted the insurance. To which his father replied in his *magistral* letter reviewing Will's "love episodes" that if he would give him title to the policy they would send him money to pay Madame off so that he could behave properly toward his wife.[61]

But before Bradford even wrote, Camille had come to Paris for a reunion that turned into a showdown that turned into a conference at which Albert Clemenceau may have been present—and she had accused Morton in writing of having mistresses, "adding in injurious terms that her confidence in him was lost." Will cabled home saying how much money to send and that he had a good lawyer.[62]

It all happened—demotion, deal with Adèle, deal with Camille, getting money from his father, getting a lawyer—in under a month.

Camille disobeyed a summons, and in November Morton was granted a divorce on the grounds of her letter.

Losing Madrid was not worse for Morton than the shock of 1902, when he learned that he was not succeeding Blowitz, nothing ever was;

but it was an aftershock of appalling magnitude. He had made the *Times* "important" there. He was aiming at return to Paris as chief. But his mission was a condensed reprise of his eleven years under Blowitz: hard work, hubris, and unwisdom.

Barrett Wendell came to lecture in France. He was followed by George Santayana. They were guests to honor and entertain at a time when Morton was trying to hide his own situation from the world.

George Meredith had invented characters doomed by the Comic Muse to lie ceaselessly in order to save face. In his *Evan Harrington,* a tailor's daughters who have married above their station go through contortions to avoid being recognized by people from their past. One of them has married a Portuguese marquis, babbles about life at the court in Lisbon, and falls into timely faints when exposure threatens. Steeped as he was in Meredith, Morton could not have been wafted to Lisbon without thinking of the novel. The vertiginous experience of fiction interfacing fact may even help explain his marriage.

His mother wrote of the pain caused by his affection for Madame, his silence, his revealing his marriage post facto and relapsing into silence. Would Camille join him? What about the furniture?[63]

He again stopped writing home as he fell into the post-Blowitz routine.

A New Dispensation

From "the splendour of the *Times* office," wrote another correspondent who held the coveted Paris assignment, he would descend to that of the *Morning Post* ("a corner table in the Café Napolitain") and, like his friend Henry James, hint at "evasive subtleties." It was fun to track their meaning, sometimes "scarcely worth" it, "and no one enjoyed the chase more than Fullerton."

But fun at the Napolitain, like merriment with Blowitz in the past, hid "perfect misery."

Morton's newspaper style was thought Jamesian by people who did not read James. James was not diffuse; Morton was. He had been told so all his life. He spurned advice, forcing subeditors in London to edit copy clogged with qualifications of parentheses. And, like James's "poor distinguished" Merton Densher, he wrote with "deplorable ease . . . it was part of his fate in the first place, and part of the wretched public's in the second."

* * *

Since the café contingent also saw Morton, less dubitably, as "the perfect *boulevardier* . . . dressed as only a man who takes a proper pride in exceptionally good looks could do," he caused a sensation when he tottered in like a "scarecrow," his top hat telescoped. He had been trapped in a demonstration and the police had stormed over him. He went home to stay in bed for a week.[64]

Home to Mme Mirecourt.

There and outside the office in general, he lived among French people, thought in French. He reviewed French writers in the new *Times Literary Supplement*—Fernand Gregh, Rémy de Gourmont, Maurice Barrès—and published travel articles in French. James had proclaimed a jealous "rage of resentment" against the companion he—in one article—"notoriously"[65] had; he cut the coy allusion to a woman when he turned the essays into *Terres Françaises*. The book came out in 1905 with an analytical table of contents (a labor of love by Aeneas O'Neill, the heroically named senior assistant) and a preface in which Morton thanked the companion who knew the names of flowers, who was with him in the Rue Fabert as he wrote.

At the *Times,* 1905: The author of *Terres Françaises* had the past "too much with him," wrote a *TLS* reviewer.[66] In 1906 the *Times* reported that the book had won the Drouyn de Lhuys medal of the Société de Géographie Commerciale and the Académie's Marcelin Guérin prize.[67]

Morton had not forgotten having been denied a Harvard fellowship for study abroad. He wrote to tell Professor Charles Eliot Norton that the "boy" who, like Apollonius Rhodius, had been scorned had won an award honoring Harvard and . . . *some* of his teachers.

By this time in my research, the woman on whose account the quest for Fullerton had been undertaken was a dimly remembered character waiting in the wings. The chase had led in other directions. But now the *Times* records bring him up to January 1907, when Edward and Edith Wharton settled at 58 Rue de Varenne in the Faubourg Saint-Germain.

The M.F. whom E.W. was about to meet was not an influential and prestigious Chief Correspondent but a man over forty hanging on by his teeth to a junior post and straining by lies and ambiguous givings-out to be seen by outsiders as Blowitz the Second.

Edith Wharton

Morton had social compensations. Mirecourt had lived in one of Zola's worlds; he lived partly in Proust's, though a world Proust (whom he never met) had quit in life and was recapturing in art. Handsome, cultivated, unencumbered, he was received by hostesses in the Faubourg Saint-Germain. The celebrated Countess Rosa de Fitz-James was, like him, a book collector, one reason, perhaps, for the "true friendship" with which she invited him to dinner "to meet Madame Wharton."[68] He was soon helping Mrs. Wharton serialize *The House of Mirth* in French.

In Massachusetts, the letter signed Apollonius Rhodius[69] had reminded Charles Eliot Norton and his family of a member of the class of 1886, and Norton's daughter Sara mentioned Fullerton to her friend and close correspondent Edith Wharton.

"Your friend Fullerton," Edith told her, "is very intelligent, but slightly mysterious, I think."[70]

Mrs. Wharton was "an admirable intelligence," Morton told his mother next day.

James was staying with the Whartons, and seconded an invitation from Edith. Make her a sign, he told Morton, "if you are not absent or *remarié!* Don't, I beseech you, be any of those things!"[71] (Morton had sent James Camille's love letter to amuse him. His style of announcing the marriage and the divorce that followed so hard on it must have made it plain that nothing was there for tears.) Leaving a reply at Edith's door, Morton strolled along to the quais and bought a book of piety for his "dearest Mamma," to whom he sent letters showing that he was often "bespoken" to the Whartons. They were "very rich," he told Julia, but *she* was "exceptionally douée with *savoir faire,* as well as being an admirable intelligence."[72]

Edith thought of Morton as a "good comrade" when she and Teddy left in June, and Morton had not yet had the idea of seducing her.

That month he reviewed Anna de Noailles' *Eblouissements* ("ardent, wasted, joyous, excited, full of a mingled asperity and sweetness")[73] and sent the comtesse the review with a florid prediction that her monument would bear an inscription of "Gratitude from Nature."[74] He may or may not have known that she was ending an affair with Maurice Barrès, another writer whom he knew and had reviewed. She kept his letter; her answer is unknown.

His compliment to Adèle in his own book had not helped much in the Rue Fabert. Whatever fraction of his father's remittance he had paid her when he moved into her new flat, a large debt remained. Impatient with his reluctance to clear it by marrying her, she let him know that she had evidence of criminal misconduct on his part.

At the *Times* that summer he knew only defeats. He got Number 7 to use a paper by a man named Laur revealing that the French statesman Gambetta had once met Bismarck, the German chancellor, in secret. It transpired that Laur had forged a key passage. "Considering," Chirol wrote, "how you went out of your way to call Mr. John Walter's special attention to the value of the contribution you had obtained through your personal relations with Mr. Laur, the poor figure he cut has been extremely disappointing."[75]

Pursuits and Captures

So Fullerton sailed to America in September. Professionally mortified, his private life a mess, he was ready to experiment on Katharine and make moves toward "having" the rich and successful, reserved and decorous, intelligent and interesting Mrs. Wharton.

After convincing Katharine, at Bryn Mawr, that he loved her, he paid an overnight visit to Lenox, where, in October, there was already snow and he and Edith noticed witch hazel growing—"the flower that blooms in the autumn!" From Brockton he sent her another sprig of witch hazel,[76] perhaps plucked in the land behind his parents' house as he resumed his experiment on Katharine. Edith began "The Life Apart," the journal of her own late flowering.

And so he returned to Paris in November, pausing in Rye, to Adèle's ultimatum: pay up or marry her, or she'd expose him. His frantic letters to his fiancée and to James about blackmail began.

Over Christmas, in Brockton, Katharine told their parents of the engagement, then returned to Bryn Mawr and waited for letters.

In Madrid, Camille sang in *Werther* at the Royal Opera and Mireille, seven, performed in the children's chorus.

The Whartons came back to Paris.

Edith kept the "Line-a-Day" diary and the secret journal I'd read so long ago, but she also wrote ordinary letters—letters once stored[77] like—indeed, *with*—the Fullerton Papers, in Morton's study in the Rue du Mont Thabor. The diary recorded encounters with Morton; "The Life Apart," her joy and sorrow in them. Her letters were the machinery that brought them about.

Straight-faced in a whirl of activity, she asked Mr. Fullerton to bring friends to cheer two solitary people at loose ends.[78] (She and Morton were at their best together when humor was possible.) He brought André Tardieu, a journalist, to tea and when invited to a dinner party Edith was giving for the new U.S. ambassador, Henry White, asked if he might bring Lavino (whom he smilingly identified to Edith as his "Chief";[79] he could not keep up his imposture with people who might meet the real Correspondent).

To a hostess, this was not the same as welcoming a friend of a friend to potluck. Edith was glad Morton had asked; he'd "found how we like our friends to treat us." But she didn't know a suitable lady for Mr. Lavino; why not bring him to tea?[80] *He* could find a lady, Morton offered. Edith gracefully regretted that as she wouldn't know the lady, the lady might not wish to come.[81]

As it happened, the Whartons dined the next night at the embassy and found that Lavino was also a guest.[82] (It was the day King Carlos was assassinated, as Edith noted in her diary; Morton had mentioned it. Of course, Lavino too had details, and it was an obvious theme for diplomatic table talk.[83]) But though Morton brought Lavino to lunch, Edith did not ask him to her dinner—a rare occasion when Morton's wish to impress a superior overrode his social tact and a rare if not unique occasion when Edith denied an express wish of his. For by now she was in love.

Morton Fullerton pursued Edith Wharton, but Edith cleared the path and beckoned him on. She planned the meetings; the devices for secrecy were hers, communicated by letter, postcard, and *pneu*. Her "M.F. took me" or "I went with M.F." usually means that he accepted an invitation from her. ("I must find someone to go with me." "We might go." "Don't feel you must—") To guard against disappointment she would back an invitation with an ancillary invitation that he *must* accept, but if he couldn't there was still a default rendezvous; this tended to be for a Saturday, Morton's free day. (The *Times* had no Sunday edition.)

He brought other friends to Edith's: his classmate Charles Loeser;[84] Victor Bérard,[85] whose concept of sociohistorical geography he profoundly admired; and John Walter of the *Times* and his wife.[86]

Camille came through with Mireille on her way to Trieste and, "still dazed and stunned"—by the assassination?—saw Morton for the first time since the divorce. He told her about his "amours with his sister," whose letters he was ignoring. From Fiume she sent love from Mireille and herself and asked to have her wig sent on.

Teddy Wharton left. James came to stay with Edith. When *he* left, she and Morton saw him off, then went to Montmorency, where they made love for the first time; and she, or he, picked a chestnut blossom, countersymbol to witch hazel, which she pressed in her journal. They went to Senlis, to Meudon. "I am mad about you,"[87] she wrote. Late in the evening he would write to her, on the cheap square-ruled paper journalists used, in a café—perhaps the Napolitain, among his bantering colleagues.[88]

On her last day in France he called in the afternoon and again in the evening, staying late.[89] She gave him "L'Ame close" to read. He returned it next morning in the boat train[90] and then wrote a letter that he posted to the Mount in Lenox, Massachusetts.

Edith and Katharine in America

In Lenox, Edith received his letter, which can be imagined:

> . . . as you loiter on the terrace. . . . I salute your acceptance of the situation. Learn to go masqued. Your work will be the deeper for your having known love. Bon retour à Lenox, Madame et chère camarade.[91]

While Katharine prepared to cross the Atlantic, Edith followed the papers for mail-ship arrivals. Ships brought three letters, which she read with eagerness—and trepidation and fortitude, reminding Morton in hers of things he had said earlier: that she pulled back, that she must fight for freedom.[92] He spoke of "the camaraderie we invented, *or, it being predestined, we discovered.*"[93]

Her "Line-a-Day" went nearly blank. Her companion was a husband confined to the society of a wife who wished him away.

Might his sister be near Lenox before sailing?[94] she asked Morton, who'd said that Katharine was coming to Europe, though not, naturally, that she intended to confront a peccant fiancé.

Naturally. Yet Katharine's engagement was not quite secret. She must have wished it were. She had grown up hearing the adults on the subject of Will's loves, from girls-next-door through his exotic landlady and exotic wife. Now *she* was exposed to Mamma's terrible speculations. ("What if Will 'chucked' *you?*"[95]) She would have welcomed the privacy Edith had in the many rooms and the arbors, gardens, and terrasses of the Mount and in the staff whose presence debarred emotional expression. (The Fullertons had one "help," Annie.)

When Morton wrote that he would not come till autumn and didn't know where he'd be next winter, when she was planning to be in Paris, Edith told him desperately not to write again. She must face the fact that it was over.[96]

Five ships had failed to bring letters when she wrote next. He hadn't even answered a letter she'd sent from her ship! She wrote with no "hidden reproach," only "tenderness and understanding."[97]

After three weeks she sent a cable.

He wrote. He liked her to be "joyous." He hoped that by autumn he could tell her his worries were over.

Edith begged his pardon for having cabled.[98]

Promotion

At the *Times*, in July 1908, routine.

In early August, suddenly and unexpectedly, Lavino died.

So, was it *now, at last,* that Morton—?

John Walter took over during an interregnum that ended with the appointment of George Saunders of Berlin as correspondent.

Morton received another cable from Edith.

He did not reply.

He received a letter. Could her friend and lover, *Henry's* friend, drop the friend, drop the friendship and treat their love as a *passade?* She would not write again unless she heard from him.[99]

He did not answer.

At the *Times*, Saunders, the new Chief Correspondent, told Bell he would like to keep Fullerton on, as first assistant:

The continuity of the work could hardly be kept up without him and, though both his judgment and his style leave something to be desired, he knows his Paris. Could you possibly arrange to give him £50?[100]

The salary was raised to £45. But Saunders's opinion of his First Assistant altered. He could not for one moment "trust his judgment in political matters—useful and, indeed, indispensable as he is in a variety of ways." In the margin before "indispensable," Saunders added: "almost."[101]

"I rack my brain; I gnash my teeth; I don't pretend to understand or to imagine," James wrote when he learned that Edith was afraid that Morton had deliberately dropped her.

> I am still moved to say "Don't conclude!" . . . Anything is more credible—conceivable—than a mere inhuman *plan*. A great trouble, an infinite worry or a situation of the last anxiety or uncertainty are conceivable. . . . Only sit tight yourself *and go through the movements of life*. That keeps up our connection with life—I mean of the immediate and apparent life; behind which, all the while, the deeper and darker and the unapparent, in which things *really* happen to us, learns, under that hygiene, to stay in its place. Let it get out of its place and it swamps the scene; besides which its place, God knows, is enough for it! Live it all through . . . but live it ever so quietly; and—*je maintiens mon dire*—waitingly! I have had but that one letter, of weeks ago—and there are *kinds* of news I can't ask for.[102]

The passage on the unapparent life stands out nobly in a letter otherwise not to be taken at face value, James's brain-racking hyperbole being due to his discomfort in prevaricating. He knew that Morton *had* "an infinite worry." But he saw that Edith didn't know about the blackmail, and he "hadn't the right," he told her later, to be more definite.[103]

At the *Times,* September. Explaining an office fire, Morton told Bell that until the staff settled in under Saunders they could not know what was expected of them. "I shall be glad" (stiffly) "to hear that you have shown this letter to Lord Northcliffe."[104]

There was a new régime in London also. Northcliffe had bought papers, built mass circulations, and become chief proprietor of the *Times*. Morton saw him as the power to be courted. But Northcliffe had "got a wrong impression" from a brief talk with him in Paris.[105]

The Second Congregational Church and the parsonage, Palmer, Massachusetts, 1876.
Courtesy of Mrs. Jane Golas, Palmer, Massachusetts.

The Rev. Bradford Morton Fullerton.
*Courtesy of Mrs. Jane Golas, Palmer,
Massachusetts.*

The O.K. Club at Harvard, 1886. At the front, left and right, Fullerton and Herbert Lyman. In the row behind them, seated, third from the left, Alanson Houghton; second from the right, George Santayana. *Courtesy of the Harvard University Archives.*

Fullerton at twenty, a Harvard senior. *Courtesy of the Harvard University Archives.*

THE

BLANCHE ROOSEVELT

ENGLISH OPERA COMPANY,
IN
"The Masque of Pandora."

THE POEM BY
HENRY W. LONGFELLOW.

MUSIC BY
ALFRED CELLIER.

Blanche Roosevelt, 1881. *Courtesy of the Theodore Roosevelt Collection, Harvard College Library.*

Henri Opper von Blowitz. *Courtesy of Times Newspapers Ltd.*

Ixo (1). *Civico Museo Teatrale "Carlo Schmidi,"* Civici Musei di Storia ed Arte, Trieste.

La Jeunesse de Louis XIV.

Adèle. From *Le Charivari*,
9 January 1879.

Ixo (2). *Civico Museo
Teatrale "Carlo Schmidi,"*
Civici Musei di Storia ed Arte,
Trieste.

View of 40 *bis* Rue Fabert.
Author's collection.

View from 40 *bis* Rue Fabert across the Esplanade de Invalides to the Faubourg Saint-Germain. *Author's collection.*

Edith Wharton, 1907. *Courtesy Lilly Library, Indiana University, Bloomington, IN.*

Henry James as painted by Jacques-Emile Blanche in Paris, spring 1908. *National Portrait Gallery, Smithsonian Institution; Bequest of Mrs. Katherine Dexter McCormick.*

The Mount, Lenox, Massachusetts, ca. 1905–1907. *Courtesy of the Lenox Library Association, Lenox, Massachusetts.*

The Fullertons' house in Brockton, Massachusetts. *Author's collection.*

Katharine Fullerton in her mid-twenties, in a play at Bryn Mawr. *Photo courtesy of the Bryn Mawr College Archives.*

C. Moberly Bell, Manager of the *Times*, London. *Courtesy of Times Newspapers Ltd.*

Mireille Chabbert with Paul Andrieux. *Author's collection.*

Fullerton, ca. 1909. *Courtesy of the Beinecke Rare Book and Manuscript Library, Yale University.*

Seated woman, with dog. Companion photograph to the one of Fullerton, seated. The inscription reads: "Mistress charges me to give you a big kiss. Your doggie, Charley." Though the handwriting is somewhat uncharacteristic, and though it seems strange to have given her lover so forbidding a likeness, the woman must be Edith Wharton. *Harry Ransom Humanities Research Center, The University of Texas at Austin.*

Mme d'Esprévint, 1913. *Author's collection.*

The Palais-Royal Theater. *Author's collection.*

The beginning of a letter from Morton Fullerton to J. L. Garvin. *Harry Ransom Humanities Research Center, The University of Texas at Austin.*

The village of Saint-Rémy, Haute Saône. *Author's collection.*

* * *

Katharine was in England. James gave her lunch at Lamb House (putting her up overnight, as an unchaperoned young lady, at an inn). He had met her at Bryn Mawr and thought her

> so intelligent that I almost thought of her as unhappy—but perhaps it was only that she *ought,* ideally, to have been. . . . I found in her great personal charm and tried to make out to myself better than I perhaps did what was becoming there of her beautiful and capable youth.[106]

They both knew about the blackmail. Morton had showed Katharine James's bracing letters, and who but she can have written the devoted letter he showed James?[107] But James can't have read any of the ones *we* have seen, passionate and marked "*Destroy,*" without stupefaction; did Morton send selected pages, or were there less ardent letters? In any case, Katharine could not have discussed Morton's problems without betraying that she now really was, as James had said she "ought, ideally, to have been," unhappy.

At the *Times,* Saunders rented space over the office for a wire service, leaving a "charmingly furnished" flat that an assistant might have free or as good as free. But Fullerton, he told Number 7, "seems wedded to his bachelor apartments near the Invalides."[108]

A chance to leave Mirecourt! Did she insist that he stay till he paid in full? Or did he think he was better off with her (he was presumably breakfasted, house-kept, and valeted) than he would be living over the shop?

Late in the year, Edith arrived in England. She had no private talk with James (who told Walter Berry that she'd been having, "after a wild, extravagant, desperate, detached fashion, the Time of her Life").[109] In December, Katharine left England for France, and "Dear Mr. Fullerton" received a letter from Edith saying that she would be in Paris for one day and asking him to return her letters, if any survived, to her brother's Paris address by registered post.[110]

He replied: "The letters survive, and everything survives."[111]

Six words were enough to atone for five months' disregard.

A Party of Pleasure

At the *Times*. Morton had not "partially" resigned in 1907 or 1908. Early in January 1909 he told Saunders he would take home leave that summer.[112]

He wrote to Edith (they had not yet met). A M. Soulié would like to read a play to her. Bring him, she replied; could Howard Sturgis (a house-guest) be there? But it might be less solemn if Soulié and she met before the reading; why not bring him to lunch first? Morton could let her know about Howard at lunch.[113]

In this typical contingency planning, Edith probably thought it would be less "solemn" for Morton and herself to meet with others present before the fraught tête-à-tête that was bound to come.

Morton had been worn out? James asked her a few days later. He had been sure there was a reason for that silence but hadn't been free to speak. "Glad am I that we 'care' for him, you and I; for verily I think I do as much as you, and that you do as much as I. We can help him—we even can't *not*."[114]

James knew that Edith had been hurt. But Edith, reticent to begin with, could not have "told all" without a pert assumption that he would sympathize. His letters do not suggest that she put such a strain on their friendship. In "we 'care'" he took up a word of *hers* that let him suppose that she too felt deep affection, only, for Morton: his repression of the erotic in his own "caring" making it the easier so to suppose. He sent Teddy "best love and a kiss—even two—inert lump of a friend as he may be moved to pronounce me."[115]

Edith and Morton did not return at once to their old footing. The quaint eccentric Howard Sturgis was there. Teddy came. Carl Snyder, a visitor at Lenox last summer, arrived. Morton went to Tours to see Katharine and visit the d'Aulbys.

Katharine admired Count d'Aulby: a thinker versed in Eastern spirituality, a musician composing an exoteric trilogy and an esoteric tetralogy.[116] He and his wife, Francesca, whom Morton had met years ago, had four children and led a pleasant provincial life of tennis, garden parties, and dinner parties for officers of the local garrison. Francesca was writing letters and poems to Morton as Edith again settled at 58 Rue de Varenne.

At the *Times*, February 1909: routine.

In Katharine's poem "Gemma to Beatrice," Dante's wife speaks for marriage and children as against the mystic love symbolized by Beatrice. Morton had Katharine copy the poem for Edith, who praised it, invited her to Paris overnight,[117] and took her, Morton, and Carl Snyder out for the evening. By now Edith was again writing Morton imprudent letters; he dropped one in her car that Snyder "picked up" and looked at "curiously" before handing it to her rather than Katharine.[118]

It calls for a pen-and-ink illustration by Charles Dana Gibson: Edith and Katharine side by side in the motor, Snyder on a jump seat, Morton in back view descending, donning his top hat, an envelope on the floor behind him. With the caption "Double Deceit."

Morton told Edith he worried about his sister's religious bent. By suggesting that she was austerely devout he could elicit Edith's opinion of her and regale himself in private.

Ignoring the whole tenor of "Gemma," Edith firmly disposed of his spurious concern. Where James had been struck by Katharine's capacity for loving, it didn't take Edith an hour to see that a religious life was "the inevitable solution, or outcome," for her.[119]

There are gossamer hints that Katharine intuited something between Will and Edith. Edith had not a glimmer of what Katharine felt; Edith was not much interested in Katharine. ("To a nunnery, go!")

Paralysis

Morton had progressed from excuses for neglect to reproaching Edith for holding back. It was agreed that they would again meet as lovers. He would let her know by Monday when and where.

He wrote letting her know—and urged her to *consider*. To *reflect*. His letter reached her on Monday, February 22, and the rendezvous he set was for that very day.

She had been "*paralyzed*," she wrote on Tuesday, "by not getting your note till 11, knowing it must have been written, and having the conviction that it must have got into the wrong hands, yet being unable to find out." Morton received her letter the same day and wrote on it: "February 23 after!!!"

!!! stood for a disaster that had left Edith shattered. In this first meeting after months of emotional turmoil and sexual deprivation, its time and place uncertain till the last moment, she must have been too tense to satisfy or be satisfied. Morton said she was "impossible," and she accepted his verdict. Think of her as the "old friend"[120] of last year, she wrote dismally.

Weeks later she would again recall his "impossible" and again say that his "consider" had "paralyzed" her.[121]

What she did almost immediately was to take Teddy for a drive to the Midi, saying that the change of air might do him good. She herself was gasping for air.

Teddy had been married to Edith for twenty-five years; he was not insensitive to her moods. Last summer at the Mount she had been in no state to fake affection, and now, miserable after ruining what she had hoped would be a renewal of joy . . .

She had married in primal ignorance. ("She told me," says Mme de Divonne, "that at I think nineteen a fiancé, before M. Wharton, kissed her on the forehead and she was afraid that she would have a child!") *SWF good family accomplished likes travel dogs riding* sought SWM, failing to add: *intelligent, makes up stories, used to own way, wants Love.*

Teddy admired the girl advertised, wanted to please her, and, it seems, accepted the inadequacy of such sex as there was, perhaps on the assumption that good women were cold. He may have turned to other women even before he became aware, after false jealousies, that his wife really was in love with someone. Whether he suspected Morton we don't know. After this motor tour, at any rate, he frequented other women with little concern for secrecy.

Edith regarded Teddy's "excitability" as a character flaw he could correct if he tried. She had no wish for a serious talk—what was there to say? What *did* they say to each other? Talking was so hard in a motor that silence wouldn't have signified as they drove through hilly vineyards behind chauffeur and maid, but there were long Lucullan meals and long evenings to get through. Even half-paralyzed, Edith could escape into reading and working. Teddy, depressed, with a family history of mental illness, had no inner fortification as he slowly went insane.

Propositions

At the *Times,* March. Lord Northcliffe was at the Paris Ritz. He thanked Fullerton for sending a copy of *Terres Françaises* and a letter of political interest from Constantinople.[122]

A few weeks after the débâcle of February 22, Morton made Edith a proposition to which she replied within hours:

> On the practical side, as to your particular suggestion, I'm not as stupid as you think. In my case it would not be "the least risk," but possibly the greatest, to follow your plan, even if I could—as assuredly I should—finally overcome my reluctance.[123]

He had put a plan to a self-despising woman who believed it might ruin her reputation but knew she would accede to any course that might satisfy her desire. "I'm not so stupid as you think" is startling in Edith Wharton: surly, even vulgar.

He had evidently proposed the whole night together that she used to sigh for. Impossible in Paris, but he was going to America that summer by way of England; they could go to a London hotel.

Morton was seeing Francesca d'Aulby, seeing the unidentified Doll, and seeing Katharine often enough for Doll to send him her *pneu* in bad French: "As you told me your little sister loves you. Don't break her heart." He also saw Camille.

Camille had been carting Mireille about Europe in a disjointed life of trains, hotels, backstage commotion, late hours, glorious music, and professional vendettas. Around this time, Paul Clemenceau proposed to her, or she to Paul Clemenceau, that he take Mireille, and she made the transfer: informing, if not consulting, Morton, who knew Georges and Albert and possibly Paul, who hadn't yet quarreled with Georges. Georges and

Albert would definitely have been interested. For a childless brother to "take charge" of a little girl was of moment to the whole family.

Was Paul Clemenceau Mireille's father, or was Carlos I? Paul could have been Camille's lover when Mireille was conceived at the turn of the century. But we'd want to know why she went to Lisbon pregnant, or with an infant, so soon after, and why Paul took the child so *long* after. Whereas we know that she was well established in Lisbon when Morton arrived there in 1903, that her claim to have been Carlos's mistress is credible, and that her giving Mireille to Paul around this time jibes with Carlos's assassination in 1908. A more recent affair with Paul might explain his taking another man's child as a favor to her and, more important, because he and his wife wanted a pet.

Mireille couldn't have remembered "Papa" from Lisbon or Madrid. What idea she had of Morton from things Camille said, or from seeing him at this crisis in her life, is unknowable. Abandonment by her mother left her silent. She would have been a subject for James: a child out of its depth in an adult situation, like the little boy in "The Pupil" who has "a whole range of refinement and perception . . . begotten by wandering about Europe at the tail of his migratory tribe" and "a sharp spice of stoicism . . . which produced the impression of pluck." But James may never have known that Morton had a stepchild.

Persuasion

Edith's sullen opposition had mellowed. She sent Morton a poem. "When you read 'Ogrin' aloud," she wrote, "are you glad that it was written for you, and *by you?*"[124] The idea of his reading it aloud (to himself?) may seem odd, but "Ogrin" was an apologia written for him, as "Gemma" was Katharine's, and she was designing a protocol. Morton praised the poem when they met, but, talking with what she thought unusual sincerity, said there must be freedom "in loving and in unloving." Edith said there must also be trustworthiness.

> If I thought that you could continue to talk to me and to *be* with me as you were this afternoon, while you had, at the same time . . . even à fleur d'épiderme [for a heart-beat], the same attitude to anyone else, I should think you had failed in the loyalty due to a love like mine.

Edith's concept was high-flown enough for a Louis-Quatorze *pré-cieuse*. She and Morton agreed that she loved more than he did. She therefore allowed him to take his "cardiac troubles" elsewhere on condition that he and she become "good comrades" again.[125] Her magnanimity entitled her to a unique place in his life; also appointed him the one who would impose carnal relations, which *she* would gladly forgo so as not to impinge on his freedom. She feared the inevitable change in *him* only because of the sorrow he would feel for her. She would turn her love and suffering "into beauty."[126] His share in the experience made him co-creator of her poetry.

A reader ignorant of the biographical setting might not sense, in the ripe relaxed "beauty" thus created, passion so deep on Edith's part that Morton's known record dissolved in a rarefied superlove, exacting veneration from both alike, in which normal human resentment could not thrive. She agreed to his proposal of a night in London. James was expecting the Whartons after Easter, Morton later.[127] Edith informed him that Teddy had gone home for a cure and that she would convey America-bound Morton as far as London.

The previous summer, James had not realized the intensity of Edith's anguish at Morton's silence. Since hearing from her that the silence had been due to fatigue, he'd assumed that all was well. Now he gathered that all had *not* been well but, not for a moment thinking of Morton, inferred that she feared Teddy's illness might be "cerebral"—which, he told Gaillard Lapsley, "is the first 'cross' I really imagine that she has had to bear."[128]

An Edict and a Commission

At the *Times,* a thunderbolt. Bell to Fullerton:

> I am told that in the National Review for May there is an article by you which deals very fully with the French political situation created by the strikes.

(In "The Crisis of the State in France" Morton argued that a Napoleonic bureaucracy thwarted representative government.)

> I think you must know that it is wholly contrary to our rules that anyone in the employment of The Times should write to any other serial publication without our permission. . . . I shall be glad to hear what you have to say.[129]

Fullerton to Bell: Colleagues of every rank wrote for magazines. His chiefs had told him he was free to do so. Now, should an essay on Henry James, soon to appear, have been submitted to Bell?[130]

Bell to Fullerton, 6 May:

... we certainly do not allow any junior correspondent to write on subjects connected with the Country in which he is serving, and if I had heard ... the practice would have been stopped earlier. At all events it must stop now, and no article on any subject whatever must appear in any review, English, American, or Foreign written by you or with your name.[131]

Blowitz, Chirol, Lavino, and Saunders had known about Morton's articles, which were mostly nonpolitical. As Lavino said, he had "plenty of literary connections."[132] He presented French writers to TLS readers in perceptive and erudite reviews. (He might have made a good professor of English at Harvard, his early ambition.) Even the cross-grained Bell respected his "thorough zeal for literature" (though: "If you will let me say so I think you are a little too inclined to manufacture a style of your own and I think it creates in many people a prejudice against you and the very solid work which is wrapt up in it").[133]

Thanks to those anonymous Times reviews (their authorship known to writers only by word of mouth), to his magazine articles in English, and to the French articles (some of which became Terres Françaises), Morton was—amazing for a foreigner—entering Les Quarante Cinq:[134] forty-five (to the Académie's forty) intellectuals and artists. Henri Bernstein, Tristan Bernard, Paul Dukas, Alfred Cortot. Many of them were friends, some of them schoolmates, some "passionate friends" of Proust: Reynaldo Hahn, Fernand Gregh, Léon Blum, Robert de Flers, Georges de Lauris, Gabriel de la Rochefoucauld. Political right and left were represented by Abel Bonnard and Léon Blum, the center by André Tardieu.

In this galaxy, if he could no longer publish under his own name, Morton risked being seen as a hack.

He would also lose a significant source of income.

But he capitulated. He withdrew "The Art of Henry James" or had the Quarterly hold it.

Edith Wharton had had a share in the essay, in which he argued that while the fiction even of other great novelists was like "the extraordinarily interesting narratives told by the kinematograph," James transmuted life into art as by "the mysterious process of radio-activity."[135] Bell's edict brought Morton's servitude home to her. A letter from London suggested a way of helping him.

Three men made her plan possible, two of them unknowingly. Francis Marion Crawford, a novelist and travel writer. Joseph Pennell, an illustrator. Frederic Macmillan, the publisher.

Pennell was going to illustrate a Crawford *Paris* for Macmillan, when Crawford died. Pennell supposed he could go on.[136] Oh, said Macmillan, the book fell through now. Though there was no contract, murmured Pennell . . . Macmillan proposed the book to Mrs. Wharton, who asked if he had thought of Mr. Morton Fullerton, whose *Terres Françaises* had been called "the best 'appreciation' of French scenery and history ever written by a foreigner."[137] Macmillan at once asked Morton if he would like to do a book on Paris, in his own way at his own time, with an advance on royalty of, say, £400?[138]

On the day Macmillan's letter reached Paris, Edith and Morton were driving from the Channel coast to London, where they were to dine with James.

"Terminus"

"Dine with Morton Fullerton and E.W. Charing Cross Hotel," June 4, James reminded himself.[139]

Railway hotels offered grand menus, good wine lists, mediocre cuisine, and a heavy dullness that suited E.W.'s wishes. No one must think that she and Morton were together. James's company was a safeguard against speculation by other people dining in the restaurant, but James too must be deceived. She and Morton would, in Donne's crabbed phrase, have "shadow'd with negligence their most respects," knowing that, while accidental discovery of their plan would discomfit James terribly, a hint by either of them would revulse him as a moral solecism.

If, for all her savoir-faire, Edith had to strain for easy conversation, a recent event may have helped. Meredith had died. James had gone to a memorial service; with mixed views of the work, he loved the man. Edith had seen the two together and "their old deep regard,"[140] while Morton of course ranked Meredith next to Shakespeare. The three friends at table can hardly *not* have talked about Meredith and indulged in mordant gossip about people who had been at the Abbey.

* * *

The "long secret night" that followed James's departure was relived by
E.W. in "Terminus" in the drowsy and voluptuous cadences of gratified desire: desire gratified in a grimy room to the music of steam locomotives.
Morton said later that she "boxed the compass of all the shades of temperament of which womankind is capable. . . . She was fearless, reckless even
in her frank response. . . . "[141] In the morning, Edith thought of other, unknown women waking beside a lover before journeying on to another des-
tination, alone. When she gave "Terminus" to M.F., he appended a note:

> [Poem written by E.W. during my month in America, and commemorating,
> in the inspiration of Goethe's *Roman Elegies,* the night which we spent at
> Charing Cross Hotel, before I sailed from Southampton. I took We had
> motored from Paris to Boulogne, & crossed to Folkestone where we passed
> the night. On the morrow we went up to London, and were met at dinner
> by Henry James. I took apartment No. 92 in which I left her alone the next
> day at 10 with only time to have sent to her room a bunch of roses. That
> evening at sea I received the accompanying telegram: M.F. Aug. 1909.][142]

(Actually, James "saw W.M.F. off to N.Y. at Waterloo [Station] 10
a.m."[143] Morton had forgotten the hour when he made his note. "I had
left her in the early morning," he wrote years later, "and as I lingered she
took up her pen to write."[144])

It must be said that, for a clandestine evening and night, the events of
June 4–5, 1909, are remarkably well documented.

"Terminus" is the poem Hugh Fullerton thought he had destroyed
after Morton's death because it would harm Mrs. Wharton's name. He
found that he still had it, and ("times change!") we met so that I could
authenticate the handwriting as a preliminary to purchase by Yale. As
late as the 1950s people could think that a sensuous though not licen-
tious poem would hurt a posthumous reputation. No wonder that the living Edith wanted no one to guess at her liaison.

"*Tu prétends que James ne savait pas. But what makes you think he
didn't know?*"
"*His character, and Edith's. His messages to Teddy.*"

James knew that Edith was mismated, but, until Teddy fell apart, took
pains not to slight him. *After* the "Terminus" night, as before, he ad-

dressed Edith as a married woman whose husband's happiness mattered to her. The hugs and "tender benedictions"[145] he sent Teddy were exaggerated, but not duplicitous; not messages he would have asked a self-declared faithless wife to deliver to a husband.

"And if he had known, would Edith have written: 'Wonderful was the long secret night you gave me, my lover'?"

Small Expectations

Morton's "month in America" was about five weeks' absence from Europe with about two weeks at home. On the voyage west, as Europe receded, family problems loomed.

His parents had not seen him since before Katharine revealed the engagement. She had been abroad since last summer. For a year and a half they had worried. Now at last they could interrogate Will. *What in the world was said?* Did he deny having led Katharine on? Later Bradford would speak of her "imagination," but Julia would say she had papers that Will wouldn't want Mr. Gerould to see.

The opacity of those two weeks in Brockton is maddening.

While he was overseas, Edith stayed in England, seeing people. She drove James about. They visited friends, dined with friends, did a theater. Macmillan was surprised at not having heard from Morton; she explained that Morton had left France before the "Paris" offer could have arrived.[146] She wrote "Terminus."

At Cherbourg, where his ship called on the return passage, and at Plymouth, where it docked, Morton found messages. Edith would be near Folkestone with the motor. Wire her his dates. She'd stayed on in case he would cross with her. Her visit to Rye might tire James; she'd given it up.[147] She sent a letter to the steamship office, for delivery when the boat train arrived, to explain that yesterday's note might have made him think she meant to fill his time. She'd meant only to make it clear that she had no plans.[148]

On Saturday, July 10, Morton wrote that he would stop over at the Charing Cross Hotel before going to Rye on Monday.

Was he in 92? (their suite last month) Edith asked brightly when she got his note. Henry urged her to come to Rye on Monday for dinner and

the night or take him and Morton to Folkestone for the night, but she felt
he'd rather have Morton alone. She might go just for tea; if she did go for
the night, she'd efface herself.[149] The letter ends; at that point she may
have heard from James.

Edith pushed away the chilling knowledge that if Morton longed to
see her he would have asked her to meet him in London. She knew it was
a grief to James that Morton had come to Rye only once before and that
having Morton *and* her would not be the same as having Morton to himself. She allowed herself to be obtuse.

In town, Morton saw Macmillan and accepted an offer of £500 (up
from £400) tentatively, stressing that he could consider it only because
there was no time limit.[150] He reached Lamb House before dinner and
was standing at the hearth with James when Edith arrived and, "dead of
joy,"[151] saw him at last, after all those weeks.

Whatever her self-effacement (a notion the other two might have
smiled at), it was as a trio that they discussed Morton's "Paris" project
and also his durance vile in the Rue Fabert, though Edith was told nothing specific about the blackmail—and, surely, neither she nor James
about his refusal of a virtually rent-free flat.

After a two-day tour (Chichester, Arundel Castle, Eastbourne, Pet-
worth, Boshan, Brighton) and another night in Rye, they lunched in Canterbury.[152] James, "red, congested and tired,"[153] took a train home. Edith
and Morton went on to Folkestone to cross, but a storm kept them, the
motor, the driver, and Edith's maid on shore that night of July 15, and
the next.[154]

On the morning of the 17th, Edith sent a note to Morton's room. He
should have his luggage ready for the omnibus, she had ordered a taxi,
she would be in the reading room. An executive memo, ending: she was
happy, was he?[155]

In Paris, Edith gave it out that her return was delayed because, with
her "usual docility," she had obeyed a wire from James saying he wished
to be taken on a motor tour and that she had left England as soon as she
dropped him at Canterbury.[156]

He had obeyed Mrs. Wharton's "unappeasable summons" to a tour,
James told Howard Sturgis, and had separated from "her" at Canterbury.[157]

Morton told Macmillan that "James and I" had spent several days in the south of England.[158]

Covert Aid, 1: An Advance

Edith's seven days, first with Morton and James, then with Morton only, opened a month of perfect happiness which began when she rejoined Morton at Lamb House and lasted till well after her return to Paris.[159] She did not date her happiness from the "Terminus" night that had been followed by weeks of hanging about England thinking how she could contrive to travel back to Paris with him.

When she hinted at the possibility that she might leave Teddy, Morton let her know that he was against the idea. Anyway, she said later, she probably wouldn't have done it.[160]

During the enforced stormy wait on shore, and on the way to Paris, and in Paris, Morton told Edith that a future £500 would not help now, while writing "Paris" would only add to his heavy load. When he read the letter from Macmillan that had been waiting for him, he hesitated.

Edith dismissed his indecisiveness firmly, [161] but not because she was unsympathetic. A plan had been forming in her mind. She asked James to ask Macmillan to pay £100 down should Morton ask for it. She would supply the money. Morton would think it came from Macmillan; Macmillan, that it came from James.[162]

Before even answering Edith, James wrote to Macmillan: His friend Fullerton supported an ailing father. To do "Paris," he might have to ask for a down payment on the advance. If he did, would Macmillan accept James's check for £100 and send it as from the firm, "independently of anything you yourselves send him"? If he proposed the money himself, Fullerton might refuse it.[163]

That done, James told Edith of his joy in her idea and promised to "breathe, nor write, no shadow of a word" to Morton. He hoped the sum to be paid "the accursed woman" wasn't very great or the interest on it "anything like as burdensome" as it had been.[164]

("Interest"—on *ransom?* So Morton was now picturing Adèle's demands as something other than plain blackmail to his friends, as he had all along to his parents.)

Macmillan preferred a genuine payment, if secured, to subterfuge. He told James not to send a check, but would he be surety for £100 if the book wasn't written?[165]—and, not waiting for an answer, offered £100 down of the agreed £500 to Morton, [166] who replied that he was "keen" to do "Paris." The £100 would "be very acceptable: the documentation of my subject is somewhat expensive."[167]

Macmillan's making the offer before James assented was not rash (if James would donate, he would guarantee); it did cause confusion. Learning that the firm had, unasked by Morton, offered £100, James thought they offered it on their own and would send £100 more if requested. Should "Paris" not be produced, he wrote, they must call on him for £100. "But I greatly *believe* in the book."[168]

Morton's acceptance was written from the Hotel Vouillemont. He had left Mirecourt that very day, August 2, paying her without waiting for the formal agreement[169] and check[170] that duly followed.

Within hours, Edith described a change in Morton which James said showed how he had been "lost to himself and lost to *us.*" Had "she" surrendered "the papers, letters, scraps of writing" with "references to people etc., which he mentioned to me, originally, that, as they were private things all, she threatened to make God knows what injurious and public use of?"

"People etc." was kept vague, since Edith knew no details. But James inferred that the change in Morton meant that he *had* got them back, which must mean "the real finishing of the affair."[171]

Covert Aid, 2: A Magnificent Combination

The affair was *not* finished. Morton still needed money. In her letter describing the change in him, Edith had also set forth a new idea which, after asking about the papers, James hailed gladly:

> As for your proposition of lending him the sum you mention, through me
> (if he can't manage to arrange it otherwise), I can only accede to the beautiful, the noble beneficence of this on your part . . . even though it puts *me,*
> poor impecunious and helpless me, in the ridiculous nominal position of a
> lender of de fortes sommes! . . . I will play my mechanical part in your magnificent combination with absolute piety, fidelity, and punctuality.

This "combination," scheme, was separate from the "Paris" plot. Again money would go to Morton ostensibly from James but really from Edith, but as a loan. Edith would get Morton to say she could tell James he would accept a loan if James offered one.

Morton's *letting* her do it, James wrote, would seem almost as beautiful as her doing it.[172] When Edith wrote that Morton *would* accept, James said he was sending "by this post" a letter in which he'd told Morton he would "give as much pleasure by accepting" the offer as by "any act" of his life.

> Of course he will *interpret*—my overture—but, frankly, I venture to hope and believe that he will, after the first step back, see the thing in a *light*—in the light in which it will have been presented. And if he does that I shall rejoice, and I am sure you deeply will. For it will mean the release of his mind, his spirit, and his beautiful intelligence from a long bondage. . . . What a harsh task master is the Times!

James supposed that "the Car" created a breeze for Edith in the stifling Paris heat. "But Teddy has my continued and intimate commiseration. He is passing a terribly *mauvais moment.*"[173]

Did Morton "interpret?" He was ignorant of his friends' part in the "Paris" plan, beyond knowing that Edith had suggested him to Macmillan. The loan was different. He knew James had no money. Did he pretend not to "interpret," and thank James only? Did he face James and Edith with their ruse but decide, as James hoped, that it would be nobler to accept than to refuse? Or did he refuse?

The rather surprising answer comes indirectly. Months later, Edith begged Morton to go motoring with her and let her pay "even if you scorn and spurn my scheme for your complete emancipation."[174]

It was without new funds, then, that Morton had his subsequent meetings with Mirecourt.

Pacts

He had left her with strings attached. He had not fully paid up, and, though Edith had taken in his books, Adèle still had his furniture and pictures. But when he informed Edith, in October, that he was going to

Rueil on Saturday, she told him indignantly not to let "her" order him about, but to meet "her" at his convenience, in the Rue Fabert. And if he did go to see a woman he thought "half-mad, or at any rate dangerous," he might take a man as witness. A "business footing" was justifiable with "her."[175]

But in all probability Mme Mirecourt appointed Rueil precisely because, under the Napoleonic Code, she had to have a man to act for her, and in Rueil, Henri-Napoléon Saint-Laurent, *rentier,* could help in a family matter involving apparently a fair sum of money.

Moreover, it was *she* who wanted a "business footing." A comment by James on "Morton's *pacte* with his fiend"[176] was not, as to the pact, figurative. Morton signed an agreement framed by the Maître Faribault who later drew Adèle's will. Morton, the *maître,* Saint-Laurent, and Adèle met in the *cabinet* where the porphyry clock still ticks that ticked through their negotiations.

Morton had signed the pact when Edith, knowing his old Harvard link with Bernard Berenson, had him invited to a luncheon given by Henry Adams so that he and Berenson could get to know each other. Afterwards "BB" told Edith he'd forgotten how nice Fullerton was. Morton did not pursue the reacquaintance. Berenson, his junior, had a villa in Italy and a name as an authority on art, while *he* was living in a hotel room, without his books, pictures, and comforts.

Moreover, his intimacy with Edith was becoming a constraint. In meeting him on a Saturday, Adèle encroached on time Edith thought hers. Sharing Saturdays was a clause in *her*—unwritten—pact with Morton. But a woman who frankly said that all the "blessedness"[177] was on her side had no power to enforce, and Morton had other demands on his day off. ("I am going to telephone you Saturday at 4.15," Francesca d'Aulby wrote from Tours.)[178] He often failed to observe Saturdays, not always giving Edith notice.[179]

She urged him to take a flat. He'd be happier than in a hotel and no longer hold her "responsible" (*sic*) for his leaving the Rue Fabert.[180] She naturally wanted, without saying so, a safe, agreeable place to meet.

Morton too wanted a flat: one with a chatelaine who, like Adèle in the old days, would make home life pleasant, but at the cost of his being unable to take other women there. While he was at the Vouillemont he tested various apartments, giving reasons why Edith could not come to him: e.g., it would scandalize his landlady—who, Edith strangely protested, "ought to be indulgent";[181] had he said the landlady was disreputable? So, they met at hotels, each of which she disliked and refused to go back to.[182]

She did go back to the Vouillemont. It was around a corner from the magnificent Crillon, where she stayed for months waiting to move into a new flat at 53 Rue de Varenne, and where (since her servants were not lodged in her suite) she and Morton also met; she celebrated the suite in a poem.[183] But the proximity operated against freedom on one side, unsuspecting ignorance on the other. When Morton sent word to her hotel that he was too ill to see her, Edith sent to his offering help, was told he wasn't there, and cried out at his not grasping that she wanted *honesty*.[184] Communication was too easy. One Saturday, Morton received a hand-delivered note asking him to return Edith's letters. *Why?* he protested in a hand-delivered reply. He'd hoped to find if she'd be free today. On Sunday he received a *pneu* and rang the Crillon to ask if Mme Wharton could lunch on Monday. She was in the act of writing to explain *why:* Saturday before last he had made love to her, then ignored her for nine days. His message was brought up from the desk. Mollified, she ended her letter by saying she'd send it to him anyway to show that the *pneu* wasn't meant to be unkind.[185]

She alluded to "rivals" with forced nobility or heavy humor.[186] She left cogent statements of grievances incomplete;[187] once she erupted in a visceral rage, the more lowering in that it's incomprehensible what she meant by saying she *remembered the elevator cage* at the *Times* building.[188] Site of some dire occurrence, but what? Blanche Roosevelt had made a scene in the earlier *Times* office. Edith avoided scenes; but had she called there; had Morton, say, embraced her, had she been recognized?

Scandal was always a threat both in fiction and in fact. Edith had created a society reporter with eyes "like tentacles"; even James's self-righteous Henrietta Stackpole "walks in without knocking at the door." Morton's 1890s notebook has

Melodion Credit Foncier had mistress Rosine Michel who played soubrette parts as Andrée. She quarreled with him because he slept with all her friends—

He'd been taking down Adèle's gossip about the artiste-cocotte milieu that had been Mirecourt's.[189] The banker Melodion had a well-born wife and the Legion. His status made the tidbit interesting to a reporter even on the priggish *Times*.

Shortly after the Rueil pact was signed, the end of October, Rosa de Fitz-James told Morton she'd heard that Mme Wharton's separation from her husband was reported in New York. She begged him to keep the calumny from their friend.[190] Berry was the "other man" in rumor, but rumor might easily be set on the right track. Indeed, Rosa would not have sent Morton the warning unless she knew him to be, at the very least, Edith's intimate friend. If she guessed the truth, she was discreet. No one else—except Teddy?—did during Edith's lifetime.

Danger notwithstanding, Edith *had* to see Morton. She became less prudent, meeting him in hotels against her better judgment. She no longer appealed to preconditions; she took what she could get.

Teddy came, announced misconduct with women and misuse of Edith's money, and left. In however bumbling and inarticulate a way, he had to make his resentment known. What was said on either side on the score of infidelity isn't recorded, but Edith disclosed Teddy's *financial* depredations to James, arousing in James, who was ill, shocked helpless sympathy and a certainty that Morton "must have devotedly rallied."[191]

He had not. That year, Edith wrote on the last day of 1909, her "Ever Dearest" had given her "some divine hours" she wanted to remember "alone tonight."[192] A loving letter, and ambiguous. She'd remember them in solitude; she'd remember them, only, of a year of mostly not divine hours. That December, she said later, his treatment of her had worsened.[193] And before that there had been November, October—

Morton's response to her reasonings, reproaches, and pleas was delphic: "I will be all you have the right to expect."[194]

The Year 1910

Lord Northcliffe was at the Ritz again and "stole" Edith's first Saturday in her new flat.[195] Morton kept it open in hope of seeing him, more anxious than ever to be known to the proprietor as an astute political analyst. He no longer tried to win Saunders's good opinion; Saunders was a churl. (Edith called on Mrs. Saunders, but the attention did not melt the correspondent.)[196] In a winter of calamitous floods, "I'm sorry for us both," Morton told Edith, who refused to be pitied. She had *him*.[197]

* * *

At the *Times*. If Morton met Northcliffe, it did him no good.

He received Katharine's plea for one word before she answered Gordon Gerould's proposal. A few weeks later he told her that she could count on his coming home that summer and that he had troubles at work. He received her cable "COURAGE DEAREST LOVE."

He received his father's harassed report: Mr. Gerould wanted to marry Katharine before Will came home and disrespectfully spoke of him not as "Mr. Fullerton" but as "Morton," though they had never met; and Katharine had things Will wouldn't want Mr. Gerould to see. It was an unimaginable experience. "Come this summer and help us through it," Julia wrote at Bradford's intense dictation, in the only appeal from Will's parents on record, underlining: "*I am very anxious to hear about your affairs—your connection with the Times, etc.*"[198]

Katharine knew that they were cold-shouldering a loving, highly eligible suitor because of his antagonism to Will, who, far from freeing her, wanted her to endure another four months of suspense.

At the *Times:* Morton took some sick leave. He was always prone to colds, bilious attacks, and gallstones.

One project that eked out his salary, a preface to the old Smollett translation of *Gil Blas,* was enjoyable. The picaresque Gil was not a con man who'd do anything at all for gain, and his creator, Alain LeSage, was "amusedly aware that the only absolute truth is that all things are relative."[199] But Morton was run down and tired.[200] He had given Edith one of his rare books, seemingly as a peace offering after a quarrel, and been told first, proudly, that she didn't want it,[201] then that she had sold it for him because she was worried about his health.[202] Relieved that he wasn't angry, she assured him that she didn't "'do good by stealth' habitually!"[203]

In point of fact, attempting stealthy good was rather a habit of Edith Wharton's. She tried to help James, with uneven success, as well as trying to help Morton via the benign Macmillan scam and the failed "Combination." But from now on her efforts for Morton were *en clair.* When he asked if she didn't resent the prospect of a life bounded by Teddy's needs, she replied that only hope of helping *him* kept her going and begged him to accept a loan and quit the *Times;* if he needed more than a year to find work, take *two.* He refused.[204]

* * *

Francesca wrote from Tours that Tom Meteyard, in Rye, said that Henry James was "quite feeble and *almost* losing his mind."[205] James *was* ill, but he took comfort in Morton's "beautiful and tender and admirable letters"; and when Edith went over to see him Morton wrote to her, too, his first letter prompting a reply with a buoyant mention of Charing Cross and a joke about a Mrs. Paine.[206] From Folkestone, near Rye, where she was tending Teddy, also ill, Edith again begged Morton to accept a loan.[207] He again refused.

"You're cross," he observed when he called on Edith after her return. "No," she wrote next day; but while she was in England he had sent love letters and she'd answered in the same vein. But she had been back for three days now, and he had ignored her:

> . . . I judged you long ago, and I accepted you as you are, admiring all your gifts and your great charm, and seeking only to give you the kind of affection that should help you most, and lay the least claim on you in return. But one cannot have all one's passionate tenderness demanded one day, and ignored the next, without reason or explanation, as it has pleased you to do since your *enigmatic change in December*. . . . [T]he pain within my pain . . . has been the impossibility of knowing what you wanted of me, and what you felt for me—at a time when it seemed natural that, if you had any sincere feeling for me, you should see my need of an equable friendship—I don't say love because that is not made to order!—but the kind of tried tenderness that old friends seek in each other in difficult moments of life.[208]

One week after sending that stately rebuke, Edith commemorated a rendezvous at the Vouillemont in a poem beginning:

> She said to me: "Nay, take my body and eat,
> And give it beauty, breaking it for bread"—

which she dated April 14 and sent to Morton, who wrote on it next day: "E.W. after her visit chez moi. . . ."[209]

He had seen Verlaine as Christ the Man of Sorrows and Dreyfus as Christ crucified. Edith saw *herself* as Christ at the Last Supper: "This is my body, which is given for you, take and eat in remembrance of me." Having sex was holy communion. When Morton left, sated, bread and wine were no longer sacramental; she felt like food cleared from the table.[210]

For Morton, however, the sequels to that visit were the poem and an invitation to a tea for ex-President Theodore Roosevelt, an old friend of Edith's who was in Paris to speak at the Sorbonne.

Henry James and Theodore Roosevelt

Morton admired Roosevelt for having boldly seized Colombian territory when "a great Frenchman, M. Bunau-Varilla, fomented a Revolution at Panama," to prevent construction of a Nicaragua Canal.[211] Edith promised him a quiet talk with TR. He'd better not tell Saunders, lest he play some dirty trick.[212]

Out of respect for the guest of honor, [213] Teddy appeared at the tea. Among the other guests was a recent ambassador to the United States, the scholar J. J. Jusserand (to whom the Ranee had introduced Morton long ago). In ten minutes' private talk, Morton caught Roosevelt's "attention by the remark that the French would have tolerated a speech like his at the Sorbonne from no one else," only to have Jusserand "whisk" him away to an official function.[214]

With or without Bell's permission, "The Art of Henry James" was out. James had told Edith that he'd write to Morton later. The day after the tea, Morton began a letter to his "Dearest of Friends":

> E.W. has sent me on your letter . . . I supplicate you not to think of me as waiting for a letter. I am waiting, we are waiting, solely for the end of this season of depression, which distresses us beyond words. Twenty times a day my imagination brings you out into the light, and that vision of you irradiates the whole field. . . . It seems to me that, however much I should regret not being able to finish this or that dream I should be so happy in the sense of the sublime and beautiful work already done that no such contretemps would trouble my equanimity for long. The chance to rest for a time after the six days of Creation, and to look back with the assurance that I should contemplate nothing that was not good, would be one that I would welcome. That is your position. Take it like a God.
>
> I have little to tell you. The prospect of doing my *Paris* seems remote unless I chuck the *Times* altogether. If I were worthy of the name of man that is what I should do. . . . I think of going to America in the autumn, but how from any point of view to afford it I do not know[.][215]

This, Morton's only extant letter to James, must be given in all its limpness. It can't represent the letters James called "celestial." Morton's mind was not on it. He let it dangle unfinished and, "browsing chez moi," "jotted" some ideas:

Roosevelt had praised men of action to *academics!* But they could take "home truths" from a man who had "justified Frenchmen to themselves [by] reconciling *raison d'état* and rights of man." The French admired a president who was a leader and a teacher:[216] their president, by constitution, could be neither.

Curious about Morton's provocative comment, Roosevelt told Edith to bring him to an embassy reception. Morton intended to go, but while "browsing" changed his mind and asked Edith to hand TR a "Note" instead. She "thought me a fool," he wrote:

> I was sure however I was right in not wishing a second meeting in an Embassy crush, where I should have fumbled with my ideas, and undone the impression made at the Wharton tea. The proof that I had been of a sage Machiavelism came on the morrow, when Mrs. W. sent me the letter herein enclosed, from R.[217]

In the letter, Roosevelt had sent "warm regards" to "an able fellow" with striking ideas.[218]

Edith was irked at what looked like perverse recalcitrance. But Morton knew what he was doing.

He had made a symbolic choice when he abandoned a letter to James to plot strategy for developing his "in" with Roosevelt. James considered Morton's bold leader a "dangerous and ominous jingo,"[219] though at a White House supper he had been struck by his "very attaching personality."[220] Roosevelt, not disliking James when they met, was still a Rough Rider who had called him a "miserable little snob" and shaken a big stick at "the undersized man of letters, who flees his country because he, with his delicate, effeminate sensitiveness, finds the conditions on this side of the water crude and raw" and "cannot play a man's part among men."[221]

In turning to Roosevelt, Morton believed he made himself "worthy of the name of man."

The choice turned his life around. He did not, however, act on it at once. He had spells of nerveless indecision; Edith, whose help he would need, was busy with Teddy; and, as usual, he preferred to be indirect, devious, sagely "Machiavellian."

A Magnificent Loan

On a Saturday in June he told Edith that he needed his freedom.

He was as free as before they ever met, she wrote after he left her. "And now let us think of your future."[222]

In a letter, he said what he had not made clear in talk.

She replied in despair at his telling *her* that no one could help him![223]

She had supposed that after they ceased to be lovers she would remain his chief helpmeet. Humble toward him, she was sure that no other woman could match her understanding of him, or her cultural *apport*. But her sense of entitlement was not very satisfying, convinced as she equally was that she did not attract love.

A woman of the world (Morton's first assessment), Edith in love gauchely invoked promises, with recalls of "you said," "I said," and argued: "You will be free, so surely you can—" All her life she had been the one to *manage*: first her family, then her husband. She discussed Morton with his doctor and advised him on his dealings with his colleagues, his ex-landlady, and his parents. A fatal combination of low self-esteem and bossiness neutralized her intelligence. Morton received letters reporting her feelings yesterday, today, and an hour ago. She assured him that she understood him, but most of all she wanted to share her experience and *be understood*.

Until now, Morton had, as she said, chosen to postpone "the reign of the spirit"[224] and, instead, make love. His reason was perhaps too hurtful for her to face. All *his* life he had been a victim of devotion. He preferred sex ad lib to a schedule in which a woman whose ideas were familiar to him would platonically occupy his prime hours of leisure. There is a paper with three lines in Edith's hand but totally unlike her verse and so remarkably like the doggerel in Morton's notebook that if they aren't by Byron—and they are not—they are pretty surely his:

> For I have always hated to be sure,
> And there is nothing I could less endure
> Than a fond woman whom I understood.[225]

He dismissed Edith not only as lover but as confidante, *éminence blanche*, dowager *maîtresse en titre*.

Such is the logical inference from that exchange in June 1910.

However, Morton's tantalizings and postcoital neglects and Edith's reproaches, renunciations, and despairs were positively last performances by perpetrator and enabler. As if nothing had happened, Morton wrote five days later to say that he was unhappy. He enclosed his mother's account of Katharine's wedding, in which she sighed: "Well, we are alone now, quite alone."[226]

Edith was all impatient common sense. He wanted his sister to marry; surely he had known that his mother would be left alone! What was the *real* reason why he was unhappy?[227]

Katharine had the good fortune to be loved by a man who took her part against the people she loved and had the strength to marry him without waiting for Will to come home and give advice.

Morton too took an important step. After his declaration that he was beyond mortal help, and after allotting Edith several days of thinking herself ousted from his life, he accepted her offer of a two-year loan and resigned from the *Times.*

The loan, amount unknown, was probably made in late July. That it *was* made we learn from a spirited and generous letter in which Edith told Morton (at the end of Year One?) that something he'd said suggested he might be tormenting himself over

> what could be done if (as the phrase goes) "anything happened" to you before the "obligation" was wiped out. . . . Don't think of it at all for a whole year, and think of it then as a small obligation, too elastic to be a burden while you live, and ceasing when you cease. . . . And now goodnight—*et ne réponds pas.*[228]

The *Times* of Brockton and the *Times* of London

At the *Times:* On August 2, 1910, Fullerton tendered his resignation to John Walter, chairman of the board.[229] It was a year to the day since he had left the Rue Fabert.

Walter wrote to him informally, and Morton replied informally that he *did* feel he ought to have succeeded Blowitz and been paid more. But he was leaving because he had never been able to save a penny, "save for a paltry Insurance." In ten years he would be

> getting *hors de combat,* with nothing to look forward to, no money coming . . . either from *Times* or parent. It seems to me to be mere equity that

in an institution where a *garçon de bureau* [office boy] like our ancient Pierre receives a life pension of 200 francs a month Morton Fullerton should not be allowed to sever his connection without being granted *at least a year's salary.*[230]

Walter put the resignation to the board as of September 3.

Buckle, the editor, gave his opinion in writing. Fullerton was leaving in his prime, voluntarily. In twenty years he had not impressed his chiefs enough to gain promotion. If, as Walter said, his "superfluities" of style had blinded them to his "zeal and knowledge," shouldn't he go to "some congenial spot" where they needed a correspondent, say, Madrid?[231]

On the 23rd, Bell wrote informing Fullerton that his resignation had been accepted. He would be hearing from Mr. Walter.[232]

Morton had been at sea. Landing in New York on the 24th, he called on the Whartons, who had just arrived, at their hotel.

Edith was out of date. She thought Morton had issued the *Times* an ultimatum: he would resign, unless—[233] Handing her a letter he'd had from Saunders before he left Paris, he made for Brockton, on tenterhooks till he should know the board's decision: the more so in that, as the letter showed Edith, the past weeks had offered scant hope of the dignified and lucrative severance he considered rightful. Saunders had refused to pay his November salary and said they might "chuck" him—"would in fact, if they could get a substitute." Edith was aghast:

> Believe me, they will give you nothing, *and never meant to;* and I should give them all the pretexts they want for not doing so! That kind of publicity in the papers will help you immensely here at this stage, and may lead to a big offer for a foreign correspondence. *Miss no chance of the sort.*[234]

Morton had other ideas about publicity. He granted the *Brockton Times* an interview.

BROCKTON BOY'S SUCCESS ABROAD
Mingles with the Greatest of the World's Statesmen

In 1902, Massachusetts papers had announced his succession to Blowitz, $10,000 a year, horse and carriage, etc. He did not correct that misimpression now when interviewed by a reporter who wrote that he had succeeded de Blowitz on his death and had since visited all the European capitals . . . executing on frequent occasions diplomatic missions of the most delicate nature . . . [enjoying] intimate relations with the most powerful influences in European politics. . . . [O]ne is immediately impressed with the trustfulness in his sincerity, and faith in his convictions. A voice of uncommon sweetness, attractive face and a winning manner, lend special charms to him as a narrator.

Mr. Fullerton had a few words for his parents' townspeople. The cause of the "Great Divide" between plenty and poverty was not economic, but "moral and religious."

"I have resigned from the regular staff of the *Times*," he said, "but I may not sever my connection entirely."[235]

Meanwhile, the *Times* of London had made up its mind.

John Walter to Fullerton, 27 September: "behalf of Board . . . accept your . . . salary . . . December 31st. . . . Directors furthermore ask . . . convey . . . appreciation . . . regret . . . token . . . beg acceptance . . . cheque. . . . Wishing you . . . "

Morton returned to New York and dined with a James bereft of his brother William, a tired Edith and a deeply disturbed Edward Wharton, and a smooth Walter Berry soon to retire from an international judgeship. At dinner he may have announced the official terms of his resignation: two months' further salary and a £200 present.

Teddy left for a world tour, with a caretaker; Morton dined with Edith, James, and Berry. Edith sailed for France; Morton lunched with Berry and James. He dined with James, then dined with James and others before returning to Brockton. James returned to Cambridge, where Morton dined with him and stayed the night in early November.[237] It was the last time he and James ever saw each other.

Morton had written two letters to John Walter, thanking him formally for the board's £200 check and informally for a private £200, which had made him feel "I can't accept it" until he saw that Walter deserved "as frank a proof of sincere friendship" on his part. "I take the gift, then, in the spirit in which you make it."[238]

The end of an era was marked in another way the following spring. Moberly Bell died at his desk at Number 7; while writing a letter he fell dead to the floor.[239]

The *Times* archives document Morton's departure. Ages ago, 1891, the church in Palmer, Massachusetts, had filed a local newspaper item:

HOW HE GOT STARTED
On the Road Which Has Led Him to $8000 a Year
from the London Times

Since William Morton Fullerton graduated from Harvard there has been a tinge of romance. . . . He located in a small town on the coast of the Adriactic sea to complete some literary work. He was accustomed to spend several hours daily on the beach, and for several weeks he noticed that as regularly as he appeared, he was followed by an unknown person who asked: "Did you ever happen to know Will Fullerton of Boston? you are a perfect picture of him as I knew him years ago." Young Fullerton replied that his name was William Fullerton . . . and the stranger introduced himself as an English nobleman.

(The seacoast of Illyria. *Enter* Lord Ruddigore.)

The acquaintance ripened during the stay abroad, and on his return home the Englishman begged Mr. Fullerton to accompany him as a companion and intimate friend. Through his friend's influence, Mr. Fullerton obtained a position on the London Times and has taken high rank upon the staff. They have remained bosom companions, and have visited this country, spending some time at Mr. Fullerton's home in Waltham.[240]

It would go far to explain, along with his style, Mr. Fullerton's unpopularity on "the other side," at Number 7 Printing House Square.

PART FIVE

Prometheus Unbound

The new freelance called on magazine editors.

It was the first time he had ever really stayed in New York. No reporters asked for interviews. He told Edith that he'd be lost without her to talk to and had a pleased, maternal reply from Paris: New York would conduce to independent work and bring out the best in him.[1] Meanwhile she pitied him for being there.[2]

Even if Morton had fully shared her opinion that the new America was repulsive, he would have muffled it, he wanted readers; but in fact he was interested in what he saw, and in "America Revisited: The Sensations of an Exile" he wrote about it amiably, identifying himself as a native who had come home only three times in the last twenty years. (Two of the visits had taken place in the past four years, but he wanted to sharpen the contrast of the skyscraper culture to the "prehistoric" life of sleigh rides and spelling bees he had known as a boy.)

New York did have a "sky-line." It was unrecognized because it shifted as buildings blended "in dun feudal, or Dantesquely violet masses"; no other urban architecture had so "subtly varied an aesthetic potentiality." Fin-de-siècle language, but Morton had toughened. The shifting silhouette was a result of modern technology—thanks to which buildings rose to the sky in no time.

Americans had come out of "dank Puritanism" into the sun. Play was no longer sinful. (Morton burdened the entire nation with a Calvinist past.) College football was an imperial game. The populace waited outside newspaper offices for scores; an actual spectator felt like a patrician.

A Mr. Gibson said *he* had not created the fine, free, athletic Gibson Girl: the nation had.

The "sheerest idealistic instruction" of the past, obscuring economic reality, had instilled an idea of equal rights that was being demolished by experience as the country became "a democracy of selected individuals . . . obliged constantly to justify their selection." In places like Lenox and Morristown, the "favorites of American fortune" had "organized a life warm with a rich comfort which only England's aristocracy had anticipated."[3]

In Princeton, near Morristown, Morton visited the newly married Geroulds.

When Hugh Fullerton heard Katharine's story he exclaimed: "That explains Professor Gerould's attitude! He never wanted to talk about Morton! Katharine was very charming. Morton taught her to write. 'I formed her,' he used to say." (PYGMALION ABUSES GALATEA.)

Happy with Gordon and their "sturdy" Christopher and "beautiful, blooming" daughter Sylvia,[4] Katharine continued to love and admire Will. But, "as you would expect," says Christopher, "Will was not a topic of much conversation in our household. In modern parlance you'd sum him up as a con man."

In his Harvard class report, Will rejoiced that his spirit was unbroken after years as "an anonymous portion of a great machine." He was now "an unattached critic of the great spectacle of things."

Incriminating Letters and a Con Man

When he returned to France he observed—as a *not* unattached critic—a spectacle produced at Tours in the Valley of the Loire.

Two years earlier, when he went there to see Katharine, Francesca d'Aulby had pirouetted into a not very serious affair with him. But her letters had saddened. Willie was sweet to have faith in her! People were trying to get her poor husband "out." A Mrs. Paine "would give *anything*" to get some letters back, "most *burning* it seems and *most* compromising to *her.*"[5] Francesca tried to "bear this great trouble as a high-spirited and (I hope) high-bred American woman should,"[6] but its effect on her children alarmed her.[7] Katharine wrote from Princeton of "poor Francesca d'Aulby."[8]

The d'Aulbys had been jailed on a suit of abuse of confidence by the widow of C. H. Paine of Boston, the Copper King. D'Aulby had sold the Paines Old Masters which Mrs. Paine alleged were fakes. Francesca was released, but the count was held for months awaiting trial.

Francesca counted on Will's help. They'd found a letter from him to her husband praising "the rare beauty of [his] canvases of the Italian school,"[9] and in Boston he had talked with people whose testimony Francesca's lawyer said would have "colossal importance."[10]

The trial was reported in Paris, Boston, and London (d'Aulby was English) shortly after the end of the Crippen trial (DENTIST DRAGGED TO GALLOWS).[11]

At Rennes, rafts of letters had been brought in for rival handwriting experts to evaluate. The courtroom in Tours was strewn with Titians, Murillos, and Corots, and art experts wrangled: genuine—copy—forgery—pastiche! D'Aulby explained that his dealings were complicated. (Among Morton's papers is the count's note on a card: "In the event of a sale, you must let me either in buying something for you, or, you doing so for yourself, give you 10%—on sale.")[12]

D'Aulby's titles, too, were allegedly false, as false as the uniform, plumed hat, and medal of the Order of Mélusine in which he had married Miss Francesca Lunt in Trinity Church, Boston.

When he took the stand, one could see how he'd charmed people, wrote Figaro's special correspondent (its theater critic). Blue eyes, sweet voice . . . He claimed to be an Italian duke?—Well, there he'd been victimized by a confidence man. But he was a count. It was a family tradition.

It was not only his Old Masters that Mrs. Paine had adored. "We entered," d'Aulby told the court, voice lowered, "into very intimate relations."

The trial was in its early days when headlines announced: MRS. C. H. PAINE A FRENCH DUCHESS. The widowed Copper Queen had just married the Duc de Choiseul Praslin, who was said to have the usual number of debts.

Francesca took the stand bravely in purple velvet, diamonds, and pearls. At first her elegance seemed "a little American," but her "tout à fait 'lady like'" way of fluttering her fan won sympathy. "I am an extremely proper straightforward woman," she stated, "very very American! I would never have tolerated anything improper in my house. I ran it not knowing where the money came from. And I hate money. I have a horror of it." ("Tumultuous applause.")

MRS. PAINE'S LETTERS READ IN COURT

HER LOVE FOR D'AULBY AN INCANDESCENT FLAME

"I wish I could sit on your knees before the fire and love you daily," read one letter, "loving while daylight's fading fires go out, but not my love. I send you my kisses, which are waiting for you, and am, darling, wholly yours, Lucy."[13]

The new duchess accused the count of forging the letters and asking $200,000 to return them. The count accused her of wanting them back because she wanted to marry a duke. ("*Emotion!*")

Defense counsel told her that her outrage to public morals must be avenged and challenged her business manager to a duel.

"Thieves, swindlers, adventurers!" she shouted at the d'Aulbys. But neighbors testified to their good reputation. And Mme d'Aulby came of an excellent family. Her uncle was a famous poet. Besides, she and her husband had no need of money. Any sum she asked for was immediately sent from Boston by her former guardian. (This was the evidence Morton had obtained.)

The public laughed at the duchess. "One always laughs at the dupe" (*Figaro*). "The confidence man carries people with him." On Christmas Eve she dropped her suit. ("*Stupeur!*") She had kept an adventurer, maybe, but a widely respected one, in jail; and when *she* was attacked, she quit?! She fled, fearful of being mobbed.

London and Boston found other news ("HOME SECRETARY CHURCHILL LEADS ATTACK IN SIDNEY STREET," "MISS ROSE FITZGERALD IS PRESENTED TO SOCIETY"). But Paris enjoyed *émotions!* and *stupeurs!* until Francesca was acquitted and the count given a month on a technicality.

The trial was still on when Morton, Edith, and Berry fêted New Year 1911 with Professor and Mrs. Barrett Wendell, who were en route to India. Edith had followed the case, warning Morton to beware of Mrs. Paine and acidly complimenting him on his friend the Comte.[14] She had met Francesca (who told Katharine, who told Will, that she didn't like Mrs. Wharton: "looks worn out and nervous and wants too much 'homage'")[15] and had bought paintings by Francesca's kinsman Tom Meteyard, who came from England to be a witness.[16]

Morton must have wondered that Edith never saw herself as Mrs. Paine, with incandescent letters in an unreliable lover's keeping, or thought "*ma semblable*, my sister." She had often asked for their return. Coldly, because he had neglected her.[17] Masochistically, to spare him pain in telling her he no longer loved her. . . . She evoked with mock horror their ending in an autograph album.[18] Her requests were usually demands for attention—he had only to reply and she would apologize— and almost pitifully transparent. In threatening to take away her letters when he offended her, rather than refusing to see him, she recognized that they were more important to him than her company.

A year ago he had had a gentle request. She had been thinking that James, since his illness, was in no state to be "custodian" of "all those old letters" in which she'd "unpacked her trunk" to Morton. "Should 'anything happen'" to Morton, it would be painful if they fell into "other hands"; she'd like to burn them.[19]

So James was expected to read her early letters (the ones written before quarrels began?). Had Morton persuaded her that he *ought* to see them, as works of art, and had she agreed? But was he to see them only after Morton's death? After *hers*? Her request is smooth, yet awkward, as if she were embarrassed at basing it on the possibility of Morton's dying before a man who was much older and in very bad health. She could simply have said: Don't give them to James. It was Morton she didn't want to have them.

Blackmail was a staple of fiction. In *The House of Mirth*, Edith had had a cleaning woman sell compromising letters. Not that she imagined that Morton would sell hers, but she knew that he had been blackmailed and may have surmised that he'd left letters about. He had once dropped a letter from her, in her motor.

In any case, she let Morton keep them. She saw how Mrs. Paine fared, yet viewed her own letters not as the potentially damning papers they were in the immediate but as part of her oeuvre.

Twenty years later, the London expert Maryon-Daulby announced that he was disposing of his Old Masters in order to found a world center for teaching his Marcotone Science of Tone Color and producing an annual festival of his music-drama heptology *The Cycle of Life*.[20] Francesca had returned to America with the four children.

"Paris," "The Statesman"

The *Times* had sent £200 plus two months' pay; John Walter, £200: in toto almost Morton's annual salary, £540. Adèle had Macmillan's £100, but Morton had Edith's loan, amount unknown. "Paris," once finished, would bring £500 less £100. And, once out, an urbane guide in which his familiarity with the modern city was enriched by his historical lore might bring in a small but steady income. He had never been so well off.

His pleasure in solvency was not unalloyed. "A gallstone," he told John Walter, "started on a stupid loafing promenade" in his insides, and "during the expedition I suffered as they suffer in Hell."[21] And the project that had freed him from Adèle was a burden. A year and a half after signing contracts, he asked Macmillan if chapters of "Paris," which was "shaping up," might come out first in an American magazine.[22]—Yes, said Macmillan, if drawings were by Pennell and could be used in the book gratis.[23]—U.S. editors, Morton suggested, might prefer photographs.[24]—The publisher replied that Pennell was "very popular there."[25]

"Shaping up" was part lie, part inert half-wish. Edith had advised Morton to get permission for periodical publication. But he failed to write a chapter to show editors. Seeing his block, wanting him to be happy, she pointed out that he could free himself from his obligation by repaying Macmillan.[26] He let matters drift. Company records show no repayment, but they list MSS received 1911–1919. (Accepted: Winston Churchill, *Speeches*. Rejected: James Joyce, *Dubliners*.) No "Paris" by W. M. Fullerton was submitted.

Not very methodically, he looked for other ways to make money. (Keep him in mind, he told Wendell, "if ever you hear of any one going about with a lantern in search of a man with my past.")[27] He contemplated but did not write a pamphlet on Roosevelt and a memoir of Blowitz; he translated a life of the courtesan La Castiglione for Will Meredith at Constable's[28] and with him forayed into "oil" but prudently retreated;[29] and, with Edith, he wasted time in a theatrical venture.

Paul Bourget, novelist and dramatist, monarchist and anti-Dreyfusist, Academician, was the lion Edith Wharton had offered guests before Teddy's illness ended her salon life. She obtained his permission for

Morton to adapt his stage success *Le Tribun* for production in English as
"The Statesman."

The tribune, in ancient Rome a defender of the plebs, is a prime minister who embodies all that Bourget hated. Reforming France as a secular
democracy in line with abstract justice, he backs workers who go on
strike, treats bishops rudely, scorns the Family. But when his son commits
a crime, he finds that he cannot bear to have him arrested as abstract justice demands. He questions the merits of Liberty, Equality, and Frater-
nity, and resigns.

The play propounded, with a "cartload of explanations,"[30] the "Vati-
canism" Morton had always opposed. But there was no time for ideology
as he and Edith lobbied actor-managers—few but powerful men, some of
whom had ties with the R. G. set. R. G.'s in-law the Duchess of Sutherland knew people; Edith approached her. Sir Herbert Beerbohm Tree *did*
recall meeting Morton with their friend Aïdé.[31] In New York the agent
Elizabeth Marbury tried Schubert.[32]

Doubtful though it was that London or New York would suspend disbelief in a father stunned by finding that a father can love a son, Sir
George Alexander was encouraging. He wanted changes (James heard
that Edith had "written in a love scene" and quipped on Morton's "Alex-
andrines").[33] All changes had to be approved by Bourget; it isn't known
which change Edith meant when she cabled Morton at the Charing Cross
Hotel—he was in London seeing editors—that Bourget was agreeable.[34]
But when all hope was lost, it was Alexander whom Edith angrily
blamed.[35]

The leading role had tempted some British actors.[36] In Paris it was
taken by the legendary Lucien Guitry. In the cast were Mmes Grumbach,
Ellen-Andrée—surely a name seen before. . . . Ellen-Andrée had been
with Mirecourt in the Palais-Royal troupe in the days when it was (said
the London *Times,* no less) "a sort of dramatic happy family, whose
strength lay in their artistic genius."[37] In *Le Tribun* she was only an old
faithful retainer, but she was named in large print.

Adèle goes to the Théâtre du Vaudeville and chats with her old friend
in the green room. Looking for her seat, she spots Morton with a woman
of a certain age, elegantly turned out, with a parure of emeralds and diamonds. She bristles.

No. Her sister Zélie had just died, and Zélie's husband not long before.

Rueil-Malmaison

The Witnesses to the Will

Adèle was in Rueil seeing the Saint-Laurents' notary, Maître Faribault, who had drawn her pact with Morton two years back. Sale of their house would explain her staying down the street, where she became so ill—an epidemic?—that the *maître* and his hastily convened witnesses came to her bedside.

Living people may remember Mme Mirecourt and her fuss about the trouble she had collecting from a tenant in Paris.

Near the bus stop a few old buildings quiver as traffic thunders by. There's the witness Roze's house, next to the dollhouse Adèle stayed in. Roze and another witness have descendants.

To reach Henri Morlat, garage owner, grandson of the witness Morlat, you follow twisting, unposted streets, cross nameless culs-de-sac. Houses no higher than the trees. No traffic. Dogs, cats. "I thought your letter was a *blague*," M. Morlat says over coffee in his fragrant kitchen, "but my wife said I should answer." Mme Morlat and a shy teenage daughter nod. "My best idea is that you get in touch with the Rozes. Old Mme Roze, you know, rented the house where your Mme Moutot stayed to an old lady, *petite et mince*. My mother was a laundress, I used to take the laundry there."

But . . . M. Morlat is too young. Even if Adèle stayed till the year she died. She was not the thin little old lady.

Today's M. Roze has a mansion stoutly walled off from the Avenue Georges Clemenceau. Brocade, candelabra, portraits. The original of one portrait sits by his side. "My mother here," says M. Roze, "still lives in our old house. When she was young, my grandmother rented the little house next door to people who made it a *pension*. Mme Moutot—Mme Mirecourt?—may have stayed there."

And must have exchanged bonjours with Mme Roze here. But Mme Roze, eighty, with brilliant dark brown eyes, head high, has no recollection of her.

The witness Dunon is still alive, but his daughter says he has lost his memory.

The man two doors down from where Mme Mirecourt stayed has only been there thirty years, but maybe the lady next door, Mme Roze— "Merci, monsieur."

Morton did not go to see Adèle then, in 1911, as he did two years later when she again seemed to be dying. He was out of the country.

Paris

Visits: The Mount, Lenox. Newbury Street, Brockton

The Whartons had spent much of the summer in Lenox. James, who was still in America, looked forward to revisiting the Mount and wrote to Edith expansively: "Please thus feel my arms open at their very widest . . . and then close about you at their very tenderest!"[38] But guests were dismayed by signs of friction as host and hostess made and unmade plans for separation, for sale of the Mount, for an income for Teddy. Teddy was reasonable, Edith told Morton, when not terrified that she would leave him.[39] On the same day, James told her that she must save her life by "a separate existence."[40]

A year ago Edith had informed Morton that Berry advised separation; what did *he* think?[41] His answer is not known. Now, as he prepared to sail, he knew that she was undergoing the "worst moral struggle" of her life,[42] that separation seemed inevitable, and that, driving from Newport to Lenox, she had called on his parents in Brockton and received a charming welcome.[43]

He must have read Edith's pleased account of her unannounced call attentively, pictured her driving into Newbury Street, a more affable Lady Catherine de Burgh, leaving her coach and coachman to wait outside— and wondered. Edith had read letters of Julia's and was predisposed to like his parents. He knew that she would not knowingly have condescended to them. But she might not have understood that they were unaware that they could be condescended to. Or that they would not necessarily accept her on *her* terms.

Julia, great-great-grandchild of a cousin of George Washington,[44] was prouder of being the daughter, wife, and sister-in-law of New England ministers (so many lords of a manor, Morton explained to the French)

but prouder still of her father's "advanced ideas" and the "native culture" of her mother's family.[45] She herself had taught at the East Tennes-
see Female Institute (a name inviting Whartonian satire) but was modest
about her own attainments. "Had I devoted my whole life to improve-
ment as you have," she observed to Will, more accepting than wistful,
"we should have been more alike."[46] She was not a caricature. Still,
"High lace mittens," Katharine's son recalls, "not that she wore them but
that was the impression. She was oh so prim and proper."

Describing Katharine's wedding, Julia had told Will that Mr. Gerould
had shocked the family by wearing not a Prince Albert, like the other
men, but a "store made" business suit. Katharine said she had asked him
to, no one knew why![47] Edith would have sympathized with her grie-
vance. But as Morton often remarked, all is relative. Friends in Paris
called Edith "prim and proper," even using the English phrase. In Brockton she was a "society woman" whose advanced ideas, propounded in
her stories, were . . . sinful. Bradford and Julia may have thanked her for
helping Katharine with "Gemma and Beatrice." But her loan to Will, had
they known of it, would have been cause for sore humiliation. And if they
had known that she was his mistress . . .

In the play Edith expected to work on with Morton at the Mount, the
tribune's son, brought up irreligiously, is the lover of a married woman.
Exposed, the woman not only prostrates herself before her husband as
his "thing" but—Bourget's abiding emphasis was on the family—also
confesses to having stolen a son from his parents. Had Bradford and Julia
known of Edith's relations with Will, it is very hard indeed to imagine
how they would have coped with her presenting herself so easily before
them. As it was, they may have made conscious allowances for the sake
of hospitality.

Morton was to have spent five days at the Mount,[48] but at the last moment he wired from Brockton that he couldn't come because of an accident to his mother.[49]

Four years ago he had made a boring train journey for the sake of two
short days and a night in Lenox. He could have snatched time now; he
could truthfully have pleaded work. But 1911 was not 1907. Since 1907
he had irreversibly changed the Whartons' lives. He had heard of Teddy's
"excitable" state from Wendell, who had seen him in India during his recent world tour.[50] He knew that James had left the Mount. Edith had
given him an idea of the atmosphere there. In the event, Edith divorced

Teddy on grounds of *his* adultery, but in 1911 it was not unreasonable for Morton to think that Teddy might divorce *her*, citing *him*. He had lived in fear of reprisal by the Rajah of Sarawak. Were he to go to Lenox . . . Even if Julia self-sacrificingly urged Will to go, he may have preferred not to be present at a marital crisis that might publicly become triangular.

He accepted another invitation to the Mount and again canceled at the last moment.[51] In September he saw Edith off from New York, did some business there, went to visit the Geroulds, and sailed for France.

Old Maids and Unmarried Women in France

When Edith handed him a *Century* commission for an article on "the old maid in France," Morton changed "old maid" to "unmarried woman." A countess had told him that she put her daughter into a convent because she couldn't afford a dowry and couldn't have a *vieille fille* about. But old maids—"social waste-stuff," nuns or nursemaids to a brother's children— were of the past now that, "against the opposition of eighty French bishops," secondary education for girls was law. Training wives and mothers was the aim; the result was that girls no longer felt bound to marry. They were leaving a "parasitic" life of "literary and social conventions" to be telephone operators, stenographers, doctors, lawyers. Anna de Noailles, Rosa Bonheur, and Marie Curie "radiated French prestige."

The article would have offended the eighty bishops (and Paul Bourget, who opposed educating even lower-class *boys*). For other reasons it may have caused displeasure in America, where editors were said to be governed "by the fear of scandalizing a non-existent clergyman in the Mississippi Valley."[52] Morton discussed single women who were not maidens: prostitutes, women "married at the [nonexistent] *mairie* of the Twenty-First," and "spinsters" like "Ninons de l'Enclos" and of "other kinds of *clos*" whose lives were "beautifully facilitated" in France. The bluestocking Ninon had advocated and practised free sex into old age; *clos = maison close = brothel*. Did editors, under the sway of that hallucinatory cleric, realize that Morton was saying something he believed would shock people who understood?

At once sociological and suave, the essay gave a more "modern" view of France than did Bourget's play, while accommodating several inconsistent attitudes: protofeminism, *c'est-si-bon* romanticizing of brothels, and deromanticizing of an idea popularized by Charles Dana Gibson: American man more than any other man revered woman, and reverence was the due of American woman, superior as she was in "beauty and mental plane" to any other. Morton demurred. Frenchmen were less religious toward women than Anglo-Saxons were, but cared for them more as "intelligent, indispensable" companions. The French woman was not only one of the most "seductive" but one of the most "competent and loyal" women in the world; and in Paris "the sentimental age" for men and women alike had been "beautifully and elastically extended well up to the fiftieth year if not beyond."

Edith Wharton, fifty, a married woman whose sentimental age had begun when she was forty-six, learned on returning to France that, while she was at sea, Teddy, contrary to their agreement, had begun the process of selling the Mount.

The Writing of *The Reef*

"Poor dear Teddy Wharton" became "poor damned Teddy"[53] as word of his lunacy spread. (Gossip would climax in James's report that on a visit to friends one of the first things Teddy did "was to say 'Have you seen my gold garters?' then to whisk up his trousers and show them in effect his stockings held up with circles of massive gold.")[54] It also became known that Teddy "kept" women on both sides of the ocean. Edith's lawyers began to seek evidence. The marriage was ending.

As for Edith's liaison . . . She showed Morton a new poem. She had once believed that he and she were as one, seeing only each other when they looked at things together. In the sensual music of "Colophon to the Mortal Lease," orgasm made "sense and spirit one," but the poem ended: "Ah close your eyes. They see not what I saw."
"Copied from Edith Wharton's ms March 1912," Morton wrote on the copy he made. "I saw not what she saw, and that's the tragedy of it." Tense, the definite past.[55]

Morton went to Luxembourg to work on a book. Edith moved about. He heard from Rome that she hoped he'd find solitude in Luxembourg;[56] from Milan, that she was worried about the book *she* was writing, which he was reading, and would like to go over with him, she'd make for a place near Luxembourg.[57] From Vevey she sent comments on his manuscript and suggested that he meet her as she passed by.[58] From Paris she suggested that he cross to England, where she would be.[59]

Morton steadfastly replied that he must stay and work.

Something held her back from going, herself, to Luxembourg.

The manuscript that Morton had been reading was *The Reef*, which Edith was revising in line with his suggestions, much improving it she said.[60]

In the novel, a room in the Gare du Nord Terminus Hotel is the venue of lovemaking by Sophy, a rash girl from a dubious milieu, and Darrow, a diplomat with time on his hands who is soon sick at having acted out of pique because Anna, whom he hopes to marry, has put off his visit. When the visit takes place, he finds Sophy there, as a governess, and lies expertly about her to Anna.

Sophy has the idealizing love of the Edith who had kept a secret journal four years ago. Darrow's pleasant ironic presence and facile mendacity are Morton's, and there is a lot of the more experienced Edith in Anna, who after a torpid marriage feels like "a slave, and a goddess, and a girl in her teens" when with Darrow, then suffers in concentrate Edith's slow disabusement and the jealousy Edith tried to deny. In her struggle between desire for Darrow and agony over his deceit, passion wins. Boldly for 1912, Edith had a "good" woman go to bed with a man who is not her husband. Unlike Edith, Anna knows that her love is returned, yet she knows she will never be sure that Darrow is not concealing another unimportant betrayal.

Edith's enraptured night in a London railway hotel had been succeeded by demeaning weeks in England waiting for Morton's return from America, and the happy month that ensued had been blurred by three subsequent years of clandestine hours in Paris hotels, railway and other, years of *angoisses de la gare et de l'amour*. Her novel would show Morton how she evaluated him when in command of herself.

Reading about Merton Densher, in whom James had censured and forgiven the vices of his style, Morton had guessed that he was a model (though not as regarded style). Interpreting Darrow did not require guesswork. That may have been why Edith was so very desirous of a meeting: she wanted to see recognition in Morton's face and set in train nuanced questions and answers that could not be monitored in marginal notes and queries.

It is mildly interesting that Morton may have helped shape a story, volatile in manuscript, concerning himself, a rare opportunity for "originals" of characters. Another circumstance makes the writing of *The Reef* positively bizarre. Morton and Walter Berry had been doing each other favors, not always at Edith's behest: Walter speaking for Morton at the U.S. State Department,[61] Morton putting Walter on to people in France who helped him find a retirement job.[62] James was soon speaking to Edith of "you and WB," "you and MF and WB." Morton asked Edith if Berry had read any of *The Reef*. Not a line, she replied. Walter took absolutely no interest in her writing.[63]

In her memoirs, Edith said that Berry "taught her how" to write. He had always read everything she wrote, but after he retired, he could "follow my work more closely . . . his reading of each chapter as it was written" and "his comments as he read" gave it "fresh life."[64]

On the face of it, Edith's published tribute to Berry's help is more credible than her denying it to Morton. One can't be sure, for she stretched the truth in exalting, almost beatifying Walter after his death; but if he read any of her manuscripts, it would have been *The Reef*; he was with her part of the time when she was writing it and discussing it with Morton by post. It would seem that both men read, ignorant of each other's roles. (Presumably Edith lied to Morton so that they would not compare notes; and if that is so, she wouldn't have let Berry know about Morton, either.) At times, Morton may have been revising Walter, and vice versa.

What James Knew

Despair over her marriage and a thwarted wish to see Morton, adamantly alone in Luxembourg, were the background of Edith Wharton's visit to England in summer 1912.

James sent Howard Sturgis a distress signal at the approach of "the Bird 'o-freedom—the whirr and wind of whose great pinions is already cold on my foredoomed brow!"[65] Berry came, but left; James and Edith were, essentially, together for three weeks.

At Ascot they were among the Ranee's guests at tea.[66] The two women had not met before. James knew the Ranee didn't know that he knew she'd had an affair with Morton, or that Morton had kept her letters, imperiling her reputation, or that Edith had enabled Morton to recover them. He knew Edith didn't know that the Ranee had had an affair with Morton or that it was the Ranee's letters that had been recovered. But, did he know about Morton and Edith?

He "knew about" the Ranee and remained fond. But *she* hadn't told him. Moreover the easygoing but perceptive Ranee drew confidences even from him; he had even "poured out" to her his feelings on the death of Constance Woolson. He and the Ranee were both impulsive and unguarded.[67]

Whereas Edith . . . His cadenzas on the demon "flight" conductor and the "silver-sounding toot that invites me to the Car"[68] conjured the mad motorist Mr. Toad of Toad Hall—the Car had even now carried James to Ascot— Would James have had the heart to be facetious had he known, and from Edith herself, of her adultery?

James noted Edith's kindnesses in his diary. But he was ill and nervously vulnerable, on the verge of shingles. Her almost constant company provoked a truly abusive outburst. She "uses up everything and every one," he told Sturgis.

> She came over . . . to help herself (and us!) through part of an embarrassing and unprovided summer. . . . [She] is like an extravagant dandy who sends thirty shirts to the wash where you and I (forgive, dear Howard, the collocation!) send one; or indeed even worse—since our Firebird dirties her days (pardon again the image) at a rate that no laundry will stand; and in fact doesn't seem to believe in the washing, and still less in the ironing—though she does, rather inconsistently, in the "mangling"!—of any of her material of life.[69]

It was three years almost exactly since Edith had indeed "used" James to fill the unprovided period of Morton's absence in America and make him invite her to Lamb House along with Morton. James may have been unleashing feelings he had repressed in 1909.

Edith's letter about James's reading her letters at some future time seemed to mean that he was ignorant of the liaison. But, percipient, with his novelist's curiosity, wouldn't the James whom Max Beerbohm sketched peering at two little shoes and two big shoes put outside a hotel room door for cleaning have been dim not to know?

On the other hand, while James knew Edith the poised, witty, bountiful woman of letters, he knew neither the forlorn damsel singing "Willow" nor the voluptuary who offered herself to a lover as a cannibal's feast. Nor did he know of Morton's experiments on human flesh and spirit in Katharine. Of his streak of *badness*. Unless . . . In *The Wings of the Dove,* Kate Croy induces Merton Densher to make the dying Millie Theale think he loves her. Did James, in imagining Merton Densher, have a subliminal sense that Morton too might, under suasion, as it were vaguely, charm a girl, with a legacy—vaguely—in mind?

James admired *The Reef.* But why had Edith set it in France? The hotel scenes didn't require "the notorious wickedness of Paris," he told her. "Oh, if you knew, how plentifully we could supply them in London and, I should suppose, in New York or in Boston."[70] To have written that knowing, and knowing she knew he knew, of her *après-dîner* at a London hotel would have been to poke her in the ribs with a leer. If he knew she didn't know he knew, he might have ventured the dig. But if he knew she knew—

With the approach of James's seventieth birthday, April 15, 1913, Morton subscribed to a fund raised in England for a Sargent portrait of the novelist, ultimately intended for the (British) National Portrait Gallery. When Edith heard, she asked people in America to donate to a fund James could spend as he wished. (She couldn't, she said later, defensively, have asked "America" to pay for a portrait meant for London—[71] though Morton and at least one other American had done so.) Although her appeal went out late, she had raised a fair sum, from Barrett Wendell and the Boston doctor Sturgis Bigelow among others, when James heard of it and reacted with a hostility of which, this time, she was cognizant. He stopped the "dreadful project"[72] short. Then, fearing that he'd angered a valued friend, he wrote a letter to Morton that he hoped would appease Edith.

She was, in fact, livid. She was convinced that her plan had been misrepresented to James (unaware that James had declared that he couldn't be beholden to Bigelow, whom he disliked,[73] or Wendell, so poor a writer for a Harvard teacher as to make him "unhappy").[74] She could not have forgiven anyone but James, she told Morton, and not even James at first.[75] What angered her most was a "lie" that she had tried to help James twice before and been stopped.[76]

The shock of James's anger revived her timidity toward Morton. In the letter James wanted Morton to show her, he had indicated that he knew that Morton was overburdened. She told Morton that she'd rather go back to her old life before she knew him than "be anything but a rest and a joy" to him.

Edith had been heedless in her project, thinking less of James than of taking command of an operation. She was irrationally angry at an irrationally angry James, irrationally lowly toward Morton. She was on edge as she awaited her divorce decree.

Morton was awaiting publication of his book.

The Duchy of Luxembourg

Declining Edith's invitations to quit his solitude, he had spent the summer of 1912 in operetta country. Franz Lehar's *Count of Luxembourg* was as melodious as his *Merry Widow;* Luxembourg was an improbable site for a study of the modern world. Yet there Morton put his experience, his diligence, and his ambition into a work entitled "International-ities" until it became *Problems of Power.*

In Luxembourg, as he read Edith's manuscript, he read her comments on his. Till now, she had always praised his writing. Now she castigated his un-English sentences. Too many notes and dates. He must return to the style of his *Patriotism and Science.*[77]

Chagrined, Morton thought she disparaged the "interest"[78] of a book that was everything to him. For if he *ought* to have written "Paris," *Problems of Power* was the book he *had* to write, as he told John Walter, passionately, in an unexpectedly moving letter:

> I have attempted a synthesis, extraordinarily up-to-date, of the modern world, focussing the influences at work. . . . There is no book just like it (I speak of the theme) now accessible. The whole question is, how I have *done* it. If you find I have done it well, there can be no doubt as to its deserving a serious sendoff in The Times. Don't feel embarrassed by my appeal. When you see the thing you will see that I had to do the book, in justification of my past, my unappreciated past.[79]

The birthday present tiff mattered nothing as Morton saw his book through the press. He had improved it in ways that Edith had suggested and with touches of his own stronger, even slangy, essay style ("the Republican crew in office and the Royalist, Imperialist, or other gangs out of office"[80]—"gibbering candidates for citizenship"[81]).

Marking time, he rented a study in the Rue du Mont Thabor. "The Unmarried Woman in France" came out in New York. The unmarried French woman with whom he had lived until four years ago lay dying. He called on her and shared Charles Alfroy's joy in her disconcerting recovery. *Problems of Power* came out in London and New York.

Problems of Power

It was subtitled "A Study of International Politics from Sadowa to Kirk-Kilissé"—that is, from 1866, when Prussia defeated Austria, to 1912, when the Ottoman Empire lost much of its Balkan territory. Fullerton maintained that there is an "art" of history:

> less a record of the vicissitudes of artificially isolated States . . . than a kind of telescopic penetration and foreshortening of the human nebulae, those agglomerations composed of bustling molecules, whose infinitely complex movements are determined by the size, the weight, and the individual drift of their myriad fellows.[82]

Two "occult powers" worked "behind the façade of Government": multinational companies and banks, and public opinion.[83]

The migrations of Phoenicians, Vandals, and Huns were continuing in "the majestic phenomenon of migration" of workers from poor nations into richer nations in search of higher wages.[84]

Morton examined the financing of the Baghdad Railway and the mining economy of the "tiny and quaint Duchy of Luxembourg." He discussed America's wish to replace "the insolent attitude of *laissez-aller*" with a "really democratic existence" and the effect of spectator sports on the American character.[85]

Economics and finance were ousting politics from diplomacy.

His political philosophy was changing. At Rennes he had called "State crimes" like the Dreyfus verdict "a standing warning of the danger which individual liberty and social justice run from the untrammelled development of military institutions." Now he suggested that a theory that the Dreyfus case had been engineered by Germany in order to harm the French military was credible, and he deplored legislation for "social betterment" because it hindered "the construction of Dreadnaughts, the equipping of airfleets, and the forming of army corps."

The populace or the mob, armed by the humanitarianism of our special form of Christian civilization, possesses, in the devices of universal suffrage and parliamentary government, sure instruments for the immediate and frequently selfish utilization of the wealth of the community, and for the satisfaction of party interests and class appetites in injudicious and often anti-national ways.[86]

Fullerton made no concessions to the populace. He gave Latin citations untranslated. He drew on government documents, abstruse studies, memoirs (and, for an anecdote about Bismark, "the private and unpublished papers of Hamilton Aïdé, in the possession of the author"[87]). Even today, when its stress on economics is commonplace and its specificity outworn, *Problems of Power* must be seen as impressive in scope, densely detailed, and severely intellectual.

It came out in the month of Edith's divorce—also "out" in the news. "All these affairs do *not* help her own reputation," Julia wrote. "She has dealt so largely in her stories with the society life of today that a report like this does not astonish people." (You wonder again about Julia's private thoughts during Edith's visit. And since then *The Reef* had been published.) The Brockton and Waltham libraries would get Will's book. His father had written to *The Congregationalist* about it.[88]

Rudyard Kipling said he would do his best to call it to the attention of Field-Marshal Lord Roberts.[89]

"Intensely interesting" (*New York Times*). "The best account we have seen" (*Spectator*) "of the understandings and misunderstandings . . . between the great powers." "In the main historically sound" (*TLS*); the author might have paid more respect to "the traditional anonymity of *Times* correspondents."[90]

But the great review was written by Theodore Roosevelt and published in his magazine the *Outlook*. "The author," he wrote,

> knows international politics . . . as few other Americans, save two or three men of exceptional diplomatic experience, do know it. His book . . . is of interest to every educated and thoughtful man in any country who is concerned with the great problems of the future. But it is of especial interest to Americans. . . . [I]t would be a good thing for all our people to read Mr. Fullerton's book.[91]

"There must have been much with which you could not agree," Morton told Roosevelt, "but you have . . . in a beautiful spirit of fair-play

given me the most magnificent chance." (He had written that, after ousting Spain, the United States with "inexperienced idealism" had given
Cuba to the Cubans. He explained to TR that he had looked at Cuba
"from very far off, or from very high up," not as an event in a decade).[92]

Private Disillusionments and Public Honors

Problems of Power took James unawares. Morton had not mentioned
what he was working on. Edith had never confessed to encouraging Morton to drop the book James "greatly believed in."[93] When James heard
from a third party that Morton had a book coming out, he "unspeak-
ably" hoped it was "the Paris."[94] He praised *Problems of Power* for its
"brilliant 'go'" but feared for Morton "a little as for a lost soul of 'Journalistic circles,' Dantean as it were."[95] They were so out of touch that
James's letter praising the new book was sent back to him from the Dead
Letter Office and he had to ask Edith for Morton's new address.[96]

Morton's fall in James's esteem, not quite Miltonic, was steep enough
if we recall James's saying that Morton's comments on *The Wings of the
Dove* had intensified his need to live for his art. ("And I *shall*, I feel,
somehow, while there's a rag left of me. Largely thanks to you.") At that
time, Morton had just learned that he was not being kept on in Paris. He
had made himself read the novel attentively—and not only because he
surmised that the protagonist was, in some measure, himself. The nadir
of his career was, on his side, the zenith of the friendship.

The correspondence over blackmail five years later left James hoping
that at last he knew about Morton's mysterious past. It also marked the
end of an exclusive relation. James's visit to Paris next spring began a triple
entente, of course imperfect. Morton and Edith hid their liaison, which
reached consummation precisely as James was rolling away in the train on
which they'd seen him off. Morton harbored his secrets and his lies. James
kept the names of those at risk in the "blackmail" from Edith. He and
Edith hid their "Paris" payment scheme and tried to hide their "combination" from Morton—with whom James, having sworn secrecy, could never
again be quite frank. And Edith undoubtedly hid her loan to Morton.

Morton's behavior under threat of blackmail also marked James's first
perception that the friend who had led a "gallant"[97] life, who had been

"heroic" at Rennes, was weak. And now James's hope that "Paris" would open to Morton the "blest *alternative* life" of art[98] was disappointed. Morton preferred the political commentary for which he had been scorned until Roosevelt's praise, salve for his wounds, assured him that he could be a freelance Blowitz enabled by friendship with heads of state to influence history. Morton's intelligence, James sighed, had "such perversities!"[99]

"But why shouldn't Morton write a book which would bring money and create him an authority? Why should Zhahms decide that he remain a petit littérateur?"
"When you put it like that . . . "

If Morton had forced himself to do "Paris," he would have stewed ever after at not having done *Problems of Power,* which could not have been postponed. He seized the exactly right, the only possibly right moment, sixteen months before the war he predicted broke out. And the book did bring money and authority. James did not realize, though he thought he did, how hard it was to subsist by "art."

But what really troubled James was not Morton's subject; it was, rather, a change of heart in his friend.

At Rennes, Morton had called the Dreyfus case a war between national security and the civil liberties that Bourget decried as "abstract justice." Now he said that both ideals were legitimate forms of patriotism and that it was not surprising, "when the idea of abstract justice seemed likely to throw the whole machine out of gear—that many a Frenchman, . . . divining, what is unquestionably the *genius* of French history, should have rallied to the side of the Anti-Dreyfusists with . . . M. Bourget, M. Barrès, and M. Charles Maurras and with ninety-nine percent of the French army."[100]

Fullerton had once thought Maurice Barrès, an exemplar of the "anti-Dreyfusard ideal of duty and heroism," an artist unconvincing as a thinker.[101] Admiration of the artist led to friendship and, as Morton repudiated his "idealistic" past, political accord. When James joked about *journalistic* hell he skirted the shift in values that drew Morton to the three men Morton named: Bourget, whose pleasing side, James said, was lost in "an abyss of corruption."[102] Barrès, for James "a *poseur* and a mystificator of the first water."[103] Maurras, a founder of the far-right Action Française.

The rank of chevalier of the Legion of Honor conferred on Morton in August 1913[104] ostensibly rewarded his service in a city-planning exhibition organized by Senator Edouard Herriot, mayor of Lyon. Recommended as U.S. Commissioner by Ambassador Myron Herrick, he went to the United States hoping, he told Roosevelt, to get Americans to show how they dealt with "the problem of rational existence in great agglomerations."[105]

Relating architecture as well as migrations to topography was a passion with him. The New York skyscraper was as "right" as the ancient theater "imbedded in a hillside with the convex of its tiers of seats backed against the afternoon sun."[106] But he had little time for his new task. Of the cities he approached, only New York had come through when President Poincaré opened the International Urban Exposition in Lyon in May 1914. He saw that the broken promises and "procrastinations" of the rest would affect Herriot's attitude in the Senate toward the "Panama question" and, his "patriotic and diplomatic energy" aroused (he told James Hazen Hyde, founder of Alliance Française), he tried to "help the general cause of Franco-American relations by making Herriot see things in a less municipal light, and by stirring up the press."[107]

Since the Panama scandals, a reorganized company had built the canal, a technological feat with controversial political aspects. Theodore Roosevelt, Charles de Lesseps, and Philippe Bunau-Varilla had opened the waterway. Morton knew not only Roosevelt but two generations of Bunau-Varillas and de Lesseps. He told Katharine that there was more to his Legion than the press was aware of.[108] Prevision of his lobbying on behalf of the French official interests backing the Panama Canal may have been the undeclared reason.

"It's news to me, and of the happiest," James wrote, "that poor dear Morton . . . has been gloriously decorated—since it appears that a glory, or an advantage, s'y attache."[109]

Teddy, Berry, and Morton were "poor dears" when they were in difficulty. But at the moment of Morton's public *success* James was benevolent—and supercilious. (The Légion isn't all that glorious.) An heir of all the ages had defected "for a riband to stick at his throat," or in this case his buttonhole. James even speculated that Morton might do better by "reAmericanizing" and doing nonliterary work in Washington[110]—that is, by quitting what was a vital necessity for James: Europe. For the moment James ignored the fact that it was a necessity for Morton too. He thought of him "yearningly,"[111] sent love, inscribed a copy of *Notes of a Son and Brother* from "his faithful old friend."[112] But nothing happened to revive his faith in Morton, as distinct from his fidelity.

A Debut and a Dinner

> Sunday matinée . . . Mlle Ixo will make her début today as Santuzza in *Cavalleria Rusticana*.
>
> —*Le Figaro,* 7 June 1914

Will sends flowers, drops into Camille's dressing room to say nice things. Imaginary. But what he did the night before is known. *Figaro* named the guests at an INTIMATE DINNER given by U.S. Ambassador Myron Herrick for LE PRESIDENT ROOSEVELT:

> Mssrs Gabriel Hanotaux, Liard, Rodin, M. et Mme Bergson, Mme Waddington, Mme Lodge, Mme Longworth, Mme Edith W. Larton [sic] MM Philippe [sic] Roosevelt, Moreton [sic] Fullerton.

Bergson was the philosopher Henri Bergson; Hanotaux, an ex-foreign minister; Liard, rector of the Sorbonne; Mme Waddington, a statesman's widow; Mme Lodge, a senator's wife; Mme Longworth, Alice Longworth. Rodin was Rodin and wasn't sure he could find a suit, Herrick recalled. "We answered that his name and his reputation entitled him to come in his pyjamas. . . . The old man appeared, however, in his morning clothes."[113]

The use of Edith's Christian name in the newspaper denoted her status as divorcée. (In *The Custom of the Country,* out the previous year, Edith had satirized the thrice-divorced Undine Spragg, who takes it as a personal insult that protocol debars a divorcée's husband from becoming an ambassador. Her own background and her friendship with Roosevelt and with the previous ambassador, Henry White, saved her from being treated as déclassée.)

After dinner the politically minded men talked late in the smoking room about the possibility of war. Next day Morton sent Roosevelt a set of statistics on the European armed forces.[114]

* * *

Camille-Ixo, looking for the notice of her debut, would have seen the mention of her ex-husband. Mirecourt would have registered both Morton's grandeur and the glory of her former rival—and registered, as the days passed, the silence that was the only critical reaction to Ixo's singing. There seems to have been no word about her either of praise or of blame.

The embassy dinner—dignitaries in white tie and decorations, women in décolleté and diamonds—was the apotheosis of Morton Fullerton's Belle Epoque career.

The First World War

Ixo's debut, Fullerton's Expo, introduced an unusually sunny European June, July, and August. "The War began," Morton wrote, "in the dazzling summer of 1914 with the 'tango.'"[115] In England tea on the lawn, and honey still for tea; in Paris, thés dansants.

Three weeks after the embassy dinner the heir to the Austro-Hungarian throne was assassinated in Sarajevo. Another three weeks, and the Socialist leader Jean Jaurès mounted to Morton's study. They had met during the Case. Jaurès, a brave Dreyfusist, argued that workers, knowing that wars only served capital, would stand together against national leaders. Fullerton disagreed, but did not expect, he said later, "to be proved right quite so soon."[116]

Proved, because on July 31, Jaurès was assassinated as a pacifist traitor by a member of Action Française; and, despite their anger, Socialists both in France and in Germany voted war credits. Austria had declared war on Serbia; now Germany declared war on Russia and France, England on Germany, Austria on Russia. Turkey, Romania, Bulgaria, Japan, Italy, and Greece, came in.

Expecting a short war, Morton proposed to John Walter that the Times send him to the Peace Conference. He would have unparalleled sources. He was in "almost intimate conversation" with Delcassé, the French foreign minister; and Sir Edward Gray, British foreign secretary, "might say, even, that my intervention was not altogether, perhaps, without influence . . . at a critical moment."[117]

The Times would keep him in mind, Walter promised. Meanwhile, would he serve again as a correspondent in France?

He could not; nor could he promise to be available to the French Foreign Ministry. To leave now would be "the greatest sacrifice" he had ever made.[118] But his father was dying.

By then German planes had flown low over the Rue du Mont Thabor. The First Battle of the Marne saved Paris.

Morton was making arrangements to lecture in America when he had a wire from home. On October 22 he applied for an emergency passport.[119] His father died the next day.

He spent almost six months in America, arguing the Allied cause and denouncing German sympathizers. "The spy" Harvard Professor Hugo Münsterberg ought to be shot, he told J. H. Hyde.[120]

He told Roosevelt that European papers called Harvard a "hot-bed of German agitation."[121] (TR, fuming at being only an ex-president, unable to lead the army to Flanders, invited him to Oyster Bay.)[122] He spoke to "bankers and clubmen of New York, and the manufacturing and social world of Buffalo and Cleveland—to chance acquaintances in smokers of the great express trains."[123]

He made no money or next to none. To learn that he was coming back "on a collapse" gave James "quite a hideous little pang,"

> leaving one afresh as it does, bang up against that exquisite art in him of not bringing it off to which his treasure of experience and intelligence, of accomplishment, talent, ambition, charm, everything, so inimitably contributes. If he comes through London, as I don't see but that he must, I do hope he won't have the infamy to pass without letting me know. But when a person is capable of *such* things![124]

Shortly before the German torpedoing of the *Lusitania,* Morton returned through submarine-infested seas to terra firma torn up by the beastliness and horror of trench warfare. James learned only indirectly of his return to Paris. There he soon "abandoned" Edith, she told James. He would reappear when she could "be of use."[125]

James—with his long habit of affection, and perhaps a grumbling feeling that, after all, Morton was *his* friend first—replied that her account of Morton's "dissociation" was "too lurid." "He is the most inscrutable of men—he will never pose long enough for the Camera of Identification."[126]

The contributors to *The Book of the Homeless,* Edith's anthology in aid of refugees, included Roosevelt, James, Sarah Bernhardt, Anna de

Noailles, Renoir, Yeats, Hardy, Cocteau, Monet, Rostand, Charles Dana Gibson ("The Girl He Left Behind Him"), Rodin. Not Fullerton. Edith probably asked him for a piece; she asked the minor prosateur Wendell, and Morton at the moment was a "name." And she had no wish to affront him. Her anger, as usual, had passed; he was helping her with publicity for her war work. George Santayana, whom she did not yet know, sent a poem "The Undergraduate Killed in Battle"; Morton may have brought him in, though too busy to prepare a contribution of his own. He was consumed, like everyone else, by the war.

Abyss of Blood and Darkness

The First World War is old newsreels of heavy-coated unshaven men trudging in the rain. Mud, corpses, rats, barbed wire, gas gangrene, shell shock, no-man's-land.

In that abyss dividing two eras:

James was appalled by the killing. One had supposed the world "to be, with whatever abatement, gradually bettering . . . to have to take it all now for what the treacherous years were all the while making for and *meaning* is too tragic for any words—"[127] He assumed British citizenship to declare his sympathy, received the rarely awarded Order of Merit, and died in February 1916 at seventy-three, a week after the battle of Verdun began.

Lord Ronald Gower, seventy-one, died a week after James.

Outside Mme Mirecourt's windows troops drilled on the Esplanade. Delicate flying machines passed overhead.

Walter Berry, like Fullerton, engaged in Allied propaganda.

Hugh Fullerton came to Paris with the YMCA.

Rob Fullerton's daughter Gertrude came as an x-ray technician.

Edith Wharton organized committees and workshops, toured the front, wrote about the war for Americans, and was given the Legion.

Teddy Wharton spent the war in a Swiss sanitarium. ("Of course he was mad," says the Vicomte de Noailles; "there was a famous story of his golden garters which was the last one heard.")

Alfred Dreyfus, who had retired, returned to active duty.

The Geroulds went to Hawaii when going there was an adventure. The war "ejected" Katharine and left her "happy on a tropic shore."[128]

The Ranee? The Rajah returned to England. When royalty visited, she joined him in his establishment, then would be off. He died at eighty-five in 1917. ("Have you sent a note of condolence?" Julia Fullerton asked her son.)[129]

When America entered the war, André Tardieu went to the United States as High Commissioner for France. In the bad period when Russia's surrender freed German armies for the Western Front before Americans could arrive, Georges Clemenceau, dogged, bulldogged, tigrish, became prime minister and carried the war to the end.

Mme Pouget. One forgets about Mme Pouget. She'd have been in her thirties during the war. Where was she, what was she doing?

Camille Chabbert toured the front, singing for the *poilus*. (Did her trajectory and Edith's ever cross?)

Her daughter Mireille spent the war years alone in a château in the Vendée. *Luxe, calme, et solitude.* One descent was made by the wife of her foster-father, Paul Clemenceau's wife, "the Austrian woman" who had a nephew in the enemy army and whose alleged attempts to arrange talks caused a breach between Paul and his Tiger brother, Georges.

Paul Clemenceau, who was in dynamite, made money.

An overage archaeologist, Joseph Déchelette, volunteered and was killed. Later Morton dedicated *Au Seuil de la Provence* to his memory. Morton lost friends. But imbuing all he wrote during the war years was indifference to human lives except as they might help crush the enemy. Grief was lost in hatred. James had compassionated the young German dead.[130] Morton Fullerton pointed his finger out of the posters and "the bells of hell went ding-a-ling-a-ling, for you but not for me."

In *Hesitations* he railed against the new American president. He fumed at Woodrow Wilson's neutrality and detested his bringing the public into decision making. Moreover, Wilson had plagiarized Fullerton's idea of extending the Monroe Doctrine.[131] *Hesitations* was poorly reviewed[132] but came out in French, with black bars marking deletions by military censors, and Morton translated Gabriel Hanotaux's book on Franco-American union into English.

He longed to be closer to the action. "If I had any money, mon cher," he told John Walter, "I might, through Roosevelt, be in our diplomatic service tomorrow."[133] But when Wilson declared war on Germany, Julia was sure that Will's criticism of the president would work against "any real government advancement" for him.[134]

The Pentagon Papers

AMERICAN EXPEDITIONARY FORCE RECORDS C-in-C Report File Folder 84 COPIES OF FULLERTON'S LETTERS ORIGINALS AND OTHER LETTERS GIVEN TO COL QUEKEMEYER FOR C IN C Classification cancelled by authority of the Adj Gen Nov. 19 1946 AGPA-G 384-(17 June 46) 8 July 46.

A big parcel so labeled comes from the Pentagon.

Of 117 reports indexed, 48 are here. "Conversation with Mr. W.M.F.," the first (missing), may have recorded the talk that led to W.M.F.'s attachment to Brig.-Gen. Dennis E. Nolan, chief of intelligence AEF, assistant chief of staff G-2 (Intelligence).

Nolan, Morton said later, "had a thorough knowledge of guerilla warfare in the Philippines but knew not one thing about the map of Europe."[135] But the new agent did not write down to him. The reports, often very long, were in Morton's usual style, even to classical citations. They were based on personal contacts both with government leaders and with conspirators. They explained, argued, and advised. The basic advice was that after victory the Allies must either dismember Germany or turn it into a "Boche 'Reserve'" like the American "Indian Reserves." They must also reintegrate a Russia purged of Bolshevism.[136]

Morton reported to G-2, after talks with Sir Valentine Chirol of the *Times* and Colonel Lawrence of Arabia, that England, "mystically idealistic," no longer held "imperialistic ambitions."[137] The *Times* staff had to use "democratic formulas" because Lord Northcliffe hoped to be prime minister.[138]

Chirol was analyzing the French press for British authorities. Morton analyzed it for G-2. He reported that *Action Française*, published by Action Française, was admirable for the "elevated patriotism" of its editors, Charles Maurras, Jacques Bainville, and Léon Daudet.[139]

He spoke of "the dazzling summer of the 'tango.'" It emerges that "tango" was a bad word. Woodrow Wilson must keep the proletariat from "indulging in tango, Bolshevistic attitudes."[140]

In a separate peace, the new Soviet government that controlled Russia had ceded Latvia, Lithuania, Estonia, Ukrainia, Finland, and Poland to Germany. Germany was telling the peoples there that Allied promises of self-government were false; the Allies would hand them to Russia. But, Morton said, victory on the Eastern Front was possible only if those peoples turned against Germany. They must be made to do so. The Allies must no longer treat them as objects of "sentimental concern" but as "instruments of war, of the same general character as gas shells, grenades, avions."

Some of them, believing in "sentimental humanitarians" like Wilson, were already "ripe for revolt."

> This rebellion should be constantly and scientifically accelerated by the employment of professional agitators, authorized to spread broadcast in these countries the gospel of the Entente's formal assurance to back them morally and materially.

To occupy "Moscovy" would mean feeding forty million people— "absolutely unthinkable, even supposing that our troops are not contaminated by Bolshevism." But Siberia must be occupied.[141]

The war was nearly over. On November 8, Morton vented his fury that Germany had been given three days in which to accept an Allied ultimatum. The Armistice signed on the 11th, which brought "the greatest stab of joy that had ever been known by waiting millions,"[142] filled him with disgust. For the rest of his life he lamented the interruption of victories that would have annihilated the enemy.

Wilson came to Paris for the Peace Conference saying: "To conquer by arms is only to win a temporary victory. To conquer the world by gaining its esteem, ah, that is a permanent conquest."

Do we still need to seek "esteem," Morton demanded, we "who have throttled, in the grandest battle of idealism that this planet has ever witnessed, such hosts of Darkness as only a Milton or a Dante had ever previously ventured to look in the face!"[143]

He told General Nolan he hoped the president would learn that the only absolute truth is that all truth is relative.[144]

He dined with Owen Wister in a "jungle of captured German guns." A graduate student at Harvard in Morton's day, a friend of Theodore Roosevelt, a family friend of Hamilton Aïdé, and already famous for *The Virginian*, the first "Western" novel, Wister had recently been guiding American readers "in the footsteps of the Hun." He gave them Morton's view of the Peace Conference:

Wister: What you're saying, if it's true, is that you and and I, sitting here at this table, are living in the presence of a tragedy that beats

Aeschylus and Sophocles and Hamlet and Lear and Othello and every
worst thing in history . . . rolled into one.
Fullerton: I think so. . . .
Wister: And here sit you and I, enjoying a good dinner!
Fullerton: Would it noticeably help matters if we abstained? The milk
is spilled.[145]

The Red and the White

Paris swarmed with diplomats, conspirators, refugees, and spies. The war
had broken up four empires—Germany, Austria-Hungary, Russia, and
what remained of the Ottoman Empire—each containing ethnic groups
bent on independence but at odds with one another.

Morton reported on the seething "cauldron" of the "jealous parvenu
little Balkan states"[146] and other Eastern European entities: The Serbian
Minister "recommended to me today the prudence of avoiding intervention in Serbo-Yugo-Slav politics." "I had a few minutes with M. Venizelos
[of Greece]. The views of the Hellenic Irredentist Committee on Constantinople seem to have met with favor in England and France." "I had an
interesting talk with M. Thomas Masaryk, President of the Tcheco-
Slovak Republic. By a happy chance, a moment after leaving him I fell in
with M. Titulesco, ex-Minister of Justice in Roumania. Knowing him
more or less intimately, I was able to verify from the Roumanian point of
view the declarations of M. Masaryk."[147]

Morton's view of the Ottoman Empire was partly formed by Ismail
Kemal Bey, "a very wise old Albanian gentleman," but he brought in a
journalist friend, Sommerville Story, to help the Bey with his memoirs, a
task made hard, he explained in a preface to Story's book, by the subject's
"patriotic preoccupations" and "spasmodic disappearances. . . . Boswell
interviewed Johnson with joy for long years. But Johnson usually kept his
appointments."[148]

Toward another refugee, Morton never allowed himself levity. Grand
Duke Alexander, cousin of the murdered tsar, rescued by a British war-
ship, arrived in Paris penniless, taxied to the Ritz, and heard that America would dictate the peace. His proposal to Wilson that they talk man to
man drew the reply that, pleasant as a talk would be, the president was

occupied by Peace Conference business.[149] Morton, however, paid a call, and soon sent Nolan a text "the Grand Duke himself" had written.

Bolshevism, Alexander explained, "encourages all the bad instincts."

> One must always remember that at the head of Bolshevism are Jews; out of 220 members in the Moscow Soviet 170 are Jews. Jews never suffer, not one Jew was ever killed since the Revolution broke out; they only profit from it, like they did during the war.[150]

Alexander complained that American officers were forbidden to talk to him because he was intriguing to restore the Romanovs. *"It might be well,"* Morton advised Nolan, *"if I were in a position to contradict this statement to the Grand Duke—if it be not true."*

> I am in a position, as you know, to affirm categorically that the Grand Duke cherishes no such intentions. All he wants is to see bolshevism crushed out, and some formal stable Government take its place. . . . I may mention, by the way, that he is thinking of sending his boys to the United States to finish their education. But he is wondering whether they would be allowed to go there.[151]

"The Keys of the Southern Gate-Way of Russia, on the Black Sea at Odessa, are handed over to Bandits who are the puppets of the Jewish accomplices of Prussia,"[152] Morton warned Nolan, passing on "An Original Scheme for Throttling Bolshevism." "Business circles" in New York, Paris, and London would fund a 100,000-man corps equipped with "heavy artillery, lance-flamme, tanks, aeroplanes for bombardment, armoured autos." This force would take Petrograd, then bomb Moscow. The army would rule till a constitution was framed.[153]

In the midst of G-2, Morton pointed out in a preface to a "definitive edition" of *Problems of Power* that if his principles had been applied in 1913 the world would not now be so confused. But "certain leaders of 'the Democracy' wantonly pandered, and, in the author's opinion, criminally pandered, to its prejudices."[154]

He never concealed from Nolan his "aversion" to Wilson, clearly knowing that the general would not object to criticism of his commander in chief. But in May the Paris *Herald* ran a story with the headline "SOCIETY OF NATIONS ADMITS BALANCE OF POWER PRINCIPLE" and the byline of Fullerton, who called the League "a flippant creation of inexperienced leaders";[155] and this article did cause disfavor. It was filed with a memo by a Colonel Cox that must have come from General Pershing: "In view of Mr. Fullerton's desire for publicity General Nolan will write him a note telling him that his services are no longer required."[156]

As at the *Times*, Morton chafed at anonymity. His Pentagon file, however, has no dismissal note from Nolan, only a request two days later for certain data and Morton's report that a campaign in the Ukraine led by Simon Petliura, whom he "knew personally," was going well. "Everyone sings the praises of my friend. . . . They call him the 'new Napoleon.'"[157] Morton did not mention (quite possibly did not know) that the campaign consisted largely of pogroms.

He sent Nolan a status report on the "Original Scheme," which now synchronized a raid on Russia with the march of Admiral Kolchak's Whites into Siberia.

Kolchak's forces, with Allied support, occupied Siberia and other regions, killing off moderate Socialists as well as Bolsheviks. They were later defeated by the Reds; but when Morton wrote, the synchronization was being managed by "an extraordinarily able and clear-headed financier, Mr. Davidoff, who is known to all the chancelleries and all the great banks of the world."

Last autumn, Fullerton had advised sending agitators to assure Russian neighbors that Allied victory would make them independent. The revised "Original Scheme" would mean adjusting that plan:

> What is to become of Lithuania, Ukrainia, and even of Poland is no longer the same question as . . . six months ago. All those who think with Mr. Davidoff would willingly give Finland any form of self-government she desires and they are ready to favor even a certain modicum of imperialism [slip for "independence?"] in Poland. But, they would not willingly accept the independence of the other Nationalities.[158]

He had achieved liberation from "sentimental concerns."

If Will came over, Katharine wrote, they'd give him a cocktail before the idiotic country went dry.[159] It was the eve of Prohibition.

Before he had her letter, the Treaty of Versailles was signed. Woodrow Wilson was given the Nobel Peace Prize. Will was promoted to officer in the Légion and appointed to the Franco-American War Affairs Commission, headed by André Tardieu.

PART SIX

After the Peace: *Figaro* in the United States

"Arrived Paris Oct. 12, 1920," Fullerton noted on a letter from Milan in which "Votre [. . . ?]" wrote: "tu vois William Helene je vous oublie pas, I not forget you."

Hélène? Mme Pouget, of course. A peasant type, Hugh Fullerton says, "but Morton was sensible to get someone like her to do his cooking." After Morton died, she went south to a niece.

Something about the Luxembourg.[1] A letter to "Helene William Fullerton" in the same hand is signed "*Votre* [?Medurdo]" and says "Helene you're still polishing the furniture. *Et toi* William . . . your statemen don't leave you a moment."[2]

The Luxembourg Palace was the Senate, but this is no "stateman."

Morton kept everything; but why date letters from an uncouth (?) Italian who tutoyers him and thinks he's married to a woman of low degree? He was now U.S. secretary-general in the League of Nations Intellectual and Artistic Cooperation Commission chaired by Henri Bergson, whom he had met at the embassy dinner for Roosevelt and who would soon be Nobel laureate in philosophy. He was also a quasi-official spokesman for the United States in the French press.

His friend Marquis Robert de Flers of the Quarante Cinq and the Académie, author of comedies in the line of *Monsieur Blondeau's Tenants*, was a power at *Le Figaro*. His friend Walter Berry, for all his very non-businessman-like persona, was now president of the U.S. Chamber of Commerce. At the initiative of Berry and de Flers, *Le Figaro* started a weekly page "Le Figaro aux Etats-Unis,"[3] which often took two pages to report engagements, weddings, and parties in the new American colony. Morton became its editor.

In bygone "halcyon" years, Morton said, the natives had taken little notice, "the infiltration of us barbarians was so slow."[4] Now there were the Cercle Interallié (he and Berry were on the board), the American Club (they were officers), the Comité France-Amérique, and British and American hospitals, churches, and libraries. The colonists were mostly businessmen and officials and their families.

The Page stopped running over and began running every other week, less "social," but as a full page. As such, astonishingly, it went on, in French, the showcase of an alien, if lately Allied, in-group.

Fullerton used half the space himself and chose the other contributors: Katharine.[5] Stéphane Lauzanne of *Le Matin,* Blowitz's nephew and adopted son. William Astor Chanler, whom Morton had known at Harvard and on Pershing's staff; his wife, Minnie; his brother Winthrop; and Winthrop's wife, Margaret Terry, a friend of Edith Wharton. The Chanlers were linked with Morton's friends Santayana (a connection of James's and Edith's Sturgis friends) and Marie Meredith (married to a Sturgis). Every fortnight, Fullerton's feature and: Talk by Berry. Speech by President of Yale conferring LL.D. on Mrs. Wharton. Article by Mrs. Gerould. Morton moved his friends about his Page, configuring Edith and Berry, Edith and Katharine, Edith and himself, Edith and himself and a Chanler.

He brought in French acquaintances: Henri Bergson, Marshal Hubert Lyautey, "organizer" of Morocco.

He printed a poem by a recent *Harvard Monthly* editor. Alan Seeger had hero-worshipped Theodore Roosevelt,[6] joined the Foreign Legion so that he could fight, written "I have a rendezvous with death," and been killed. "Well as I knew them," Morton wrote when Seeger's father sent him a book of his poems, "I abandoned everything . . . to bathe in the brightness that they radiate."[7]

At the brightness falling from the poems of that war, often inexpert, written in the knowledge of statistically imminent extinction, eyes dazzled. "Comrades," Seeger wrote in "Returning to the Front after Leave," "you cannot think how thin and blue / Look the leftovers of mankind that rest, / Now that the cream has been skimmed off in you." The fittest men of a European generation had been wasted. Seeger's translator dedicated her work to her fiancé, killed at the Somme.[8] For survivors of the war the world would never be the same again.

Le Figaro's New World

On an ocean liner the first-class passengers looked third-class. "Varied racial features not yet amalgamated" made for a "heavily amorphous" American face.[9] Morton contrasted the new immigrants with owners of "founders' shares" who believed that if America ceased to belong to them it would lose its "*raison d'être* and its unity."[10] Katharine, a descendant of Miles Standish and John Alden, deplored the influx of an "inferior population."[11] Untypically, Morton was not sure. He spoke of "gibbering candidates for citizenship" but liked the melting-pot idea of "the admirable Jewish writer Zangwill." Perhaps the true American was not yet born.[12]

Katharine Fullerton Gerould was placed in the "school"[13] of Mrs. Wharton and Mr. James. Tenser and drier than Wharton, she recalls James, Meredith, and above all Conrad, from rhythms to exotic sets: writing with careful wit of nature, society, the Ambiguities. Her tale of a shipwrecked man and woman forced into bodily though not sexual intimacy to stay alive is anything but "romance." After their rescue the woman breaks with her fiancé; abjures men forever.[14]

A reviewer noted, casually, a rebellion against that school by unnamed Left Bank expatriates. Fitzgerald, Miller, Hemingway, Stein were writing. Berry's Crosby relatives were running the Black Sun Press. Five years after *Figaro*'s American page began, the *New Yorker* began Genêt's letters from Paris. There were some social encounters. Morton met Janet Flanner, *dite* Genêt, and perhaps (at the Anglo-American Press Club) Hemingway. Sylvia Beach of Shakespeare and Company at least knew *of* him and connected him with *Le Figaro*. But nothing in the "Dean of the American Colony" spoke to the new writers, and it was not from Morton's Page that French readers learned of *them*. Enclave of a square circle, it had the opinions of his friends at home. Barrett Wendell when young had made Santayana think of Shelley, but in his forties he had incensed Katharine by insisting that Harvard remain "a school of manly virtue" by keeping women out; and in the 1920s, a Late George Apley, he held views that were stuffier yet, as reported by a hostile press. (Walt Whitman: "hexameters trying to bubble through sewage." The West: inferior to the East.)[15]

* * *

Fortunately not prescient, Katharine felt "burglarized"[16] when fans asked personal questions. "Fan" had come in from baseball. Her *Conquistador* became a film starring Ramon Navarro. Movies were in. Jazz was in. On ocean crossings, Morton was put off by "African" music, musicians, and dances.[17]

He made no concessions to the new male look, grooming moustaches only slightly diminished as gravely as did Hercule Poirot (who came in), and continued to attract.

It was harder on women who had disguised their bodies with crinoline, bustle, low-slung shirtwaist, and hobble skirt when the bobby-haired flapper sashayed onto the dance floor in waistless frock ending above the knee. Still, the Edith Wharton photographed as accommodating sensibly to the new line is more sympathetic than the grande dame hung with pearls. More vulnerable.

Subtleties of Parisian Life

Yet the people who remember Mrs. Wharton knew her then, and they remember her as both abnormally rigid and abnormally fussy. Abel Bonnard said "something ravishing," says Mme de Prévaux: His friendship for her was "a rose-bush, but a rose-bush planted facing north." When another man heard that she had had a lover, a balloon issued from his head, almost, full of exclamation points. "I could have sworn—! Maybe Monsieur Wharton touched her; I am not sure she'd have let *him!*" He had wondered if she was a Lesbian, because in his youth he'd propositioned her and she had declined.

At the Cercle Interallié, Marshal Lyautey's nephew begins to laugh. "I must tell you a story my uncle told me. A Général Gross didn't grasp *les subtilités de la vie parisienne.* There was a luncheon, fourteen persons, and he said to Berry during a pause: '*Cher ami,* do you know Mme Edith Wharton?' and—there was not a word. Everyone looked at his plate. The general was very important, you know. But there was *a silence!*"

"Berry was *horrid,*" says the Baronne de la Grange. "He had a corps of lovely ladies. I can't imagine why she loved him. I used to see Fullerton

at Minnie Chanler's. Charming and all that, always coming or going. Of
course I knew nothing of a liaison."

Knowing both Edith and Berry, Morton must have covered a smile,
hearing talk. He spoke later of the "myth" of her "frigidity."

*"To speak of a myth" (Marc) "he had to know there was a myth. He
knew what was said in talk at which he was present. Talk among men.
Did he talk, himself?"*
"He'd have risked a lot."
*"Eh oui, le code du gentleman. But to dissent when they said that she
was frigid, that would not be gentlemanly."*

Edith loved two men who were sophisticated and intelligent: one asex-
ual, the other a satyr, both loveless, both selfish, who got on well together. Morton praised Walter in print. Hearing of Morton's first rise in
the Légion—"the best act of the Herriot government"—Walter "rushed
to the telephone," couldn't get him, "So just this word to say how glad I
am. . . . All my congratulations, old man."[18]

When Camille was in Paris she'd have asked Will about people on his
Page, especially her ex-sister-in-law, whose letters she would later take by
force along with letters from the high officials he cited when direly hint-
ing at treason, strategems, and espionage.

Around this time her daughter was degraded—epaulettes ripped off,
sword broken—and left France. "And so we nieces and nephews became
the heirs," Albert Clemenceau's daughter had explained to me in all simplicity. A child without a family threatened *la Famille*—a force greater
than the Austro-Hungarian empire that had been affected by Szeps, the
father of Paul Clemenceau's wife. She was the woman Georges Clemenceau accused of conspiring with Austria during the war, and if the danger
to the family inheritance posed by Paul's protégée came up in talk with
Georges or Albert, Morton would have been more interested in the alleged activities of Paul's wife.

Private Armies and Public Forums

"I always supposed he was a spy," Mme de la Grange volunteers.

The inconclusive conclusion of his G-2 record: A command to
Brigadier-General Nolan from General Pershing to fire him, a command

not obeyed. Indexed reports that stop in 1919 and are declassified, not twenty-five years after that date, but twenty-five years after that date plus two. Hugh Fullerton has "no doubt that Morton's contributions were valuable to the State Department."

The Chanler connection: William Astor Chanler, big-game hunter and "ardent Anti-Semite," had helped put down a tribal revolt in Africa and, a relative says, "ran a private international secret service, fomenting counter-revolution," in which Morton had a part.[19] This operation may have grown from the private army Morton advocated in 1919. In a perhaps separate endeavor a Fullerton associated with the Times is said to have worked with a White Russian judge on investigating the tsar's murder.[20]

While some of Morton's covert activities remain covert, acres of newsprint document his open exertions. As at the Boston Advertiser, high in a cubicle in a turret he meted judgment to the world below, dealing now not with books but with principalities and powers, proud that, like Blowitz, owing allegiance to no country, he was "sought out by the representatives of all."

In an affidavit to "explain protracted foreign residence and overcome presumption of expatriation" he deposed that he had worked for the New York Times.[21] He doubtless lied only to avoid red tape, but his patriotism, New England parochialism, had of course faded. France's was "the most fascinating and human of all histories."[22]

Morton's basic premise was that Germany must be kept weak by Anglo-Franco-American entente. Obstacles to entente were America's isolationism and England's forgiving and forgetting.

Repayment of Allied war debts to the United States was a bitter issue. (Grand Duke Alexander saw in Paris a sign saying the French had Uncle Shylock to blame for their woes and a sign in California saying roads could not be repaired because France didn't pay up.)[23] Morton argued that it would be simple justice and sound economy for the U.S.A. to cancel the debts. One of his editorials to that effect filled five columns of a six-column page.[24] His advocacy brought promotion in the Legion to commander.

He had said in Problems of Power that although a centralized state "fosters Antisemitism" and enacts "excessive" laws against anarchists which can also be applied to "crimes of opinion," its advocates have "amiable defects," its opponents "odious merits."[25] This rightward trend accelerated.

The new American president, Calvin Coolidge, had "suppressed an-
archy and revolt" during the Boston Police Strike. "It was Mussolinism
before the letter, in the best tradition of New England."[26]

The impartial study of the origins of the war called for by J. M.
Keynes, H. G. Wells, G. B. Shaw, Arnold Bennett, and Gilbert Murray
would only "add momentum to the seething masses."[27]

A "Renew the Reich" movement waxed as the League of Nations
waned. Morton loathed Renewal but despised the League. The leaders of
the democratic Weimar Republic lied when they said that Franco-
German economic union was the way to peace. Germany must be walled
in with a "military, naval, air, and chemical alliance."[28]

When Morton's classmate Alanson Houghton became ambassador extraordinary in Berlin, Morton reprinted one of his *Harvard Monthly*
poems.[29] In the same capacity in London, Houghton proposed international suffrage and a referendum before a country declared war, and
Morton (who now disparaged even *national* suffrage) cried: "Idealism,
what crimes . . . !"[30] "Even if we are not cavemen hurling flints," he
wrote later, "the 'prehistoric principle' holds."[31]

Pessimism in the line of Machiavelli and Hobbes has a welcome tang
after the saccharine. But Morton believed that he could cause and control
as well as predict; and, by whatever concatenation of genes and circumstances, for him to be powerful meant to denounce, not to argue or per-
suade. It was "thunder, nothing but thunder."

What had happened between the conservatism of *Problems of Power*
and his strident French editorials was G-2. For four years he had written
on matters of great importance with no outside check, no informed readers, only the respectful General Nolan—to whom he passed on without
caveat Grand Duke Alexander's views on society. He had had power (a
degree of power) without responsibility.

Mme Mirecourt's Heirs

With distancing from the war came *All Quiet on the Western Front, No
More Parades, A Farewell to Arms, Siegfried et le Limousin, In Parenthe-
sis.* Disillusionment and generosity. *La Grande Illusion.* Morton intensified his vilification of Germany for "the aggressive gluttony, land-hunger,
and thirst for wassail that had characterized the race from Attila on."

These *Figaro* articles explain Eugène Fleuré's amazement that Morton was not taken by the Gestapo during World War II.

His hatred of Germany, no stronger than, say, Berry's, went deeper. He had lived with a Frenchwoman from a region invaded in an earlier war. Had the Hun driven Adèle's family from their home?

She died in 1924, when Morton was consolidating his Page. It was three days before they found her. Neighbors may have talked.

Mesdemoiselles Louise and Angèle Bouvier, sisters, still live in the Rue de la Comète, around a corner from the Rue Fabert.

An ironing board up and laundry on it, orange peels drying on a radiator, a picture of the pope, and two sweet-faced, mystified, very old ladies. They don't know the names Moutot, Mirecourt, and they have lived here all their lives!

"There aren't many who'd remember that far back."

"There was the baker across the street, but he's dead."

"Yes, he's dead."

Who inherited Adèle's money? The inside pages of her will were not for my eyes, Maître Radet had said, but . . .

Rueil-Malmaison

"Why, there is no reason why you shouldn't see," he says. "It was never probated. But I wonder if it is still here."

The cabinet déjà vu: fireplace, mirror, curtained bookcase. The marble base of the bronze lioness on the mahogany desk is a pen-and-ink stand. The porphyry clock ticks.

This is where Morton and Mme Mirecourt signed their pact on a Saturday begrudged them by Edith Wharton, dipping pens into that inkwell with Henri-Napoléon Saint-Laurent looking over their shoulders. The chair I am in, by the desk, is the chair of honor (cf. Nero Wolfe's red leather chair). Adèle sat in it; *she* was Maître Faribault's client. He, at the desk, reduced eighteen years of love and rage to a schedule of payments, and two years later went to that tiny house to draw her will—*Is* it still here?

A man in a *blouse* brings it in.

I appoint Charles Albert Alfroy my universal heir to execute the following bequests: To Mme Bellotte, Rueil, 5000 francs. To Mme Louise Bavoux, Widow Buisson, 36 Rue de Maistre Paris, my furniture, clothes, pictures, and jewels. I desire him to give Mme Buisson's children such gifts and do them such kindnesses as he pleases, relying on his sense of honor.

Alfroy! "A friend," I told Maître Radet. "It was in tracing him that I found you, Monsieur. But he died before she did."—"That's why this will was never probated. She must have made a new one. And Mme Belotte?"—"She rented the house from your friend M. Roze's mother and took in guests; perhaps she'd been kind when Mme Moutot was so ill. And Bavoux—Mme Moutot's mother was a Bavoux."

Paris

Pictures, furniture, jewels. Mirecourt did better than Ixo in providing for her old age, apart from any money left by Zélie. And she had Morton's payments.

Three years after Adèle made her will Morton told Edith Wharton that Julia was exhausted by nursing his father, and she rebuked him for not sending *them* the money he was giving a woman who might deserve some compensation, but not for life. A "clever lawyer" might free him; he should fight, now that he was not afraid of a scandal at the *Times!* (So, he'd told Edith that it wasn't sheer blackmail.)

But he kept on paying. *In person.* Can he have hoped that Adèle, a *donna mobile,* would make him her heir? After Alfroy died, *did* she? No. Obviously she chose the widow she'd named in the will that became invalid, mother of children who were obviously minors and may be alive today! Finding them should be a breeze.

Weeks divided between the Persepolis Conference on Literacy and ladders in *mairie* storerooms.

Two Bavoux from Saint-Rémy were here in the 1890s. Comb current voting lists for Bavoux's who are of an age to be their children and may know the terms of Morton's *pacte* with his "fiend."

There are fifty of them. And the Buissons, so easy to find? Buisson, Bush, is one of the commonest names in France.

Nothing, nothing. *Tipota.*

Cubism and Politics

Morton had studied art history at Harvard. He had known artists, attended the official Paris salons (not the Rejects'), discussed Old Masters with Comte d'Aulby with some assurance. Recently he had helped Thomas Meteyard arrange a Paris show, and reviewed it. (The "seductive keynote" of the paintings was "taste" in composition and in "harmony of tone.")[32] But his approach was literary. Art was not a passion—and it never comes into his editorials. When *Le Figaro* for 1927 glided and bumped down the screen and "Cubisme et Politique" by W.M.F. appeared, the article cried for attention.

It's not about art. He says that modern statesmen, like Cubists, consider the past a mere set of conventions. They want to represent the entire content of human experience "once and for all and all at once," a scientific impossibility. Woodrow Wilson died of defying diplomatic conventions by appealing to the populace. "Medardo Rosso of course survives and will live forever as a miraculous exception. But in general cubism political and cubism aesthetic have the same value—absolutely nothing."[33]

One of those barbarous letters to "William Helene" is signed Rosso and the other—

Medardo Rosso. Sculptor, 1858–1928;[34] friend of Degas, Zola, Dalou. Exchanged works with Rodin; his *Laughing Woman* is in Musée Rodin. *Impressionisme plastique*. Photographs of his statuary, stunning, could be photographs of paintings: Everyday subjects, groups, people in a bus. Suggestion of background, atmosphere, light and shadow. Insertion of a real light in *Kiss under Lamp Post*.

Morton had been the lover of a sculptor. But R.G.'s work, guiltless of aught that could offend or perplex, was light-years distant from Rodin's and Rosso's. Morton speaks of "Cubism" with incurious ignorance; he might as well have said "modernistic." His *Figaro* colleague, the art critic Camille Mauclair, though better informed, also damned innovation. Prizes went to "the weeds in the field of Bolshevist painting." Expressionism was Socialism.[35] Morton praises Rosso only because he knows him personally. Knows him well. Rosso calls him and Mme Pouget "my other family."

When Rodin unveiled his grand *Balzac*, Rosso accused him of stealing his style. They were enemies when Rodin died in 1917; and Rosso had new cause for anger when he wrote to "William Helene," for, at Clemenceau's initiative, the nation had bought two Rossos, but they were withdrawn from display at the Luxembourg Museum.

That's why he asked William Helene to "go to the Luxembourg and find out what they've done not saying nothing." Not to the Senate but to the museum that was part of the palace complex.

"He considered his friends to be his true family," says a student of Rosso. "He was a creature of extremes in his art and life, very impulsive and warm and generous but also incredibly closed and secretive about his art and life, and he held long grudges when he felt he had been betrayed."[36]

Rosso accused the Rodin family and the museum director of conspiracy and complained to Clemenceau—in good French. Morton may have helped him. Rosso sculpted Clemenceau. Morton may have known Rosso and suggested to Clemenceau that he buy some Rossos and have Rosso sculpt him. Less likely, he knew Rosso through Clemenceau. Or through . . . Poor old thing, no; not the artistic type.

The Mission to Madrid: Sixth Time Around

Politically, Fullerton remained absorbed by the war's beginning, which in his opinion was the formation of the Entente Cordiale.

(To recapitulate: he had learned in 1902 that France and England were secretly negotiating claims to Africa, excluding Germany. The *Times* rejected the story at first, but in early 1903 let him wire it from Madrid two months before his post as Madrid correspondent began. Just before taking up the post he went to Lisbon for the visit of Edward VII to Carlos of Portugal. The secret talks he had reported led to the Entente Cordiale, which decided alignments in the First World War.)

The war was barely over when he told John Walter that the *Times,* out of "modesty, ignorance—or jealousy," was "losing a beautiful occasion to affirm its authority" by not reminding people of a wire

> which not only was the first mention of negotiations towards that Entente which was to "save civilisation," but was also an essential and conscious part of the mechanism devised . . . for preparing public opinion. . . .
>
> Few journalistic achievements, it seems to me, are more honourable than this, and I feel that the *Times* may, without indelicacy, take credit to itself now for an act of which the German war has shown the wisdom.[37]

Reporting adumbrations of the entente had become the entente, the "act." The *Times*—Fullerton—had saved civilization. Later he expanded on his scoop:

from an observation post in Madrid, where I was detained on a prolonged and urgent mission, I saw over beyond Gibraltar, in the heart of Morocco, the weaving of that net of intrigue which the great Delcassé [French foreign minister], the Richelieu of the Third Republic, was already secretly undoing.[38]

That passage had stood out in the first skimming of Morton's life. Now we know that he was sent to Madrid because the *Times* had nothing else to do with him, except sack him, and that he had already "seen" the intrigue in Paris. Like his being Chief, it was a lie. But a rectificatory lie. He created a background more worthy of his dispatch than his real ignominious sojourn in Spain.

It was a fairly safe lie (whereas you wonder how he got away with the other one). It appeared in 1923 in *Au Seuil de la Provence*—travel sketches few *Times* people were likely to read, at a time when even fewer knew or cared about a long-retired junior staff member. French readers, on the other hand, would relate the mission to the wartime intelligence which Morton did not keep very secret.

Last remakes of the wire: 1925. The *Times* ran a story on the entente. In a flash, *Le Figaro* responded: The *Times* might have made a "discreet allusion" to a wire it had refused to print at first, Morton now said, because he would not give his source, which he now gave: Paul Cambon, French ambassador in London.[39] In 1927, new detail: for months before sending it he had been "in almost daily contact" with the *corps diplomatique* in Madrid.[40] In 1928, reprint.[41] In 1929, suggestion that the *Observer* print it: "That wire is history."[42]

But as he improved his story, government archives were being opened, and more became known about the background of the entente.[43] They reveal that he had unwittingly been present at the next phase of maneuvers when he covered the frivolous royal visit to Lisbon. That visit was an "essential and conscious" part of the secret negotiations, planned in London to blunt interest by governments and press when the king went on to Paris for another social visit—and secret agreement of the entente with the president of France.

The details of the Paris visit were arranged in Lisbon by the French minister, who offered Morton hospitality, and the British minister, who praised an "appreciation" of the Lisbon visit Morton sent the *Times*. For some reason, Cambon had had him leak one piece of information, but the diplomats concerned with King Edward's so to speak secret mission hoodwinked him.

When the wire appeared, the *Times* was ridiculed and accused of printing "bogus" news. Morton's chiefs must have known that his story would be seen as a ploy of the French Foreign Ministry (as, evidently, it was). Why did they decide to use it? Possibly because Lavino, who succeeded Blowitz in 1902, persuaded Morton to name his source, with the result that London had him wire it from Madrid, to deflect attention from Paris.

During later negotiations Morton was in Spain, no international nerve center. Lavino would have handled the continuing story from Paris, and the likelihood that he had sponsored the wire is borne out by the fact that (though Morton may not have known it for decades), when the Entente was formally signed, Lavino was congratulated by Valentine Chirol on his "share in the Anglo-French agreement—and it was no inconsiderable one."[44]

As facts dribbled out, Morton did not claim personal knowledge of the behind-the-scenes activity in Lisbon. But there was no cause for embarrassment. His story and the scaffolding he erected about it, his additions and repairs, were associated with Madrid; he had publicized his stay in Lisbon so little that almost no one knew of its chief consequence, his marriage.

When Camille turned to Paris cabaret, she and Will were friendly enough, but at some point—perhaps when she learned that he was with another woman—she began to assert that she was his wife. Mme Pouget, of course, denied it furiously. Hugh Fullerton assumes that it was absurd, and I've accepted his view, but . . .

Camille and Will both knew the divorce was fraudulent. Moreover, Camille belonged to a church that denied the validity of *any* divorce. She could certainly argue that she was still married. And she had no reason to lie when she said that Morton had recognized her child, thereby making her legitimate. She made the statement at the end of her life, when Mireille, Mireille's daughter, and Morton himself were dead. Even if the divorce had been valid, Mireille would have remained legitimized.

But Camille did not appeal the divorce; and when Mireille married, she did not take advantage of her right to name Morton as father.

Riding High

From the mid-1920s through the mid-30s, Morton carried all before him. When *Figaro* dropped the American page in 1929, he was in effect promoted. From then on, every other week he had the first two or three columns on page one in which to air his views, a prominence he shared with Henri de Montherlant and Abel Bonnard. He consorted with statesmen, generals, and industrialists. From this period date most of his papers signed "bien sincères remerciments, Edouard Herriot" (prime minister), "affectueusement, André Tardieu" (prime minister), "Meilleurs souvenirs," Raymond Poincaré (prime minister and president). His memoirs, the Marquis de Chambrun, senator, wrote in 1935, "would be very useful for a history of the last thirty years."[45]

He moved among the beautiful people: leisured, chic, and rich. The Duchesse de Talleyrand. Anna Gould. (*Had* she been one of his wronged fiancées?) Her ex-husband the playboy Marquis Boni de Castellane. Prince Dominic Radziwell. The Maharajah of Kapurthala.

Julia Fullerton told the family with modest pride that, in New York, Will stayed at the Waldorf Astoria. When Queen Mary came to Paris she always had him to tea, because King George had called him to London in 1914 to ask his advice about declaring war.

Julia died at ninety-two.

Katharine's son Christopher Gerould came to Paris with a dimmer view of Will than the Fullerton side of the family's. He knew that the amethyst ring Will gave his mother was "a gift from his old boy friend Ronald Gower." He did not know—*she* never did—the extent of the contempt Will had shown for her, joking about his "amours with his sister" to Camille and to the "Doll" who sent him a *pneu* when the "little sister" was in Paris. ("Don't break her heart . . . I'm talking morals to you—!")

In July 1930 the Geroulds, in Princeton, could read in the *New Yorker*'s Paris Letter of a fancy-dress party given by a duchesse. Present "was Miss Dolly Wilde in the habiliments of her uncle, Oscar Wilde, and looking both important and earnest."[46]

In England, Wilde's niece read the article and sent thanks to its author Janet Flanner, *dite* Genêt.[47]

Dolly. Was "Doll" Dolly Wilde? A tempting idea—and had Morton kept in touch with her all those years? When in Paris, Dolly Wilde lived in a set of Lesbian expatriates, literary and artistic, like Nathalie Barney, Djuna Barnes, Romaine Brooks, and Flanner herself. She committed suicide in London in 1941, early in the second war.[48]

Janet Flanner knew Morton, but she doesn't want to talk about him. And he may have known Wilde's niece.

But she was not Doll. Not possibly. Doll's handwriting has no resemblance to hers, and Doll's *pneumatique* is postmarked 1909, when Dolly Wilde, Dorothy Ierne Wilde, was only thirteen years old.

Teddy Wharton died. Rosso. Walter Berry. Thomas Meteyard.

Morton spoke of Berry's "fine culture and high irony" and "immense and varied contacts with life, of which he is a rare connoisseur"[49]—surely the self-portrait he'd have drawn. In Meteyard he recognized a man unlike himself, "of a singular modesty, utterly unconcerned with the arts of self-promotion. All those who knew him will suffer at heart from his going; for he was charming and extraordinary, and an unfailing friend."[50] Morton concealed his less savory qualities from Meteyard as he did from James.

A newer friend was the nonagenarian millionaire Edward Tuck. Morton may have met the Tucks, Americans, during the war, when they entertained fifteen thousand doughboys in their Paris house and took the wounded into a hospital they built in Rueil.[51]

An old friend, André Tardieu, came into power—three times prime minister. Probably the most gifted man of his generation, in Morton's opinion. Disdainful of mankind, for vulgarity pained him, but kind to individuals.[52] Tardieu, right of center, may have slightly braked the influence of extremists on Morton—who wrote incessantly of politics.

November 1932: In the United States the Great Depression and an election, Herbert Hoover versus Franklin Delano Roosevelt.

Though Morton told the French it would make no difference who won, Americans crowded into Pershing Hall to listen to the radio. News, adjournments to a bar, and rumbas alternated until "resounding hurrah's broke out, a gramophone started la Star-Spengel [*sic*] Banner, and champagne corks popped in a salvo of honor."[53]

In the *Figaro* the ghost of Theodore Roosevelt visits the White House, where Franklin Delano Roosevelt is explaining war debts to the outgoing Hoover. "*Voilà,* Herbert," Morton had FDR conclude—"and Teddy is listening!"[54]

* * *

In the *Tout Paris* directory: W. Morton Fullerton, C***. Mme Wharton, née Edith Jones, O**. Lt. Col. Alfred Dreyfus, O**. Paul Clemenceau (and Mme née Szeps). Mme Pola Negri, artiste.

"Camille-Ixo artiste lyrique" or "Ixo-Camée" (in phone books, she didn't make *Tout Paris*) was singing and partying in Paris and Nice with friends like Maître Théodore Valensi of the Chamber of Deputies, who sent her a portrait-card of himself: legal robes, cap, stock, coquettish twinkle.[55] His nephew recalls her as "rather eccentric, with heavy make-up, a bit Folle-de-Chaillot, the kind of woman my uncle liked." She knew the film star Pola Negri, who boasted Chaplin and Rudolph Valentino among her lovers. Valentin Mandelstamm (*Last Flight to Lisbon*) wrote about Pola on Morton's page.[56] Pola lived in a chateau in Rueil. Edward Tuck gave the French nation a chateau in Rueil near Josephine's, using another himself. Pola knew Mandelstamm and Camille. Morton knew Camille and Mandelstamm, and it was partly through Tuck that he knew the *huppé* international set in Monaco and elsewhere. Camille, too, might have moved in that circle but that her raffishness, no drawback in itself, was marred by lack of money. Even so, from her flat in Nice, a mile along the coast from Monte Carlo, she could as in Paris to some extent keep track of the man she had met in Lisbon, reborn. A personage.

Edith Wharton recoiled from the glitter Morton enjoyed. (At sixty-odd, C***, he would write that he "must rush off to dress for the ball at the Embassy.")[57] Her *Tout Paris* address was the Pavillon Colombe, the house she bought in Saint-Brice-sous-Forêt, north of Paris.

The Forêt bordering Saint-Brice is Montmorency Forest, where she and Morton lunched the day they first made love. She chose not to forget him, though her eyes had cleared. He could still hurt her: as when he let her know that he had not followed her work, in a late proof of what she called, with surface playfulness, his "total rejection of your E."[58] Only with him and with Berry had she wanted "total" friendship,[59] she told him. She consulted him over problems that arose after Berry's death.[60] When he was ill, she gently offered hospitality that he did not accept.[61] Morton never visited her winter place near Hyères, where she said he might "get another delightful chapter for the new 'Terres Françaises,'"[62] but he did go to Saint-Brice. Arranging a last meeting, in June 1931, she wrote that she would walk to the station to meet him.[63] Afterward she wrote that her old servant Gross had said that M. Fullerton was still the same. *Was he?* Edith asked.[64]

Concealments

Morton's published address was his study. He would go there from the
Batignolles, then to the *Figaro*, dot-dotting with his cane, as Eric Hawkins at the *Herald-Tribune*, the first person I met who had known Morton, used to see him ("always alone"). Then on to sit for the painter Brisgand,[65] to dinner at Maxim's, to an assignation, to supper; and after
supper, or next morning, back to Mme Pouget.

He had some people meet this "charwoman type," others not. Hugh
Fullerton met her only after the Second World War and took her to be a
prudential acquisition of Morton's old age, but by 1930 she was his con-
cubine or common-law wife: they'd been together over ten years. He
once took her to America. He had a V.I.P. friend obtain a tobacconist's license for one of her cousins.[66] Ambassador Lewis Douglas took her and
Morton to lunch. She was named with Mr. and Mrs. Hugh Fullerton in
the notice of Morton's death and with them "received" at the funeral.

But like Mirecourt before her Hélène, while a true companion, not a
mere housekeeper, was a base from which Morton hunted women.

Of course Eric Hawkins of the Paris *Herald-Tribune* was dumbfounded at hearing of a marriage, not because, as I naïvely supposed, he
thought Morton "a bachelor type," but because everyone knew him to be
the very opposite.

It explains why Morton kept a room in the Elysée Hotel between the
wars. He needed a place to take women to. And men.

Hugh Fullerton shakes his head. "He was so tangled up with women
he couldn't have had the time or energy; he was physically frail. He didn't
have that name or I would have had wind of it. He gloated over his tri-
umphs over great ladies. They appealed to his vanity, which was inordi-
nate when he was at the top of his stride, though he always descended to
the *bas-fonds* at the same time. I remember a detailed report on a Maha-
ranee. He crept into her room in a friend's mansion and pounced on her."

Confusion with Margaret Brooke, Ranee of Sarawak? No. Mr. Hugh
Fullerton has two black-jade elephant bookends. "the Maharajah of Kapurthala presented them when Morton visited him in India."

There *had* been men, though Hugh Fullerton did not know it; but it is
hard documenting homosexuality, at a time when homosexuals had to be

secretive, in a man as elusive as Fullerton. "Slightly mysterious," Edith Wharton had said soon after they met, which was also soon after Aïdé left him his papers ("I *trust you*. I say no more"). Reading them, Morton wrote on a card: "My relations with Aïdé; His Note Books/ Aïdé on me," listing dates in 1889.[67] (The notebooks have gone.)

My early investigation of Morton's American life had uncovered friends his own age, men he knew while he was Samuel Longfellow's protégé, before his intimacy with Aïdé and R.G. and acquaintance with Wilde. Some of them were homosexual. Santayana was, in orientation, romantically. He wrote a love poem to a classmate, Ward Thoron. After college he was close to another classmate, the art critic Charles Loeser (said to have been in love with Berenson). Loeser, like Santayana, kept up with Morton, who went to Chantilly with him to look at paintings[68] and introduced him to James, perhaps to Aïdé (who introduced him and Berenson to R.G.)[69] and to the Whartons. And in France Morton met Bertram Goodhue, friend of the architect Ralph Adams Cram, and Richard Hovey, friend of Thomas Meteyard and Bliss Carman.

Cram's biographer places Cram (whom Morton did not know), Hovey, Goodhue, Meteyard, Carman, and Santayana in a "Bohemia" that flourished within the confines of the stereotypical, puritanic fin-de-siècle Boston. They were men of talent, medievalists, Anglo and Roman Catholics, "Visionists"; and so many of them were homosexuals as to have formed "an emerging gay subculture"[70] that was smothered when the overseas scandal of Oscar Wilde's trial and sentence made aestheticism, and even high-church Episcopalianism, suspect as Decadent and brought visits by Boston police.

Morton left for London while the "Bohemians" were only becoming acquainted; and he left London, before Wilde's fall, for Paris, where, a few years later, his refusal of Wilde's request for a loan drew the barbed: "Sentiment, my dear Fullerton, need not borrow stilts." The most telling comment on his attitude is his own note on the ex-convict's letter: "*Parbleu!* What he called stilts were the Johnsonian tongs." No "There but for the grace of God," though *he* had had homosexual relations for which he would be blackmailed seven years later.

Only a few weeks after his exchange with Wilde, Morton went to Rennes as champion of another victim of prejudice. His homoerotic admiration of several military witnesses at the Dreyfus trial seems strangely unguarded, given the post-Wilde climate in London. (Was that why he was sent a private wire: "REMEMBER BRITISH PUBLIC RESENT HIGH colouring"?) But he was under too much pressure to dissemble, and his feeling for male beauty was as much *him* as was his indignation (at Rennes) at injustice. The handsome officers were pro-Dreyfus; beauty was truth, truth beauty.

Ranging Paris at will, Morton may have had any number of male lovers among high-placed men like the friends of Proust in the Quarante Cinq and among less notable bourgeois. He may also, as with women, have found, in what Hugh Fullerton called the "lower depths," partners in one-hour stands.

Edith Wharton saw Morton so preeminently as *her* lover, and a lover of other women, she can hardly have been aware of his range of sexuality in the years when they were intimate unless he told her himself, to shock her—which cannot be ruled out, though the cruel things she rebuked him for saying seem to have been comments on *her* character rather than revelation of his. But toward the end of her life, after his 1931 visit, she had a glimpse of an early, probably gay friendship when he asked her opinion about publishing some poems by Bliss Carman for which he had written a preface.

Carman, fair, flamboyant, very tall—born in mid-April, he called himself "a cross between an April Fool and a Maypole"[71]—Carman was always rapturously in love; but after two engagements, one of nine years and one of four, he warned adoring women that he could go only so far because of a "Unitrinianism"[72] influenced by Santayana: the "love passion" must be inspired by physical beauty but must become mystic. He ended his one known heterosexual liaison so as to remain friends with both his mistress and her husband.[73] He and Morton saw each other in the 1890s, and during the First World War he met "the beautiful Fullerton all unexpectedly . . . one of the very few that I have always held in very fond remembrance which not even my own vile neglect could impair. There he was, handsome as ever, and we had a heavenly luncheon together in a little New York French restaurant."[74]

Carman was a well-known poet ("revered" in his native New Brunswick)[75] when he died in 1929. His manuscript "Songs before Sunrise" may have been in Morton's hands for years, to judge by Edith's contrasting their "golden glow" to the gray present. She saw no reason not to publish, she told Morton, blandly adding: "You might tone down your tribute to the poet's photograph, and a few other personal touches (personal to yourself) in which Carman is not concerned."[76] Perhaps with nothing more in mind, she needled him for susceptibility to male beauty as well as self-centeredness.

* * *

By that time (which was when Hugh knew him), Morton may have been conserving energy by concentrating on women, always his dominant interest, or may only have been more discreet with men.

He had feared that the Wilde association would become known, and he was blackmailed over R.G. Why did he choose to run risks? His was not the predicament of men for whom love meant secrecy or obloquy. His attraction to men did not debar attraction to women. He experienced nothing like the anguish of the W.M.H. whose letter was in Aïdé's papers or of James in letters to the sculptor Hendrik Andersen. His easy enjoyment of pleasure and obvious talent for giving pleasure, undifferentiated as to men or women, were less about love, or even sex, than about control. As you mouse about the Fullerton files, *power* keeps appearing on the screen. As an unusually beautiful youth he found that he could exert influence over older, well-to-do, important men who took him to Europe, took him to Greece and Egypt, found him a professional position beyond his qualifications. With younger men, was he passive or a predator? "Everyone knew" (Hugh Fullerton says) "he dropped his mistresses like hot cakes." Were men, too, drawn by vows of love and stricken by casual dismissals?

Perhaps not. With the misogyny of the Don Juan, he had a higher opinion of men's intellect and conversation than of women's. With men he could give and maintain the "equable friendship" Edith despaired of receiving; he was a better friend to men, perhaps not seeing even attractive males automatically as potential conquests. As a consequence, we can't know from his letters whether a friendship with a man was more than friendship.

After his death, Camille said that Morton had been a *pédéraste*, not saying *when*. Had he had male lovers in their short marriage? Or did he reveal his same-sex affairs to an unshockable artiste later, as he did his amours with his sister; did she tell Mireille, did Mireille tell Robert Lainé, and so on? The Lainé search dragged its length along, Lainés wrote from Drury Lane and Wimbledon, from Lille and from Saint-Saviour's, Channel Islands.

Forget it. Mireille was eight or nine when Camille dumped her. Keeping after them would be crazier than hunting for Mirecourt.

Hunting for Mirecourt. Time-devouring, back-breaking, mind-stultifying, funds-depleting labor hard on soles and heels. Fees, letters, stamps. Fares. Madness. Forget Mirecourt.

A Shock of Nonrecognition

The post brings a copy of the official biography of Edith Wharton, inscribed to me "with enduring gratitude."

The biographer says that the "hard research" of his Paris associate disclosed the fact that the woman who had blackmailed Fullerton was probably a "certain Henrietta Mirecourt."[77]

Stupeur.

Henrietta?

Henrietta Mirecourt (the "probably" disappears) lived with Fullerton at 2 Rue de Chausée [*sic*] d'Antin. "From references to her, she appears to have been an intelligent, even a cultivated, person, and perhaps part English."[78]

Emotion.

Half an hour—hours—later—There was a Daffis de Mirecourt, *femme de lettres.* I had told the biographer so, with a "maybe Mme Mirecourt was a kind of French Henrietta Stackpole." A character in a James novel.

But surely . . .

But the creation of a "Henrietta Mirecourt" who lived with Fullerton at the *Times* office at number 2 Rue de la Chaussée d'Antin was only one surprise among many, for me, in the official biography of Edith Wharton.

What do you do when you find that the results of long, hard, unpaid labor have been tossed into the *poubelle,* rubbish, garbage, and you are fulsomely praised for distortion of the facts?

Eventually, you get back to work. And sometimes there are random but apt rewards.

La Belle Mirecourt

The dream of finding an aged person who would bring out photos of Aunt Adèle—"There she is in her Venus costume, there she is holding me"—that dream had faded. *Tant pis.* To the Arsénal Library for a weary check of the satiric magazine *Charivari.*

In winter 1878/79, Adèle played in *Tant Plus Ça Change.* Revues normally had very short runs, but the editor of *Charivari* was co-author of this one and indefatigably kept it before the public. As part of his bold-faced puff he produced a center spread with drawings of the cast.[79] Including Mirecourt.

It's not a photograph. But the face of Lhéritier, the famous comedian beside her, exactly resembles his face in photographs.

In the revue, a visiting American *femme libre,* liberated woman, makes a speech to a group of Parisiennes: "Ladies—dear martyrs—too long have we endured the tyranny of Man!" They take her to see *The Youth of Louis XIV,* a burlesque of a serious play that was having a successful run that season. Historically, Louis fell in love with Marie Mancini. In the skit, his attempts to *tromper,* seduce, her are drowned out by hunting horns. The caption to the drawing is a pun: "La belle Mancini-Mirecourt trompée—trumpeted/deceived—by Lhéritier-Louis XIV."

Marie (seated on a bench, pulling the petals from a daisy): He will marry me, a little, a lot, passionately, not at all—
Louis: O Marie, how beautiful you are! O Marie, I love you! Will you have my throne and a lock of my hair? *(The trumpeter sounds his horn.)* Pay no attention, Marie. Etiquette requires it when I am hunting.
Marie: Sire, your Majesty is fickle.
Louis: Marie!
Marie (seriously): History tells us so.
Louis: I'll give you diamonds, Marie—
(The horn interrupts again, and so forth.)

La belle Mirecourt. The fair-haired landlady of the Rue Vignon twelve years later. James's "brutal slut" thirty years later, the ill cantankerous old woman later still who would answer Alfroy only by *oui* or *non.* The body that later still was moved from its fine and private grave and thrown into the common pit.

New York

Fullerton's Family Again

A roomy apartment at West Eighty-fourth Street off the park houses Gordon Gerould's scholarly works (e.g., *The Gratefull Dead*) and thrillers, inscribed to Katharine, and her books, inscribed to him. "Will was keen on my becoming literary too," says Christopher Gerould (who became science editor of *Life*). His wife, Mireille, as a child, met Edith Wharton ("I was afraid, she was so stiff and disapproving"), and her father, U.S. consul-general in Marseille, knew Will.

Gay Fullerton, living close by on Central Park West unbeknownst to the Geroulds and they to her, remembers her cultivated, modest grandfather, Rob. Rob worked with his son Bradford on a bibliography of American literature[80] but refused to be called co-author.

On the phone from Connecticut, Rob's daughter, Mrs. Gertrude Worcester: She visited Uncle Will in Paris in World War I when she was in the Red Cross, and again in the '20s. "He had an affair with Isadora Duncan. It was interesting to see them fall by the wayside. Of course his mistress was Mme Desprévint; that was very open. Everyone knew."—"Mme Desprévint?"—"He was anxious to marry her, but she wouldn't; thought it would be bad for him."—"I thought there was a Mme Pouget?"—"I think she was Mme Pouget-Desprévint. She was a lovely person, I think she had been an opera singer."

Oh, *no!*

Paris

Protestantism

"Could Mme Pouget have been an artiste?" I asked.

Hugh Fullerton: "Oh, no. Much more a cleaning-woman type."

Mrs. Fullerton: "Mind you she was very witty, very droll."

Hugh: "She knew he was philandering and she didn't care. He used her as a cook-housekeeper, any port in a storm. She had the aspect and manners of an amusing sly old French peasant."

At least the firm negative as to her career is a relief.

"She thought the Protestant church in the Batignolles was proper for the funeral, because his father had been a minister."

A world unfamiliar to many people even here in France, where dictionaries give the antonyms of Catholic as "unbeliever, pagan, heretic." The Société Historique du Protestantisme, near Walter Berry's house, displays the tiny "chignon" Bibles Huguenot women used to hide in their hair when they went to prohibited meetings, and relics and prints of mas-

sacres—the Saint-Bartholomew, La Rochelle—and martyrs: Albigen-
sians, Cathars, Vaudois, "slaughtered saints whose bones / Lie scattered
on the Alpine mountains cold."

Morton may have reminisced about his childhood so wistfully that
Mme Pouget quelled her Roman Catholic scruples and determined to
give him a Protestant send-off.

A letter comes from the daughter of Mme Pouget's niece. Her mother
has died, Mme Eldin writes. *She* would love to talk, and yes, her great-
aunt Hélène had used the name Desprévint.

Go, at last, to Alès *du côté de Nîmes.*

Alès, near Nîmes

La Belle Hélène

At dawn the train is rolling south through the gorges and rugged crags of
the Garrigues. At noon in the Alès hotel, men in different-colored cardi-
gans are seated four of a color to a table, and at each table a different language is being spoken. "Why?" I asked.

"But it's the International Boules Competition!" the waiter says.
"France, Italy, Spain!"

Some of the *sportifs* have gray hair. "On va faire un *massacre!*" says
one. "It'll be a bloodbath."

The hotel people point the way to the Eldins' house.

"We have had hotels all over," Mme Eldin says; "we've been no-
madic. And my Aunt Hélène's father was an army officer, in charge of
uniforms, so they moved from garrison to garrison."

A pretty salon with ivy trained down an arch and, over the fireplace, a
portrait of a stunning woman: black hair, dark red gown, pearls, fur.
Near it the portrait of a man. At last, what people have said about
Morton's personal effect is believable. Smashing! Come-hither eyes.
("*You'd* have fallen for him," Hugh Fullerton told me; and, if one didn't
know so much about him . . .)

"Mme Pouget came to see her mother every year. With M. Fullerton
several times. I remember when I was fourteen. We knew he'd written
books, lectured. We'd been told to behave. Then he was very nice, did

tricks for us, corks up his sleeve, champagne cork in his nose. Handsome, with big blue eyes—"

"Not all that handsome." (M. Eldin)

"Oh, you saw him late. *She* was beautiful—and her body was beautiful. Très bien bâti.

"No, she wasn't on the stage. She had a brother in Paris, and she went there to be *gouvernante* of some children or *vendeuse* in a bookshop, or both. He was a tax inspector.

"Those portraits are by Brisgand, and Rosso gave them a wax head they sold at auction. It was worth a lot.—Oui, elle était modèle, she was a model! For painters and sculptors. My great-grandmother was very pious, played the harmonium in the temple. She was very poor, and Mme Pouget was a very very good daughter. All her life she sent her a *rente*—money every *trimestre*."

M. Eldin: "We saw them after the war, 1946, in Paris."

Mme Eldin: "The apartment was very pretty."

"They had a maid's room" (M. Eldin) "and we found three cubic meters of *plastrons,* dress-shirt fronts, which were M. Fullerton's! C'est la vérité!"

Mme Eldin: "They were very very *malheureux* during the war. He was beginning to be a little handicapped. They gave us the impression of a very close-knit old pair even though my aunt said he was selfish and she'd suffered from him.

"Oh, no, when he died she didn't leave Paris. She had a nice room at the Hotel Terminus of the Gare Saint-Lazare."

"Fullerton had dinner there with Paul Verlaine," I say.

Mme Eldin nods. "She didn't want to regularize the situation; he knew such distinguished people . . . So, she fed pigeons. Then the manager wrote that she was too ill to stay. My brother and I went and brought her back in a *wagon-lit*. She had gangrene.

"My aunt said he gave women money. She wanted it all. She said he was *avare* to her and generous to others. My aunt said it was *incroyable* the number of women he knew. My aunt said to me once, 'In forty years I have not deceived him.' My aunt said Fullerton told her he had never loved anyone but her, never in his life, but at that point he was absolutely dependent on her, all the other women had abandoned him. But above all she had always loved him.

"My mother was shocked because she posed nude for sculptors. You know, here in the Cévennes, with Huguenots, it was, simply, scandalous.—Yes, we are Protestants. A minority, now. And Hélène had not married M. Fullerton! That *is not done* in the Cévennes. Especially among Huguenots."

On my journey back to Paris, like the train departures scrolling on the station monitor, surmises and assumptions alter.

Hélène, so long kept down on her knees with pail and scrub brush by an ignorant casting director, had posed for Rosso and probably Rodin. Posed for painters. Bearded men, palettes and chisels, smocks, berets, tobacco smoke. Hélène *dite* d'Esprévint.

She broke with the strictest moralists in France, supported a mother who wouldn't let her stay in the house when she came home. *And* she knew Morton before the First World War!

Mme Eldin has *Problems of Power* in French, inscribed "à Hélène Pouget en souvenir du soleil de notre été de Luxembourg, où, à côté d'elle, ce livre fut enfanté, Morton Fullerton, 4 mars 1916."

In memory of their "sunny summer in Luxembourg where by her side this book came to birth." Not this French edition inscribed by Morton (he didn't do the translation) but the original book, published in April 1913. He and Hélène were lovers by the summer of 1912.

That spring he had written of Edith: "I saw not what she saw, and that's the pity of it." Edith was writing *The Reef*, drawing on their affair with a mind to his comments, hoping that Luxembourg provided the solitude he wanted, and visiting James, who perceived with ire that she had come because she was at loose ends.

Hélène's friend Rosso had been so poor that he had slept in the Colosseum, and he was socially conscious. William was against humanitarianism; on the other hand, Rosso was not a nobody. Rosso may have thought William a political genius but a well-intentioned ignoramus when it came to art.

At the embassy dinner for Theodore Roosevelt on the eve of Camille's début, Rodin was a guest, as well as Henri Bergson and sundry diplomats and appendages and Edith and Morton. For Morton, being at table with the enemy of his and Hélène's friend Rosso must have added spice to an already savory evening.

Hélène, who had (probably) posed for Rodin, stayed home.

She and Fullerton were together for forty years. It was the longest-sustained personal association of both their lives.

Paris

Children and Parents

Hélène was thirty-seven that summer in Luxembourg. Photographs show a glowing woman. You wonder who her previous lovers had been. Whether she had children, wanted children—"Do you think Morton had children?"—"Well!" says Hugh Fullerton. "He may have had. I'd be surprised if he hadn't. Birth control wasn't very reliable."

She was much younger than Edith, who'd have thought her handsome but common. She'd have thought Edith . . . not a person to put you at your ease.

But even upper-class women felt that. "She made a girl feel her hair was wrong," says Mme de Prévaux, "She was very intimidating."

"Because she was intimi*dated*," says a younger woman, the writer Claude Silve, who was fond of Edith and gasped when she heard of a lover: "I never suspected! I felt merely that she lacked love. She always suffered from her lack of *amadouement*, lovableness."

Like Hélène Pouget, Philomène *dite* Claude Silve, daughter of the Duc de Lévis Mirepoix, rebelled against an exclusive society; but *hers* is still notable for frank curiosity about "amours," keen observation, total recall, and pleasure in imparting information. She wrote a novel—"very bold!" one lady told me (and crowned by the Academy); eloped to South America with a married man; returned with a child she kept with her, affronting the Faubourg; and was taken up for rehabilitation by Mmes de Béhague and Wharton, who decided that she should marry their friend Robert Norton. ("Very magnanimous, especially of Mme Wharton," murmurs another lady.)

This rebel (who married a man of her own choosing) would have sympathized with Edith's affair, which was neither bold nor unusual; but Edith did not confide in her, even on a rainy-day visit she made at Saint-Brice when Edith talked by the fire of her girlhood in New York. "I had the impression that her mother did not understand her. Had she known him—the man—in New York?"

"He lived here. They were both in their forties."

"She was here as a child, she told me, under the Second Empire. She gave me a subject for a story: a kidnapped child who is happier with the kidnappers than with his family. It was the bitter side Mme Wharton liked."

The narrator in Claude Silve's *Un Jardin vers l'Est*, A Garden to the East, tells a story told her by an old woman she visits in the 1930s whose only *amour* has been a passion for "reliving"[81] and who in the 1860s is also the cousin of Peter, the kidnapped boy.

In the memoirs she was writing at the time of Claude Silve's visit, Edith relived a childhood vision in Paris of a "beautiful lady in a beautiful open carriage . . . center of a sumptuous spectacle": the Empress Eugénie.[82] Watching the empress the children in the novel are lost in the crowd and Peter is abducted. He comes home, ransomed, only to die. He has been in a desert garden with orange trees, gazelles, and little foxes, the "garden planted to the east in Eden" of Genesis. The story is not bitter but magical. Peter was a willing hostage, having been told that he is a prince left temporarily with ordinary people for reasons of state, which fits his dreams. He dies from loss of happiness.

Perhaps when, a year or so before the visit, Mireille Chabbert married, she did not name Morton as father because she believed her father was a king. A dream children have, rarely with such probable cause.

Was it Edith's idea that the kidnapped boy should believe he was a prince? She more than half-believed that her mother's husband was not her father; an idea that, after decades of academic disbelief, has been shown to be almost certainly true.

Whereas Katharine knew her real father but legally rejected him, an action children rarely take. She saw him sometimes. He notarized the passports[83] when her foster parents took her to Paris, where she spent a year with Will/Morton, in loco parentis at twenty-six, an acting father/brother who would later turn himself into a lover.

His stepdaughter Mireille was singing on a gas-lit stage one moment, *et O ces voix d'enfants,* the next she was demoiselle of a greenwood chateau . . . where her foster father and his Austrian wife married her to their village-boy godson ("they had a wedding and he married us"). Her real marriage took place in a London registry office. She had been unrecognized by a father, recognized and dropped by a stepfather, abandoned by a mother, expelled by foster parents, rejected by a lover; but the name she gave the baby born eight weeks later, Mirabelle, must mean that in spite of all she was a romantic who hoped to give her child what *she* hadn't had from Camille or any of her fathers, not knowing that in eighteen days she would leave her to a father who had not wanted her.

Morton was lapped in love from birth. But it's as if he had been an alien disabled by lack of affect. Edith's "If only I could rely on *some feeling* in you" echoes. The charm that inspired love was a specific against loving and disappointment in love. Other setbacks hurt. Not getting a fellowship. Not being promoted. His parents trusted him to excel not only morally ("like our beautiful example Christ") but in the world. Even if loveless, he was vulnerable in his vanity, and his parents' expectations were always there.

PART /EVEN

From Postwar to Prewar

Long ago at Ville d'Avray, Morton had noted that the willows were growing out of Corot's frame. In the 1930s he continued to view a world
close to explosion point in the ungiving cadre of the Belle Epoque. 1933:
"It took me a year to get Cambon's revelations to me about the Entente
Cordiale published in *The Times!*"[1]

Still harping! *Obsessed,* he was, by that wire.

Mirecourt's kid brother Auguste Moutot? I know only, my dear Wat-
son, that he was obviously a typographer and had but one eye. And that
he married a laundress, Henriette Tourenne. Trace *her!*

En avant, crablike: *procureur's* anteroom, *huissiers* with racing sheets,
procureur, mairie counter, *mairie* archive. Auguste died; Henriette married an upholsterer who died, then an upholsterer who outlived her. Her
death *acte* records only marriages two and three.

HITLER CHANCELLOR — BECOMES MASTER OF GERMANY

*"If she'd had living Moutot descendants, they'd have made sure the
certificate was correct — don't you think?"*

"Tu n'es pas un peu folle? Art thou not a trifle loony?"

AN INTERNATIONAL INFAMY

The Nazis demonstrated "the great modern fact," Morton wrote.
Germany was "a scourge fantasized by belief in her racist right to sub-
merge the world."[2] He denounced the German Americans who went
"home" to vote for Hitler. But then, unexpectedly: Though expulsion of
Jews and concentration camps "have not kept the 'liberal' nations of
Europe from giving the Führer loads of presents, a whole German-
American world has been profoundly shocked."[3]

It was not a palinode. Morton did not connect the anti-Nazis to the democratic Germans of the early '20s whose existence he had denied when he opposed food and economic aid, demanded immediate war reparations, and helped prepare the way for Hitler, who, he now wrote, "divided the planet between countries where Jews cannot live and those where they are forbidden to enter." This movement, comparable to "the great migrations of history," angered America. "She will not soon forget to whom she owes this new difficulty."[4]

By ascribing outrage at the refugees' plight to self-interest, Morton degraded the motives of anti-Nazis, as if to placate anti-Semites. But he was inconsistent. Arguing that "hostility to aggressive minorities" was partly justified by their opposition to centralized power, he cited Freemasons and Protestants as minorities inviting hostility,[5] but not Jews—Why did he falter?

Since Rennes, he had liked the Berlin newspaperman Theodore Wolff, "of a race in which independent criticism is second nature." When Wolff queried Germany's sole guilt for the war, Morton blasted him as a "former friend."[6] Persecuted by the Nazis, Wolff regained favor.[7] Morton may have wished not to offend him again, or to offend Henri Bergson, or even Léon Blum of the Quarante Cinq, who was both a Jew and a leader of the Front Populaire, loathed by the right.

Still less, however, did he wish to offend anti-Semitic friends.

Even before the war, Morton had called the theory that Germany "created" the Dreyfus case so as to compromise the French general staff impressive "above all" to one who, like himself, had witnessed events "from the trial of Zola to the tragic August at Rennes."

That theory proved useful. Intelligence and vanity alike would have made it hard for him to revise his analysis of the court-martial. His "tragic" elliptically reasserted Dreyfus's innocence. But by harboring the idea that a foreign enemy—*the* foreign enemy—had exploited a domestic conflict he evaded the moral issue without offending his friends of Action Française, which, though royalist and Roman Catholic, had been under ban by Pope Pius XI since 1926.

Backward Glances

Morton repudiated his early politics; he confirmed a literary credo formulated in his youth. He is called a disciple of James, but George Meredith was the god of his idolatry. Backsliding once, he called Meredith only "the greatest *natural* genius since Shakespeare." He had been his disciple and, more, his apostle, in America and had an investment in a reputation he had helped build.

But even if James was only "the greatest of our American artists in prose"—stress on "American"—Morton talked more and more about his personal friendship with James. He began to imply, perhaps believe, that his elegy of the 1890s on an unnamed man who was probably Samuel Longfellow commemorated James. ("Yet gone he is, and I am left alone.")[8]

A figure in books on Meredith even before Meredith's death, otherwise, with trifling exceptions,[9] he was passed over by people who might well have mentioned him. Arthur Symons recounted Verlaine's London visit without naming the Paris friend who had helped, though he printed Morton's long letter about the visit in full.

Wharton's *Backward Glance* and the Ranee's *Good Morning and Good Night* came out close together. Neither woman spoke of Morton. The Ranee may have forgotten her fling with a caddish American. Full of life, she had young friends. ("The Ranee? Oh, yes, she was a friend of Guy's [Burgess]," says Dennis Proctor.)

Wharton's pleasant, anodyne memoir is rich in fibs and lapses of memory. Her omission of Morton was not forgetful. She cut him from her pages on James, though her closest experiences with James involved him; from pages on men whom she knew through him—Tardieu, Wendell, Abel Bonnard—and who were closer to him than to her.

Yet she left a record of him that discloses layers of her being from celebration to barely verbalized sobs. She left erotic poems written for him and erotic poems she chose to think were written *by* him as well as by her. Morton left unfinished a "dream" of making love to a quasi-goddess. Edith's "Beatrice Palmata" narrates an act of incestuous oral sex. Whereas his fragment is impressionistic, conventional, and subjective, hers is explicit, depersonalized, and darkly polished. The seducer/father's style is Fullertonian. The fragment also ludicrously recalls Daisy Ashford and Mr. Salteena.

He had inspired in her, then vitiated, a belief that she was lovable. She knew he valued her letters more than he did her. But *she* valued them more than she did *him*. Deeper than self-doubt was certainty of the importance of her self. It took a powerful ego to think that her every word was worth saving. She had an elemental will to survive in posterity, to superlive. "Medea superest."

But how did Morton obtain her papers?—Not the letters she posted or the poems she presented to him, but the undated and unsigned scraps of paper she covered with jottings of self-abasement? For they, like those letters and poems, were among *Morton's* papers in *Morton's* study when she died. Was there an encounter at which she said, "Take them; they'll show you what you've done"?

As Morton revised his career, forging lies, Edith made up a happy love story. His essay on James had contained a whimsical variation on his favorite theme: No "epic movement of peoples" matched the invasion of Europe by American women backed by "their indispensable heads of commissariat, the silent, clean-shaven American men. The emigration required its Homer, and Mr. James was there."—[10] "'The Conquerors,'" Edith told the vicomte de Noailles, was about "young ladies coming from America like Crusaders." In her Buccaneers, as they became, she drew on real girls who married lords; but the independent, imaginative Nan, who runs away from a dull duke, was partly Edith Jones as seen by Edith Wharton.

Claude Silve, to whom Edith gave a subject, kidnapping, gave in return something toward a character. Nan was *also* a French girl who in real life ran away from a ducal family, though readers could not know it, when *The Buccaneers* came out, any more than they could know that the man Nan runs away with had a touch of Morton Fullerton as the author had once imagined him to be. Like Darrow in *The Reef*, Guy Thwarte thinks of a woman as a musical instrument a man can play, but unlike Darrow and M.F. he is "loyal and tender."

One day at Saint-Brice, Edith Wharton and Leon Edel talked about a best-selling "memoir in the form of a novel." Morton, too, read it. From his 1936 Harvard class report:

> I have no story to tell. It is already told immortally in Santayana's *Last Puritan*, which I hold to be the most remarkable book that has ever come out of America. I stake my reputation on that verdict. I can only ask you to see for yourselves.[11]

They had been intimate enough in their youth for Santayana to lambaste Morton's character unceremoniously (Morton shouldn't get "mad" at him for saying that, having "gone in for success," he could not say what he really thought),[12] and to ask his opinion on sex. In the 1890s, Morton sent a "Founders' Issue" of the *Monthly,* from Paris, an essay on The Beautiful with a long preface addressed to Santayana.[13] Katharine, at Radcliffe, knew that Mr. Santayana, with his "godlike serenity" and "philosophical, abstract glare," would rather lose a vacation than miss a visit by Will.[14]

After Santayana settled in Italy, he and Morton remained in contact, though their ways of life had diverged. Morton had indeed gone in for success. He moved among important people at the center of action. Santayana lived a life of austere meditation. He was a revered thinker and a respected poet when he published *The Last Puritan* in 1935. He called the book a memoir and introduced real Harvard teachers—Barrett Wendell and, archly, himself—into the story of Oliver, the Last Puritan, and his mostly Harvard friends, especially Mario.

To Mario, even as a child, a room full of women "was vastly exciting, like an orchestra." Caught in bed with a girl, he leaves college. He goes to war serious yet "deeply elated": "That must be the way he looks" (thinks Oliver) "when he is making love." Mario is given the understated ardent flattery with which Morton charmed women and men (though Mario, like James's Merton Densher and Wharton's George Darrow and Guy Thwarte, is entirely heterosexual).

Whatever Santayana's intentions, it is unlikely that his self-referential classmate would have found the book vastly exciting unless he believed that Mario was himself observed.

Finances

Thrilled by the novel, Morton worried about his *Figaro* job. "Vladimir d'Ormesson was there." (Hugh Fullerton) "They were deadly enemies. Morton told me, 'He goes or I go!' Well, Morton left; you know where d'Ormesson went!" (To ambassadorships. To the Académie.) On the microfilm, d'Ormesson columns supplant Morton's. At last, even on American issues d'Ormesson took precedence.

The Marquis de Flers, a sponsor on *Le Figaro,* had died. André Tardieu vanished from life, stricken with a disease that left him a physical and mental wreck.

Hugh Fullerton is sure Morton was sacked. At the *Figaro* they know only that he was not an employee; he was paid by the piece. *Oh oui,* he could easily have had his own office there, even so.

"Old Man Tuck," says Hugh, left Morton stock worth $30,000. "But money went through Morton's fingers like water of course."

His parents wondered how he managed. Bradford's long-ago homily on his duty to discard Mirecourt and cherish Camille was about money, and in the course of it he said something strange. "*Consider well what has been said to you about the third person. While this third person must know something of the facts it is unnecessary to expatiate here upon your sense of obligation.*"[15]

Solemn, as if the name, like Jehovah's, must not be used. Or the sex revealed. Bradford avoids a *he* or a *she*. *Person*, like *personne*, is noncommittal. Someone who had helped Will financially and would continue to do so contingent upon his good conduct? Mystery.

Will did not take the easy course, for him, of marrying money. His perpetration of marriage to a single mother just beginning a career in opera was not for profit. He may have discouraged Edith Wharton from jeopardizing her marriage from fear not only that Teddy might sue him but that Edith might want to marry him.

If James sensed subconsciously that Morton, like Merton Densher in *The Wings of the Dove,* might make a dying girl think he loved her, implicit in his imagined man is capacity for self-scrutiny and remorse. Densher is "blest and redeemed" by refusing Millie's legacy. He tells Kate that he will marry her if she agrees that they not accept it. If she wants it, he will make it over to her. The rupture is absolute. But Morton, liking money, abominating marriage, would have kept Millie's legacy—and not married Kate.

Who paid the bills in the Batignolles? Morton was still making payments to Mirecourt when he began living with Hélène, who was tenant of record. And when Mirecourt died in 1924 we don't know how much money she left to—maybe—the Widow Bavoux née Buisson, whose children she had hoped her original legatee Alfroy would help. Money Morton may have hoped she'd leave to him.

And did she? Suppose that an old, ravaged, hard-bitten Millie Theale made a noble benefaction to a man who had ill-treated her. Mirecourt remains a significant unknown.

Her mother was Jeanne Bavoux. A Marie-Jules Bavoux came here from Saint-Rémy with his parents when Adèle was on stage. Could they have come to Paris and not looked up kinfolk? *And* he was here, on record as a wine merchant, in the 1890s, when Adèle took Morton as a lodger. He may have witnessed her metamorphosis from actress to landlady.

"Yes," says Mme Perrot, company director, "he was my father. He died twenty years ago; unfortunately we always went to my mother's. . . . I can try to find his sister. She might know."
But her aunt, and her aunt's husband and daughter, are all dead.
All the more reason to go to Saint-Rémy.

The Trojan War Will Not Take Place

Le Guerre de Troie n'aura pas lieu came to the stage. Morton and Hélène may have seen Jean Giraudoux's illustration *allegro ma non troppo* of the folly of war over Helen or anything. (Quel est le motif de votre guerre?) Morton, *realpolitiker,* had boxed himself in with the romantics of Giraudoux's Troy—and of Shakespeare's Troy, in *Troilus and Cressida.* Shakespeare's Hector would return Helen to the Greeks to avert war. For Troilus, she is a theme of honor and renown.

> *Hector:* Brother, she is not worth what she doth cost
>   The holding.
> *Troilus:* What is aught, but as 'tis valued?

But Hector argues for an objective criterion. Value consists

> As well wherein 'tis precious of itself
> As in the prizer. 'Tis mad idolatry
> To make the service greater than the god.

At seventy, Fullerton talked of glory, honor, power, pride, and revenge. He glamorized a past soldiery. In the First World War the French War Office had asked him to pass on to the U.S. commander in chief, General Pershing, police reports of unexampled acts of violence, even use of revolvers, by U.S. doughboys.[16] Now, an American Legion convention in Paris brought "crusaders back to the scene of their heroic exploits."[17]

In July 1937 the press reported the announcement at a Cercle Interallié reception that a memorial to the late Jacques Bainville, a distinguished contributor to *Action Française,* was planned by his friends Morton-

Fullerton, Charles Maurras, Maurice Maeterlinck, Abel Bonnard, Paul Valéry, Léon Daudet, and others.[18]

In late August the press reported the celebration of Edward Tuck's ninety-fifth birthday.[19]

Between festivities, on August 12, Edith Wharton died.

The news was received "not without emotion"[20] in the literary world, reads an item in *Le Journal des Débats* possibly contributed by Morton, who was writing for the paper by that time.

The *Journal* had passed its prime when he joined it; it was a step down. He had, however, the same relative importance as at *Le Figaro*, with his own frequent, long, front-page editorials.

He published some still classified G-2 reports and drew on others in discussing a sorry world map. Too many minorities had become nations.

England had been corroded by liberalism and France poisoned by democracy. "Wake Up!"[21] he had urged the English. But now they were awake; he ceased hectoring (noteworthy etymology) and began explaining their ways to the French.[22]

He refrained from attacking the second Roosevelt because, though he pampered the masses, FDR saw the danger of Hitler and upheld (a recidivist slip?) the ideals of "fair-play," democracy, and "racial amity" that had inspired the civilization France, England, and America wanted to save.[23]

But today few Americans could rise in life. Morton cited Joseph Kennedy, ambassador in London, as authority. Workers were "galvanized by Bolshevik money."[24] Not only the "lost generation" but a whole people was confused. Still, "what a propitious moment for a leader" (he used the English word) "who would offer a new patriotism."[25]

Attacking Hitler, Fullerton defended other dictators.

Salazar's New State was repressive? Portugal was a laboratory where Salazar sought vaccines against the Bolshevizing plague.[26]

Mussolini invaded Ethiopia? Action against a fanatical mob. If he had faults, France and England were to blame for ignoring his vast thoughts about power in the Mediterranean.[27] Edward Tuck had restored a monument to Augustus Caesar; Morton rejoiced that before dying his great compatriot had sent a photograph of the restoration to the emperor's successor, Il Duce.[28]

As the microfilm of dirty, illegible old newspapers unwound. . . .

A political sympathizer ought to take over.

In the 1890s, which culminated in the trial at Rennes, Morton had "a thirst for experience and knowledge which is simply almost intolerable in its insistence."[29] In a change of heart not unrelated to his failure at the *Times,* he changed allegiance till, by the 1930s, he had rejected "the perennially young and revolutionary France adventurously curious as to ideas and enamoured of progress"[30] and had allied himself with the Action Française he had attacked in the years when Henry James, who "cared for goodness,"[31] was a touchstone.

Pope Pius XI had condemned not only Communism but Nazism and Fascism and with them Action Française. His successor, Pius XII, lifted the ban in the year the Second World War began.

The Second World War

Hitler was allowed to take part of Czechoslovakia. Morton blamed the "humiliating confusion" of Munich on years of Wilsonianism.[32] When Hitler took the rest of Czechoslovakia, Italy invaded Albania; and at last Morton lost faith in the Duce. "There is Italy placing herself shamelessly beside Germany, that same Italy who declared she was satisfied after the conquest of Ethiopia!"[33]

The Danzig Corridor, which had been part of Poland since World War One, separated Germany from East Prussia. On September 1, 1939, German troops entered Poland.

On September 2, Fullerton wrote in the *Journal des Débats* that war must be averted—and there was a way! His friend Colonel Bunau Varilla, the Panama Canal engineer, had just suggested a scheme. A canal should be dug through the Danzig Corridor.[34]

On September 3, England and France declared war on Germany.

On September 17, Fullerton asked: "WHAT WOULD GENERAL PERSHING SAY?" and replied: He would say, "Do not repeat the error of 1918. When the Germans are beaten, they must not be allowed to go home flags flying and bands playing."[35]

The *Journal des Débats* changed from a seven- to a four-column page, with blanks where the censor had removed type. The contents were official communiqués. This format continued during the months of the Drôle de Guerre, the Phoney War.

Things were so quiet, Rob Fullerton in the States wished he could run in on Will.[36]

* * *

Then 1940. Débâcle. Blitzkrieg. Invasion. Dunkirk.

The last issue of the *Débats* was dated 11 June. Next day the Germans were at the city gates. The last free paper published was a one-sheet *Herald* put out by Eric Hawkins, whose first story had been the sinking of the *Lusitania*.

Marshal Philippe Pétain formed a new government, which signed an armistice with Germany on June 22.

A month after Paris fell the *Journal des Débats* reappeared, printed near Vichy and carrying an appeal by Pierre Laval, minister of state in the new government, to obey Marshal Pétain.[37]

From London, General Charles de Gaulle announced the creation of Free France and exhorted his countrymen to fight on.

Paris like Troy was occupied, pillaged, and enslaved.

1940–1944: The Occupation of France

All efforts to reach Fullerton in Paris have failed. I have asked assistance of Sumner Wells of the U.S. State Dept., and the only thing received has been a memorandum of expense connected with attempted communication. A friend returning from Paris in January, 1941, reported meeting him at the United States Legation, but this is the only positive news. (John M. Merriam, secretary, Harvard class of 1886, 1942 report)

People outside learned what was going on in Paris only after the Liberation, and then only slowly and partially.

The Vichy government changed LIBERTÉ ÉGALITÉ FRATERNITÉ to TRAVAIL FAMILLE PATRIE—Work, Family, Fatherland. In a Palace of Sports no distance from the Maison des Dames du Calvaire, thirty thousand Jews were rounded up for transport to death camps.

Charles Maurras called Hitler's victory a "divine surprise." Stéphane Lauzanne edited *Le Matin,* which was owned by Maurice Bunau-Varilla, as a collaborator. Abel Bonnard became Vichy minister of education. ("Ah, Abel Bonnard," M. de Margerie said gravely when the name came up. "He ended badly.")

Other acquaintances of Morton's were not visible. Léon Blum, Socialist and Jew, was sent to Buchenwald. Edouard Herriot of the Urban Exposition, lately prime minister, first supported, then differed with Vichy and was deported. Henri Bergson registered with the police as a Jew; died the next year.

Camille Chabbert was one of the millions of Parisians who migrated to unoccupied France. From Nice she sent Morton "inter-zonal" post-cards with multiple-choice messages in German and French that the sender could tick. ("I am in good health, slightly ill, seriously ill, wounded.")[38] The report that she let Jews hide in her Paris mansarde for money was hearsay and perhaps a canard. Her granddaughter Mirabelle died in the London Blitz.

In the Gironde Department, Maurice Papon sent four convoys of Jews, including two hundred children, to be gassed. Jean Moulin, prefect of Chartres, refused to obey Vichy orders and escaped to Marseille in the unoccupied zone, where the U.S. consul general, Hugh Fullerton, gave him a visa enabling him to cross into neutral Spain and Portugal and join de Gaulle in London.[39]

So weird had been Morton's idea of digging a canal the day before war began, it would not be surprising to learn that he had temporarily lost his wits, from sudden fear. And he did apply for a visa for Spain and Portugal.[40] Lisbon, rich in personal associations, was a neutral port of transit to safety for enemies of Hitler. As in *Casablanca*. But he changed his mind and stayed, although soldiers with swastika armbands patrolled the deserted streets.

"But the soldiers were correcte." (Marc) "There were crimes, but they were committed by the Gestapo and by the French who collaborated, who were worse. They urged the Germans to do more."

A letter Morton wrote in 1940 was held in transit for five years.[41] The American Friends Service Committee in Marseille learned that he was "watching without impatience or dismay to see things logically through."[42] When America entered the war in 1941, he was interned with other enemy aliens and "almost taken as an 'eminent hostage'"[43] but was allowed to return to the Batignolles.

Jean Moulin parachuted into France to coordinate the Resistance. Betrayed, captured, and tortured, he died in 1943.

Liberation

In July 1944, ten weeks after the first Normandy landings, insurrection
was proclaimed. Throughout Paris today, ICI EST MORT, here died,
plaques name fallen *résistants*. There was fighting in the Batignolles; the
Eldins saw bullet holes ("in a wardrobe, very clear"). When Free French
tanks came in, the Germans surrendered.

Leon Edel entered Paris with de Gaulle. ("That is, I was somewhere in
the rear of the procession.") Learning at *Le Figaro* that Fullerton still
went to his study every day—"this was in wartime"—he mounted the
five flights.

> It gave me something of a shock to see this still handsome old man who had
> always been . . . a fashion plate, dressed in shabby clothes, and those fine
> moustaches now ragged and unkempt, his eyes bleary. . . . But he was
> charming and melancholy; the charm was always there. . . . He took me
> around the room and showed me the piles of boxes . . . and said, "there you
> are—there is my life."[44]

Morton deposed at his reopened embassy that the Swiss embassy had
given him identity papers. "Now on account of my age I have completely
discontinued activities, except that I am writing my own book and memoirs. I have no one left in the U.S. except my brother who is no longer
young. All my interests are in France."[45]

"Of all his vast acquaintance," says Hugh Fullerton, "not one, with
the brilliant exception of Lewis Douglas, our ambassador to Great Britain, had lifted a finger to help."

Rob's daughter Gertrude had sent Morton CARE parcels; Paul Blanchette, a friend in Vermont, had offered part of his salary;[46] Berry's sister
Nathalie Alden had left him $2,000 in a will filed only after the Libera-
tion[47]—attempts at aid he probably didn't know of when Hugh Fullerton, returning to Paris as consul-general, found him and Mme Pouget in
need of food and fuel.

Like Verlaine, with one coal burning.

Perhaps he had not used his visa because he did not want to leave
Hélène on her own.

On "The Night before Christmas 1944," Morton sent Hugh Fullerton
a "sumptuous" copy of H. W. Longfellow's *Hyperion*, bequeathed him
by Samuel Longfellow, which he'd meant to give Hugh as a present:

You have anticipated me, by the largesse of the multiple rich things—
oh, I don't forget the cigars—that have filled with gratitude the heart of
Mme Pouget, and mine . . . The Barrett Foster vignettes will tell you of a
Germany that was! . . . I call on the Erynnies, on all the Furies, to draw and
quarter the Demons who have sullied the romantic world that Longfellow
loved. I thank you again, dear Hugh. . . . It's a great joy for me to feel that
you are there, that you are there. . . .[48]

Soon afterward, at the request of Morton's class secretary, a navy officer
who had never met Morton went to his study and found him "with his hat
and coat and muffler on, trying to keep warm." But he looked "surpris-
ingly young, with his hair still black, and his mustache neatly waxed." The
officer was offered some prewar Johnny Walker and gathered that except
for a relative he was the first American Morton had seen. Asking about his
classmates, Morton learned that Santayana was alive, in Italy, and had just
published an autobiography. He was interested, the officer wrote, saying
that before the war Santayana came to see him whenever he was in Paris.[49]

In August 1945, Morton received a letter—it had taken two months to
cross the ocean—from his cousin LeRoy Phillips (whose mother had
spilled the beans about Mirecourt half a century back). His reply was uninhibited: "Six years ago I was still a valiant lover. (I hope you are).
Today, alas, I'm helpless and ashamed."

Phillips was a bibliographer of James and knew Leon Edel. Morton
told him he was sorting his "archives" for "documents . . . for such fanat-
ics as Edel and you (and myself) . . . if you could see the letters written to
me by Santayana . . . from Berlin, Dresden, and Avila, you would be jealous of my possessions."

> The five years through which I have "lived" . . . had nothing new to tell
> me, author of *Problems of Power* and of some thousands of pages in maga-
> zines and newspapers. . . . All that has happened is the fulfillment of my vi-
> sion of international conditions. I'll even risk another prophecy, to wit: If
> the "Allies" fail to assume the obligation, accept the *corvée*, of garrisoning
> Germany *during, perhaps, some 50 years*, the world will explode in an-
> other war, which no counter-irritant, even of the atomic bomb variety, will
> be capable of preventing.[50]

It was too soon, sixteen days after Hiroshima, to know that "international conditions" would never be the same again.

A Political Elegy

Morton did not speak to Phillips of what was going on outside his study:
discovery of death camps, trials for war crimes.

Charles Maurras was sentenced to life imprisonment for collaboration
with the Nazis. "Dreyfus has had his revenge," he said. He was freed before his death. Abel Bonnard fled; sentenced to death in absentia, he returned and had his sentence commuted to ten-year exile, but when the
term ended chose to remain in Franco's Spain. He and Maurras were expelled from the Académie.

Somehow, Morton managed to go to the Midi. He called on André
Tardieu's widow, and on his return to Paris wrote "Rereading André Tardieu." Besides mourning a friend, he wrote, he was suffering for France.
"*Mon pays,*" "still shaken by internal convulsions," faced her "greatest
crisis in centuries."

(The fall of France had ended the Third Republic. A National Assem-
bly was debating the constitution of the Fourth.)

Tardieu would have been the man for the day, Morton wrote. Even
some on the left admitted that he was not antirepublican, still less Hitlerian. But "a sort of silence" reigned over "certain ideas, certain men, who
displease a sect or a party."[51]

Morton offered no ideas of his own in this subdued essay. "Internal
convulsions" was neutral. Why did he write? If he wanted to resume
journalism—was testing the water—Tardieu was a name to invoke. He
had no war record, having been hopelessly ill for years. "*Mon pays*" was
politic; but Morton had earned the right to say "my" country, having remained in peril of the Gestapo and, amazingly, survived. But, whatever
became of his singularly joyless article, he did not return to journalism.

Next year the *History of the Times* for the period of his service came
out.[52] His 1903 wire was cited, with his name, as the first public notice of
the Entente Cordiale, and *Problems of Power* was called a "penetrating
study on realistic lines." On the other hand, the "tremendous explosion
of public indignation in England" that followed the Rennes court-martial
was discussed without identification of the Rennes correspondent.
Lavino's importance in the Entente story was brought out, and Morton's
arch-foe Saunders was lauded.

Tantae ne Animis Caelestibus Irae?
Can Godlike Philosophers Feel Such Spite?

"I share your natural gaiety and refuse to die before embracing you," Morton told LeRoy Phillips. The two of them must seize Time "by the forelock—as in a Dürer drawing."

> Men of my age are lonely survivors in a cruel new world. . . . My dream is to write a "Gil Blas" which will be a synthesis of the vanished New England, the old, the beautiful old England of before 1900, the France that, too, is dead.[53]

Morton was not, however, declining into nostalgia. His navy visitor had sent him Santayana's autobiography from London.

Morton had supposed that Mario in *The Last Puritan* was modeled on himself and had extravagantly praised "the most remarkable book that has ever come out of America." It was natural to expect a direct portrait in the new work.

In detail Santayana recalled Harvard. The *Monthly:* he named its editors, all but Fullerton. The Okay: a club sans Fullerton. Under "College Friends" came "closest friends," then men "in the front rank" of friends. No Fullerton. Then a Herbert Lyman. "I mention him here lest he should seem to be forgotten in my catalogue of College friends."[54] In a second volume, Santayana omitted Fullerton from a chapter on his American friends in Paris.[55]

It was the snub absolute, as cutting as the ostrakon shard that ostracized an ancient Greek, and was meant to be seen as such by all the few survivors of the class of 1886.

Morton, in Paris, got the message. His letter to LeRoy Phillips modulated from the minor elegiac to the snappy colloquial:

> Santayana has had the nerve to save his honor in the production of two masterpieces of autobiography. If he had been more honest still he would have asked me to give him copies of the pornographic letters he wrote me from Germany in 1889 to 1900.[56]

In the "sketch" he contributed to the 1946—sixtieth—report of the class of 1886, Morton wrote that he was arranging his papers for the Harvard Library.

> It is something, at all events, to have saved from the Gestapo letters of a Theodore Roosevelt and a Clemenceau, and of several hundred other

personages of the half century before 1940—and let me not forget those of our *eminentissime* comrade, Santayana.[57]

Morton certainly meant Santayana's letters on diarrhea and on amatory instincts. They were not pornographic; parts of them were ribald, irreverent, and earthy. It takes an effort of the historical imagination to realize that in the 1940s expressions like "wipe thine ass" and "dogs stuck together" and "whorehouses," used by one young man to another, might have embarrassed an old man with an international reputation for spirituality. As Santayana had said in one letter, "angels don't have wet dreams."[58]

Santayana may have happened to remember the letters when he began his autobiography and asked for them back. Or had Morton written praising *The Last Puritan,* received the deflating response that he was *not* Mario and/or that Mario was a bad man (Santayana did think he was),[59] and reminded Santayana of his letters? What, beyond the letters themselves, did he have on Santayana?

Or did Santayana simply find it intolerable that concrete vestiges of a long-past, less guarded self still existed?

Scholars seem to agree equally that Santayana was homosexual and that he almost certainly had no physical affairs. If he had had a *passade* with Fullerton, it would have been after college, for in his superficially facetious treatise on sex he didn't think of his friend as gay—rather, had an uneasy respect for his prowess with girls. Did Morton have knowledge of a same-sex affair with someone else? There is no evidence. It is Santayana's extreme reaction to whatever it was that Fullerton said or did that raises the question. *Tantae ne animis . . . ?*

Santayana's memoirs, serene and finely cadenced, have every appearance of candor. When he disparaged friends (Wendell: "no real distinction"), he did so dispassionately, as from Olympus. "The sun and the planets have their times for shining; we mustn't expect them to be always in our hemisphere," he wrote apropos of a friend who had cooled toward him. The "eclipse of friendships" left him untroubled. Having "chosen a place for the time being, I lived as best I could with the human souls that inhabited it. Not at all in bitterness; not with any painful sense of disappointment. . . . And in each person I catch the fleeting suggestion of something beautiful, and swear eternal friendship with that."[60]

Fullerton's response to Santayana's invisible vindictive retaliation for an unstated offense was to give him notice that his letters would be laid open to the public—and *at Harvard.*

* * *

LeRoy Phillips must have known what Morton meant by Santayana's "saving his honor," but it looks as if no one now does. In talking with the younger men who were to write about him, Santayana apparently made no mention of Fullerton, or none they thought worth recording.

The treatise on amatory options has been printed, and Morton's praise of *The Last Puritan* in 1936 has been noted, without divination of a past close friendship between the two men. Morton's 1946 reference to the *"eminentissime"* Santayana has been taken at face value. But for the chance survival of Morton's letters to Phillips, it would continue to be seen as a compliment, and Santayana's deletion of a friendship from his life as he wished his life to be seen by posterity would remain undetected.

Given people's interest in Santayana, letters that will illuminate Santayana–Fullerton relations between the wars may turn up somewhere. At present all that's certain is the hatred. It was verbal combat by ricochet— from Rome to publishers in London to Paris, from Paris to the Alumni Office in Cambridge, Massachusetts, to Rome—by ex-friends, octogenarians, each knowing the other would read his words.

"As to memories of 1886," Santayana wrote in *his* 1946 sketch, "I have written them out, and need not repeat them, but wish the survivors a happy and peaceful sunset." (Was he—a logical problem—repeating his omission of one survivor?)

Forty-one classmates of 1886 were listed in that sixtieth and last report. One hundred and ninety-four had died along the way. Some survivors were loaded with honors and wealth. The address for one magna cum laude was the Home for Aged Men, Boston. But was any other sketch as loaded with private meaning as was Fullerton's, with its threat, in the guise of admiration, to Santayana—whose own sketch was almost saintly? The near-success of Santayana's attempt to alter the historical record is a reminder of how fragile Veritas can be.

A Matter of Perspective

But the message to Santayana was only a tailpiece with a sting in it to a sketch that Morton said he was free to write only by "miracle."

> During the five anxious years of war I remained Parisian, exposed to the harassing surveillance of a German secret-police, whose reckless caprices

no one could foresee nor foretell. I escaped the concentration camp. At my age I was not a dangerous character. There was, in fact, nothing new to learn about me. In books and by daily articles, in the press of three countries, during more than a quarter of a century, I had clearly defined my attitude as to German international behavior. If it was not irrational to suppose, for instance, that I might possess clandestine facilities for thwarting German policy it was reasonable to believe that, rich in canny professional habits, I would prudently refrain from wanton hectoring of Nazi invaders.

To be sure, the Europe of the recent five years was no place for an elderly hedonist. He might have fled to his favourite refuge, Monte Carlo. . . . But it wasn't easy for him not to follow his bent, not to pursue, by *vitesse acquise, inertia,* the old habits of his sixty and more journalistic years . . . devoted to the recording and interpretation of salient events. You will admit, moreover, that, to this end, Paris offered to the chronicler of *Problems of Power* an ideal point of view. In spite of the tyranny of the censorship he could watch from there the flux and flow of the drifting world and quickly reassemble the flotsam and jetsam left by the flood-tide that had all but submerged Europe. The author, too, of *Terras* [sic] *Françaises* was keen, moreover, to learn on the spot, at whatever personal risk, just what was befalling France. He knows now what, had he looked from afar, optical illusion would have distorted. For History the perspectives of the Gallic future remain the same. All will soon go well with France if England and the United States acknowledge their blunders of 1918. France is a cosmic isthmus whose security concerns the world.[61]

There was nothing new to learn about him, and, as he'd told Phillips, the five years of war had had nothing new to tell him. He blamed England and America for the fall of France. He spoke of the Gestapo. Not of Vichy.

For four years, in the dichotomy he had used as a schema since the 1890s, it was Vichy, Pétain, Pierre Laval versus the Free French, de Gaulle, Jean Moulin. Collaborators versus *résistants.* As the war of ideals became murderous actuality, what he had called the "elevated patriotism" of men who gave priority to raison d'état, national interest, eventuated in collaboration with the enemy of *la patrie.*

After the Liberation, Marshal Pétain, whose motives in forming the Vichy government are disputed—some officials believed they could best serve France by remaining in place and not giving Germany free rein—— presented himself for trial and received a death sentence that was com-

muted to life imprisonment. Laval, whose motives were clear, was captured in Austria by Americans. He died before a French firing squad.
Abel Bonnard and Charles Maurras were found guilty. Half a century
later, Klaus Barbie and Maurice Papon were, are, still unpunished.

Morton says nothing about the events inside France that led to those
trials and sentences. The "sketch" by the member of Harvard 1886 best
placed to convey the French experience of the war was dated July 1946,
as was the muted Tardieu piece produced for French consumption. But
unlike that piece the sketch is satisfied and pompous and, like Morton's
letter to Phillips, gives only personal information.

If Morton supposed, when he wrote, that he had escaped "optical illusion" in a conquered city where talk was dangerous, he would seem to
have realized later that he hadn't had the access to "sources" required for
an authoritative history. Though he had eight years in which to write
about the Occupation, he did not do so.

I had to remind myself that he was old and that he'd been in danger.
Eugène Fleuré was amazed that the Gestapo had let him go free, age notwithstanding, yet he stayed in Paris rather than go to America—no, to
Monte Carlo, but allow a lot for a show of jauntiness as rebound from
fear.

Nonetheless, it is chilling, his talk of "personal risk" and his high detachment from the risk, bereavement, imprisonment, torture, death, at
best the unhappiness, of the "flotsam and jetsam," that is, of most of the
people around him during the Nazi Occupation.

*"Nous étions humiliés." (Marc) "We wanted the Germans to be
beaten, except some who sincerely were partisans of entente and all
along would rather have Hitler than Bolshevism. Like Fernand de
Brinon, who had been an editor of the* Journal des Débats *and created a
Comité France-Allemagne and became representative of the Vichy
government to the German authorities in Paris."*
"Le Journal des Débats?"

Fernand de Brinon. H'mn. Editor 1920–1932—well before Morton
came in. Founded his committee in 1935. Escaped to Germany when the
Allies entered but was brought back and tried. Executed 1947.

But *someone* on the *Débats* put out Vichy news and views during the
Occupation. Someone in the management, not Fullerton.

But that contorted sentence in his class report: If it was not irrational to suppose that he might possess clandestine facilities for thwarting German policy, it was reasonable to suppose that, rich in canny professional habits, he would prudently refrain from wanton hectoring of Nazi invaders.

Could he have been laying the basis for a defense?

His leitmotif had been hatred of Germany—not a nation but a criminal Asiatic horde. Fanaticized Huns and Vandals.

But for years he had consorted with men who preferred Hitler to the republic.

Mme Lauzanne de Blowitz lives in the Rue Vignon, near where Morton lodged with Mme Mirecourt in a building later demolished. She showed me portraits of her great-uncle Blowitz and a painting of his Normandy villa by John Walter, Morton's friend on the board of the *Times*. Her father, Stéphane Lauzanne, often talked of M. Fullerton.

"Do you know about my father? Well, he was put in prison. It was held that he had been a collaborator, but he was amnestied. A friend of his who knew M. Fullerton knows the inside story of the world press. He edits this review."

The review lays bare the international Israeli conspiracy against President Nixon and the control of the world by the United Nations and London Israeli bankers.

"My father is in the family tomb with Blowitz. There is only room for me. I used to visit every All Souls' Day. Now I send a garçon in a taxi with flowers."

"Is it possible that friends in high position protected him?"

Unhappily, Mr. Hugh Fullerton replies: "There did develop, as I know, a certain aberration in Morton's political views during the Occupation. I came across (and burned a long time ago) some letters from Jacques Doriot, the Pétain and Laval minister who was later executed or assassinated, I don't remember which. He was certainly not a Gaullist at any time. As to the Action Française people, I frankly do not know."

"Doriot! Non! He had been a great patriot in the '14–18 war. But during the second war, he was completely Hitlerian. He founded a party. He ran the Legion of French Volunteers against Bolshevism, l'LVF, which fought in the German army on the Eastern Front. You don't know what the letters were about?"

"Only that there were letters, c'est tout."
"C'est beaucoup. If Morton was en relation with Doriot, he had nothing to fear from the Gestapo."

In 1944, when things looked bad for them, Hitler and Ribbentrop wanted Doriot to become governor of Paris. But he was killed in Germany when his car was blown up, by whom is uncertain.

Rather horribly, it forces a reconstruction of Morton's last years.

After the Liberation, he saw what was happening to his French friends of choice. Maurras, Bonnard, Lauzanne de Blowitz. The revenge of Dreyfus. He could without paranoia fear that one of the men who were being hunted, arrested, and tried would mention him. Therefore, planted in a foreign publication read by a few octogenarians a reference to his conduct during the Occupation so convoluted that none of them would think it worth deciphering, but which could if necessary be adduced as exculpation in France.

As time passed and accusations were not forthcoming, he would have felt safer: but would also have realized that any firsthand account of the Occupation, even after the turmoil and vengefulness of the early Liberation passed, would be severely scrutinized.

His authentic sources would have incriminated him. A proponent of alliance against Germany for forty years, he had more reason to be afraid after the Allied victory over Germany than before.

Did what James called the "exquisite art in him of not bringing it off" apply even in Morton's "canny" correspondence with Jacques Doriot? He and Mme Pouget continued to be short of fuel and food; he didn't gain much by his treason.

"Except his life, except his life, except his life."

Which was not yet over.

Decline

In her last years, Edith Wharton had had a devoted friend in Elisina Royall Tyler, an acquaintance of Morton's in the 1920s. After her death, Mrs. Tyler found letters from Morton that Edith had kept in a "small velvet casket"; she seems to have destroyed them.[62] Then or later she discovered that Morton was in possession of poems by Edith, and after the war she wrote to him.

"So," he replied in November 1946:

I know now that you know, and the certainty is a relief, placing me, after all consolingly, before a "certainty," as I say, that . . . burns up the worry I have felt during all these years while I thought of you as the custodian of Edith's papers. But, before writing you frankly I must reflect. Now, with tears in my eyes I would blur the page. . . .

In sincerest gratitude for your letter, your

Morton Fullerton[63]

From New York, another old acquaintance wrote to Morton. Alive by miracle, penniless, joyful, Valentin Mandelstamm was full of scenarios and novels. Could Morton put in a word for him with Messmore Kendall, who was "*ultra-important*" at Loew-Metro-Goldwyn?[64]

But Mandelstamm wrote to a man who was no longer riding high.

"In the end he was just finished and out," Hugh Fullerton says. "You know you have a certain position and brilliance, and you think it's going to last forever. And it vanishes. That's what happened to him. I remember he invited me and the president of some bank to lunch, and when he reached for his wallet he hadn't any money."

Death and Letters

In 1950, three and a half years after hearing from Mrs. Tyler, Morton, "painfully hampered and embarrassed" in moving, dared not accept a rendezvous she proposed. "True, I stagger daily to my Thabor attic to pursue with a secretary the task of arranging my papers. But I have had to refuse all other engagements."[65]

"Fullerton *se porte bien,* he's all right," Mme Pouget told Eugène Fleuré. "I mix a little water with his wine."

"He needed a cane," Mme Eldin says, "and it was hard for him to move. He was very difficult. He didn't understand aging. My aunt would get up at night, and even had to keep him clean. She was very very good to him."

"The only counsel I can vouchsafe," he told Mrs. Tyler, "is to beg you to seize the event, however delicate the problem, to destroy the myth of your heroine's frigidity.

She was not only a great lady, but also a great woman—she boxed the compass of all the shades of temperament of which womankind is capable. In love she had the courage of George Sand. She was fearless, reckless even, in her frank response to her companion[?] [*bienfaiteur?*].

I shall send you soon a striking proof of this in a long poem addressed to me on the morning of the long night we spent together in Charing Cross Hotel. I had left her in the early morning and as I lingered she took up her pen to write.[66]

He knew that the ostensibly complimentary likening to Sand would outrage Mrs. Tyler. He did not tell her that he was the custodian of countless letters from Edith. He may not have known that Edith had saved *his* letters or that Mrs. Tyler had destroyed them.

He met Mrs. Tyler, gave her the poem "Yseult," and let her read (?) "Colophon" and (allegedly saying it was "worth money"[67]) (?) "Terminus." In July he assured her that he had not forgotten his "promise to communicate a precious document."[68] Then, in August:

By what incredible misunderstanding—surely by no stray word of mine—have you harboured the idea that I was "considering" the parting with the poem I showed you!

Moreover, what you saw was a copy. The original should be in your possession already if Edith herself did not destroy it. I showed you also the letter of Edith saying "I beg you, dear, send back the poem soon. . . . "

I gave you a characteristic manuscript of hers, but others, precious ones, I mean to keep sacredly. I hope you are making happy progress in your pious task in which you have all the sympathy of

Morton Fullerton[69]

It is not clear whether he and Mrs. Tyler were talking about the same poem or whether one meant "Colophon" (or another poem), and the other "Terminus."

Mrs. Tyler had a lawyer, Max Shoop (like Fullerton an ex-officer of the American Club), write to him saying that the poem he had was part of Edith's oeuvre; Mrs. Tyler alone was entitled to dispose of it; Fullerton had no right to give it or a copy of it to anyone else; would he please give it to her.[70]

Morton relished suavely, caddishly thwarting Mrs. Tyler. But Shoop was uncandid. The physical manuscripts Morton had were Morton's property. (And Edith had named Gaillard Lapsley her literary executor.)

There correspondence ended. Early next year, Morton, already ill, broke his hip; was taken to one hospital, then to another.

Hugh Fullerton had been away. "When I got back, they told me at the American Hospital his divorced wife had made such a scandal they said they couldn't have any more of that."

"It was the hospital that made him leave?"

"Yes."

(So that's why Morton told Hugh about his marriage. They told Hugh a woman said she was Morton's wife, and Hugh asked him, and he said, well, as a matter of fact . . .)

"The Clinique was rather run down. I found Morton in a room he shared with a retired teacher he evidently considered of inferior class as he completely ignored him—wouldn't speak to him although their beds were side by side."

"Mme Pouget came every single day with fresh linen." (Mrs. Hugh Fullerton) "His room was incredibly different from the rest."

The people at the Protestant funeral service in the Batignolles church, August 1952, were nearly all French. Hugh Fullerton: "I remember the pastor said we should not weep for the dear departed; we could hope to join him in Paradise! Mme Pouget paid for the stone. Even to the last he had charm for women. My wife always stood up for him despite everything. . . . Well, poor old boy."

Camille went to the deputy mayor and came back and told the concierge, "He gave me a thousand, I can buy some liqueur!"

George Santayana died.

Rob Fullerton died.

Hélène was evicted from the Batignolles flat. Calling to say good-bye, Hugh Fullerton saw two suitcases with papers.

Later Camille took them at revolver point.

"Amazing!" says Hugh Fullerton. "Pouget hated her guts. I'd have expected her to throttle the woman, even if there was a gun!"

Hugh thought Mme Pouget was leaving Paris, but she stayed for several years before going south, to die. "She remained *très coquette*," says Mme Eldin, "wouldn't let anyone into her room till she was *bien coiffée* and so on—but she suffered terribly."

Camille died. From the Champs-Elysées to the Elysian Fields.

"She was afraid of being thrown into the common pit," said Maître Guerre.

Camille's English tenant saved the papers she had seized. Hugh Fullerton had others that Morton had given him earlier; destroyed letters from Jacques Doriot, and came close to burning "Terminus."

Almost every morning, for a few weeks in the Belle Epoque, Edith

Wharton found on her breakfast tray a letter from Morton, which she read by delicious stages.[71]

In *Monsieur Blondeau's Tenants,* the tenor Riflardini goes through his post:

> This one's from the Vicomtesse. Tears, gnashing of teeth. I'm heartless, ungrateful. (*Throws the letter away.*) Ancient history, dear! (*Another*) A declaration of love from that red-head with the freckles. You're wasting your ink, my pet. (*Another*) "Dear, adored Jules, I, bound in wedlock, ought no longer to think of thee but the effort is beyond me and this very day wilt thou receive my visit. Signed, *La dame voilée.*"

The play has more than one "veiled lady"; but in due course Mlle Mirecourt enters, throwing back her veil. Mme Mirecourt, who was to shed tears and gnash teeth for Morton.

Vallombrosan leaves. A rani writes letters to Morton; a landlady threatens to make them known; Edith enables Morton to buy them back and destroy them; he keeps them. A count demands that a duchess, widow of a Yankee king, pay for the return of her letters; she refuses; they are read aloud in public; she is ridiculed and runs away. The count does not know that Morton has letters from the countess. Morton publicly threatens George Santayana as to private letters. Edith keeps letters by Morton, Elisina Tyler destroys them. Elisina Tyler wants to recover poems personally compromising to Edith, Morton teases her. Morton gives Hugh Fullerton a poem by Edith; Hugh almost destroys it; Hugh sells it; it is printed with the consent of Elisina Tyler's successor. Hugh burns letters politically compromising to Morton. Morton keeps letters by Edith; they go through the hands of a sculptor's model, an opera singer, a businessman, and a writer, and end up overseas. Inside an illuminated capital O fabulous beasts, sable, gules, vert, and argent, wheel counterclockwise, gnawing at each other's tails.

Lies, Errors, and Madness

A regular biography should discuss Fullerton's concept of France as a cultural isthmus. Ferret out the "third person" of his father's 1903 letter and the two unidentified women named there. And who was Doll? Investigate his Panama Canal theory and his bisexuality. Address problems not yet known to exist.

But first our notions of Fullerton, Wharton, and James must be cleared of lies and errors. Fullerton lied, and a biographer of Wharton accepted his lies and misrepresented accurate data, contaminating later studies.

Although the biographer's failure to give his sources aroused comment, most reviewers relied on the bona fides of an academic. But examine his sources and his book is like an architectural drawing by Escher: coherent at first glance, but follow a corridor or a staircase and you are in a world of unreason.[72]

Errors will be corrected. As to ascertaining the truth, great areas of ignorance remain.

Mirecourt knew what Morton said about the Ranee, Lord Ronald Gower, and Camille, maybe about Katharine and Edith. We have everyone's version of events but that of the one person Morton could not be indifferent to.

If we could only see the pact she and Morton signed.

I stared long and hard at her signature—the ink had turned brown—on her 1911 will. It gave away no secrets.

No matter if she was the Wicked Witch of the Franche Comté. Or an angel of light. What *really happened*?

Some *why*s are infinitely recessive. Why didn't Telemachus take better care of his father's dog? But is it impossible to learn what happened between Morton and her and Camille and James and Edith? That known, we may get at the "greatly dark and moving why they did it" (Robert Burns understood the problem). Adèle of Saint-Rémy may hold one end of the straw that is the clue and it is maddening after all this time not to know her side of things.

She must have talked to her conjectural legatee Louise Buisson née Bavoux about Morton and the prima donna he married and the rich *Américaine* who chased him. Louise may have told her children. If she had a son living in Paris, his military record will be in the Archives de la Seine.

The shelves mount ten feet. Climb on a stool, tug at a volume. Not a straw, a leaden block immovable.

Twenty thousand and two Buissons were called up over a twenty-five-year period. Try another volume. No use. Go home to the Left Bank, to the Quinzième.

Go to Saint-Rémy.

EPILOGUE TO A
DETECTIVE STORY

Saint-Rémy, Haute-Saône

The Haute-Saône in the Franche-Comté was on the route of eastern invaders from the Huns and Vandals on. With a visit to Saint-Rémy scheduled, go beyond vague guesses to *The Franco-German War 1870–71*, by Generals and Other [German] Officers Who Took Part in the Campaign.[1]

Their map puts Saint-Rémy at two miles from a major "line" of march that was in fact a broad swathe. They could not move in parade because of the natives. General von Widdern, writing on "Guerrilla Fighters," complained that partisans attacked railways and communication routes "stealthily and by surprise." The Germans were forced to deal with them. They put captured partisans and an equal number of local civilians to death; they took hostages; they torched villages: "Let us hope," the general concluded primly, "that a future campaign will find us better and more thoroughly prepared for the duty of protecting the railway lines; the army of 1870/71 left much to be desired."

Malt does more than Milton can, General von Widdern does more than Morton could to make one understand how the French felt when 1914 came around.

Adèle's brother Auguste Numa Moutot, who had lost an eye by the age of twenty, was seventeen when the Prussians moved through. It is still only speculation, but not vapid speculation, that the Moutots emigrated as a result of the war and that Adèle Moutot did something to instill in her foreign lodger a hatred of Germany that outlived their intimacy by two world wars.

So, night train to Vesoul; by car at morning into undulating hills with pastures, some *vignes*, some fruit trees, few signs of habitation, the blue line of the Vosges in the distance.

"Que penses-tu trouver? What do you think you'll find?"
"I don't know. I know they'll think I'm a lunatic."

A DANGER sign. Saint-Rémy is a hill town with steep curving streets. Population, four hundred. Church, shop, *mairie.*

"Beautiful, *oui,*" says the deputy mayor, "but it used to be a very very poor village. There is a hospital now and a lot of work. But Saint-Rémy used to be *misérable.* Many people left—and left the other villages—for Paris."

He leads the way to M. Georges Bavoux's. Cages of rabbits. Huge old tiled fireplace with a modern stove inside it. Mme Bavoux is making a *tarte* on a long oilcloth-covered table.

M. Bavoux: stout, balding, ruddy-faced, in a sleeveless *pull* (= cardigan) and conventional baggy *pantalon.*

His family are of a different line from the Bavoux who was Adèle Moutot's mother. He doesn't know the name Moutot. He used to farm, but he had a tractor accident, *"c'était grave,* the village was very very poor, *misérable.* Now, thanks to the hospital, there is work. At first we were a little nervous . . . seeing them. . . . *C'était normal, quoi?* But it's brought work."

"Oh, it has transformed the economy," the deputy mayor says. "The main building is the château. Eighteenth century, *oui.* The Comte de Gramont was Baron de Saint-Rémy. And we have an annex in another château at Clairefontaine. This will tell you."

A glossy colored brochure.

CENTRE PSYCHOTHÉRAPIQUE DE SAINT-RÉMY

Quiet relaxed atmosphere, psychiatrists, psychologists, electroencephalography, kinesitherapy, ergotherapy, workshops offer manual activities aiding in rehabilitation.

The mayor of Saint-Rémy is director of the Psychiatric Hospital. The deputy mayor of Saint-Rémy is deputy director of the Psychiatric Hospital.

Floral wallpapers, cheerful two-bed rooms. Beauty shop. Cafeteria. Patients drinking red wine, *c'est la France,* and gazing at the green mountains.

A pale young man rises and strikes out across the lawn.

"But are they, is it safe to let them . . . *se promener,* go about?"

"*Mais,* Monsieur, it is not a locked unit, these ones aren't dangerous. They have *des problèmes.* Many *dépressifs,* some delusions, obsessions . . . "

A telegram from Madrid, a head from King Charles, an artiste from Saint-Rémy, golden garters, lutes and lobsters.

"But so many, from a region so unpopulated?"

"Ah, but Monsieur we are registered for all of France. They send many from Paris. We receive many many mentally ill from the *Région Parisienne*."

The hilltop is springy underfoot, the morning air mild. Emptiness. No trace of the hordes that pushed through here, pushed on by hordes behind them (problems of power) from the Mongol steppes to the Atlantic. If there is a golden mean in scholarship and at one extreme is brutish indifference to the truth, at the other . . . Hector was right, 'tis mad idolatry to make the service greater than the god.

A Short List of Fullerton's Writings

Fullerton wrote industriously all his life. He produced books, articles, poems, prefaces, translations, and lectures, in addition to his newspaper work. A few examples are given here.

1882–1888
Articles and verse, *Harvard Advocate, Harvard Monthly, Unitarian Review, Traveler's Record.*
Weekly "Letters about Books," *Boston Record/Advertiser.*
1890
"English and Americans," *Fortnightly Review,* Feb., May.
"Bion of Smyrna," *Nineteenth Century,* Sept.
"Some Notes on George Meredith in America," in Richard LeGallienne, *George Meredith: Some Characteristics,* with a bibliography by John Lane (London: Elkin Mathews).

1891–1910
Daily correspondence for the *Times* (London).
1891
"Impressions in Cairo," *English Illustrated Magazine,* illus. Percy Anderson, March.
In Cairo (London and New York: Macmillan). "Impressions in Cairo," revised.
1893
Patriotism and Science: Some Studies in Historic Psychology (Boston: Roberts Bros.) Contains "On a Certain Danger in Patriotism at the Present Time," "English and Americans," "Democracy, with Reference to a Recent Book."
"Monsieur de Blowitz," *McClure's Magazine,* July.
1894
"To the Brink of Pirene," *National Review,* Sept.
"George Meredith" (sonnet), *Yellow Book,* Oct.
1896
"Three Sonnets," *Scribner's Magazine,* March.
1897
"At Arcachon," *Fortnightly Review,* Oct.
1899
"The Dreyfus Trial," *Times* wires from Rennes, Aug.–Sept.

1902–1910
Unsigned book reviews, *Times Literary Supplement.*

1903
"France, England, and Morocco," *Times* wire from Madrid, 2 Feb.
"Before Homer: Sea-Power and the Odyssey," *Cornhill Magazine,* Feb.
1905
Terres Françaises: Bourgogne, Franche-Comté, Narbonnaise (Paris: Colin).
Revue de Paris essays of 1903 and 1905, revised.
1907
"Monsieur Clemenceau," *National Review,* Feb.
1909
"The Crisis of the State in France," *National Review,* May.
1910
"The Art of Henry James," *Quarterly Review,* April.
"Mr. Roosevelt and France," *Scribner's Magazine,* Sept.
1911
"America Revisited," *Scribner's Magazine,* June.
1913
"The Unmarried Woman in France," *Century Magazine,* April.
Problems of Power: A Study of International Politics from Sadowa to Kirk-Kilissé (London: Constable; New York: Scribner's). New and revised ed., New York, 1915. Third definitive ed., London, June 1920. [Preface dated April 1919]. Reputed German and Japanese translations, not traced.
1916
Hesitations: The American Crisis and the War (New York: Doubleday; London: Constable).
La Guerre européenne: Les-Etats-Unis et la guerre. (Paris: Imhaus et Chapelot). Translation of *Hesitations.*
Les Grands Problèmes de la politique mondiale: Problems of Power, trans. B. Mayra (Paris: Imhaus et Chapelot, two eds.).
1917
Ce qu'un français doit savoir des Etats-Unis. With Emile Boutroux, Jules Lepain, Firmin Roz (Paris: Grasset).
"Morning in Achaia: Poem," *Scribner's Magazine,* April.
1919 ff.
Unpublished reports submitted to AEF, G-2 (Intelligence).
1920
Introduction to *The Memoirs of Ismail Kemal Bey,* ed. Sommerville Story (London: Constable; New York: Dutton).
1922–1935
Bimonthly signed columns, *Le Figaro* (e.g., "Les Deux Croisades," 3 May 1923; "Ce que dit le Président Coolidge," 14 Dec. 1923; "Le Nationalisme ouvrier: De Karl Marx à Samuel Gompers," 11 July 1924).
1923
Au Seuil de la Provence: Le Rhône Cévénol Revision of *Revue de Paris* essays. (Paris: Nouvelle Librairie Nationale).
1936–1940
Bimonthly signed columns, *Le Journal des Débats* (e.g., "Les Mystères de Moscou," 21 May 1937; "La 'Sea Power' et Les Américains," 21 May 1939; "Répondez à l'Appel du Maréchal!" [7 July] 1940).
1936 ff.
Untraced articles, *L'Echo de Paris.*

Notes

Abbreviations

AL	Kenneth M. Price and Phyllis McBride, eds., "'The Life Apart': Text and Contexts of Edith Wharton's Love Diary," *American Literature*, Dec. 1994
AT	Archive of the *Times* (London)
BA	*Boston Advertiser*
BL	British Library
BMF	Bradford Morton Fullerton
BN	Bibliothèque Nationale
BR	Blanche Roosevelt
BW	Barrett Wendell
CC	Camille Chabbert
CMB	C. Moberly Bell
CNHJ	Leon Edel and Lyall H. Powers, eds., *The Complete Notebooks of Henry James* (New York and Oxford, 1987)
ERT	Elisina Royall Tyler
EW	Edith Wharton
EW	R. W. B. Lewis, *Edith Wharton: A Biography* (New York, 1975)
FD	Francesca d'Aulby
Fig.	*Le Figaro*
FM	Frederick Macmillan
FP	Fullerton Papers, Beinecke Library, Yale University
GM	George Meredith
GS	George Santayana
HA	Hamilton Aïdé
HCA	Harvard Class Archives
HCL	The Houghton Library, Harvard University
HJ	Henry James
HJEWL	Lyall H. Powers, ed., *Henry James and Edith Wharton Letters: 1900–1915* (New York, 1990)
HJL	Leon Edel, ed., *Henry James Letters*, vol. 4 [1895–1916] (Cambridge, Mass., and London, 1984)
HP	Hélène Pouget
JD	*Le Journal des Débats*
JF	Julia Fullerton
JW	John Walter

KFG   Katharine Fullerton Gerould
LC   Library of Congress
LChr   Alan Gribben, " 'The Heart Is Insatiable': A Selection from Edith
          Wharton's Letters to Morton Fullerton, 1907–1915"; Clare Colquitt,
          "Unpacking Her Treasures: Edith Wharton's 'Mysterious
          Correspondence' with Morton Fullerton," both in *The Library
          Chronicle*, 1985 (Harry Ransom Humanities Research Center, Uni-
          versity of Texas at Austin)
LE   Leon Edel
LEW   R. W. B. Lewis and Nancy Lewis, eds., *The Letters of Edith Wharton*
          (New York, 1988)
MB   Margaret Brooke
NYHS   New-York Historical Society
PofP   William Morton Fullerton, *Problems of Power* (New York and Lon-
          don, 1913, 1914, 1920)
PP   "Pentagon Papers" (American Expeditionary Force Records, Depart-
          ment of Defense, Washington, D.C.)
PU   Robert H. Taylor Collection, Princeton University Library
RMF   Robert Morton Fullerton
SC   Simmons College Library
SL   Samuel Longfellow
TF   William Morton Fullerton, *Terres Françaises* (Paris, 1905)
TLS   *Times Literary Supplement*
TR   Theodore Roosevelt
UI   Lilly Library, Indiana University
UR   Reading University Library
UTA   Harry Ransom Humanities Research Center, University of Texas at
          Austin
UV   Special Collections Department, University of Virginia Library
VC   Valentine Chirol
WB   Walter Berry
WMF   William Morton Fullerton
YU   Beinecke Library, Yale University

Prologue (pages 1–7)

1. HJ to WMF, 7 Nov. 1902, *HJL*, 246–49.
2. WMF, "A French Poetess," *TLS*, 14 June 1907.
3. Jean Cocteau's adjective.
4. For 30 April, 1888, General Reference Branch, National Archives, Washington, D.C.

Part One (pages 9–65)

1. Preface, *TF* (Paris, 1905).
2. "America Revisited," *Scribner's*, Sept. 1910.
3. Notebook in possession of author.
4. WMF, *PofP* (London, 1920), 54n.
5. Accent marks effaced in this entry are supplied. (In the text, the amper-
sand and contractions are written out, with the arbitrary exception of passages

where they suggest the writer's haste or informality. When the style and/or transcription of a manuscript vary in different published editions, I have used my own reading.

6. Preface, *Au Seuil de la Provence* (Paris, 1923).

7. Ibid.

8. EW, "Line-a-Day," 18 Feb. 1908, UI.

9. Ibid., 25 Mar. 1908.

10. "The Life Apart" ["L'Ame close"] 21 Feb. 1908, *AL*, 671.

11. Ibid.

12. Ibid., 20 Apr. 1908, *AL*, 673.

13. Ibid., 3 May 1908, *AL*, 675.

14. Ibid., second entry for 3 May 1908, *AL*, 676.

15. For details of trains and inns, see Karl Baedeker, *Paris and Its Environs* (Leipzig, 1907).

16. "The Life Apart," 13 May 1908, *AL*, 678.

17. Ibid., 19 May 1908, *AL*, 679.

18. Ibid., 13 May 1908, *AL*, 677.

19. *PofP* [1913] (London, 1920).

20. London, 1928.

21. *In My Time* (London, 1938), 211.

22. From number 33 to number 99, between 1933 and 1950.

23. This decree is the authority for the statement in *EW* (189–90) that CC "charged [WMF] with maintaining several mistresses and 'of having, as a result, refused to grant her his caresses.'"

24. HJ to WMF, 14 Nov. 1907, *HJL*, 4:472–74.

25. HJ to WMF, 26 Nov. 1907, *HJL*, 4:477–80.

26. HJ to WMF, 29 Nov. 1907, *HJL*, 4:480.

27. Wilde to WMF [June 1899] in Wilde, *Letters*, ed. Rupert Hart-Davis (New York, 1962), 803.

28. WMF to Wilde, 23 June [1899], in Wilde, *Letters*, 803–4.

29. Wilde to WMF, 25 June [1899], in Wilde, *Letters*, 803–4.

30. See Marie Belloc-Lowndes, *The Merry Wives of Windsor* (London, 1946), 208.

31. See Philippe Jullian, *Oscar Wilde* (Paris, 1967).

32. Wilde to *St. James's Gazette*, 26 June [1890] in Wilde, *Letters*, 258–59.

33. Lord Ronald Sutherland Gower, *Old Diaries, 1881–1902* (London, 1902).

34. "Chabbert" and "Chabert" both appear in letters and official records, "Chabbert" more frequently. Camille's daughter used "Chabbert" in her marriage license.

35. Stéphane Wolff, *Un Demi-Siècle de l'Opéra Comique* (Paris, 1953).

36. KFG to WMF, 5 Jan. 1910, FP. Unpublished FP letters are in the Yale Collection of American Literature, Beinecke Rare Book and Manuscript Library, Yale University.

37. HA to WMF, 27 Nov. 1900, FP.

38. WMF, "In Craigie House," *BA*, 28 Mar. 1887.

39. WMF to Marian, 28 Jan. 1888, FP.

40. *DNB* (*Chambers' Biographical Dictionary* gives 1830).

41. See Hesketh Pearson, *Beerbohm Tree* (New York, 1956).

42. WMF to HA, 14 Dec. 1899, FP. Aïdé served in the army, but he retired at twenty-seven (*DNB*).

43. WMF to HA, 18 Aug. 1889, FP.

44. WMF to HA, 4 July [1895], FP.
45. MB to WMF, Mon. [from 12 Hans Place after 31 Mar. 1890], FP. Most MB letters are dated only tentatively.
46. MB to WMF, Fri. 7 P.M. [Apr. or later, 1890], FP.
47. WMF to MB, 2:30 A.M. Fri. [1890?], FP.
48. MB to WMF, Sun. [1890], letter beginning "My darling—our last conversation," FP; cf. MB to WMF, Tues. [early 1891], FP.
49. MB to WMF, Mon. 8 P.M. [1890], FP.
50. MB to WMF, "8 Aug." [error for Sept.?] [1890], FP.
51. MB to WMF, Mon. [after Mar. 1890], from 12 Hans Place, FP.
52. WMF to MB, 2 A.M. [Sept. 1890], FP.
53. WMF to MB, 12 Sept. 1890, FP.
54. MB to WMF, 11:30 P.M., 8 Jan. [1891], FP.
55. MB to WMF, Thurs. evening [late 1890 or early 1891], letter beginning "My darling—I don't wish," FP.
56. MB to WMF, Tues. 8 P.M., FP.
57. MB to WMF, Sat. [?11 Apr. 1891] letter beginning "My dearest—Alice is all right," FP.
58. See MB to WMF, Thurs. [2 Apr. 1891] and Sat. [?11 Apr. 1891], FP.
59. WMF to HA, 4 July [1895], FP.
60. MB to WMF, Wed. [3 June 1891], FP.
61. MB to WMF, 8 Apr. [? 1892], from Hotel Marini, Rome, FP.
62. HA to WMF, 16 May 1893, FP.
63. JF to WMF, 6 Feb. 1893, FP.
64. WMF to MB, [early Sept. 1890], FP.
65. JF to WMF, 28 Nov. 1897, FP.
66. JF to WMF, 24 Jan. 1898, FP.
67. JF to WMF, 9 Apr. 1899, FP.
68. JF to WMF, 11 July [1897], FP.
69. JF to WMF, 20 Sept. [1897], FP.
70. JF to WMF, 11 July [1897], FP.
71. JF to WMF, 23 Aug. [1897], FP.
72. Quoted in KFG to WMF, 22 Nov. [1907], FP.
73. KFG to WMF, 20 June 1897, FP.
74. KFG to WMF, [15 July 1897], FP.
75. KFG to WMF, [1898], FP.
76. KFG to WMF, 1 Mar. 1898, FP.
77. JF to WMF, 16 Oct. [1898], FP.
78. KFG to WMF, [early 1898], FP.
79. JF to WMF, 17 July [1898], FP.
80. JF to WMF, 16 Oct. [1898], FP.
81. KFG to WMF, 14 May 1899, FP.
82. KFG to WMF, [21 Aug. 1899], FP.
83. KFG to WMF, 13 and 15 May [1900], FP.
84. WMF to HA, 2 Feb. [1897], FP.
85. WMF to HA, 9 Oct. 1902, FP.
86. JF to WMF, 25 May 1894 [error for 1904], FP.
87. Albert Clemenceau to WMF, Nov. 1904, FP.
88. Ella Clapp to WMF, 19 Mar. 1905, FP.
89. KFG (A.B. Radcliffe, 1900; A.M., 1901) was reader in English at Bryn Mawr, 1901–10.

90. KFG to WMF, Thurs. [Oct. 1907], FP.
91. KFG to WMF, 1 Nov. [1907], FP.
92. See HJ to KFG, 5 Dec. 1907, PU.
93. EW, expecting WMF on Friday afternoon, 18 Oct., or Saturday morning, after his Bryn Mawr talk, sent her car to meet two New York trains, but delays in the mail caused a mix-up. On the 19th she wrote to Brockton: she and Teddy must leave early on the 22nd; if WMF cared to come only for the afternoon/evening of the 21st, would he wire? He did so. Early on the 22nd she dropped him off at Westfield and continued on a drive with Eliot Gregory. He would have been back in Brockton that evening. See EW to WMF, 15 Oct. [1907], 53.1 UTA (*LEW* 116); EW to WMF, 19 Oct. [1907], YU; EW to Sara Norton, 26 Oct. [1907], YU. When JF spoke of him and KFG as spending "three weeks under the same roof" (KFG to WMF, 7 Jan. 1908, FP), she spoke loosely. For the lecture, which WMF also gave at Harvard, see HJ to KFG, 5 Dec. 1907, PU.
94. KFG to WMF, Fri., [8 Nov. 1907], FP.
95. KFG to WMF, Sat., 9 Nov. 1907, FP.
96. KFG to WMF, 23 Nov. [1907], FP.
97. "The Life Apart," 27 Nov. 1907, *AL*, 671.
98. KFG to WMF, 11 Dec. 1907, FP.
99. KFG to WMF, 13 Dec. 1907, FP.
100. RMF to WMF, 9 Jan. 1908, FP. The statement (*EW*, 201) that KFG and WMF "agreed . . . to discuss it all with the older Fullertons" in Brockton and "were, it seems, formally engaged [there, the elders being] persuaded to give their approval and consent" is mistaken.
101. KFG to WMF, 7 Jan. [1908], FP.
102. KFG to WMF, 10 Jan. 1908, FP.
103. WMF, quoted by EW, "The Life Apart" 7 May 1908, *AL*, 677.
104. KFG to WMF, Fri., [?2 Oct.] [1908], FP.
105. KFG to WMF, Sun. [?27 Dec.] [1908], FP.
106. FD to WMF, 1908–1910, passim, FP.
107. KFG to WMF, Tues., [early winter, 1909], FP.
108. Doll to WMF, [early winter 1909], Paris postmark "[19]09," FP. The text reads: "Chèr ami! Vous êtes donc tout le temps avec votre soeur. *Vous jouez trop avec le feu.* Comme vous m'avez dit votre petite soeur vous aime. Ne brisez pas son coeur si vous êtes incappable de vous atacher à elle. Je vous fait la morale!! Mercredi ou jeudi mon ami arrivera. Il restera 8–10 jours. Aussitôt seule j'espère vous revoire Je vous embrasse tendrement Doll."
109. KFG to WMF, 5 Jan. [1910], FP.
110. Cable in FP.
111. BMF to WMF, 22 Mar. 1910, FP.
112. JF to WMF, 24 June 1910, FP.
113. KFG to WMF, 17 Feb. [1913], FP.
114. KFG to WMF, 5 Feb. 1940, FP.
115. CC to WMF, 22 Mar. 1908, FP. This is described in *EW* (p. 248) as "a worried, affectionate letter urging [WMF] not to trifle with his sister if he were not serious."
116. CC to WMF, 10 Mar. 1908, FP.
117. KFG to WMF, 10 Jan. [1908], FP.
118. BMF to WMF, 13 May 1904, FP
119. HJ to WMF, 20 Aug. 1909, *HJEWL*, 120–21.

Part Two (pages 66–82)

1. HJ to WMF, 27 Jan. 1900, bMS Am, 1094.1 (65), HCL. Unpublished HCL letters are quoted by permission of the Houghton Library, Harvard University.
2. Information from Daria d'Arienzo, Amherst College archivist.
3. See John Cody, *After Great Pain: The Inner Life of Emily Dickinson* (Cambridge, Mass., 1971).
4. *History and Manual of the Second Congregational Church* (Palmer, Mass., 1895).
5. He was secretary of the Society of Inquiry and, for one term, class president. He won prizes in declamation. He weighed 115 pounds, "the least of any classmate." Information from Violet Kellogg, archivist, Phillips Academy.
6. BMF to WMF, 13 May 1904, FP.
7. Letter communicated to the author by Judge Edward Dwight Fullerton's son Dwight. A note reads "Ans'd 5/7/1900."
8. KFG to WMF, 2 June [1914], FP.
9. WMF, *Patriotism and Science* (Boston, 1893).
10. WMF to JF, 22 Apr. 1907, UV. Fullerton Letters (9040). Quoted by permission of the Special Collections Department, University of Virginia Library.
11. Others overlapping with WMF were Larz Anderson, Frederick Atherton, George Pierce Baker, Winthrop Chanler, Alanson Houghton, and Mark de Wolfe Howe.
12. WMF to BW, [?1895], bMS Am 1907.1 (487), HCL. By permission of the Houghton Library, Harvard University.
13. WMF, *College Themes*, HCA.
14. GS, *The Last Puritan* (New York, 1935).
15. WMF, "The Duchess Emilia," *Harvard Advocate,* 24 Apr. 1885.
16. WMF, "Stedman's Poets of America" (review), *Harvard Monthly,* Jan. 1886.
17. *Boston Advertiser,* 11 Jan. 1881. See *The Masque of Pandora*, by Henry W. Longfellow (music by Alfred Cellier; arranged for the stage by Bolton Rowe; . . . produced for the first time at The Boston Theatre, by the Blanche Roosevelt English Opera Company, 10th January, 1881) (Boston, 1881).
18. GS, *Persons and Places* (London, 1944).
19. WMF to BW [1895?], HCL. By permission of the Houghton Library, Harvard University.
20. WMF, "Bion of Smyrna," *Nineteenth Century,* Sept. 1890.
21. WMF to BW [1895?], HCL. By permission of the Houghton Library, Harvard University.
22. WMF to C. E. Norton, 1 July 1906, bMS Am 1094.1 (33), HCL. By permission of the Houghton Library, Harvard University.
23. *Boston Sunday Record,* 5 June 1887.
24. WMF, "Letters about Books," *BA,* 31 Jan. 1887. The *Advertiser* exists in microfilm at the Boston Public Library. Original issues of the *Record* at the Massachusetts Historical Society are so brittle that pages flake into dust when touched; the *Record* will not survive much more research.
25. For WMF on GM, see "Some Notes on George Meredith in America," in Richard Le Gallienne, *George Meredith: Some Characteristics,* with a bibliography by John Lane (London, 1890). GM's son, W. M. Meredith, published GM

letters to WMF in *Scribner's* (1912). C. L. Cline, ed. *The Letters of George Meredith* (Oxford, 1970) contains letters to and about WMF.

26. "George Meredith: At the Great Novelist's Home. . . ."*BA*, 17 Dec. 1888.

27. See KFG, "The Newest Woman" in *Modes and Morals* (New York, 1920).

28. *BA*, 10 Jan. 1887.

29. Ibid. 31 Jan. 1887.

30. Ibid. 10 Apr. 1887.

31. Information from Thomas Meteyard's son, Robert Meteyard, Douglass Shand-Tucci, Nicholas Kilmer, and Kilmer's *Thomas Buford Meteyard: Paintings and Watercolors* (New York, 1989).

32. See Muriel Miller, *Bliss Carman: Quest and Revolt* (St. John's, Newfoundland, 1985), 45.

33. Carman to Muriel Carman, 8 Mar. 1887, *Letters of Bliss Carman,* ed. H. Pearson Gundy (Kingston and Montreal, [1981]), 14–15.

34. GS to WMF, 9 Sept. 1886 and 10 July 1887, UTA. Unpublished UTA documents are cited by permission of the Harry Ransom Humanities Research Center, The University of Texas at Austin.

35. GS to WMF, 10 July 1887, UTA.

36. GS to WMF, 31 Aug. 1887, UTA.

37. GS to WMF, 28 Dec. 1887, UTA; John McCormick published the greater part of the letter in *George Santayana: A Biography* (New York: 1987), 70–71.

38. GS to WMF, 31 Aug. 1887, UTA.

39. WMF to Marian, 28 Jan. 1888, FP.

40. *Literary World,* 16 Apr. 1887.

41. In *A Few Verses of Many Years* (Cambridge, Mass., 1887), SL dedicated "The Cascade" to WMF, "To whom I owe half the lines."

42. *Through the Year with the Poets,* November vol. (Boston, 1890).

43. Dedication, Paris, 26 July 1891. See Joseph May, *Samuel Longfellow: Memoir and Letters* (Boston and New York, 1894).

44. See Edward Wagenknecht, *Longfellow: A Full-Length Portrait* (New York, London, Toronto, 1955). SL made no reference to BR's stay with the family and her book on Henry Wadsworth Longfellow.

45. JF to WMF, 14 Nov. 1897, FP.

46. Preface to "The Notion of the Beautiful," *Harvard Monthly,* Oct. 1895.

47. "George Meredith," *BA*, 17 Dec. 1888. Largely reprinted in A. Hammerton, *George Meredith* (Edinburgh, 1910).

48. Citations are from "Impressions in Cairo" and *In Cairo* (slight textual differences).

49. WMF to BW, [1895?], HCL.

50. WMF, "Theocritus: With Special Reference to His Supposed Obligations to the Septuagint," *Unitarian Review,* July 1886.

51. WMF, "To the Brink of Pirene," *National Review,* Sept. 1894.

52. WMF, "Before Homer," *Cornhill,* Feb. 1903.

53. GM to Louise Lawrence, 20 May 1889, in Cline, *Letters of George Meredith,* 2:959.

54. MB to WMF, 11:30 P.M., 8 Jan. [1891], FP.

55. HJ to WMF, 4 Mar. 1891, bMS Am 1094.1, HCL. Unpublished letters of HJ are cited by gracious permission of Leon Edel and Deborah Edel.

56. WMF to HA, 18 Aug. [1889], FP.

57. Arthur Symons, "The Decadent Movement in Literature," *Harper's New Monthly Magazine,* Nov. 1893.

58. Symons to WMF, 20 Nov. [1891], FP.

59. Le Gallienne, *George Meredith.*

60. It is still so listed in library catalogs.

61. WMF, "George Meredith" (sonnet), *Yellow Book,* Oct. 1894.

62. WMF, "Impressions in Cairo," *English Illustrated Magazine,* Mar. 1891.

63. WMF, "English and Americans," *Fortnightly Review,* Feb. 1890.

64. HJ to WMF, 4 Feb. 1890, bMS Am 1094 (37), HCL.

65. HJ to WMF, 31 Mar. [1890], bMS Am 1094 (20), HCL.

66. HJ to FM, 4 Mar. [1891], BL. BL letters are cited by kind permission of the British Library. Macmillan archives are at the BL and at UR, which rescued thousands of letters the publishers were about to scrap for lack of room. They are quoted by permission of the British Library and the Reading University Library.

67. WMF to FM, Thurs., [Mar. 1891], BL.

68. WMF to FM, [Mar. 1891], BL.

69. HJ to WMF, 22 Mar. 1900, *HJL,* 4:136–37.

70. HJ to WMF, 14 Nov. 1907, PU; *HJL,* 4:472–74.

71. The book was not, as is said in *EW* (p. 185) about "new departures in scientific thought."

72. WMF to FM, 17 Feb. 1893, BL.

73. WMF to FM, [1893], BL.

74. Quoted in WMF to FM, [1893], BL.

75. HJ to WMF, 20 Oct. 1896, bMS Am 1094 (55), HCL.

76. *Boston Journal,* [1891] (archive of Second Congregational Church, Palmer, Mass.).

77. WMF to John Lane, 25 June [1890], YU.

78. GM to Louise Chandler Moulton, 9 Mar. 1890, in Cline, *Letters of George Meredith,* 2:992.

79. Alice James, 19 Apr. 1891, in *The Diary of Alice James,* ed. Leon Edel (New York, 1982), 193–94.

80. *Proceedings, International Congregational Council* (London, 1891); information from Congregational Society, Boston.

81. WMF notebook.

82. *BA,* 16 May 1887.

83. George Dwight Pratt of Springfield, 19 June 1895, Massachusetts State Archives.

84. WMF to SL, [early 1892], SL Papers, Longfellow Family Correspondence, H. W. Longfellow National Historic Site. (Marcel Terrié of the Fondation Salomon de Rothschild has no record of WMF correspondence.)

Part Three (pages 83–144)

1. Thousands of ephemeral plays, some of them one-night stands, survive because pamphlets hawked at the theater, now in the BN, gave not only the cast but the entire script. From 1872 to 1879, Mirecourt appeared in *La Cocotte aux Oeufs d'Or, grande féérie parisienne* (Clairville, Grangé, & Koning; music by Hervé, Coedès, Raspail, & Patusset), Théâtre des Menus-Plaisirs, 31 Dec. 1872–24 Mar. 1873. *La Mariée de la Rue Saint-Denis, folie-vaudeville*

(Clairville, Grangé, & Koning; music by Hervé & Raspail), Menus-Plaisirs, 4 April–20 May 1873. *La Comète à Paris: Revue en 3 actes et 10 tableaux* (Monréal & Blondeau; music by Chautagne, Planquette, & Patusset) Théâtre Déjazet, 5 Dec. 1874–8 Feb. 1875. *Pif-Paf, féérie* (Clairville, Monréal, & Blondeau; music by Matz-Ferrare), Théâtre du Château d'Eau, 4 Oct.–2 Dec. 1875. *Les Echos de l'Année, revue*, Château-d'Eau, 31 Dec. 1875–6 Feb. 1876. *Tant Plus Ca Change, vaudeville-revue* (Gondinet & Véron), Palais-Royal, 28 Dec. 1878–23 Jan. 1879. *Un Scandale, vaudeville* (Duvert and Lauzanne) and *Les Gommeux de l'Assommoir, "à-propos"* (Burani; skit on Zola's *L'Assommoir*), Palais-Royal, 17 May–early June 1879. *Les Locataires de Monsieur Blondeau, vaudeville en cinq étages* (Henri Chivot), Palais-Royal, 11 June–28 Aug. 1879; revived 30 Oct.–3 Nov. 1879.

2. *La Cocotte aux Oeufs d'Or*; see note 1.

3. *La Comète à Paris*; see note 1.

4. See *Le Figaro*, 2 Jan. 1873; *Le Constitutionnel*, 6 Jan. 1873; *Le Gaulois*, 4 Apr. 1873. For reviews of plays, see also *La Gazette de France, Le Petit Journal, Le Journal des Débats, Le Théâtre, Le Spectateur, La Scène, La Vie Parisienne, Le Temps, Le Charivari*, etc.

5. "Et l'on serait heureux sur terre / Si le monde où nous combattons / Ne connaissait pas d'autre guerre / Que la guerre que nous faisons." *La Comète à Paris* (n. 1).

6. Undated article, Rondel Coll. Miette, Bibliothèque de l'Arsénal.

7. HJ, "A French Watering Place," *Parisian Sketches, 1875–1876*, ed. Leon Edel and Else Dusoir Lind (New York, 1957).

8. WMF to SL, [early 1892], SL Papers, Longfellow National Historic Site.

9. WMF, "Monsieur de Blowitz," *McClure's Magazine*, July 1893.

10. WMF notebook.

11. "A Bomb Thrown in the French Chamber," *Times*, 11 Dec. 1893.

12. "The Panama Bribery Trial," *Times*, 9 Mar. 1893, was probably WMF's first story to be printed in his own words. He pasted a cutting of it in his notebook facing notes he had made in the courtroom.

13. Evan Charteris, *The Life and Letters of Sir Edmund Gosse* (London 1931). Gosse had told the story, not naming HJ, in "A First Sight of Verlaine," *Savoy* (ed. Arthur Symons), Apr. 1896, below.

14. For the Verlaine incident, see Verlaine "My Visit to London," *Savoy*, April 1893; *Correspondence*, ed. Ad. Van Bever (Paris 1919); V. P. Underwood, *Verlaine et l'Angleterre* (Paris, 1956); Symons, "Some Unpublished Letters of Verlaine," *North American Review*, Nov. 1915. Symons tells the story and prints WMF's letter without naming WMF. Stuart Merrill, *Vers et Prose: Oeuvres Posthumes* (Paris, 1925), says, "Robert Sherard was given the responsible task of seeing [Verlaine] on to the night train" (p. 316); cf. Joanna Richardson, *Verlaine* (New York, 1971). Sherard, *Twenty Years in Paris* (London, 1925), does not state that he escorted Verlaine but invites the inference that he did. WMF also recalled the meal with Verlaine in a letter to J. L. Garvin, 25 Nov. 1934, on the letterhead of the Café Terminus, Gare Saint-Lazare (UTA). Christopher Gerould recalls WMF's showing him a postcard that Verlaine sent from England, saying "Quelle douleur s'en aller sur la mer!" The story is also told in Eugène Fleuré's manuscript memoir of WMF.

15. The postcard, dated 10 Feb. 1894 (BN), is printed in Verlaine, *Oeuvres Oubliées*, vol. 1, ed. Maurice Monda (Paris, 1926). Both sides of the card are

shown, between pp. 64 and 65. Monda thanked WMF for showing him the card. See W. B. Yeats "Verlaine in 1894," *Savoy,* Apr. 1896, reprinted in Yeats, *Autobiography* (New York, 1938). The entry in WMF's notebook has not been known till now. In 1894, Verlaine was writing an article (unfinished) for *Cosmopolitan* (Van Bever, *Correspondence,* 3:160–61). The magazine was edited by WMF's college acquaintance A. S. Hardy; WMF may have suggested the piece.

16. *Times,* 11 Dec. 1893.

17. WMF began three novels, or one novel with three titles: "New England," "Guy Temple," "Richard Trunnier." Family letters allude to his collaboration on a novel with a "Druse Prince," perhaps the same as a mysterious emir; work was halted, he told Aïdé, when the emir had a hernia repaired at a hospital for paupers. "France, a psychological study," and a "libretto" on Napoleon were lost or stolen. WMF also translated an unidentified play, *Jeune Turquie.*

18. "Three Sonnets" *Scribner's Magazine,* March 1896. These must be the "two sonnets on HJ in an American magazine" mentioned in an obituary of WMF, signed "W.S." *Times,* 1 Sept. 1952.

19. HJ to WMF, 4 Feb. [1893], *HJL,* 3:405.

20. Carman to WMF, 4 Feb. 1892, Gundy, *Letters of Bliss Carman,* 42.

21. For Hovey, see Allan Houston MacDonald, *Richard Hovey: Man and Craftsman* (Durham, N.C., 1957).

22. Information from Robert Meteyard and Nicholas Kilmer.

23. BR to WMF, [1890s], FP. In *EW* the letter is paraphrased as follows: BR "was telling Fullerton firmly that she would not again visit him in his rooms alone 'unless expressly invited' . . . only to add yieldingly: 'When am I to see you again, Adonis'?" (p. 186).

24. Information obtained by Virginia Boegli. "Progressive Men of Montana," Merrill G. Burlingame Special Collections, Montana State University Library; "History of the Belt Slauther House" in *Cascade County History and Description,* WPA Project, 15 Sept. 1941; "Long Journey" *Montana Magazine of History,* summer 1954; W. Turrentine Jackson, *Wells Fargo Stagecoaching in Montana Territory,* Montana Historical Society Press, 1979.

25. Dedication, *Stage-Struck* (New York and London, 1884).

26. Arsène Houssaie, preface to *La Vie et les Oeuvres de Gustave Doré,* by BR, trans. M. du Seigneux (Paris, [?1886]).

27. Harris, *My Life and Loves* (New York, 1963), 443.

28. See Houssaie, note 26, above.

29. BR, *Elisabeth of Roumania* (London, 1891) and *Victorian Sardou* (London 1892). W. Beatty-Kingston wrote, in the preface to *Sardou,* that Hugo's judgment of her was confirmed when she became "the first American authoress" to be decorated by the Académie Française. See also Francis Steegmuller, *Maupassant* (London, 1950) and Marcello Spaziani "Lettere inedite di Maupassant," in *Studi in onore di Vittorio Lugli e Diegago Valeri* (Venice, [1961]), vol. 2.

30. HJ to WMF, 14 July [1893], *HJL,* 3:419.

31. *Times,* 7 July 1892.

32. See BR, "Guy de Maupassant," *Woman's World,* Nov. 1888.

33. François Tassart, *Souvenirs sur . . . Maupassant* (Paris, 1911).

34. She died 10 Sept. 1898 of cerebral thrombosis, Bright's disease, and cirrhosis of the liver (death certificate, St. Catherine's House, London).

35. BR, *Verdi: Milan and 'Othello'* (London, 1887), 248.

36. JF to WMF, 9 Apr. 1899, FP.

37. WMF to HA, 21 Nov. [1896], FP.
38. WMF notebook.
39. *Times*, 7 Jan. 1895.
40. WMF, "Monsieur de Blowitz," *McClure's Magazine*, July 1893.
41. WMF, "At Arcachon," *Fortnightly Review*, 1 Sept. 1895.
42. WMF to BW, [1895], HCL.
43. WMF to HA, 2 Feb. [1897], FP.
44. Reports datelined Rennes 5 Aug.–9 Sept. 1899; printed in the *Times*, 7 Aug.–11 Sept. 1899 (greatly condensed here). WMF showed Eugène Fleuré a calendar, *Dante il Giorno in Giorno*, with a Dante quotation for every day of the year. WMF had asked each of the "chief actors" at Rennes to write something on the page for his birthday. Demange, Dreyfus's lawyer pro tem., frowned when he saw his quotation, took it as a sign of failure, and refused to make a contribution.
45. HF to WMF, 30 Nov. 1899, PU. Unpublished PU letters are quoted by permission of the Robert H. Taylor Collection, Princeton University.
46. London records give Mireille's age as twenty-nine in Feb. 1930 and thirty in May 1930. Despite evidence that Mireille was born in 1900 and that Camille made her first and last appearance at the Opéra Comique in 1914, it is stated in *EW* that Camille was "already making a name" there when, perhaps because she was pregnant, WMF married her in 1903 and that Mireille was born "of the match" (pp. 189–90).
47. HJ to WMF, 2 Oct. 1900, UV; *HJL*, 4:168–70.
48. BMF to WMF, 13 May 1904, FP.
49. WMF, "Georges Clemenceau Prime Minister of France," *Everybody's Magazine*, Feb. 1907.
50. WMF, preface, *Terres Françaises*.
51. See p. 12 above.
52. HJ to WMF, 7 Nov. 1902, UV; *HJL*, 4:248–49.
53. The wire is reprinted in *PofP*, 59n.
54. *PofP*, 58.
55. WMF annotation to Wilde letter of 25 June [1899], HCL.
56. HJ to WMF, 12 Mar. 1901, HCL. By permission of the Houghton Library, Harvard University.
57. Blowitz, Maurice Barrès, et al., *Léon XIII devant ses contemporains* (Paris, 1892), 213. WMF repeated Blowitz in *Patriotism and Science* (11n.) and later said that the pope had died "broken-hearted" at not having reconciled church and state in France (*PofP*, 93).
58. On 12 Mar. 1892. See *Memoirs of M. de Blowitz* (New York, 1903) and Frank Giles, *A Prince of Journalists* (London, 1962).
59. Librairie de la Société des Bibliophiles François (Paris, 1870).
60. Quoted from letters of JF, KFG, HJ.
61. Quoted from letters of WMF, Alfroy.
62. "En Bourgogne," *Revue de Paris*, 1 Feb. 1903.
63. Sarah Phillips to WMF, 19 Sept. 1897, FP.
64. Communal and departmental records.
65. WMF, *Terres Françaises*, 222.
66. Military conscription records.
67. WMF, *Au Seuil de la Provence*, 7.
68. From the Museo Teatrale, Civici Musei di Storia ed Arte, Trieste.
69. Also in the *Corriere della Sera, Gaceta de Madrid, Le Figaro*, and undoubt-

edly in other newspapers in various countries. But CC is absent from histories not only of La Scala and Covent Garden but of houses where she is known to have sung with éclat. See C. Fishovic, *Stara Kazaliste I Rijeci* (Zagreb, 1953) and G. Policastro, *Il Teatro Siciliano* (1924) for the ambiance of tours that may have taken her to Algiers and even Saigon.

70. Henri Mordacq, *Clemenceau* (Paris, 1939).
71. For the visit, see *Times,* 2–7 April 1903.
72. HJ to WMF, 14 June and 2 July 1903, PU. The Robert H. Taylor Collection, Princeton.
73. See *Times,* 3–8 Feb. 1908.
74. Mireille Chabbert's London life is recorded in Westminster City Archives, Poor Rates, and GPO directories and at St. Catherine's House.
75. Information about the Hall and church records obtained by Terence and Prue Bird.

Part Four (pages 145–91)

1. AT letters are quoted by kind permission of Times Newspapers Ltd.
2. CMB to WMF, 2, 20 Apr. 1891, AT.
3. CMB to WMF, 2 Dec. 1891, AT.
4. Blowitz to CMB, 28 Feb. 1892, AT.
5. WMF, "Monsieur de Blowitz."
6. W.S., WMF obituary, *Times,* 1 Sept. 1952.
7. Blowitz to CMB, 26 Oct. 1894, AT.
8. GM to WMF, 21 Aug. 1895, Cline, 2:1206.
9. HJ to WMF, 2 Oct. 1900, HJ Letters 9040, UV.
10. WMF to CMF, 16 Apr. 1899, AT.
11. CMB to WMF, 21 June [1899], AT.
12. WMF to CMB, 23 June 1899, AT.
13. HJ to WMF, 16 Sept. 1899, bMS Am 1094.1 (68), HCL.
14. VC to Blowitz, 31 Aug. 1899, AT.
15. VC to WMF, telegram, [Aug. 1899], AT.
16. VC to WMF, [?14] [Aug. 1901], AT.
17. VC to WMF, 26 Aug. 1901, AT.
18. VC to WMF, 28 Aug. 1901, AT.
19. HJ to WMF, 17 Nov. 1901, HCL; *HJL,* 4:214–15.
20. Blowitz to CMB, 20 June [1902], AT.
21. CMB to WMF, 8 July 1902, AT.
22. WMF to CMB, 9 July 1902, AT.
23. Blowitz to CMB, 10 July [1902], AT.
24. E.g., 22 July 1902, AT.
25. Blowitz to CMB, 17 July 1902, AT.
26. 23 July 1902, CMB to WMF, AT.
27. WMF to CMB, 25 July 1902, AT.
28. CMB to WMF, 25 Sept. 1902, AT.
29. WMF to CMB, 5 Oct. 1902, AT.
30. CMB to WMF, 14 Oct. 1902, AT.
31. WMF to HA, pp. 50–51 above.
32. Lavino to CMB, 14 Mar. 1903, AT.

33. WMF to CMB, 26 Mar. 1903, AT.
34. WMF to CMB, 9 May 1903, AT.
35. VC to WMF, 6 Apr. 1903, AT.
36. CMB to WMF, telegram, AT.
37. CMB to WMF, telegram, AT.
38. HJ to WMF, 14 June, 2 July 1903, PU.
39. CMB to WMF, 13 May 1903, AT.
40. WMF to CMB, 13 May 1903, AT.
41. WMF to CMB, 17 May 1903, AT.
42. *Times,* 15 June 1903.
43. VC to WMF, 4 June 1903, AT.
44. CMB to WMF, 23 May 1903, AT.
45. WMF to CMB, 26 May 1903, AT.
46. HJ to WMF, 7 Nov. 1902, *HJL,* 4:248–49.
47. CMB to WMF, 22 Sept. 1903, AT.
48. CMB to WMF, 1 Oct. 1903, AT.
49. WMF to CMB, 29 Jan. 1904, AT.
50. CMB to WMF, 2 Feb. 1904, AT.
51. VC to WMF, 4 Feb. 1904, AT.
52. VC to WMF, 8 Feb. 1904, AT.
53. CMB to WMF, telegram, 22 Feb. 1904, AT.
54. CMB to Lavino, 6 Apr. 1904, AT.
55. Lavino to CMB, 9 Apr. 1904, AT.
56. CMB to WMF, 13 Apr. 1904 (copy made by WMF), AT.
57. WMF to Walter, 15 Apr. 1904, enclosing copy of CMB to WMF, 13 Apr. AT.
58. CMB to WMF, 21 Apr. 1904, AT.
59. Lavino to CMB, 22 Apr. 1904, AT.
60. André Rivoire to WMF, 12 Apr. 1905, FP. Cf. HJ to WMF, 2 Dec. 1905, PU. A "roundabout report" "out of Löser [Loeser] by Sturges" represents WMF "as living at a great railway hotel."
61. BMF to WMF, 13 May 1904, FP.
62. JF to WMF, 25 May ["94" error for 1904], FP.
63. JF to WMF, 25 May [1904], FP.
64. H. Warner Allen, "Mr. Morton Fullerton," *Times,* 2 Oct. 1952, AT. Paris colleagues included G. A. Raper, J. W. Ozanne, J. N. Raphael, Laurence Jerrold, W. E. Lonergan; see Lonergan, *Forty Years of Paris* (London 1907).
65. HJ to WMF, 14 June and 2 July, 1903, PU.
66. "A Scientific Traveller in France," *TLS,* 21 July 1905.
67. *Times,* 22 Mar. and 30 June, 1906.
68. Gutmann Fitz-James to WMF, [Jan. 1907] 59.4, UTA. As a widow, Comtesse Rosa de Fitz-James used her maiden name.
69. See p. 72 above.
70. EW to Sara Norton, 21 Apr. [1907], YU; *LEW,* 112–13.
71. HJ to WMF, Mon. 22 [Apr. 1907], 59.55, UTA.
72. WMF to JF, 22 Apr. 1907, UV. Special Collections Department, University of Virginia Library.
73. "A French Poetess," *TLS,* 14 June 1907.
74. WMF to Anna de Noailles, June 1907, BN, in Edmée de la Rochefoucauld, *Anna de Noailles* (Paris, 1956), 115.

75. VC to WMF, 29 Aug. 1907, AT.

76. "The Life Apart," 29 Oct. 1907, *AL, 671.*

77. After *EW* appeared and EW's love affair became known—and readers were regretting that so few of her letters to WMF remained—suddenly hundreds of those letters descended in a meteoric shower. The Harry Ransom Humanities Research Center of the University of Texas at Austin (UTA) bought them from Zeitlin & Ver Brugge, Belgian booksellers in Los Angeles representing a François Chamonal of Paris who had apparently bought them from, or represented, an unnamed owner or owners. (*LChr* 7–10; information from Cynthia Farar, Associate Librarian, UTA.)

I think there can be no doubt that the Texas papers were once in WMF's study, together with the ones now at Harvard and at Yale. (Pending cataloging, they can be viewed only a few at a time and so are often hard to date and even count.) Except that the pages of a given letter are usually together, they are in the same disorder as the Yale papers when I first saw them in Paris. They have, as a collection, the same spectrum as those at Yale: from important to trivial, from disquisition to débris. As in the Yale collection, stamps have been removed from some envelopes. But whereas the Yale collection—the Fullerton Papers—consists of hundreds of items associated with WMF and only one EW-to-WMF item, Texas has (1) over 300 EW letters to WMF; (2) a smaller number of EW letters to and from other people, all relating to WMF; and (3) letters to and from WMF that have nothing to do with EW (e.g., a letter from John Walter). None of the Texas papers relates to EW in other than a Fullerton context.

The EW-to-WMF letters at Texas date from 1907 to 1935, those at Harvard from 1916 to 1932. Yale's EW-to-WMF letter is of 1931. (The statement in *EW* (p. 11) that there are no EW letters in the Yale collection is inaccurate.)

It appears that someone began to pull EW's letters from WMF's collection but did not complete the process, leaving some of her papers among his and many of his among hers. (Hers may already have been more or less together, as they were dumped from their boxes, though mixed up.) But who got them—and when?

Possibilities to consider: (1) WMF kept the Texas papers in some place other than his study and they were obtained by a person unknown; (2) Hélène Pouget took the Yale papers from the study but left the Texas papers, and a person unknown took them before Hugh Fullerton went to the study around the time of WMF's death; (3) HP took all the papers from the study and sold the ones now in Texas before or after CC seized the ones now at Yale; (4) CC took all the papers from HP and sold the ones now in Texas before she died, leaving the rest to be salvaged by Nolan and sold to Yale.

There are obvious objections to those theories. (For one thing, EW letters were of no interest then. In 1953, Hugh Fullerton—not WMF, as is said in LEW, p. 11—sold Harvard 22 EW-to-WMF letters for $100.) It seems much more likely that CC took all the papers from HP and that Mr. Nolan did not show me all the papers he had saved (he had no obligation to do so) and later sold the residue, indirectly, to Texas.

Hugh Fullerton is not sure whether he saw one suitcase or two in HP's flat. The Texas and Yale papers combined could have been contained in one big suitcase. If there were two cases, and if CC took only one (it might have been hard to lug two while brandishing a revolver), the second may have held the Texas papers but more probably held the papers, some of them WMF's, that went to Alès.

One cogent reason for thinking that the papers all remained with CC till her death is that Nolan said that he had found "two or three" letters by Henry James in CC's mansarde, which he had thought of framing. The papers sold to Yale contain only one HJ letter (to Aïdé). The Texas papers include two HJ letters and two HJ wires.

78. EW to WMF, Thurs., [9 Jan. 1908], 53.12, UTA.
79. EW to WMF, Fri., [31 Jan. 1908], 53.11, UTA.
80. EW to WMF, Thurs., [30 Jan. 1908], 53.10, UTA.
81. EW to WMF, Fri., [31 Jan. 1908], 53.11, UTA.
82. EW, "Line-a-Day," 1 Feb. 1908.
83. Ibid., 2 Feb. 1908. In Sept. 1909 the New York *Times* and other newspapers reported that the exiled Prince Miguel of Braganza was renouncing his claim to the throne in order to marry Anita, daughter of William Rhinelander Stewart. Stewart was EW's second cousin.
84. Ibid., 29 and 30 Mar. 1908.
85. Ibid., 7 Feb. 1908. For WMF's admiration of Bérard, see his "Before Homer: Sea-Power and the Odyssey," *Cornhill Magazine*, Feb. 1903, an attractive reinterpretation of mythology and scholarship after encountering the reality of Greece. "Common sense, ingenuity and imagination, and . . . plucky daring have enabled this scholar and traveller to steer his bark gaily across the floating sargasso sea of weedy erudition which, under the name of archaeology and philology, encumbers the great open ocean of science."
86. EW, "Line-a-Day," 10 May 1908.
87. EW to WMF, 1.6, UTA, *LEW*, 145.
88. EW, "The Life Apart," 5 May 1908, *AL*, 677.
89. EW, "Line-a-Day," 22 May 1908.
90. Ibid., 24 May 1908, *AL*, 681.
91. Pastiche.
92. EW to WMF, 1 July [1908], 5.1 UTA, *LEW*, 156–58.
93. Quoted in EW to WMF, 8 June [1908], 72.1, UTA, *EWL*, 150–53.
94. Ibid.
95. See KFG to WMF, 7 Jan. [1908], FP.
96. Quoted in *AL*, 12 June [1908], 682–83, and in EW to WMF, 19 June [1908], 42.2, UTA, *LEW*, 154–55.
97. EW to WMF, 19 June [1908], 42.2, UTA, *LEW*, 154–55.
98. EW to WMF, 1 July [1908], 6.1, UTA, *LEW*, 156–58.
99. EW to WMF, 26 Aug. [1908], 5.1, UTA, *LEW*, 160–62.
100. Saunders to CMB, 23 Sept. 1908, AT.
101. Saunders to CMB, 7 Nov. 1908, AT.
102. HJ to EW, 13 Oct. 1908, *HJEWL*, 101–2.
103. HJ to EW, 11 Jan. 1909, *HJEWL*, 106.
104. WMF to CMB, 24 Sept. 1908, AT.
105. WMF to CMB, 13 Oct. 1908, AT.
106. HJ to WMF, 2 Dec. 1905, PU. The Robert H. Taylor Collection, Princeton University Library.
107. See p. 28 above.
108. Saunders to CMB, 11 Nov. 1908, AT.
109. HJ to WB, 12 Dec. 1908, *HJL*, 4:505–6.
110. EW to WMF, 19 Dec. [1908], 47.1, UTA, *LEW*, 170–71.
111. Quoted in EW to WMF, Fri., 31 Dec. [1909], 68.39, UTA.
112. See Saunders to CMB, 25 Apr. 1909, AT.

113. EW to WMF, Wed., [6 Jan. 1909], 30.4, UTA. See also EW to WMF, 68.69 [1908] and 15.23, UTA.
    114. HJ to EW, 11 Jan. 1909, YU; *HJEWL*, 105–6.
    115. HJ to EW, 31 Jan. 1909, *HJEWL*, 108.
    116. KFG to WMF, Sun., [27 Dec. 1908], FP.
    117. EW to KFG, Fri., [3 Feb. 1909], 53.16, UTA.
    118. EW to WMF, Sun., [Feb. 1909], 15.4, UTA.
    119. EW to WMF, Tues., [1909], 68.55, UTA.
    120. EW to WMF, 52.1, UTA, *LEW*, 138–39. This letter (*One* to simplify) and *Two*, below, are very important in the EW–WMF liaison. EW dated *One* "Sunday morning." In *LEW* it becomes "Sunday morning [early April 1908]." EW knows how "tiresome and 'impossible'" she has been:

[A]s to your particular suggestion, I'm not as stupid as you think. In my case it would not be "the least risk," but possibly the greatest, to follow your plan, even if I could—as assuredly I should—finally overcome my reluctance. . . . [T]hat letter you wrote a few weeks ago paralyzed me . . . when you said "réfléchissez" to me whose curse it has always been to do so too much and too long. . . . I'm not worthy to write to or to think about. . . . I'll let you know the moment I am free. It might be Monday or Wed.—(if your sister comes on Tuesday).

This painful letter is assigned to a period when EW was happily in love. "Plan" is explained (*LEW*, 39n.) as "a much-discussed plan . . . to go away together, as EW once put it . . . 'to a little inn in . . . a green wood.'" But the only record of that wish (not "plan") is an entry (p. 14 above) in "The Life Apart" for 3 May 1908—weeks after the "early April" day by which time the editors say it was "much-discussed." Moreover, this plan is repugnant to EW.
    "April 1908" is also impeached by "if your sister comes on Tuesday." In spring 1908, Katharine was in America. In spring 1909 she was in Tours and sometimes came to Paris. The evidence incontrovertibly points to 1909 as the year for *One*. The month is given by letter *Two*.
    121. *Two*, EW to WMF (59.30 UTA), dated "Tuesday" by EW, has a note by WMF showing that it was written and received on February 23. In *LEW* it is dated "Tuesday [February 1909]."

Am I not wrong [in asking about dinner] when I know how stupid, disappointing, altogether "impossible" you found me yesterday?—Alas, the long isolation has made me inarticulate. . . . And then yesterday morning I was *paralyzed* by not getting your note till 11, knowing it must have been written, and having the conviction that it must have got into the wrong hands. (p. 176)

The letter received "yesterday morning" had so "paralyzed" EW that when she met WMF in the afternoon he had found her "impossible." It is surely the WMF letter she referred to in *One*. And if this 23 February letter *Two* preceded *One* by "a few weeks," *One* must have been written in March 1909, almost a year later than its date in *LEW*. The "plan" EW called "risky" would have been WMF's proposal that she go with him as far as London, as she was to do in June.
    Two other letters (UTA, 59.28, 44.1) dated May 1908 in *LEW* (144, 145) are jaded—sadly experienced. (Sometimes after love-making EW feels "like a 'course' served and cleared away!") Neither is consonant in tone or substance with the EW of spring 1908, and reference to her secret journal, her "Line-a-Day," and the calendar for 1908 shows that these letters, too, were indisputably written later.
    It is stated in *LEW* that in EW's letters we see her relationship with WMF pass

"recurringly through several distinct phases." In 1908 there were "hangings back" and "surgings forward"; in 1909 and 1910, "the pattern repeated itself," with EW "constantly moving . . . from the hopeful to the wretched" (11–12, 15).

The hangings back and wretchedness adduced as evidence for 1908 (until EW left France and WMF stopped writing to her) are expressed in letters that were written months, a year, two years later. *All* of the unhappy letters dated March, April, May 1908 in *LEW* were written later. The "pattern" in 1909 and 1910 is correspondingly invalidated by omission of the letters assigned to 1908.

122. Northcliffe to WMF, 9 Mar. 1909, FP.

123. EW to WMF, Sun., [Mar. 1909], 52.1, UTA. Misdated "early April 1908" in *LEW* (138–39).

124. EW to WMF, Tues. eve., [? May 1909], 15.1, UTA.

125. EW to WMF, Wed. night, [May 1909], 64.1, UTA, *LEW,* 179–80.

126. Cf. EW to WMF, Fri. 29, [Apr. 1910], 31.1, UTA, *LEW,* 213–14.

127. See HJ to EW, 31 Jan. 1909, *HJEWL,* 107–8.

128. HJ to Gaillard Lapsley, 4 May 1909, bMS Am 1094.4 (49), HCL. By permission of the Houghton Library, Harvard University.

129. CMB to WMF, 30 Apr. [1909], AT. For the article, see the *National Review,* May 1909.

130. WMF to CMB, 5 May 1909, AT.

131. CMB to WMF, 6 May 1909, AT.

132. Lavino to CMB, 14 June 1905, AT.

133. CMB to WMF, 12 Oct. 1897, HCL. By permission of the Houghton Library, Harvard University.

134. Membership list provided by Hugh Fullerton.

135. WMF, "The Art of Henry James," *Quarterly Review,* Apr. 1910.

136. See Pennell to FM, 3, 5, 11 May 1909, BL; FM to Pennell 5, 8 May 1909, BL; FM to EW, 17 May 1909, BL.

137. EW to FM, 29 May [1909], BL.

138. FM to WMF, 3 June 1909, BL.

139. HJ pocket diary, 4 June 1909, CNHJ, 301. The "champagne, dim red lamps, laughter," etc. (*EW,* 258), are embellishments.

140. *EW, A Backward Glance* (New York, 1934), 254.

141. WMF to Elisina Tyler, 30 Mar. 1950, UI. Unpublished UI letters are cited Courtesy Lilly Library, Indiana University, Bloomington, IN.

142. "Terminus" MS with WMF's comment is in YU. The telegram is not extant.

143. HJ pocket diary, 5 June 1909, *CNHJ,* 301.

144. WMF to ERT, 30 March 1950, UI. Is this the source for the statement (*EW,* 259) that WMF "looked back to see Edith, propped up in bed with a writing-board across her knees, scribbling the first words of a poem," and the subsequent place of the writing board in EW iconography?

145. HJ to EW, 24 Nov. 1909, *HJEWL,* 127–28.

146. EW to WMF, Fri., [9 July 1909], 9.19, UTA, *LEW,* 183–84.

147. EW to WMF, [Thurs.], 8 July 1909, 11.1, UTA.

148. EW to WMF, Fri., [9 July 1909], 9.19, UTA, *LEW,* 183–84.

149. EW to WMF (fragment), "Tues. eve." [error for Sun., 11 July 1909], 68.50, UTA.

150. WMF to FM, 2 Aug. 1909, UR. WMF arrived on Mon., 12 July; see EW to WMF Thurs., 12 Aug. 1909, 68.49, UTA, *LEW,* 189.

151. See EW to WMF, Thurs., 24 Mar. [1910], 27.1, UTA.
152. HJ pocket diary for 12–15 July 1909, *CNHJ*, 305.
153. EW to WMF, Fri., [18 Mar. 1910], 3.1, UTA, *LEW*, 199–201.
154. HJ pocket diary, *CNHJ*, 305.
155. EW to WMF, [Sat., 17 July 1909], 68.51, UTA.
156. EW to John Hugh Smith, 21 July [1909], BL; *LEW*, 187–88.
157. HJ to Howard Sturgis, 16 July 1909, *HJL*, 4:526–27.
158. WMF to FM, 2 Aug. 1909, UR.
159. EW to WMF, 12 Aug. [1909], 68.49, UTA, *LEW*, 189. According to *LEW*, EW and WMF spent "a memorable night together in London [in June], and later a summer month in England"—a "month-long English fling." "A peak of erotic consummation and emotional fulfillment was reached in the summer of 1909, beginning with ["Terminus" night] in London and going on through a month of traveling in England" (*LEW*, 615, 122, 15). In fact, on 3 June, WMF, EW, and EW's entourage spent a seasick night in Folkestone. After "Terminus" night, 4 June, WMF was on a train or a ship or in America until 11 July. On 12 July he and EW met in Rye and stayed the night. Touring with HJ, they passed one night at an inn, one at Rye; then, without HJ, two in Folkestone. Of the three and a half days and five nights in England that composed the month-long "English" fling after "Terminus," only 15 and 16 July seem likely to have offered opportunity for erotic fulfillment.
160. EW and WMF, Thurs. eve., [?5 May 1910], 41.1, UTA, *LEW*, 215–16.
161. EW to WMF, Sun., [25 July 1909], 68.42, UTA.
162. See HJ to EW, 26 July 1909, PU; *HJEWL*, 114–15.
163. HJ to FM, 26 July 1909, BL; *HJL*, 4:529.
164. HJ to EW, 26 July 1909, PU; *HJL*, 4:527–28, and *HJEWL*, 114–16.
165. FM to HJ. This and the following letter are missing but can be reconstructed from the replies.
166. FM to WMF; see note 165, above.
167. WMF to FM, 2 Aug. 1909, UR.
168. HJ to FM, 3 Aug. 1909, BL; *HJL*, 4:531–32.
169. FM to WMF, 10 and 12 Aug. 1909, BL.
170. WMF to FM, 10 and 13 Aug. 1909, UR.
171. HJ to EW, 3 Aug. 1909, PU; *HJL*, 4:529–31; *HJEWL*, 117–18.
172. HJ to EW, 3 Aug. 1909, PU; *HJEWL*, 117–18.
173. HJ to EW, 15 Aug. 1909, *HJEWL*, 118–19.
174. EW to WMF, Thurs. ev., [?summer 1910], 23.8, UTA.
175. Thurs. [?Oct] [1909], 42.1, UTA, *LEW*, 182–83 (misdated May 1909). The account in *EW* and *LEW* of the rescue from blackmail, in italics below, can be compared to the documented version on pp. 172–73 and 176–80 in this book.
On 13 July 1909, some six weeks after "Terminus" night, 4 June, HJ, WMF, and EW began a motor-tour. *EW* reads:
"During the trip to Chichester EW consulted with HJ and WMF about a plot she had been hatching . . . to rescue [WMF] from the menace of Henrietta Mirecourt." She recommended WMF to Macmillan. WMF was commissioned and got £100.
EW had recommended WMF in a letter she dated 29 May 1909. There is no evidence as to what was said during the tour of Chichester and five other towns.
At Chichester, EW "further" proposed a way for WMF to get "an additional"

£100. "*The method of payment worked out was remarkably roundabout. EW was to write [HJ] a check.... HJ in turn was to suggest [to Macmillan] that he, HJ, should supply funds for a second advance which would come as though from the publisher*" (EW 263).

In fact, EW made her *only* proposal to HJ for an "advance" just before 26 July, on which date HJ made the suggestion to Macmillan.

"*Into this charade HJ entered with enthusiasm....*"

The "charade" did not involve Macmillan. That plot had already succeeded. The charade was EW's "magnificent combination" to provide HJ with money to offer to WMF as a loan.

"*Before [August] was out,*" HJ heard that WMF had "*recovered his possessions*" (EW, 264; cf. *LEW*, 183n.).

In fact, HJ heard of the recovery *and* of EW's new scheme on 2 Aug., and offered the loan on Aug. 15.

A letter EW dated "Thursday evening" (UTA 42.1) is "Thursday evening [May 1909]" in *LEW*. WMF was to see Mirecourt. If getting all his things back would mean another meeting, EW wrote, let her keep them—"*Anything, of course, but papers; and I understand you have all of these that you actually know of*" (*LEW* 182–83).

"*Judging from [this] letter [WMF] had regained most of the papers*" (*LEW* 183n).

This scenario has WMF regaining the papers in May, long before 13 July, when, purportedly, EW hatched the plot that enabled him to regain them.

"*[The] money made available to WMF—see the preceding letter to Macmillan—was nonetheless to be deployed ... to settle his accounts [with the black-mailer]*" (*LEW* 183).

The letter immediately preceding this "Thursday [May 1909]" letter was EW's fully dated letter of 29 May 1909 (*LEW* 180–81). But May 29 was a Saturday, and the Thursday it preceded was 3 June, when EW and WMF were bound for England, not to return to Paris till mid-July. The "Thursday [May 1909]" letter could not have been written before 2 Aug., the day WMF left Mirecourt; in point of fact it was written that fall, most probably in October, just before he met her in Rueil (184–85 in this book).

The biographer's summing-up of the rescue operation is oracular:

"*There is no doubt whatever that WMF knew all about it, and had been privy to the plot from the outset.... One can only marvel at the exquisite scruples of all three persons as they participated in this circuitous undertaking; Edith might have quietly put the money into Fullerton's hand. But one surmises that such an act would, for Edith, have verged on the sordid*" (EW 263–64; cf. *LEW*, 182n).

The idea, inherently grotesque, that HJ and EW—and WMF—"consulted," and thereafter only *made believe* to one another that WMF was ignorant of the plot, has no basis whatever in the sources.

176. HJ to EW, 29 Oct. 1909, *HJEWL*, 125–26.

177. See, e.g., EW to WMF, [autumn] 1909, 38.1, UTA; *LEW*, 189–90.

178. FD to WMF, Thurs., [1909], FP.

179. See, e.g., EW to WMF, [?22 April 1910], 68.41, UTA.

180. EW to WMF, Thurs., [Aug. 1909], 15.10, UTA.

181. EW to WMF, [1910], 68.46, UTA. Furious at not having had a letter, she asked herself, "'C'est donc vrai—?' et je me suis rappelé la cage du No 10 Chaussée d'Antin!"

182. EW to WMF, Tues., [1909], 59.45, UTA.

183. EW to WMF, Fri., [?31 Dec. 1909], 36.8, UTA; *LEW,* 195.

184. Tues., [?late Feb. 1910], 69.1, UTA (*LEW* 196–97).

185. EW to WMF, Sun., [?28 Nov. 1909], 38.5, UTA (from the Crillon, not 53 Rue de Varenne) (*LEW,* 197–99).

186. E.g., EW to WMF, Fri., [1909], 59.48, UTA.

187. EW to WMF, Tues., n.d., 59.32, UTA.

188. EW to WMF, Fri. morn., n.d., 68.46, UTA.

189. This passage, at the top of a notebook page, is followed by two unrelated items and then by the *locus classicus* "Adèle and I Ville d'Avray . . ." Lettering, pencil softness, and even—over a century later—degree of indentation on paper, show that WMF ran out of room at the bottom and went up to the top to write "Melodion. . . ."prefixing "He" with an "S" and writing "him" over "her" as he translated Adèle's chatter. It was live recording, not a conversation recollected and written down later.

190. Gutmann [Rosa de] Fitz-James to WMF, postmarked 18 Oct. 1909, 59.4, UTA.

191. HJ to EW, 24 Dec. 1909, *HJEWL,* 131–34.

192. EW to WMF, Fri. ev., 31 Dec. [1909], 68.39, UTA.

193. See EW to WMF, Fri., [1910], 68.41, UTA, and Thurs., [21 Apr. 1909], 48.1, UTA (*LEW* 206–8).

194. Quoted in EW and WMF, Tues., [winter 1910], 69.1, UTA (*LEW,* 196–97).

195. EW to WMF, Fri., [31 Dec. 1909], 36.8, UTA (*LEW,* 195).

196. EW to WMF, Tues., [1910], 53.5, UTA.

197. Quoted in EW to WMF, Sat., [?8] [Jan. 1910], 68.56, UTA.

198. BMF to WMF, 22 Mar. 1910, FP. See p. 183 above.

199. "Gil Blas," *Quarterly Review,* Oct. 1911.

200. See EW to WMF, 42.19, 70.1, 15.11, UTA.

201. EW to WMF, Wed. [16 Feb. 1910], 17.16, UTA.

202. EW to WMF, Mon. ev., [21 Feb. 1910], 68.67, UTA.

203. See EW to WMF, Tues. morn., [22 Feb. 1910], 15.11, UTA, and EW to WMF, Tues. even., [22 Feb. 1910], 15.26, UTA.

204. EW to WMF, Tues. morn., [22 Feb. 1910], 15.11, UTA.

205. FD to WMF, 2 July 1910, FP.

206. EW to WMF, Fri., [18 Mar. 1910], 3.1, UTA (*LEW,* 199–201).

207. EW to WMF, Thurs., [24 Mar. 1910], 27.1, UTA; see also EW to WMF, Tues. morn., [1910], 68.61, UTA.

208. EW to WMF, Thurs. [7 April 1910], 25.1, UTA. This important letter was written before the "mid-April" date in *LEW* (206–8). On 21 March (note 151 above), EW told WMF that she would tend her "two invalids" for the next ten days, which gives Thurs., 31 March, for her departure from England and Mon., 4 April, for her first full day in Paris. Her letter charging WMF with ignoring her for the three days since her return must have been written on Thurs., 7 April.

209. EW to WMF, [15 Apr. 1910], 15.30, UTA; Clare Colquitt, *LChr* 87.

210. EW to WMF, Tues., [17 May 1910], 59.28, UTA. Misdated Tuesday "[May 17, 1908]" in *LEW,* 145.

211. *PofP,* 172.

212. EW to WMF, Sun., 17 Apr. [dated 1910 by WMF], 65.1, UTA.

213. EW to WMF, 27 Apr. [1910], 23.1, UTA. (*LEW,* 212).

214. WMF memo, [28 Apr. and 26 May 1910], 59.39, UTA. For the speech, see TR, *African and European Addresses,* ed. Lawrence F. Abbott (New York, 1910), 31–71.

215. WMF to HJ, fragment, 28 Apr. [1910], 59.39, UTA.

216. WMF memo, [28 Apr. and 26 May 1910], 59.2, UTA. In a postscript dated 26 May, WMF added that EW had wired *Scribner's* "to announce an article by me on R." For a president as teacher, see *PofP,* 34–35. André Tardieu, another guest, was to recommend strengthening the executive along American lines.

217. WMF memo, note 216, above.

218. TR to EW, 27 Apr. 1910, 59.54, UTA.

219. HJ to Jessie Allen, 19 Sept. 1901, *HJL,* 4:202–9.

220. HJ to Jessie Allen, 16 Jan. 1905, *HJL,* 4:538–40.

221. *True Americanism* (New York and London, 1897).

222. EW to WMF, 25 June [1910], 1.7, UTA (*LEW,* 218).

223. Wed. ev., [29 June 1910], 71.1, UTA (*LEW,* 219).

224. EW to WMF, Sunday, [28 Nov. 1909], 38.5, UTA. Appears as [Winter 1910] in *LEW,* 197–99.

225. Verse, n.d., 23.2, UTA. For the hand, see, e.g., EW to WMF, 23.20, 26.1, 59.30, UTA.

226. JF to WMF, 24 June 1910, p. 57 above.

227. EW to WMF, [?5] [July 1910], 36.5, UTA.

228. EW to WMF, Mon., [?1910], 36.10, UTA.

229. WMF to Walter, 2 Aug. 1910, AT.

230. WMF to Walter, 3 Sept. 1910, AT.

231. Buckle to Walter, 21 Sept. 1910, AT.

232. CMB to WMF, 23 Sept. 1910, AT.

233. EW to WMF, Fri., [July?] [1910], 36.15, UTA.

234. EW to WMF, Sat. morn. [WMF note "Oct. 1910"], 39.1, UTA. See also EW to WMF, Sat. night [WMF note "Oct. 1910"], 39.2, UTA. Both letters probably 29 Oct. 1910.

235. See pp. 124–26 above.

236. Walter to WMF, [27 Sept. 1910], AT.

237. HJ expected WMF on 2 Nov. (HJ to EW, 2 Nov. 1910, *HJEWL,* 173–74). He did not record the visit in his pocket diary, but at that time, instead of noting engagements, he often used only X's, "a nervous release . . . and a substitute for words" (*CNHJ,* 319–20).

238. WMF to Walter, 31 Oct. [1910], AT.

239. *The History of the Times,* vol. 3, *The Twentieth Century Test, 1884–1912* (London 1947).

240. From the *Worcester Telegram,* n.d. Mistakes about WMF's *Times* career began when he joined the staff. Their proliferation is largely due to errors in *EW* and *LEW.*

Several sources were known to the *EW* biographer at the outset: (1) 1902 newspaper reports that WMF had succeeded Blowitz; (2) his announcement in his 1911 class report that he had (in 1910) resigned; and (3) a newspaper interview about his resignation, with a patently wrong notation "1907" (124–25, 193, and 125–26 in this book). When a letter WMF wrote in 1902 saying that he had *not* succeeded Blowitz (50–51) was found in Paris, the biographer revised his curriculum vitae: [After 1902,] "WMF was in effect made [Blowitz's] successor [and] remained the chief Paris spokesman for the London *Times* until 1907" (*EW,* 196). Rightly concluding from point 2 that WMF resigned in 1910, but failing to see that point 3, the "1907" interview, took place in 1910, the biographer determined that in 1907 WMF "partially" resigned.

In June 1908, WMF sent EW a letter in which EW (*AL,* 682) discerned uncertainty about his future movements. He had "resigned as the regular Paris correspondent," the biographer explains (*EW,* 229), silently moving the "partial" resignation up to 1908. In *LEW* the "complete" resignation is moved to 1911, perhaps because of an error in the *Times* history (which however makes it clear that WMF never was Chief (Part Seven, n. 52). To reconcile the new date with 1910, it is stated that in 1910 WMF was "on the verge of taking a long leave of absence" (*LEW,* 225).

It was a continuous process of altering, guessing at, or imagining facts to accommodate the conflicting dates and other data that kept appearing.

Part Five (pages 192–223)

  1. EW to WMF, 25 Oct. [1910], 14.1, UTA, *LEW,* 223–25.
  2. EW to WMF, Tues., [Oct. 1910], 36.6, UTA, and EW to WMF, Sat. night, WMF note: "Oct. 1910," 39.2, UTA.
  3. WMF, "America Revisited," *Scribner's* (June 1911) was reprinted in *PofP* (1913).
  4. KFG to WMF, 25 June 1919, FP.
  5. FD to WMF, Wed., [early 1910], FP.
  6. FD to WMF, 2 July 1910, FP.
  7. FD to WMF, Wed., [early 1910], FP.
  8. KFG to WMF, 1 Nov. [1909], FP.
  9. FD to WMF, Sun., [from Paris], [1910], FP.
  10. Maître de Maratray to WMF, [?14] Sept. 1910, FP.
  11. See *Fig., BA, Boston American,* etc., 21 Dec. 1910–15, Jan. 1911.
  12. Note on calling card of Comte and Comtesse d'Aulby de Gâtigny; envelope postmarked 2 June 1910, FP.
  13. "Love Letters of a Boston Duchess," *Boston American* [?14] Dec. 1910.
  14. EW to WMF, Tues., [26 April 1910], 59.53, UTA, *LEW,* 210–11.
  15. KFG to WMF, [1 Nov. 1909], FP.
  16. Information from Robert Meteyard and Nicholas Kilmer.
  17. See EW to WMF, 38.3, UTA (*LEW,* 193); 38.4, 59.40, 68.15, 68.45, 68.54, UTA.
  18. EW to WMF, 31 Mar. [1908], 59.40, UTA (Gribben, *LChr* 23). See also 38.3, 38.4, UTA.
  19. EW to WMF, Mon., [? Aug. 1910], 68.54, UTA (Colquitt, *LChr,* 73).
  20. See J. Paul Richter, ed., *A Descriptive Catalogue . . . of a Selection of Old Masters from the Maryon-Daulby Collection* (London, [1931]). See also *Marcotone. The Science of Tone-Color . . .* (Boston 1924). The BL catalogue gives the author as "Maryon (Edward), pseud. (i.e., John Edward Dalby [*sic*], afterwards Maryon-Daulby)."
  21. WMF to JW, 21 Jan. 1911, AT.
  22. WMF to FM, 18 Mar. 1911, UR.
  23. FM to WMF, 23 Mar. 1911, BL.
  24. WMF to FM, 25 Mar. 1911, UR.

25. FM to WMF, 27 Mar. 1911, BL.
26. EW to WMF, WMF note "March 4 1911," 23.5, UTA.
27. WMF to BW, 18 Nov. 1910, HCL. By permission of the Houghton Library, Harvard University.
28. *The Romance of a Favourite* (London, 1912). Translation of Frédéric Loliée, *Le Roman d'une favorite. La Comtesse de Castiglione* (Paris, 1912).
29. W. M. Meredith to WMF, 6 July 1911, FP. Cf. EW to WMF, 24 May [WMF note "1911"], 23.24, UTA.
30. HJ to EW, 21 July [1911], *HJEWL*, 183–84. The play was published in *Illustration Théâtrale* (Paris), 3 June 1911.
31. Tree to WMF, 21 Nov. 1912, FP.
32. James L. Campbell Jr. to WMF, 14 Mar. 1912, FP.
33. HJ to EW, 19 Nov. 1911, *HJEWL*, 196–99.
34. EW to WMF, 9 July [1911], 53.6, UTA.
35. EW to WMF, Wed., [1912], 17.11, UTA.
36. Tree to WMF, 21 Nov. 1912, FP. For *Le Tribun*, see also M. B. Grylls to WMF, 24 Nov. 1912, FP; EW correspondence with WMF et al. 12.1, 17.6, 17.8, 17.11, 17.14, 17.15, 23.24, 42.17, 54.1, 68.4, 68.5, 68.25, 68.27, UTA.
37. *Times*, 23 June 1880.
38. HJ to EW, 27 June 1911, *HJEWL*, 179–81.
39. EW to WMF, 19 July 1911, 53.4, UTA.
40. HJ to EW, 19 July 1911, *HJEWL*, 181–82.
41. EW to WMF, 5 May 1910, 41.1, UTA, *LEW*, 215–16.
42. EW to WMF, 5 July [1911], 56.1, UTA.
43. EW to WMF, [30 July 1911], 54.1, UTA.
44. JF to WMF, 5 Dec. [1897], FP.
45. JF to WMF, 10 Apr. [1894], FP.
46. JF to WMF [26 Feb. 1899], FP.
47. JF to WMF, 24 June 1910, FP.
48. EW to Sara Norton, 26 Aug. [1911], *LEW*, 254–55.
49. EW to WMF, 20 Aug. 1911, UV.
50. See EW to WMF, 4 Mar. 1911, 23.5, UTA, and EW to BW 5 Mar. [1911], HCL (*LEW*, 234–35).
51. See EW to WMF, 31 Aug. 1911, 59.43, UTA.
52. EW, *A Backward Glance* (New York, 1934), 139.
53. HJ to Mrs. Henry White, 23 Feb. 1913, / bMS Am 1237.16, HCL. By permission of the Houghton Library, Harvard University.
54. HJ to Mary Cadwalader Jones, 31 Jan. 1913, bMS Am 1094.1, HCL. By permission of the Houghton Library, Harvard University.
55. In SC.
56. EW to WMF, 19 June [1912], 50.1, UTA, *LEW*, 270–71.
57. EW to WMF, 25 June [1912], 42.13, UTA, *LEW*, 271–72.
58. EW to WMF, 27 June [1912], 51.1, UTA (Gribben, *LChr* 66–67).
59. EW to WMF, Sat., [July 1912], 17.15, UTA.
60. EW to WMF, Wed. ev., [1912], 17.11, UTA.
61. EW to WMF, Thurs. [postmark 6 May 1910], 40.1, UTA.
62. WB to WMF, 1 Aug. [1912], 28.2, UTA.
63. EW to WMF, 27 June [1912], 51.1, UTA (Gribben, *LChr* 66–67).
64. EW, *Backward Glance*, 118.
65. HJ to Howard Sturgis, 20 July 1912, *HJL*, 4:620–21.

66. HJ pocket diary, 29 July 1912, *CNHJ*. See also HJ to Howard Sturgis, note 65.

67. See *Henry James: The Middle Years* (Philadelphia and New York, 1962), 359–60; William Rothenstein, *Since Fifty* (New York, 1940).

68. HJ to EW, 4 Oct. 1907, *HJL*, 4:461–63, and *HJEWL*, 74–76.

69. HJ to Howard Sturgis, 9 Aug. 1912, *HJL*, 4:622–23.

70. HJ to EW, 4, 9 Dec. 1912, *HJEWL*, 237–41.

71. EW to Gaillard Lapsley, 2 Apr. [1913], *LEW*, 290–91.

72. HJ to William James III, 29 Mar. 1913, *HJL*, 4:653–54.

73. HJ to Mrs. William James, 1 and 16 Apr. 1913, *HJL*, 4:656–62.

74. HJ to William James, 30 Sept. 1895, *HJL*, 4:19–21.

75. EW to WMF, Sun. morn., [mid-May 1913], 23.7, UTA.

76. EW to WMF, 3 May [1913], 67.1, UTA (*LEW*, 300–01).

77. EW to WMF, Sun. morn., [mid-May 1913], 23.7, UTA.

78. See EW to WMF, Sat. [1913], 17.10 UTA; EW to WMF Sun., [?Oct] [1912], 22.1, UTA, *LEW*, 281–82; EW to WMF per Anna Bahlmann, 27 Dec. 1912, 23.22, UTA; EW to WMF, [late Nov. 1912], 36.1 UTA, *LEW*, 283.

79. WMF to JW, 27 Feb. 1913, AT.

80. *PofP*, 79.

81. Ibid., 19.

82. Ibid., xxxix.

83. Ibid., 3.

84. Ibid., 203.

85. Ibid., 20–26.

86. Ibid., 103.

87. Ibid., 266m.

88. JF to WMF, 11 May 1913, FP.

89. Rudyard Kipling to WMF, 28 Apr. 1913, HCL.

90. "World Policy and the Power of Finance," *TLS*, 1 May 1913.

91. TR, "PofP," *Outlook*, 24 May 1913.

92. WMF to TR, 8 June 1913, LC. A copy of the book inscribed to TR is in the Roosevelt Collection, HCL. The *Harvard Bulletin* reported that *PofP* received the Drouyn de Luhys prize of F2000. For Cuba, see *PofP*, 318.

93. See EW to WMF, Mon. eve [1910], 68.67, UTA.

94. HJ to EW, 3 Feb. 1913, *HJEWL*, 245–47.

95. HJ to EW, [7 June 1913], *HJEWL*, 253–56.

96. HJ to EW, 24 July 1913, *HJEWL*, 261.

97. HJ to WMF, 19 Feb. 1896, bMS Am 1094.1 (52), HCL.

98. HJ to WMF, 19 Nov. 1907, PU; *HJL*, 4:474–75.

99. HJ to EW, 29 June 1912, *HJEWL*, 224–27.

100. *PofP*, 100.

101. WMF, "The Problem of Alsace-Lorraine," *TLS*, 18 May 1905.

102. HJ to William and Alice James, 29 Dec. 1893, *HJL*, 3:449–53.

103. HJ to Grace Norton, 20 Aug. [1893], *HJL* 3:429–33.

104. *Times*, 11 Aug. 1913.

105. WMF to TR, 8 June 1913, LC.

106. WMF, "America Revisited," *Scribner's*, June 1911.

107. WMF to J. H. Hyde, 20 May 1914, NYHS. Hyde, aide to High Commissioners ARC, founded Alliance Française.

108. KFG to WMF, 19 May [error for Aug.] [1913], FP.

109. HJ to EW, 10 Sept. 1913, *HJEWL*, 265–66.
110. HJ to EW, 16 Sept. 1913, *HJEWL*, 267–68.
111. HJ to EW, 1, 2 June 1914, *HJEWL*, 283–86.
112. Inscription dated April 16, 1914. Information from Prof. Munroe Beattie, Carleton University, Ottawa.
113. T. Bentley Matt, *Myron T. Herrick, Friend of France: An Autobiographical Biography* (New York, 1930).
114. WMF to TR, 29 Sept. 1914, LC.
115. "The 'State of Grace' of England," PP, 29 Jan. 1919.
116. Eugène Fleuré, unpublished memoir of WMF.
117. WMF to JW, 15 Sept. 1914, AT.
118. WMF to J. H. Hyde, 26 Sept. 1914, NYHS. See also WMF to JW, 23 Sept. 1914, AT.
119. Sworn at the U.S. embassy, Paris, 22 Oct. 1914. WMF gave his permanent residence as Brockton, Mass.; he was "temporarily sojourning" in the Rue du Mont Thabor. Suitland Reference Branch, National Archives.
120. WMF to J. H. Hyde, 26 Sept. 1914, NYHS; WMF to JW, 28 Sept. 1914, AT.
121. WMF to TR, 29 Sept. 1914, LC.
122. Information from Mary Pitlick.
123. Preface to *Hesitations. The American Crisis and the War* (Garden City and London, 1916).
124. HJ to EW, 23–24 Mar. 1915, *HJEWL*, 330–34.
125. EW to WMF, 11 Aug. [1914], *HJEWL*, 349–50.
126. HJ to EW, 13 Aug. 1915, *HJEWL*, 350–51.
127. HJ to Howard Sturgis, 4–5 Aug. 1914, bMS Am 1094, HCL.
128. KFG to WMF, 13 Sept. [1915], FP.
129. JF to WMF, 18 May 1917, FP.
130. HJ to Hugh Walpole, 21 Nov. 1914, *HJL*, 4: 727–31.
131. "Echoes of a Symposium of the 'Society of Nations,'" PP, 27 Feb. 1919; "En remontant le cours de l'histoire: De Wilson à Monroe," *Fig.*, 4 Feb. 1929.
132. An "arraignment" of Wilson "lost in verbal morasses," *TLS*, 19 Oct. 1916.
133. WMF to JW, 3 Sept. 1910, AT.
134. JF to WMF, 25 May 1917, FP.
135. "Les Etats-Unis oseront-ils?" *JD*, 9 Dec. 1937.
136. "The Problem of German Unity," 24 Dec. 1918, PP.
137. "The 'State of Grace' of England," 29 Jan. 1918, FP.
138. "The Problem of German Unity," 24 Dec. 1918, PP.
139. "A Short Guide to the French Press," 20 Jan. 1919, PP.
140. "While Pres. Wilson Is on the Sea," 9 Dec. 1918, PP.
141. "The Problem of Russian Nationalities," 24 Sept. 1918, PP.
142. Ford Madox Ford, *A Man Could Stand Up* (London, 1948) Pt. 1, chap. 1.
143. "A Critical Month," 13 Nov. 1918, PP.
144. "While President Wilson Is on the Sea," 9 Dec. 1918, PP.
145. Dialogue version of conversation recorded in Wister, *Neighbors Henceforth* (London, 1922), 283.
146. "The Balkan Cauldron," *World's Work*, Feb. 1916.
147. PP, passim.
148. WMF, preface to *Memoirs of Ismail Kemal Bey*, ed. Sommerville Story (London, 1920).

149. Grand Duke Alexander, *Always a Grand Duke* (New York, 1933).
150. "The Grand Duke Alexander on Bolshevism," 4 Feb. 1919, PP.
151. "The Grand Duke," 22 Mar. 1919, PP.
152. "While 'His Self' Is on the Sea," n.d., PP.
153. "An Original Scheme," 24 Apr. 1919, PP.
154. WMF note dated 15 Apr. 1919, 3rd definitive ed. (London, 1920), xii.
155. "Society of Nations Admits Balance of Power Principle," *New York Herald* (Paris ed.), 3 May 1919.
156. Memo, 3 May 1919, PP.
157. Untitled report, 6 May 1919, PP.
158. "The Policy of the Entente towards Russia," 17 May 1919, PP.
159. KFG to WMF, 25 June 1919, FP.

Part Six (pages 224–52)

1. 1."Votre [?]" to WMF, received 12 Oct. 1920, FP.
2. [?Medurdo] to WMF and Mme Pouget, 2 July 1922, FP.
3. *Fig.*, 25 May 1922.
4. WMF, "De la Xénophobie," *Fig.*, 24 July 1925.
5. E.g., "La Liberté au pays des hommes libres," *Fig.*, 26 July, 3 and 10 Aug. 1923.
6. Seeger wrote, "I would go through fire and shot and shell / And face new perils and make my bed / In new privations, if ROOSEVELT led; / But I have given my heart and hand / To serve, in serving another land. . . ." "Message to America," in *Poems by Alan Seeger*, introduction by William Archer (New York, 1916).
7. WMF to Charles L. Seeger, 26 Jan. 1923, bMS Am 1578.3 (3.19), HCL. *Letters and Diary of Alan Seeger* was edited in 1917 (London). HCL has three boxes of Seeger papers.
8. See Odette Raimondi-Mathéron, trans. *Alan Seeger: Le Poète de la Légion étrangère* (Paris, 1917). (Seeger was translated for *Le Figaro* by André Rivoire.)
9. WMF, "Méditations à bord d'un transatlantique," *Fig.*, 4 Apr. 1926.
10. WMF, "Le Duel des deux américanismes," *Fig.*, 18 Apr. 1927.
11. KFG, "The Extirpation of Culture," in *Modes and Morals* (New York, 1920).
12. WMF, "Le Duel des deux américanismes," *Fig.*, 18 Apr. 1927.
13. Maurice Bourgeois, review of *Conquistador, Fig.*, 11 July 1924.
14. KFG, "The Penalties of Artemis," *Harper's Magazine*, Dec. 1915, reprinted in *Valiant Dust* (1922).
15. See newspaper clippings, BW file, HCA; Mark de Wolfe Howe, ed., *Barrett Wendell and His Letters* (Boston, 1924).
16. KFG, "The Personal Touch," in *Ringside Seats* (New York, 1937).
17. WMF, "Méditations . . . ," *Fig.*, 4 Apr. 1926.
18. WB to WMF, 14 Apr. 1925, 59.3, UTA.
19. John Winthrop Aldrich, letter to author, 11 Nov. 1975. See Mrs. Winthrop Chanler, *Roman Spring* (Boston, 1934).
20. Tony Summers to Gordon Phillips, *Times* archivist, 2 Jan. 1975, communicated to author by Mr. Phillips.
21. In May 1925 in a jumbled affidavit to "explain protracted foreign residence and overcome presumption of expatriation," WMF said he had worked for

the *New York Times* in England and Spain till 1905 and for the London *Times* in Paris from 1905. Passport Services, U.S. Department of State.

22. *PofP*, 32.
23. Grand Duke Alexander, *Always a Grand Duke* (New York, 1933).
24. WMF, "La Duperie des Dettes," *Fig.*, 22 Aug. 1926.
25. *PofP*, 100–101.
26. WMF, "Recueillement aux Etats Unis," *Fig.*, 10 Aug. 1923.
27. See WMF, "Le Piège de Genève," *Fig.*, 5 Sept. 1924 and "Les Illusions dangereuses," *Fig.*, 25 Dec. 1925.
28. WMF, "L'Alliance de la paix," *Fig.*, 22 Aug. 1927.
29. WMF, "Canicule: Poème par l'Ambassadeur des Etats-Unis à Berlin," *Fig.*, 22 Aug. 1924.
30. "Sécurité et Idéalisme," *Fig.*, 8 July 1927.
31. Cf. "La loi de la Jongle," *Fig.*, 8 July 1935.
32. *Fig.*, obituary, 21 Mar. 1928, translated by Robert Meteyard and preserved in his scrapbook.
33. "Cubisme et Politique," *Fig.*, 26 June 1927.
34. Information from Rosso's great-granddaughter, Danila Marsure Rosso, and from Sharon Hecker, who points out that Rosso "rarely used models [priding] himself on this anticlassical conception of making sculpture without nudes." See Nino Barbantini, *Medardo Rosso* (Venice, 1950), etc.
35. See *Painting Gone Mad* (*Fig.* articles by Mauclair), trans. Frank L. Emanuel (London, 1931).
36. Information from Sharon Hecker.
37. WMF to JW, 23 Dec. 1920, AT.
38. See p. 12 above.
39. "Les Origines de d'Entente Cordiale: Comment 'Le Times' écrit l'histoire," *Fig.*, 23 Jan. 1925.
40. "L'Angleterre vide ses archives," *Fig.*, 30 Oct. 1927.
41. "Vingt-Cinq ans après," *Fig.*, 6 Aug. 1928.
42. WMF to J. L. Garvin, 24 Mar. 1929, UTA.
43. In *King Edward VII*, vol. 2 (New York, 1927), 226, 243, Sir Sidney Lee mentioned arrangements in Lisbon for the Paris visit, which Berlin did not think important. Roosevelt's sympathies were with France; see Allen Nevins, *Henry White: 30 Years of American Diplomacy* (New York and London, 1930). From 1926 to 1938, Harold Temperley (an acquaintance and correspondent of WMF) and George P. Gooch edited *British Documents on the Origins of the War*, 11 vols. (London, 1926–38). The Madrid wire and Cambon's "inspiration" of it were later studied by Keith Eubank, *Paul Cambon: Master Diplomatist* (Norman, Okla. 1960); Christopher Andrew, *Théophile Delcassé and the Making of the Entente Cordiale: A Reappraisal of French Foreign Policy, 1898–1905* (London and New York, 1968; P. J. V. Rollo, *Entente Cordiale: The Origins and Negotiation of the Anglo-French Agreements of 8 April 1904* (New York, 1969). Andrew identifies WMF and cites *PofP* in his bibliography. Though the wire was called bogus, press attention led to secret discussions of an "Anglo-French exchange of interests." Andrew says that WMF revealed Cambon's role in *L'Echo de Paris*, 14 June 1937; he had in fact revealed it in *Le Figaro* in 1925.
44. *History of the Times*, 3:391.
45. Marquis de Chambrun to WMF, 23 Apr. 1935, FP.
46. Janet Flanner, "Paris Letter," *New Yorker*, 16 July 1930; reprinted in *Paris Was Yesterday: 1925–1939*, ed. Irving Drutman (New York, 1972).

47. Dorothy Wilde to Janet Flanner, [1930], LC.
48. Dorothy Wilde died 9 April 1941 (death certificate, St. Catherine's House). Flanner's note to Wilde's letters in LC says that she died a suicide. See also Flanner, "Oscar Wilde's Niece," *Prose* (spring 1973): 37–42.
49. WMF, "Walter Berry" (on occasion of WB's retirement from American Chamber of Commerce), *Fig.*, 21 Dec. 1922.
50. WMF, *Fig.*, obituary of Thomas Meteyard, 21 Mar., 1928, trans. Robert Meteyard.
51. WMF was instrumental in arranging the deposit of Tuck's papers in the Dartmouth College Library. (Information from Prof. Franklin Brooks.)
52. WMF, "En relisant André Tardieu," FP.
53. *Fig.*, news article, 9 Nov. 1932.
54. WMF, "Ce que M. Roosevelt ne dira pas à M. Hoover," *Fig.*, 22 Nov. 1932.
55. Photograph card of a portrait by Louise Galand-Legendre shown at the 1948 Salon, FP. The FP also contain a note introducing Mme Ixo to another deputy, Paul Brulet, whom she "brûle de connaître," is dying to meet.
56. "Pola Negri Ecrivain" *Fig.*, 10 July 1925. Just when the Ixo-Negri friendship flourished is not clear.
57. WMF to J. L. Garvin, 16 Dec. 1933, UTA.
58. EW to WMF, 16 Nov. 1930, HCL; *LEW*, 530.
59. EW to WMF, 11 Jan. 1931, HCL.
60. See, e.g., EW to WMF, 28 Sept. 1931, 42.6, UTA.
61. EW to WMF, 8 Feb. 1931, HCL; *LEW*, 533–34.
62. EW to WMF, 6 Jan. 1932, HCL.
63. EW to WMF, 10 June 1931, *pneu*, HCL.
64. "'Il est toujours le même.' L'est-il?" EW to WMF, 16 June 1931, HCL.
65. Gustave Brisgand to WMF, *pneu*, n.d., FP. "Votre portrait vous attend! It has been very patient. When will you come to be finished?"
66. Marquis de Chambrun to WMF, 23 Apr. 1935, FP.
67. Loose card in WMF notebook.
68. WMF notebook.
69. See Gower, *Old Diaries, 1881–1901* (London, 1902), 240.
70. See Douglass Shand-Tucci, *Boston Bohemia, 1881–1900* (Amherst, Mass., 1994).
71. See Allan Houston MacDonald, *Richard Hovey: Man and Craftsman* (Durham, N.C., 1957). After collaborating with Hovey on *Songs from Vagabondia,* with designs by Thomas Meteyard (Boston, 1894), Carman published many books of poetry and prose before his posthumous *Collected Poems* came out in 1931 (New York). H. D. C. Lee published *Bliss Carman* (doctoral thesis, University of Rennes, 1912), in Carman's lifetime. See also William Ingliss Morse, *Bliss Carman. Bibliography* (Windham, Conn., 1941); Odell Shepard, *Bliss Carman* (1923); James Cappon, *Bliss Carman* (Toronto, 1930); Muriel Miller, *Bliss Carman. Quest and Revolt* (St. John's, Newfoundland, 1985); and Donald Stephens, *Bliss Carman* (New York, 1966).
72. See H. Pearson Gundy, *Letters of Bliss Carman* (Kingston and Montreal, 1981), 190 pass.
73. Ibid., 144.
74. Carman to Maude Mosher Robertson, 11 July 1916 (of a 1915 meeting), Gundy, 239. See also Miller, note 71, pass.

75. Stephens, note 71, 128.
76. EW to WMF, 26 July 1931, FP.
77. *EW*, 541.
78. "WMF was living at 2 Rue de Chausée [*sic*] d'Antin. At the same address, and possibly the owner of the building, was a certain Mme Henrietta Mirecourt" (*EW*, 189). Number 10 Rue de la Chaussée d'Antin became the *Times* office in 1904, succeeding 35 Boulevard des Capucines.

Since the sources for *EW* were not named, few readers could assess the book's accuracy. In 1988–89, a controversy developed in the *TLS* and other journals over its misrepresentation of data. (Marion Mainwaring, "The Shock of Non-Recognition," *TLS*, 6–22 Dec. 1988. Mary Pitlick, "*EW*," *TLS*, 30 Dec. 1988–5 Jan. 1989. R. W. B. Lewis, "*EW*," *TLS*, 17–23 Feb. 1989. James W. Tuttleton, "The Feminist Takeover of EW," *New Criterion*, Mar. 1989. Mainwaring, "Feminists and EW," *New Criterion*, June 1989. Pitlick, "EW Redux," and Tuttleton, "EW Redux," *New Criterion*, Oct. 1989. Also in 1989, correspondence by Christoper Herzig, Ruth Bernard Yeazell, and Marion Mainwaring came out in the *London Review of Books*. In Dec. 1993, Kenneth S. Lynn's "EW's Abuser," in a different vein, was published in the *American Spectator*.)

The charges against his work, R. W. B. Lewis wrote ("Edith Wharton," *TLS*, 17–23 Feb. 1989), "have mostly to do with wrong street addresses and proper names in Paris. These have no bearing on the portrait of Wharton (they relate to the Paris doings of her lover) . . ." However, in *EW* and *LEW* not only grave errors but trifling ones, compounded, distort the character of EW as well as of other people important in the story. (A "pattern" in the WMF-EW liaison rests on misdated letters. WMF and EW enjoy a passionate month of love while on opposite sides of the Atlantic. HJ, WMF, and EW engage in nonsensical behavior to foil a nonexistent woman.)

The self-contradictory narrative in *EW* and *LEW* may be compared to the documented version in this book. For WMF's marriage and divorce, see note 23 to Part One and note 46 to Part Three. For his career, notes 240 to Part Four and 52 to Part Seven. For the EW liaison, notes 120, 121, and 159 to Part Four. For the blackmail story, note 175 to Part Four. For KFG, cp. *EW* 200–2, 248–50, and 286–87 with 52–57, 162–63, 165–67, 183, and 188 in this book.

79. *Charivari*, 9 Jan. 1879.
80. Bradford M. Fullerton, *Selected Bibliography of American Literature, 1775–1900,* introduction by Carl Van Doren (New York, 1932).
81. "Revivre, était chez elle un goût plus puissant que vivre: un goût-passion." Claude Silve, *Un Jardin vers l'est* (Paris, 1938), 13.
82. EW, *A Backward Glance* (New York, 1934), 39–40.
83. On 17 June 1891, Charles D. Fullerton notarized the application by JF for travel, to be accompanied by Katharine Elizabeth Fullerton (National Archives). He had already notarized an application by his half-brother, BMF.

Part Seven (pages 253–78)

1. WMF to J. L. Garvin, 2 Dec. 1933, UTA.
2. "L'encre peu sympathique," *Fig.*, 31 Jan. 1935.
3. "L'exception . . ." *Fig.*, 19 Feb. 1935.
4. "L'art d'exaspérer les américains" *Fig.*, 17 July 1938.

5. *PofP*, 102.
6. "Les Nostalgies de Théodor Wolff," *Fig.*, 20 Mar. 1927, and "La France au Carrefour," *Fig.*, 27 Nov. 1925.
7. "Un Grand Historien," *JD*, 7 Nov. 1937.
8. WMF to Leon Edel, 11 Feb. 1932, communicated to author by Mr. Edel. WMF wrote: "Do you know my quick, and first, reaction on contemplating the impressive, wide-margined pages of the two volumes you have devoted to the greatest of our American artists in prose? It is this: I must be off and show them to James." The citation is from "Three Sonnets." See p. 95.
9. E.g., Joseph May, ed, *Samuel Longfellow: Memoir and Letters* (Boston and New York, 1894) who spoke of WMF as "a young friend . . . in whose society [SL] took great pleasure" in his last years.
10. WMF, "The Art of Henry James," *Quarterly Review*, Apr. 1910, 398.
11. WMF, 1936 class report, HCA.
12. GS to WMF, 10 July 1887, UTA.
13. WMF, "The Notion of the Beautiful," with a preface addressed to GS, *Harvard Monthly*, Oct. 1895.
14. KFG to WMF, [early 1884], FP.
15. BMF to WMF, 13 May 1904, FP.
16. "Our Troops in Paris," 15 Dec. 1918, FP.
17. WMF, "Le Retour des Légionnaires," *JD*, 3 Oct. 1937.
18. "Le Buste de Jacques Bainville," *Fig.*, 29 July 1937.
19. *Fig.*, 22 Aug. 1937.
20. *JD*, 14 Aug. 1937.
21. "'Wake Up England!'" *Fig.*, 6 Oct. 1932.
22. "Le Roi George," *Fig.*, 7 May 1938.
23. "Les Conséquences américaines de la paix de Munich," *JD*, 12 Nov. 1938.
24. Le Jingoisme des Ouvriers," *JD*, 10 Oct. 1937.
25. "Une Amérique nouvelle," *JD*, 5/6 Dec. 1938.
26. "Aide-toi, et le ciel t'aidera," *JD*, 26 Sept. 1937.
27. "Delcassé a sa revanche," *JD*, 24 Apr. 1938.
28. "L'axe Rome-Berlin vu de Monte Carlo," *JD*,15 May 1938.
29. WMF to SL [1892], courtesy H. W. Longfellow National Historic Site.
30. WMF, Dreyfus report, *Times*, 7 Aug. 1899, p. 101 above.
31. Joseph McElroy, letter to the author.
32. "En aurons-nous la sagesse?" *JD*, 6 Nov. 1938.
33. "Un cul de sac sans sortie," *JD*, 19 Mar. 1939.
34. "Une Suggestion du Colonel Bunau-Varilla: De Panama à Dantzig," *JD*, 2 Sept. 1939.
35. "Que dirait le Général Pershing?" *JD*, 17 Sept. 1939.
36. RMF to WMF, 26 Nov. 1939, FP.
37. "Répondez à l'Appel du Maréchal!" [?7 July 1940], *JD*.
38. Cards in FP.
39. Milton Dank, *The French against the French* (Philadelphia and New York, 1974).
40. In 1941. He was then holding a U.S. passport issued on 3 June 1937. Passport Services, U.S. Dept. of State.
41. A letter written on 30 July 1940 to "Ken" Rand, secretary, class of 1894, reached Rand after 16 Mar. 1945 and was quoted by Merriam, secretary for 1886, in a mimeographed class newsletter of 3 July 1945, HCA.

NOTE/ TO PART /EVEN

42. In a message from WMF to the Marseille office of the American Friends Service Committee, forwarded to the Philadelphia office and sent on to Merriam, who quoted it in the class newsletter of 3 July 1945.

43. In a letter to Rand of 16 Mar. 1945, quoted in the class newsletter of 3 July 1945, WMF said that he had been penniless and that his checks had been compounded.

44. Leon Edel to the author, 18 Apr. 1975.

45. Affidavit sworn 4 Dec. 1944, Passport Services, U.S. Dept. of State. A message from the Paris embassy, forwarded to the State Department in Washington, was sent to Merriam and reported in his newsletter of 1 Dec. 1944.

46. Paul O. Blanchette, letter to author, 21 Nov. 1973.

47. Will filed 8 Sept. 1944, Washington, D.C. Superior Court. Information from Mary Pitlick.

48. WMF to Hugh Fullerton, 24 Dec. 1944; letter in possession of author. SL's will (Registry of Probate, Middlesex Co., Mass., 1892) does not list the bequest. A gift?

49. Letter from a "Boston Navy Lieutenant Commander" quoted by Merriam, class newsletter, 22 Mar. 1945.

50. WMF to LeRoy Phillips, 22 Aug. 1945; letter communicated to author by Leon Edel.

51. "En relisant André Tardieu," FP.

52. *History of the Times*, vol. 3, passim. Produced under unfavorable publishing conditions immediately after the war, the book contains inaccuracies even about Blowitz (WMF was identified as assistant under Blowitz "*1891–1909*" (italics added). *Times* obituaries and a *Fig.* obituary (James Coquet, 29 Aug. 1952) were based mainly on vague recollections of what WMF himself had said long ago: he had come to Europe under the auspices of H. W. Longfellow, had been in charge of the office after Blowitz left, had resigned in 1911 because he was unhappy with Blowitz's successor, etc.

53. WMF to LeRoy Phillips, 20 Mar. ("45" mistake for "46"); postmark 1946; letter communicated to author by LE.

54. GS, *Persons and Places* (London, 1944), 235.

55. GS, *The Middle Span* (London, 1945).

56. WMF to LeRoy Phillips, 20 Mar. [1946]; communicated to author by LE. The UTA letters dated 1886–87 must be the ones in question. They are in Austin, Texas (not at Harvard; WMF's plans went agley). Two letters or cards that GS sent to WMF in the 1920s or 1930s, found in Paris in the 1970s and bought by Yale, have vanished. WMF's side of the correspondence is not extant.

57. WMF, 60th report, class of 1886, HCA.

58. GS to WMF, 28 Dec. 1887, UTA. Largely printed in John McCormick, *George Santayana: A Biography* (New York, 1986) 70–71.

59. McCormick, n. 58, 128. Cf. Anthony Woodward, "'Pagan aestheticism' has a 'spokesman,'" in Mario. *Living in the Eternal: A Study of George Santayana* (Nashville, Tenn., 1988), 128.

60. GS, *The Middle Span* (London, 1944), 171, 150, 111.

61. Report of the class of 1886, HCA.

62. Shari Benstock writes that ERT "told her son [William Royall Tyler] that she planned to burn [the letters], feeling they had no literary value; but she first asked him to read them." *No Gifts from Chance: A Biography of Edith Wharton* (New York, 1994), p. 498, n. 51.

63. WMF to ERT, 1 Nov. 1946, UI. Courtesy Lilly Library, Indiana University, Bloomington, IN.

64. Mandelstamm to WMF [1940s], FP.

65. WMF to ERT, 30 Mar. 1950. UI The Lilly Library has a typescript copy and a copy handwritten by ERT.

66. Ibid.

67. See ERT to Max Shoop, 11 Apr. 1951, UI.

68. WMF to ERT, postcard 16 Jul. 1950; typescript copy, UI.

69. WMF to ERT, postcard 21 Aug. 1950; typescript copy, UI.

70. Max Shoop to WMF, 17 Apr. 1951; carbon of typescript copy, UI. Shoop and ERT refer to WMF's promises "of last July and August" to give ERT the original. But WMF had promised to "communicate," not to "give"; and if "Colophon" was at issue, it is true that he had only a copy, made when he returned the original to EW. He gave that copy and the original of "Terminus" to Hugh Fullerton, who sold the latter to Yale and gave the former to the present author. It is now in SC.)

What became of the original "Colophon" is unclear. It is stated in *EW* (pp. 255–26) that WMF, "in the handwritten copy of 'Colophon' that Edith sent him, with a dedication to 'M.F.,' added a postscript: 'I saw not what she saw, and that's the tragedy of it.'" However, the manuscript with that postscript was not dedicated to EW, and it is entirely in WMF's handwriting; in fact he wrote at the end, "Copied from Edith Wharton's ms March 1912" (p. 203 above), a comment the biographer omits.

71. "The Life Apart," 27 Apr. 1908, *AL,* 675.

72. The irrationality in *EW* is less spatial than temporal, the narrative often consisting of impossible sequences of events. See n. 78 to Part Six, pp. 312–13.

Epilogue (pages 279–81)

1. *The Franco-German War 1870–71* by Generals and Other Officers who took part in the Campaign, trans. and ed. Maj.-Gen. J. F. Maurice et al. (London [1900]).

Letters of William Morton Fullerton are published by kind permission of Hugh S. Fullerton; letters of Bradford Morton Fullerton and his family by kind permission of Dr. James Worcester; letters of Katharine Fullerton Gerould by kind permission of David Gerould.

Archival Sources

Many of the sources specified in the Notes are to be found in the following archives:

In France, the Bibliothèque Nationale; the Bibliothèque Historique de la Ville de Paris; the Bibliothèques de l'Arsénal, de l'Opéra, and des Postes et Télécommunications; the British and American Libraries in Paris; the Conservatoire de Paris; the Archives de la Seine; and other departmental and communal records.

Elsewhere in continental Europe, the Real Conservatorio Superior de Musica, Madrid; the Biblioteca Nazionale Braidense, Milan; the Museo Medardo Rosso, Barzio; and the Civici Musei de Storia ed Arte, Trieste.

In the United Kingdom, the British Library, the National Library of Scotland, the University of Reading, the Archive of the *Times*, Westminster City Archives, the London County Council, the Public Record Office, Somerset House, St. Catherine's House, and local and county archives.

In the United States, the Library of Congress, the National Archives, the Department of State, and the Department of Defense in Washington, D.C.; state and local records; the Houghton, Widener, Fogg, Pusey, and Business School libraries of Harvard University; the Schlesinger Library, Radcliffe; Harvard and Radcliffe class archives; the Harry Ransom Humanities Research Center, University of Texas at Austin; the Lilly Library, Indiana University; the Beinecke Library, Yale University; the Canaday Library of Bryn Mawr College; the Libraries of Princeton University and the University of Virginia; the New York and Boston Public Libraries; the Massachusetts, Montana, and New-York Historical Societies; records of the Second Congregational Church, Palmer, Massachusetts, and the Congregational Society, Boston; and the H. W. Longfellow National Historic Site in Cambridge, Massachusetts.

Index

A., 85, 116, 118
Adams, Charles Francis Adams, 70
Adams, Henry, 180
Adams, Oscar Fay, 75
Adèle, 12, 16, 85
Aeschylus, 127
Agoult, Marie (Comtesse d'), 19
Aïdé, Charles Hamilton, 41, 43–44, 46,
   50–51, 77, 78, 83, 91, 93, 100, 108,
   125, 198, 210, 220, 241, 243
Albert I of Monaco (Prince), 43, 46
Alcott, Louisa May, 74
Alden, John, 226
Alden, Nathalie (née Berry), 264
Alexander, Sir George, 198
Alexander, Grand-Duke, 40, 221–22, 230
Alexandra (Queen), 134
Alfroy, Charles Albert, 66, 113–15, 117,
   119, 121, 129, 209, 231–32, 245, 258
Alger (Times assistant), 147, 149
Alice of Monaco (Princess), 43, 46
Andersen, Hendrik, 243
Anderson, Percy, 43–46, 61, 78–80
Andrieux, Paul, 141–43
Annie (the Fullertons' maid), 52, 163
Apollonius of Rhodes, 71–72, 158–59
Arabian Nights, 69
Arnold, Matthew, 71, 80
Asquith, Herbert, 29
Aston, Sir Arthur, 127
Aulby, Comte d', 55, 166–67, 193–96,
   232
Aulby, Francesca (Comtesse d'), 55, 73,
   96, 166–67, 169, 180, 184, 193–96
Auriol, Eugénie. See Chabbert, Eugénie
Auriol, Vincent, 104

Bainville, Jacques, 219, 259
Balfour, Arthur, 29
Ball, Julia. See Fullerton, Julia
Balzac, Honoré de, 69

Barbie, Klaus, 271
Barnes, Djuna, 238
Barney, Nathalie, 238
Barrès, Maurice, 112, 158, 159, 212–23
Bavoux, Georges, 280
Bavoux, Jeanne, 258
Bavoux, Louise. See Buisson, Louise
Bavoux, Marie-Jules, 258–59
Bavoux family, 232
Beach, Sylvia, 226
Beal, Boylston Adams, 70
Beardsley, Aubrey, 42
Beecher, Henry Ward, 68
Beerbohm, Max, 206
Béhague, Mme de, 250
Bell, Charles Moberly, 146–55, 162,
   164, 171–73, 189, 191
Bellotte, Mme, 231–32
Bennett, Arnold, 230
Bérard, Victor, 162
Berenson, Bernard, 70, 73, 76, 100, 180,
   241
Bergson, Henri, 214, 224, 225, 249, 263
Bergson, Mme Henri, 214
Bernard, Tristan, 172
Bernhardt, Sara, 216
Bernstein, Henry, 172
Berry, Walter, 1, 2, 17–18, 19, 67, 165,
   224, 225, 227–28, 231, 238, 239
Bibescu, Prince, 54
Bigelow, Sturgis, 207
Bigelow family, 70
Bismarck, Otto von, 160
Blanchette, Paul, 264
Blowitz, Henri Opper von (or de), 2, 10,
   22, 46, 48, 50–52, 81, 83, 91–92,
   99, 101, 102, 112–13, 124–25, 145–
   51, 188, 189, 212, 225, 236, 272
Blum, Léon, 112, 172, 254, 262
Bly, Nellie, 62
Bonheur, Rosa, 202

Bonnard, Abel, 172, 237, 255, 260, 262,
    271, 273
Boreham, Superintendent, 143–44
Boswell, James, 221
Bourgain, Maître, 26–27
Bourget, Paul, 197–98, 201, 202, 212
Bouvier sisters, 231
Bretaud, Mme Gabrielle Roy, 138–39,
    141, 142
Brinon, Fernand de, 271
Brisgand, Gustave, 240, 248
Brooke, Adeh, 46
Brooke, Sir Charles. *See* Rajah of
    Sarawak
Brooke, Lady Margaret. *See* Ranee of
    Sarawak
Brooks, Romaine, 238
Bruvis, Malte, 85, 114, 115
Buckle, George, 146, 150, 189
Buisson, Louise (*née* Bavoux), 231, 278
Buisson family, 232, 278
Bulteel, Miss, 93
Bunau-Varilla, Maurice, 262
Bunau-Varilla, Philippe, 185, 213
Burgess, Guy, 255
Burne-Jones, Sir Edward, 45
Burne-Jones, Lady, 45
Burns, Robert, 278
Byron, Lord, 187

Cabot family, 70
Cambon, Paul, 235–36, 253
Carlos I of Portugal (King), 14, 133–37,
    140, 141, 170, 234
Carman, Bliss, 73–74, 95–96, 142
Carrière, Major, 102
Castellane, Boni (Marquis de), 237
Castellane, Anna (Marquise de; *née*
    Gould), 237
Castro, 99
Chabbert, Abbé, 26
Chabbert, Antonin, 35
Chabbert, Camille (*dite* Ixo), 25–27, 32,
    34–41, 51–52, 58–61, 5, 66, 83, 84,
    87, 91, 94, 104–7, 110, 121–23, 124,
    128–42, 214–15, 218, 228, 236–37,
    239, 243, 258, 263, 276, 278
Chabbert, Eugénie (*née* Auriol), 34, 104

Chabbert, Mireille, 40, 59–60, 66, 84,
    104, 107, 131–32, 136–44, 251,
    228, 236, 243, 251–52
Chab(b)ert family, 26, 27, 123
Chambrun, Marquis de, 237
Chanler, William Astor, 225, 229
Chanler, Mrs. William Astor ("Min-
    nie"), 225, 228
Chanler, Winthrop, 225
Chanler, Mrs. Winthrop (Margaret,
    "Daisy"; *née* Terry), 225
Chaplin, Charles, 239
Chirol, Sir Valentine, 146, 148, 152,
    153, 154, 160, 172, 219, 236
Choiseul Praslin, Duc de, 194–95
Choiseul Praslin, Duchesse de. *See* Paine,
    Mrs. C. H.
Christ, 47, 82, 92, 94, 95, 252
Churchill, Winston, 195, 197
Clapp, Ella, 41, 52
Clarence, Duke of, 127
Clemenceau, Albert, 26, 27, 52, 83, 100,
    102, 106, 107, 130, 131, 139, 140–
    41, 156, 169–70, 228
Clemenceau, Annette. *See* Langlois-
    Bethelot, Annette
Clemenceau, Georges (statesman), 26,
    58, 100, 106, 107, 130, 131, 132,
    139, 140–41, 169–70, 218, 228,
    233–34, 267
Clemenceau, Georges (grandson of the
    statesman), 131, 132, 138, 140–41
Clemenceau, Mme Georges (wife of the
    statesman; *née* Plummer), 106
Clemenceau, Mme Paul (*née* Szeps), 131,
    138–39, 141, 142, 218, 228, 239,
    251
Clemenceau, Paul, 131, 132, 138–42,
    169–70, 218, 228, 239, 251
Clemenceau family, 10, 106, 129, 139,
    140
Cocteau, Jean, 217
Conrad, Joseph, 226
Cook, T. A., 109
Coolidge, Calvin, 230
Cortot, Alfred, 172
Cox, Colonel, 223
Cram, Ralph Adams, 241

Crawford, Francis Marion, 173
Crosby, Caresse, 226
Crosby, Harry, 226
Crown Prince of Portugal, 14, 136
Curie, Marie, 136, 202

Dalou, Jules, 233
Daudet, Léon, 219, 260
Davidoff (financier), 223
Davis, Richard Harding, 92
Déchelette, Joseph, 218
Degas, 233
Delcassé, Théophile, 12, 109, 215, 235
Demange, Edgar (Maître), 102
Densher, Morton, 3, 108–9, 148, 157,
    204, 207, 258
Desprévint, Mme, 246, 247
Dickinson, Emily, 68
Disraeli, Benjamin, 150–51
Doll, 55, 94, 169, 237–38, 277
Donnelly, Lucy, 54–55
Doriot, Jacques, 272–73, 276
Douglas, Lewis, 264
Dreyfus, Alfred (Captain), 10, 119, 130,
    184, 217, 239, 266
Dreyfus Case, 4, 10–11, 49, 98–104,
    106–7, 130, 145–47, 209, 241–42,
    254
Dukas, Paul, 172
Duncan, Isadora, 246
Dunon, 199

Edel, Leon, 3, 67, 256, 264, 265
Edward VII (King), 110, 134–35, 152,
    235–36; as Prince of Wales, 42, 44, 93
Eldin, M., 247–48, 264
Eldin, Mme Ginette (née Roux), 247–
    49, 264, 274, 276
Ellen-Andrée, 198
Emerson, Ralph Waldo, 71, 77
Ernestine, la Belle, 11
Escher, M. C., 278
Esterhazy, Marie-Charles (Major), 98,
    100, 101
Eugénie (Empress), 251
Everard, Zadoc, 73, 74

Faribault, Maître, 119–20, 180, 199, 231

Fauré, Gabriel, 106
Fitzgerald, F. Scott, 4, 226
Fitzgerald, Rose, 195
Fitz-James, Rosa (Comtesse de), 5, 159,
    182
Fitz-James, Gutmann. See Fitz-James,
    Rosa
Flanner, Janet (dite Genêt), 226, 237–38
Flers, Robert (Marquis de), 172, 224,
    257
Fleuré, Eugène, 112–13, 271, 274
Foster, Barrett, 265
Fragonard, Jean-Honoré, 127
Franco, Francisco, 266
Franz Ferdinand (Archduke of Austria),
    131, 215
Franz Joseph (Emperor), 131
Freystätter, Martin (Captain), 103
Frontier, Dame, 126
Fullerton, Adelbert Morton, 67
Fullerton, Bradford Morton (son of Rob-
    ert Fullerton), 245
Fullerton, Bradford Morton (Rev.), 4, 9,
    48, 49, 50, 56–57, 60–61, 67, 68–
    70, 71–72, 76, 77, 81, 84, 105, 116,
    156, 159–60, 175, 183, 200–202,
    216, 252, 258
Fullerton, Charles, 69
Fullerton, Dwight, 67
Fullerton, Elizabeth, 69, 70
Fullerton, Gay, 246
Fullerton, Gertrude. See Worcester,
    Gertrude
Fullerton, Hugh, 2, 10, 16, 20, 23–24,
    31–32, 34, 84, 106, 129, 174, 193,
    217, 240, 242, 243, 246, 250, 263,
    272, 276–77
Fullerton, Mrs. Hugh, 240, 246
Fullerton, Julia (née Ball), 4, 47–48, 49,
    50, 51, 53, 54, 57, 61, 68–70, 76, 81,
    95–96, 116, 124, 159, 163, 175, 183,
    188, 200–202, 210, 218, 252
Fullerton, Katharine. See Gerould, Kath-
    arine Fullerton
Fullerton, Mabelle, 67
Fullerton, Robert Morton, 47, 49, 54,
    56, 68–69, 72, 77, 88, 217, 246, 257,
    261, 264, 261

Fullerton, William Morton: family, 9,
47–50, 52–58, 60–61, 67–71, 81–
82, 124, 200–202, 245–46; Figaro,
3, 22, 37, 224–26, 229–33, 235,
253–54, 257, 260; friends, lovers,
and enemies (see under individual
names); Harvard and Boston, 70–76,
241; Journal des Débats, 260–62;
London life, 42–45, 78–81; Madrid
mission, 12, 50–51, 108–10, 134–
36, 151–56, 234–36; Problems of
Power, 5, 21–22, 208–12, 222, 229–
30, 249, 265, 266, 270; Terres
Françaises, 12–13, 107–8, 116, 117,
158, 169, 172, 173, 239; Times, 1, 9–
10, 22, 49, 50–51, 81–82, 91–92,
124–26, 134–35, 145–60, 163–67,
169, 171–73, 182–83, 188–91, 215,
219, 266 (see also Dreyfus Case; Madrid mission, above; Zola, Emile);
World War I and aftermath, 4, 58,
215–23, 225, 229; World War II and
aftermath, 4, 58, 112–13, 261–66,
269–73
Fullerton (unidentified, connected with
Times), 229

Gambetta, Léon, 160
Gaulle, Charles de (General), 262, 263,
270
Genêt. See Flanner, Janet
George V (King), 237
Gerould, Christopher, 193, 195–96,
237, 246
Gerould, Gordon, 53, 56–57, 124, 175,
183, 193, 201, 217, 245
Gerould, Katharine Fullerton, 42, 47,
48–50, 52–58, 59, 67, 69, 70, 73, 77,
81, 83, 84, 86, 124, 125, 160, 162–
63, 165–67, 170, 175, 183, 188,
193–94, 201, 202, 207, 217, 223,
225, 226, 227, 237, 245, 251, 257
Gerould, Mireille, 246
Gerould, Sylvia, 193
Gibson, Charles Dana, 92, 167, 193,
203, 217
Giraudoux, Jean, 259
Godfernaux, André, 108

Goodhue, Bertram, 241
Gosse, Edmund, 12, 92–93
Gould, Anna. See Castellane, Anna
(Marquise de)
Gould, "old" (Jay?), 50
Gould (unidentified woman), 61
Gourmont, Rémy de, 158
Gower, Lord Ronald, 11, 30–31, 53,
77, 78, 83, 85, 93, 94, 110–11, 217,
237, 241, 243
Gramont, Comte de, 280
Grant, Ulysses S., 92
Gray, Sir Edward, 215
Gregh, Fernand, 158, 172
Gross, Catherine, 239
Gross, General, 227
Grumbach, Mme, 198
Guerre, Maître, 132–33, 135, 276
Guitry, Lucien, 198

Hahn, Reynaldo, 172
Hanotaux, Gabriel, 214, 218
Hardinge, W. M., 41, 243
Hardy, Thomas, 217
Harris, Frank, 78, 79, 97
Harris, Mrs. (dite Henrietta Mirecourt),
244
Hawkins, Eric, 22–23, 25, 84, 240, 262
Hawthorne, Nathaniel, 71
Hearst, William Randolph, 70
Hemingway, Ernest, 4, 226
Henri IV (King), 128
Henry, Colonel, 99, 100, 119
Hensler, Elisa Frederica, 136
Herrick, Myron, 213, 214
Herriot, Edouard, 213, 237, 262–63
Hitler, Adolph, 253–54, 260, 261, 262,
263, 272, 273
Holbein, 114, 115
Holmes, Oliver Wendell, 75
Hoover, Herbert, 238
Houghton, Alanson, 70, 230
Hovey, Richard, 95–96
Howe, John, 69
Hubbard, 149
Huddlestone, Sisley, 22
Hugo, Victor, 97, 130
Hyde, James Hazen, 213, 216

Ismaïl Kemal, Bey, 221
Ixo. *See* Chabbert, Camille

Jacquet. *See* Mirecourt, Eugène de
James, Alice, 81
James, Henry, 1, 2, 3, 4, 6, 11, 13, 14–
  15, 22, 24, 27–32, 43, 45, 53–54, 63,
  67, 75, 78, 79–82, 84, 90, 93–94,
  95–96, 104, 108–9, 110–12, 115,
  117, 135, 137, 145, 147, 48, 152–53,
  157, 159–60, 162, 164–67, 170,
  171, 172, 173–80, 182, 183, 184,
  185–86, 190, 196, 198, 200–201,
  203, 204–8, 211–14, 216–17, 218,
  226, 241, 243, 245, 249, 254–55,
  256, 257, 261, 265, 273, 278
James, William, 95, 190
Jaurès, Jean, 112, 221
Johnson, Samuel, 111, 221
Jones, Edith. *See* Wharton, Edith
Jones, Henry E. ("Harry"), 17
Jones, Lucretia, 73, 250
Josephine (Empress), 120
Joyce, James, 197
Jusserand, J. J., 185

Kapurthala, Maharajah of, 240
Kellogg "affair," "lamentable,"61
Kellogg, Fred, 69
Kellogg, Marian, 61, 69, 75, 81, 82
Kennedy, Joseph, 260
Keynes, J. M., 230
Kipling, Rudyard, 210
Kolchak, Admiral, 223

Labori, Fernand (Maître), 100, 102
La Forest Divonne, Comtesse Jules de
  (*née* Lévis Mirepoix; *dite* Claude
  Silve), 168, 250–51, 256
La Grange, Baronne de, 227–28
Lainé, Mirabelle, 143–44, 251, 263
Lainé, Paul, 40, 84
Lainé, Robert Pierre, 40, 84, 143–44,
  243
Lainé family, 84, 123, 243
Lane, John, 79
Langlois-Berthelot, Annette (*née* Cle-
  menceau), 130, 131, 228

Lansdowne, Lord, 109
Lapsley, Gaillard, 275
La Rochefoucauld, Gabriel de, 172
La Rochefoucauld, Mme de, 5
Laur, 160
Lauris, Georges de, 172
Lauzanne, Stéfane, 225, 272
Lauzanne de Blowitz, Mme, 272
Laval, Pierre, 262, 270–71, 272
Lavino, William, 50–51, 125, 149, 151,
  152, 154, 155, 161, 163, 172, 236, 266
Lawrence, T. E. (Colonel; of Arabia), 219
LeGallienne, Richard, 78–79
Lehár, Franz, 208
Lenclos, Ninon de, 202
Leo XIII (Pope), 112–13
Leopold, Prince, 41
LeSage, Alain, 183
Lesseps, Charles de, 213.
Lévis Mirepoix, Duc de, 250
Lévis Mirepoix, Philomène de. *See* La
  Forest-Divonne, Comtesse Jules de
Lhéritier, 245
Liard, 214
Liszt, Franz, 19
Lodge, Mme, 214
Loeser, Charles, 70, 162, 241
Longfellow, Henry Wadsworth, 9, 42,
  71, 264
Longfellow, Mr., 42
Longfellow, Richard, 9, 70, 76
Longfellow, Samuel (Rev.), 47, 75–77,
  82, 91, 95, 147, 264
Longworth, Alice, 214
Lorne, Marquis of, 11, 29–30, 46, 78, 93
Louis XIV (King), 245
Louise (Mère), 33, 132
Louise (Princess), 11, 29–30, 93
Lunt, Francesca. *See* Aulby, Francesca
  (Comtesse d')
Lyauté, Hubert (Marshal), 225
Lyauté (nephew of the marshal), 227
Lyman, Herbert, 267

Macchetta d'Allegri, Marchesa. *See*
  Roosevelt, Blanche
Macmillan, Sir Frederick, 79–80, 173,
  175, 176, 177–79, 183, 197

Maeterlinck, Maurice, 260
Mancini, Marie, 245
Mandelstamm, Valentin, 239, 274
Manet, Edouard, 106
Marbury, Elizabeth, 198
Marcus Aurelius, 92, 95
Margerie, Mme Jeanne de (née Rostand), 18
Margerie, Roland de, 18–19, 106, 262
Maria Amalia (Queen of Portugal), 133–34, 136
Maria Pia (Queen Mother of Portugal), 134, 135
Marian (Morton's correspondent), 42
Marie-Antoinette (Queen), 30
Mary (Queen), 237
Masaryk, Thomas, 221
Massenet, Jules, 129
Mauclair, Camille, 233
Maupassant, Guy de, 11, 43, 97–98
Maurras, Charles, 100, 212–13, 219, 260, 262, 266, 271, 273
Melmoth, Sebastian, 30
Melodion, 181
Meredith, George, 7, 23, 73, 74, 76, 78–79, 81–82, 92, 145, 147, 157, 173, 226, 254–55
Meredith, Marie, 78, 225
Meredith, William Mackse ("Will"), 78, 197
Merriam, John, 262
Melodion, 181
Meteyard, Marian, 96
Meteyard, Thomas, 73, 96, 184, 196, 238
Michel, Rosine (dite Andrée), 181
Miller, Henry, 4, 226
Minnaert, Abbé, 127
Mirecour, Mme Daffis de, 62, 244
Mirecourt, Eugène de (dit Jacquet), 63, 85
Mirecourt, Henrietta. See Harris, Mrs.
Mirecourt, Mme Jeanne de, 62
Mirecourt, Mme, 61–65, 66, 83–90, 93–94, 98, 105, 106, 108, 110–11, 113–22, 126–28, 145, 156, 157, 158, 159, 160, 165, 178–82, 197–200, 215, 217, 230–32, 243, 244–45, 253, 258–59, 272, 277, 278, 279

Monet, Claude, 73, 217
Monnet, Maire, 39, 121–22, 128
Montbars, 90
Montherlant, Henri de, 237
Mordacq, Henri, 132
Morgan, J. P., 70
Morlat, Camille Constant (witness), 199
Morlat, Henri, 199
Morlat, Mme Henri, 199
Moulin, Jean, 263, 270
Moutot, Adèle, 85–86, 118–21, 122, 123–24, 126–28, 232, 258–59, 232, 258–59, 279
Moutot, Auguste Numa, 118–19, 121, 253, 279
Moutot, Mme Auguste (Henriette, née Tourenne), 118, 253
Moutot, Berthe Adèle, 119
Moutot, François, 126
Moutot, Gabriel, 119
Moutot, Marie Alphonsine, 127
Moutot, Pierre, 126
Moutot, Zélie. See Saint-Laurent, Mme Henri Napoléon
Moutot family, 85–86, 123, 126
Mühlfeld, Mme, 5
Münsterberg, Hugo, 216
Murray, Gilbert, 230
Mussolini, Benito, 260, 261

Napoleon, 120
Navarro, Ramon, 227
Negri, Pola, 38, 239
Nixon, Richard, 272
Noailles, Anna (Comtesse de), 5, 54, 159, 202, 217
Noailles, Anne-Jules (Comte de), 5, 18
Noailles, Vicomte de, 18, 256
Nolan, Dennis E. (Brigadier-General), 219, 220, 222–23, 228, 230
Nolan-Whyatt, George, 37–40, 41, 58, 66, 276
Northcliffe, Lord, 164, 169, 182–83, 219
Norton, Charles Eliot, 71, 72, 76, 158, 159
Norton, Robert, 250
Norton, Sara, 159

O'Neill, Aeneas, 154, 158
Ormesson, Vladimir d', 257

Paine, C. H., 194
Paine, Mrs. C. H., 194–95
Papon, Maurice, 271, 263
Parkman, Francis, 75
Parsons, Adeline Treadwell (mother of Francesca Lunt), 73–74, 75
Parsons, T. W., 73–74
Pennell, Joseph, 173, 197
Perrot, Mme, 258–59
Pershing, John (General), 223, 259, 261
Pétain, Philippe (Marshal), 262, 270, 272
Petliura, Simon, 223
Peyrot, Maître, 26
Phillips, LeRoy, 265–66, 267, 269, 271
Phillips, Rev. ("Uncle"), 48, 116–17
Phillips, Sarah ("Aunt"; née Ball), 48, 116, 265
Picquart, Georges (Colonel), 100, 102, 119
Pierre (office boy), 189
Pius XI (Pope), 254, 261
Pius XII (Pope), 261
Plummer, Mary. See Clemenceau, Mme Georges
Poincaré, Raymond, 213, 237
Poitou-Duplessy, Jacqueline, 39, 51, 60
Pouget, Etienne, 33
Pouget, Hélène, 23–24, 27, 32–33, 38, 40, 58, 84, 123, 124, 129, 218, 224, 240, 264, 265, 273, 274, 276
Pouget, Jeanne, 33
Prévaux, Mme Blondine de, 19, 227, 250
Proctor, Sir Dennis, 255
Proust, Marcel, 19, 159, 172, 242

Quarante Cinq, Les, 172, 242
Queen Mother of Portugal. See Maria Pia
Quekemeyer, Colonel, 219

R[——], the, 28–29
Radet, Maître, 119–20, 231–32
Radziwell, Prince Dominic, 237
Raimondi-Mathéron, Odette, 225
Rajah of Sarawak (Sir Charles Brooke), 45, 111, 218

Ranee of Sarawak (Lady Brooke), 43–46, 47, 51, 61, 79–80, 81, 82, 83, 110–11, 186, 205–6, 218, 240
Ravachol, François, 10, 92
Reinach, Joseph, 107
Renoir, 115, 217
Reverberator, The (novel by Henry James), 81
R.G., 28–30
Ribbentrop, Joachim von, 273
Richards, T. W., 70
Richelieu, 235
Ricquet, Père, 113
Rimbaud, Arthur, 94
Roberts, Field-Marshall Lord 210
Robinson Crusoe, 74
Rodin, Auguste, 214, 233, 234, 249
Roosevelt, Blanche, 50, 71, 97, 181
Roosevelt, Eleanor, 97
Roosevelt, Ferdinand, 97
Roosevelt, Franklin Delano, 238, 260
Roosevelt, Nelson, 97
Roosevelt, Theodore, 97, 125, 185–86, 210–12, 213, 214, 216, 218, 220, 224, 225, 238, 249
Rosay, Sieur, 126
Rosso, Medardo, 233–34, 248, 249
Rostand, Edmond, 18, 217
Rothschild, Salomon de (Baronne), 82
Royot, Sieur Pierre, 126
Roze, Henri, witness, 199
Roze, Mme Henri, 199–200
Roze (son of witness), 120, 199
Rudolph (Archduke of Austria), 131
Russell, Bertrand, 55
Russell, Mrs. Bertrand (Alys; née Pearsall Smith), 55
Russell, W. F., 32

Saint-Laurent family, 118–19, 123
Saint-Laurent, Henri Napoléon, 118, 120, 121, 180, 198–99, 232
Saint-Laurent, Mme Henri Napoléon (Zélie; née Moutot), 118, 120, 121, 198, 232
Salazar, Antonio, 260
Sand, George, 275
Santayana, George, 4, 23, 70, 71, 76, 96,

Santayana, George *(continued)*
    217, 225, 226, 241, 256–57, 265,
    267–69, 276, 277
Sariac, Maitre de, 132, 133
Saunders, George, 163–64, 165, 166,
    172, 182, 189, 266
Saunders, Mrs., 182
Schubert (impresario), 198
Schwartzkoppen, Max von (Colonel), 99
Seaman, Bob, 113
Seeger, Alan, 225
Seeger, Charles L., 225
Ségur, Marquis de, 5
Sewell *or* Swell. *See* Mirecour, Mme.
    Daffis de
Shaw, G. B., 230
Shoop, Max, 275
Silve, Claude. *See* La Forest Divonne,
    Comtesse Jules de
Smith, Adam, 69
Snyder, Carl, 166, 167
Socrates, 94, 95
Soulié, 166
Stackpole, Henrietta, 62, 181, 244
Standish, Miles, 226
Steed, W[ickham?], 149
Stein, Gertrude, 4
Storchio, 128
Story, Sommerville, 221
Stowe, Harriet Beecher, 68
Sturgis, Howard, 166, 176, 205–6
Sturgis family, 225
Sutherland, Duchess of (mother)
Sutherland, Duke of, 30, 46
Sutherland, Millicent, Duchess of, 198
Symons, Arthur, 78, 94–95, 255
Szeps, daughter of Moritz. *See* Clemen-
    ceau, Mme Paul
Szeps, Moritz, 131, 133, 228

Talleyrand, Duchesse de, 237
Tardieu, André, 161, 172, 218, 223,
    237, 238, 255, 266, 271
Tardieu, Mme, 266
Thompson, Mr., 52
Thoron, Ward, 241
Titelescu, 221
Tree, Sir Herbert Beerbohm, 198

Tuck, Edward, 238, 258, 260
Tuck, Mrs. Edward, 238
Tucker, Blanche. *See* Roosevelt, Blanche
Turgenev, Ivan, 97
Tyler, Elisina Royall, 273–75, 277
Tyler, William Royall, 2

Ulman, Geraldine, 61
Uzès, d', family, 18

Valensi, Maître Théodore, 239
Valentino, Rudolph, 239
Valéry, Paul, 260
Venizelos, Eleutherios, 221
Verdi, Giusepppi, 98
Verlaine, Paul, 11, 94–96, 112, 184,
    255, 264
Verlaine, Mme, 94
Vetsera, Marie (Baroness), 131, 133
Viardot-Garcia, Pauline, 35, 97
Victoria (Queen), 30, 43, 46, 151

Waddington, Mrs., 214
Walter, Arthur, 146
Walter, John III, 146
Walter, John IV, 146, 155, 162, 163, 188,
    189, 190, 197, 208, 215, 218, 234, 272
Walter, Mrs. John (IV), 162
Washington, George, 42, 200
Wells, H. G., 230
Wells, Sumner, 262
Wendell, Barrett, 71, 72, 100, 157, 195,
    197, 201, 207, 217, 226, 255, 268
Wendell, Mrs. Barrett, 195
Westminster, Duke of, 46
Wharton, Edith, 1–6, 13–16, 17–19,
    21, 23–25, 28, 41, 53, 54, 55, 59, 63,
    65, 66, 70, 73, 83–84, 86, 91, 121,
    125, 136–37, 158–90, 191, 195–96,
    197–98, 200–208, 210, 211, 216–
    17, 225–28, 239, 241, 242, 249,
    250–52, 255–56, 258, 260, 273–75,
    276–77, 278
Wharton, Edward ("Teddy"), 1, 2, 5,
    13–14, 17, 19, 73, 158, 159, 161,
    162, 168–69, 171, 174–75, 179,
    182, 183, 184, 185, 197, 200–203,
    213, 227, 238, 258

Whistler, James McNeill, 42
White, Henry, 161, 214
Whitman, Walt, 226
Whittier, John Greenleaf, 75
Widdern, General von, 279
Wilde, Constance, 45
Wilde, Dorothy, 237–38
Wilde, Oscar, 23, 30–31, 43, 45, 71, 78, 97, 111, 237, 241, 243
Wilson, Woodrow, 218, 220, 221, 223, 233, 261
Wister, Owen, 220–21

Wolff, Theodore, 254
Woolson, Constance Fenimore, 75, 206
Worcester, Mrs. James (née Gertrude Fullerton), 217, 246, 264

Yeats, William Butler, 95, 217
Yorke, Alec, 43, 50

Zangwill, Israel, 226
Zola, Emile, 10, 26, 88, 98, 100–101, 107, 145